INVESTIGATING
SEXUAL ASSAULT CASES

Arthur S. Chancellor, MCJA

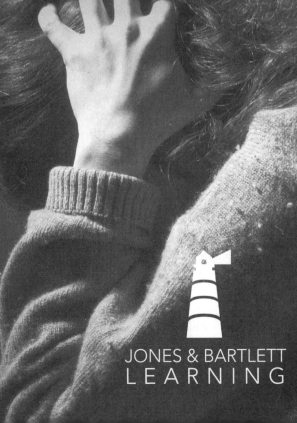

JONES & BARTLETT
LEARNING

World Headquarters
Jones & Bartlett Learning
5 Wall Street
Burlington, MA 01803
978-443-5000
info@jblearning.com
www.jblearning.com

Jones & Bartlett Learning books and products are available through most bookstores and online booksellers. To contact Jones & Bartlett Learning directly, call 800-832-0034, fax 978-443-8000, or visit our website, www.jblearning.com.

Production Credits
Publisher: Cathleen Sether
Acquisitions Editor: Sean Connelly
Editorial Assistant: Caitlin Murphy
Production Editor: Amanda Clerkin
Marketing Manager: Lindsay White
Manufacturing and Inventory Control Supervisor: Amy Bacus
Composition: Lapiz
Cover Design: Kristin E. Parker
Cover Image: © Emin Ozkan/ShutterStock, Inc.
Rights & Photo Research Assistant: Ashley Dos Santos
Printing and Binding: Edwards Brothers Malloy
Cover Printing: Edwards Brothers Malloy

Library of Congress Cataloging-in-Publication Data
Chancellor, Arthur S.
   Investigating sexual assault cases / Arthur S. Chancellor.
      p. cm.
   Includes bibliographical references and index.
   ISBN 978-1-4496-4869-5 -- ISBN 1-4496-4869-X
1. Sex crimes--Investigation.   2. Sexual abuse victims.   3. Sex offenders.   I. Title.
   HV8079.S48C43 2013
   363.25'953--dc23
                                        2012017920

6048
Printed in the United States of America
16 15 14 13 12   10 9 8 7 6 5 4 3 2 1

BRIEF TABLE OF CONTENTS

JONES & BARTLETT LEARNING GUIDES TO LAW ENFORCEMENT INVESTIGATION SERIES

Death Investigations

James M. Adcock

Investigating Sexual Assault Cases

Arthur S. Chancellor

TABLE OF CONTENTS

SERIES EDITOR INTRODUCTION

Investigating Sexual Assault Cases is the second in a series of books on the investigative process associated with the *Jones & Bartlett Learning Guides to Law Enforcement Investigation* Series. Steve Chancellor has well over 30 years of experience as an investigator and investigative supervisor. He brings with him a series of special talents and experience relating to violent crimes, and in particular, sexual assaults.

This book incorporates very important and relevant information that all investigators should read, understand, and adhere to when investigating sexual assault cases. It all begins with the victim of this atrocious act and how the investigator should proceed so as to minimize the trauma to the victim, yet gain all the physical evidence and behavioral information necessary to prepare for court and achieve a conviction of the offender.

Investigating Sexual Assault Cases should be on the shelf of all law enforcement officials, from first responders, to detectives, to supervisors. It is an A–Z guide of how sexual assaults should be investigated and will serve to increase the effectiveness of such investigations. Please read this book carefully and follow the guidelines.

James M. Adcock, PhD
Series Editor
Jones & Bartlett Learning Guides to Law Enforcement Investigation Series

PREFACE

Arthur S. Chancellor

Writing this text has been one of my major professional life goals, and I can trace its genesis back to one specific case in 1984 when I was assigned to investigate a reported rape. Upon receiving the initial complaint from a victim I was convinced it was a false complaint, and it was only because my agency protocol required a full investigation on every single complaint that I even went forward with a preliminary investigation. Needless to say, just a few minutes into the preliminary investigation, it became clear that the victim's report and complaint were accurate and truthful. This case was eventually solved, with the offender identified and later convicted of what turned out to be a very brutal rape. But, this one event showed me that I did not have a clear understanding of these crimes and it changed my whole perspective on the concepts of rape and sexual assault. I was determined never to make such a mistake again, so I began my own personal goal to learn everything possible about rape and sexual assault. I've had a rare opportunity to attend several training classes conducted by some of the original members of the FBI Behavioral Science Unit including Robert (Roy) Hazelwood, Ken Lanning, Robert Ressler, and Russ Vorpagel. Through these courses I began to understand the dynamics of these events, the importance of physical and forensic evidence, and the value of working together as a team with the police, the medical professionals, and the prosecutor. Most importantly, I learned about the offenders and the value of recognizing *offender behavior* through their interactions with the victim and their actions at the crime scene.

This book is written with the police detective in mind and intentionally concentrates on the *investigative aspects* of these crimes and how to resolve them, and not on some of the more technical areas such as forensic laboratory analysis. It is designed to acquaint a new detective or college student with the most important investigative concepts, and for more experienced detectives it provides a new perspective on how to look at the victims and offenders.

Chapter 1 presents the historical view of rape, and the origin of many of the rape myths and beliefs are discussed. It is interesting to see that throughout human civilization, rape has always been considered a criminal offense and eligible for the most severe and sometimes even bizarre punishments, but there has also always been a fear of males of being falsely accused of rape. This fear has resulted in a mistrust of the victim and placing heavy requirements on the victim to produce evidence of his or her truthfulness. In many instances, this mistrust and uncertainty of victims exists today.

Chapter 2 is dedicated to victims and how the crime affects them before, during, and after the incident, including aspects of rape trauma syndrome (RTS) and counterintuitive behaviors—that is, when victims do something that does not seem to be consistent with the events they are reporting—that are the basis of so many misinterpretations by police and beliefs that the victim is lying. Chapter 3 follows up with identifying special victims, those persons who are generally not thought of when we think of rape and sexual assaults. These are males, the mentally handicapped, and the elderly, who are routinely sexually assaulted but are not always considered as potential victims by society or the police.

In Chapter 4, we focus on the importance of the victim interview. Specifically, we focus on how to best employ Hazelwood's *behavior-orientated interview technique* to gain necessary information, not just about the criminal offense, but also to look at the offender through his displayed behavior. Other important aspects about the victim are covered in Chapter 5, where we focus on the victim's background through a *victimology assessment*. This is our chance to evaluate the various risk factors of the victim to ever become a victim of a crime and a chance to look at the victim through the eyes of the offender. Although this topic is addressed briefly in many different texts, this valuable investigative concept is covered in great detail in this chapter.

In Chapter 6, the focus turns to the offender and understanding how great a role fantasy plays in the sexual offenders' actions and how their deviant sexual interests or behaviors are developed. Chapter 7 is devoted to identifying the various categories of sexual offenders, their individual characteristics, and physical, verbal, and sexual behaviors. Chapter 8 examines other offenders who do not match exactly with the more commonly established offenders previously discussed. This includes acquaintance rapists or those who are actually known to the victim, along with female sexual offenders, adolescent offenders, child molesters/pedophiles, and juveniles. Chapter 9 describes interview techniques to be used with the various offender types and tactics that can best be employed to obtain information about the incident.

Chapters 10 and 11 shift the focuses to the crime scene examination, the medical examination of the victim and offender, and the importance of working together with a SANE (sexual assault nurse examiner) professional. Other investigative tools included are investigative plans, use of timelines, use of various national databases, linking cases together, and coordinating with neighboring jurisdictions.

The last chapters cover such important special topics as: "Drug- and Alcohol-Facilitated Sexual Assaults," "False Rape Allegations," "Working with Prosecutors," and "Common Investigative Mistakes"—mistakes frequently made during the course of an investigation that lead to unresolved cases or failure to proceed to prosecution and/or conviction.

I hope that this book will fill a void in the topic of rape and sex crime investigation by providing a fresh approach to the topic. Many previous writings, while informative, do not address all of the investigative processes necessary for an investigation to be thorough and complete. In fact, this book will go a long way toward augmenting those writings and will make the reader much more attuned to the needs of the victim, a much better team player, and a better detective. It is my wish that any detective who is ever asked to look at my loved one as a victim of rape or sexual assault will treat him or her the same way as I would treat his family member if I were called to investigate.

This text does not reflect the opinion or official policy of the U.S. Army or the U.S. Army Criminal Investigation Command.

ACKNOWLEDGMENTS

No venture of this nature can be successful without the assistance from many individuals. My wife and family have been very supportive in this project and had to put up with a lot, and had to do without a lot, while it was being put together. I want to especially thank two special professionals who were very influential in my career after I retired from the U.S. Army and started to develop my Sex Crimes training courses. The first is William Haggerty (FBI, Retired) who helped me smooth over some rough edges in my presentations and shared a great deal of his own material with me. I am very grateful for his time, guidance, and friendship. Secondly, I want to thank my friend and mentor Richard Walter, who I still call on from time to time. And, despite his sometimes sharp, critical tongue experienced by many, Richard has never been too busy to take a few minutes to listen and provide some guidance, suggestions, or to share a joke or two. To Bill and Richard, thank you, both.

I also need to acknowledge James M. Adcock, PhD, the series editor, and Sean Connelly and the editorial staff at Jones & Bartlett Learning for their hard work helping me to get this book off the ground and published on schedule.

CHAPTER ONE

Introduction to Rape and Sexual Assault

Without a doubt there are few categories of crime that affect the community and their victims as much as rape, sexual assaults, and the other so-called sex-related or sex crimes.[1] The impact of rapes and sexual assault crimes can be seen in the very way we live our lives and raise our children because they affect our overall sense of safety. We see this in a constant barrage of sex and violence in the media; one need only to read newspapers or watch TV to see examples of it. Media coverage of sex crimes becomes particularly saturated when there is a high-profile crime involving a well known victim or offender, or when there are especially gruesome aspects of the crime. Perhaps even worse is the community response and fear when there are reports of a serial offender operating within a particular jurisdiction, with multiple victims. Whenever these crimes are reported, the public becomes riveted to every sala-cious detail of what happened; much like our reality TV programs, these events can be both captivating and repulsive at the same time. However, the problem with rape and sexual offenses is far more complex than just the ter-rible nature of the crimes themselves and the fear they bring to so many. It is the combination of the crime and the community's reaction, coupled with the many myths and victim stereotypes that make this type of crime so difficult to investigate and even more difficult to prosecute.

Lanning and Hazelwood[2] address several important concepts in the prob-lem of investigating and prosecuting these types of crimes. First, they address the general societal attitude of *denial* concerning aspects of child sexual abuse, child prostitutes, rape, and other sexual crimes. Denial in this context means

---

[1] The terms *sex-related crimes* and *sex crimes* are used interchangeably to describe the many offenses involving sex acts. What constitutes these offenses may differ by culture, jurisdiction, and legal definition. However, they generally include but are not limited to any forced sexual acts or other offenses including sodomy, incest, and child pornography, and may include status crimes such as carnal knowledge.

[2] Lanning, K. V., & Hazelwood, R. R. (1988, September). The maligned investigators of criminal sexuality. *FBI Law Enforcement Bulletin, 57*(9), 1–10.

that people simply do not want to believe or accept that these things happen in our society or that reputable, well known, and respected people are sometimes involved. The second problem is the general stereotypical under-standing of the term *sex crimes*. Because when we hear the word "sex" we think of terms like pleasure, ecstasy, warmth, sharing, love, and emotion, which of course are generally pleasant and comforting to us. But the word "crime" is associated with violence, anger, devastation, and fear, which are often linked to physical harm and punishment. The two words really do not go together and for laymen what is generally heard or understood is the *sex* part of the term. Lanning and Hazelwood offer a much better description of these crimes as *interpersonal violence* or *criminal sexuality* because these terms better reflect what these crimes are actually about.

Another example of one of the many difficulties revolving around rape and other so-called sex crimes is to compare them with other criminal acts. All we have to do is think of our own individual response or imagine the public's response to any of the more common crimes such as the theft of a motor vehicle, the burglary of a home, or even physical child abuse. In each of these crimes the public can almost always accept and empathize with the victim, because no one wants to lose their possessions, no one wants to see another person, particularly a child, injured, and certainly there is a great deal of general animus by the public toward the offenders and their criminal acts. But what is missing from these types of crimes is the general suspicion on the part of the public and police that the person making the complaint is making a false report. Generally speaking, these events are almost always accepted at face value as presented by the victim. Unfortu-nately, this is not necessarily the case with rape and other sex-related crimes. As we will cover in more detail throughout this text, sex-related crimes are the only ones where we, culturally or as a society, tend to more readily *disbelieve* victims when they make a report of their sexual victimization; and before their complaint is taken seriously, we almost insist that victims be able to prove *they* are not lying. It is also one of the few crimes where police and other researchers are concerned with statistics of false reporting, or what is often referred to as *unfounding*.[3] The statistics on the number of cases that are determined to be unfounded by the police have been batted back and forth for years by different groups with varying agendas. The police may use them to reflect the difficulties in working these types of cases and to reflect a

---

[3] The term *unfounded* has no standard definition in the law enforcement community and the term has come to mean different things to different agencies. For instance, it could mean an investi-gation that was closed without prosecution, was closed based on lack of cooperation by the victim, or the victim requested not to proceed any further with the investigation. To most agen-cies and detectives, this term is used to describe allegations that were determined to be based on a false report. Therefore, based on their investigation the offense never happened and was thus "unfounded." The difficulty when conducting research into this aspect of rape investiga-tions is determining which definition was used by a particular agency.

much lower incidence of occurrence. For instance, if 100 incidents of rape were reported in a community in 1 year, but 30 of these cases were determined to be unfounded or never to have happened, then the police can report only the 70 rape offenses actually occurred during that particular reporting period. One purpose of collecting these statistics is to show the community was safer with only 70 victims than it might seem if the number of victims reported was 100. Various male groups have also use these same unfounded statistics in order to reflect the number of false reports confronting men, while feminist groups use these statistics to reflect the callous treatment of victims by the male-dominated police, criticize a particular study and how it was conducted, and respond with one of their own studies to show a much lower rate. From personal experience of the author, there are far more instances of people falsifying theft or accident reports in order to make fraudulent claims against their insurance company than false rape complaints; however, there are neither statistics created or collected nor any real discussion on this particular topic. The concept of false rape reports, however, is a such problem for detectives that it is generally covered in nearly every text written on this subject and thus is addressed in greater detail in a separate chapter of this text.

Unfortunately, when dealing with any discussion of rape and sexual assault, the victim, the offender, the criminal act, and the effect on the local community can be lost in the mix with the various competing groups arguing between each other. These divergent groups may seem well intentioned with their particular philosophical beliefs, but they often lose sight of what our responsibilities as a society and particularly the police should be—that is, protect the victims; identify, prosecute, and punish the offenders; and prevent future assaults.

▶ Historical Perspective

There are numerous texts already written covering the concept of rape and sexual assault and postulating various theories on why rape occurs. Which theory is correct is beyond this particular text because we are concerned with the actual investigation of the offenders. However, it is important to give a brief historical context to rape and forced sexual assault in order to understand how the concept of rape and its victims affects our culture and community. Rape and forced sex has actually played a part of human history probably since the beginning of time and although we have no actual evidence, it would be conceivable that our very early human ancestors such as Cro-Magnons, Neanderthals, and early *Homo sapiens* also overpowered females from their clans or other groups and forced sex upon them.

Historically there are essentially *two versions* or concepts of rape: one is through war, and the other seen as a criminal offense within individual societies. Although they are essentially the same violations of the victims, they have been seen in different light throughout human history.

War Rape

In what we generally think of as ancient history, the rape of women of a conquered city by the victorious army was considered a part of the "spoils of war." The plunder and theft of any valuables or personal effects, along with the rape of women or taking of the surviving population of the defeated city as slaves or the taking of women as concubines, was considered a normal and expected result of victory and the penalty of defeat. It was also a way for generals and governments to "pay" or reward their soldiers for their service. The rape of women of a defeated city or army was not just about the carnal lust of the victorious army or individual soldiers; it was also considered as another way to completely humiliate and subjugate the defeated country and society. It was also not unheard of for the male survivors of the defeated army to be sodomized as an additional humiliation to their manhood.

Such conduct would also serve as a reminder to the defeated civilization of the potential retribution for any future act of rebellion against the victorious army and, just as important, would serve as a stark warning to any other cities or civilizations of the price of resistance. Such early forms of terror succeeded in either fortifying the resolve to fight or caused the capitulation of many cities to their enemies to avoid the results of defeat in battle. Examples can be found within the Bible: Numbers 31:1–18 described how Moses ordered the slaughter of all Midianite males after a battle but the 32,000 female virgins were spared to become slaves or given to soldiers as captives of war. Deuteronomy 21:11–14 even outlined instructions to shave a captive's head and allow her to mourn the loss of her family for 30 days; afterward the captives were required to submit sexually to their captors. We can assume that most victims submitted against their will, but that was their lot for being taken captive.

Mythology and ancient legends are also full of other examples of women being ravished by the gods or other civilizations. The Greek God Zeus, for instance, was notorious for using different tricks, guile, and deceit to have sex with mortal women. Whether or not actual force was used, the essential result was overcoming the woman's hesitancy or will to have sex. One other very important historical legend is known as the *Rape of the Sabine Women* as noted in **Case Study 1-1**.

Case Study 1-1

Most of what we know of the early history of Rome comes from Plutarch and Livy,[4] including the well known story of the *Rape of the Sabine Women*. This incident is supposed to have occurred shortly after Rome's establishment by

---

[4] Titus Livius (traditionally reported to have lived from 59 BC to AD 17), perhaps better known as Livy, was a Roman historian who wrote a monumental history of Rome, *Ab Urbe Condita*, from its traditional founding (roughly 753 BC) through the reign of Augustus in Livy's own time.

Romulus. According to legend, after the Romans had build their impressive city, they realized their shortage of women destined them to decline within a generation because there would be no children to take their place. Therefore, they needed to seek wives to create families, raise children, and keep their city growing.

The Romans attempted to peacefully negotiate with the surrounding tribes including the Sabines in order to merge their communities together through marriage. The Romans were unsuccessful however, because the Sabines feared the emergence of Rome as a rival society. Unable to negotiate peacefully for women, the Romans simply turned to force and planned to abduct Sabine women and take them as their wives. In furtherance of this plan, Romulus devised a ruse to lure in the Sabines with the festival of Neptune Equester, inviting all of Rome's neighbors to attend and show off his city. Many people of Rome's neighboring tribes, including the Sabines, attended and marveled at the city. According to Livy, at a particular point in the festival Romulus gave a signal by raising his cloak, at which time the Romans literally began abducting the Sabine women and spirited them away. The Sabine males, furious at the act, departed back to their own cities to raise an army. However, the indignant female abductees were addressed by Romulus to accept the Roman men as their husbands and according to legend no real sexual assault took place. On the contrary, Romulus is supposed to have offered them free choice to remain or return and further promised both civic and property rights to the women if they stayed. According to Livy, Romulus promised that if they remained, "they would live in honorable wedlock, and share all their property and civil rights, and dearest of all to human nature would be the mothers of free men."[4] The legend continues that eventually the Sabine men returned to Rome, intent on war to rescue their daughters, but instead the captured women ran in between the two forces aligned for battle and begged their fathers not to fight their new husbands.

FIGURE 1-1 The Rape of the Sabine Woman by Nicolas Poussin, Rome, 1637–1638.
Source: SuperStock. © Peter Willi/SuperStock

The problem with this particular legend is that the concept of a forced abduction of women that turned out all right does not fit with the reality of an abduction of women. In this legend the victims eventually grew to love their abductors and did not wish to return to their former lives, which is a fantasy of some kidnappers. This concept in which a certain type of offender will fantasize that their forced sex on a victim will somehow work out to become a lasting relationship with the victim is explored later in the text.

When we first consider this concept of women and rape being the accepted *spoils of war*, we most often think about ancient warfare and civilizations such as the Assyrians, the Babylonians, the Greeks, and the Romans. However, this concept was fairly well accepted and used throughout human history. In what we think of as modern times—the 20th and 21st centuries—mass rape has not necessarily been state or governmental policy (with some exceptions), but it has still occurred. We only have to go back as far as World War II history to find examples of atrocities committed by various armies as they fought in nearly every theater of war. Examples include German soldiers who reportedly routinely raped Russian woman, as they rolled through Russia and other defeated countries. A few short years later, Russian soldiers returned the humiliation by committing their own whole-scale rape of German women as they entered Germany. The Russians however were not concerned with the age of the women, and both the very young and the very old were routinely assaulted as they plundered through Germany.

Perhaps the most blatant example during World War II was the *Rape of Nanking*, perpetrated by victorious Japanese soldiers against the population of Nanking, China. The Rape of Nanking (also called the Nanking Massacre) included not only the horrific rape of thousands of Chinese women and girls, but also the slaughter of thousands of Chinese men, women, and children as the Imperial Japanese Army exhibited an undisciplined rampage through the city without any real reason or mercy. The Japanese Army's treatment of prisoners of war and of the many conquered peoples was an additional element of the various atrocities they committed.

One atrocity was more of a state or officially sanctioned policy than other individual murders or other acts of rape. This involved the so-called "comfort women" who were literally taken from their homes in Korea and other Southeast Asian countries and pressed into prostitution to service the Japanese soldiers in the field. These comfort women were brought to the front-line troops as prostitutes. They were expected—that is, they were forced—to "service" or have sex with any number of Japanese soldiers every day. These actions resulted in literally thousands and thousands of rapes, all officially sanctioned by the Imperial Japanese Army and Japanese government. The Japanese commanders did not consider this repeated victimization of the so-called "comfort women" as being wrong or anything other than a way to improve the morale of the front-line troops [5] and keep them from assaulting local women in the occupied area.

Such instances of mass rape as noted in World War II still occur in the world today, but they are now the exception rather than the rule. There are still some very clear examples of rape being used as a method of terror against other ethnic groups by governments or armies. Perhaps the most recent examples were the Serbian efforts of *ethnic cleansing* in Kosovo, where the intent was basically to commit genocide or otherwise drive out the Muslim residents of Kosovo to absorb their property and country into the Serbian nation. To achieve this purpose, the Serbian army or special police units used organized rape, wherein the Muslim or other ethnic women were brought to special camps or other locations for the sole purpose of being raped or sexually tortured. Again, this was not based on a general unsatisfied carnal lust of the soldiers, but used as an instrument of terror against the population, forcing them to flee the country to escape victimization.

Many similar events that have taken place in various locations in Africa as one tribe attempts to subjugate or drive out another tribe, or corrupt, despotic leaders attempt to terrorize their own populations. Sadly, it is still very likely for these and other similar events to be repeated in the future, because they unfortunately do achieve their purpose of terrorizing the population. For the most part, rape in war is unlikely to ever be totally stopped, but it is now more generally limited to individual acts perpetrated by individual soldiers with individual victims rather than as part of a widespread, official state policy.

The Criminal Offense of Rape

The offense of rape has historically been considered a criminal offense and the prohibitions and penalties have been documented as far back as the Code of Hammurabi, long considered to be the first written law. However, when reading these ancient historical texts, it appears the offense was not always perceived as a crime against the female victim as much as it was seen as an offense against the husband or father of the victim. For instance, under ancient Hebrew law as documented in the Bible in the book of Deuteronomy, the crime of rape or even consensual intercourse with a virgin without permission of a father had specific punishments. Either incident was viewed as a crime against the dominant male within the family. As punishment for rape, the offender paid a sum of money to the husband or the father, because they were the ones considered to be wronged by the act. It is important to remember that in many ancient cultures women were considered to be the property of their fathers or husbands. Rape was considered not so much as a crime against a person but almost like the offense of trespassing.

---

[5] Hicks, G. (1994). *The comfort women: Japan's brutal regime of enforced prostitute.* W.W.Norton and Company Inc, NY: New York.

Although harsh and confusing by today's standards, the concepts of marriage, sex, and the family were viewed far differently. A father's property and possessions were passed down to his children, and it was vitally important to society that such customs were observed. Further, both sons and daughters were used to bond different families together within the tribe or community, much in the same manner as royal families intermarried to bind countries together. In some societies it was common to pay the father for the bride, while in others it was the father who was expected to put forth a dowry or provide something for his daughter to bring to her new family and serve as a form of protection for the new wife against the possibility of ill treatment by her husband as an incentive to the husband not to harm her.

The concept of proof and punishment as noted in the Bible may seem to be in striking contrast with our concept in modern times. Many who read the modern translation of the Christian Bible conclude that the Hebrews and God may have excused or condoned rape, even to the point of punishing the female victim equally as the offender. This comes from Deuteronomy, chapter 22, where if a man raped a virgin within the walls of a city and she was already betrothed to another man, both she and the rapist should share the same fate of stoning to death. The rationale was if the victim had actually offered resistance and screamed for help, she would have been heard and therefore rescued. Failing to do so therefore justified her own punishment for having sex outside of marriage. Concerning the offender, the ancients believed he had "humbled his neighbor's wife"[6] and therefore was subject to communal punishment for his transgression. However, if a woman was assaulted outside the city or while she was laboring in the fields where no one could hear her screaming, only the rapist was put to death. In this case, it was accepted that being alone and outside of any protection no one could have heard her cry out and therefore was held essentially blameless. Other punishments are outlined, including payment of 50 shekels of silver or forcing the male to marry the victim without being able to divorce her for the rest of his life.

What is missing in much of the critique of the Biblical passages is an understanding of the living conditions and societal demands of the time. During those times it was almost unheard of for an unmarried female to go out into the community or walk around the area at night without another male member of her family to accompany her; the typical "city" or town was so small and the houses were so close together that it was assumed that any attempt to call attention to an event would have been heard by someone else. What is also often missing in discussions about these and other passages in the Bible is consideration of the severe penalties prescribed for these offenses. There were no prisons or involuntary confinement back then and 50 shekels of silver was an enormous amount of money; never being able to divorce the victim might not sound like much of a punishment for the offender and

---

[6] Deuteronomy 22:23–29.

certainly not a positive result for the victim either, but in effect the offender had to be responsible for the victim for the remainder of her life and the whole community would hold him to his responsibility toward the victim. Although not so important in our modern times, community acceptance was very important at the time and, because the villages were so small, everyone in the village would know about the act. It is probable that this particular law was written, like many laws today, to influence people not to commit a particular crime because of the possible punishment. Lastly, in some instances even the death penalty was prescribed for rape, but before this punishment was inflicted there was a requirement for other witnesses to testify as to what happened. The requirement of additional witnesses besides the victim as defined in other scripture passages is not about not believing the victim and her rape complaint; it was a requirement under the legal code for all serious criminal offenses that other witnesses must be produced in order to inflict the maximum punishments.

Before the Norman conquest, the punishment for rape was extremely severe and included both death and possible dismemberment of the offender. In fact, under ancient Saxon Laws[7] as provided by Henrici de Bracton,

> If a man were to throw a woman upon the ground against her will, he forfeits the King's grace; if he shamelessly disrobes her and places himself upon her, he incurs the loss of all possessions; and if he lies with her, incurs the loss of life and his members.

Specifically, punishment could include:

> Even his horse shall to his ignominy be put to shame upon its scrotum and its tail, which shall be cut off as close as possible to the buttocks. If he has a dog with him, a greyhound or some other, it shall be put to shame in the same way; if a hawk let it lose its beak, its claws and its tail.

Although the law allowed extreme punishments for an offender, in reality they were seldom applied and although rape was still considered a serious offense during this time it was seldom charged.

During the next 700-plus years, legal concepts about the offense of rape continued to develop but many rape myths still influenced our society, and more importantly, the police and the courts. MacFarlane,[8] in his treatise entitled "Historical Development of the Offence of Rape," covers how the

---

[7] From Henrici de Bracton in *De Legibus et Consuetudinibus Angliae, Libri Quinque*, written between 1250 and 1260.

[8] MacFarlane, B. A., *Historical Development of the Offence of Rape*, [Originally published by the Canadian Bar Association in a book commemorating the 100th anniversary of Canada's criminal code, titled: "100 years of the criminal code in Canada: essays commemorating the centenary of the Canadian criminal code," edited by Wood and Peck (1993)]. MacFarlane was the Deputy Minister of Justice, Deputy Attorney General for the Province of Manitoba, Canada.

offense of rape was viewed under ancient and English common law. What is interesting is not just how the offense was viewed throughout history—because it is clear that forced rape was always viewed as a horrible crime and thus severe punishments were prescribed for the offense—but that there has *always* been a lingering suspicion or fear of potential false reports that has influenced the investigation and prosecution of this offense. We see this suspicion and fear in some of the laws and procedures enacted to ensure this was not the case. For example:

> In the 12th century a new law entitled "An Appeal Concerning the Rape of Virgins" insisted that the report of rape must be made shortly after an assault took place and the victim required to present her torn or bloodstained clothing to the crown law officials. The thinking was that if this was a true case of rape, the victim would immediately report the incident and thus seek justice and punishment for the assailant. This actually resulted in the shifting of responsibility away from the offender and onto the victim who was also required to have her body examined by law-abiding women who would attest if she were in fact a virgin and defiled or not. *If* proved to be defiled then the trial would continue, but if not, then the charges were likely dropped and the victim herself taken into custody. Whereas this particular law was designed to protect virgins, the rape of all women was still prohibited, but the possible penalty assessed actually revolved around the victim herself, meaning, if a nun, a widow, a chaste woman, or youth was raped then punishment could be severe. If the woman was of low character or a prostitute then the punishment may not be so severe.[9]

Interestingly, in cases of multiple rape, the first offender was likely to receive more punishment than other offenders who also raped the victim, under the theory virginity could only be lost once. Again, the loss of virginity was considered a more serious offense than the rape itself. It was not until 1285 that the virginity of the victim was no longer a consideration in the act or punishment of rape and was no longer considered a misfortune to a family and their potential land and property rights but seen as a criminal act requiring action by the state. The death penalty for rape, which had been suspended for a number of years, was returned and could be applied equally regardless of the status of the victim.

By the 17th century the concept and definition of rape were firmly established as being sexual intercourse by *force and against a woman's will*, and further that *consent* could not be forced or obtained through threats or fear of harm. While the definition of rape broadened, the concept of a vengeful, lying victim still permeated the courts, which resulted in trials almost always turning to the conduct and background of the victim and her own credibility and moral

---

[9] MacFarlane, B. A. (1993). Historical development of the offence of rape. In *100 years of criminal code in Canada: Essays commemorating the centenary of the criminal code of Canada* (Eds. Woods & Peck).Canadian Bar Association. Ottawa, Canada.

standing rather than focusing on the conduct of the defendant. In the 17th century, other very important concepts were introduced, such as a husband could not legally *rape* his wife. He could be charged and convicted of other assaultive behavior toward her but not rape. The belief during this time was that a woman by her matrimonial consent essentially waived any future nonconsent, as it was assumed to be the husband's right to sex with his wife.

The concept that rape must include use of force and be against a woman's will lead to the idea that the man must have used overpowering force to overcome the victim's resistance and further, that the woman must resist using all means at her disposal or must be in dread or fear of death. Thus, the following rape myth developed: *An otherwise healthy woman can prevent being raped if she truly wants to.* Similarly, the concept came into being that if a pregnancy resulted from a rape, then it was not rape. This was the result of the belief at the time that no woman could conceive if she did not consent to the act.

Perhaps the most striking and long-lasting statements on this subject came from Sir Mathew Hale, a noted English jurist who in 1670 wrote his famous "History of the Pleas of the Crown[10]":

> It is true rape is the most detestable crime, and therefore ought severely and impartially to be punished with death; but it must be remembered that it is an accusation easily to be made and hard to be proved, and harder to be defended by the party accused though never so innocent.

We see this same caution and fear in numerous previous laws that were enacted by several states in the United States, such as an insistence that some form or type of corroborating evidence must be presented in order to validate the victim's complaint. This once legal requirement has now been eliminated by every state but attests to the same fear and mistrust of the victim that is still present in our own court system today.

During the Victorian era the background of the victim and her chaste character were again important in court proceedings; women who were chaste were considered to be reputable and those who were promiscuous were not. These background and moral concerns were not brought out on issues of consent or even force, but rather they were used to validate or impugn the credibility of the victim. This was also seen in courts in the United States until the 1990s, when the rape shield laws and other rules began to generally prohibit these types of questions from being asked of the victim. Most of our legal concepts for criminal acts are based on English common law and when looking briefly through the history of rape offenses, we can see where some of our own processes, prejudices, and rape myths originated.

The major change in the way we started to view these offenses really started back in the 1970s during the rise of the feminist movement, when we finally started to study the offenders and started looking at the victims and

---

[10] Hale, M. (1670). *History of the pleas of the crown.*

how these offenses impact their lives. Until the late 1980s to 1990s there were no police departments with specialized investigative sections to deal with rape and similar offenses and there was not much specialized training. In fact, before this time period, a detective's assignment to investigate sex crimes was considered the last stop for the burnouts, disciplinary problems, incompetents, or malcontents within a department. It was where bad performers were assigned before they quit, retired, or were fired. This section dealt with weirdos and perverts and crimes that most other detectives were uncomfortable hearing about.

It was also prior to this time that rape victims were almost considered as untouchables, meaning no one wanted to have anything to do with them—not the police, not prosecutors, nor even medical personnel. They were somewhat like damaged goods that no one truly understood. With all the rape myths so well established within the police ranks, if victims presented with no real injuries, no one really believed them or had any interest in working on their cases. There was a time when even emergency room doctors would go out of their way to avoid doing any work or treating rape victims—not just out of a lack of compassion, but because they did not want to be called to court or grilled on their findings by defense attorneys. So, victims were often made to spend endless hours in the emergency department waiting room with other patients, and it was not unusual for them to give their initial police statement in the waiting room because the hospital did not have an examination room available for them to get them away from the public. They were frequently examined by male doctors and most emergency room doctors only had a rudimentary amount of training in the collection of evidence. It was often a hit-or-miss experience, depending on who was on call at the hospital, if the evidence was ever located, and if it was collected correctly.

The last hurdle to jump for victims was the prosecutors and, like the police and medical personnel, they also did not like prosecuting the majority of rape and sex crimes unless they were "good rapes"—that is, they had evidence that included injuries to the victim, other witnesses, forensic evidence, and especially a confession from the defendant. Prosecutors often declined to even consider taking cases to court in which:

- There were no injuries to the victim.
- The victim was involved in drinking alcohol or using drugs.
- The moral and sexual background of the victim could be called into question.
- The victim was a known prostitute, hitchhiker, or sexually indiscriminate.

Until the 1980s and 1990s it was very rare for a victim who was not severely beaten and without the physical or forensic evidence available to ever have her day in court. Again, it was not any single component but rather the entire criminal justice system that was hesitant to become involved in these cases. Our thought process and approach to these crimes and toward the victim have changed dramatically since the 1970s, and it is encouraging to note that this is not how the police, medical personnel, prosecutors, the courts, and even the various state legislatures look at these crimes during the 21st century.

This brief historical look at rape and sexual assault explains the background or origin of some of the rape myths that we will discuss in greater detail throughout the text and the rationale behind some of the investigative steps we suggest. One final perspective we need to address in the introduction of this subject is the extent of the problem; we must ask: "How prevalent are these crimes in the United States today?"

▶ Extent of the Problem

One of the other problems associated with rape and other sex crimes is determining the extent of the crimes, or how many are actually committed each year and who the victims are. Like *unfounded* statistics discussed earlier, the extent of the problem, or how many rapes actually take place in the United States every year, may devolve into another hotly contested subject between the same groups mentioned earlier in an effort to show that rape or sexual assaults are a lesser or a greater problem in our country and society. This should not be that difficult because the Federal Bureau of Investigation (FBI) collects annual crime statistics from law enforcement agencies across the United States and then publishes them annually as part of their Uniform Crime Report (UCR). So, theoretically we should be able to go to the UCR and look up the crime of rape to determine how many acts were reported during a specific year and also be able to determine through comparisons with other years how the crime trends and if the crime rate is rising, staying the same, or is going down. The UCR for 2009 is shown in **Table 1-1**; it is based on the statistics for previous years. The offense of rape and other crimes of violence continue to show a general downward trend, with minor fluctuations, from the number of reported rapes and other violent crimes from the mid-1990s.

According to the preliminary results that were assembled for 2010's UCR, all four of the violent crime categories, which include murder and nonnegligent manslaughter, forcible rape, robbery, and aggravated assault, again show a decline nationwide when compared with 2009 data. The 2010 UCR reflects an additional decline of 4.4% of murder and nonnegligent manslaughter, a forcible rape decline of around 4.2%, a decline in robbery of 9.5%, and also a decline in aggravated assault of around 3.6%. The UCR provides a good idea of how many crimes are being reported across the United States and we therefore could get an idea of the problem. Unfortunately, the FBI's UCR only collects statistics from those incidents that were actually reported by participating law enforcement agencies. However, rape and sexual assault offenses are widely recognized by almost all experts as one of the most underreported crimes in the United States; therefore, these official statistics do not necessarily reflect *all* of the rapes that were committed during any year, only those which were officially reported to the police.

TABLE 1-1 Crime in the United States: By Volume and Rate per 100,000 Inhabitants, 1990–2009

Year	Population[1]	Violent crime	Violent crime rate	Murder and nonnegligent manslaughter	Murder and nonnegligent manslaughter rate	Forcible rape	Forcible rape rate	Robbery	Robbery rate
1990[2]	249,464,396	1,820,127	729.6	23,438	9.4	102,555	41.1	639,271	256.3
1991	252,153,092	1,911,767	758.2	24,703	9.8	106,593	42.3	687,732	272.7
1992	255,029,699	1,932,274	757.7	23,760	9.3	109,062	42.8	672,478	263.7
1993	257,782,608	1,926,017	747.1	24,526	9.5	106,014	41.1	659,870	256.0
1994	260,327,021	1,857,670	713.6	23,326	9.0	102,216	39.3	618,949	237.8
1995	262,803,276	1,798,792	684.5	21,606	8.2	97,470	37.1	580,509	220.9
1996	265,228,572	1,688,540	636.6	19,645	7.4	96,252	36.3	535,594	201.9
1997	267,783,607	1,636,096	611.0	18,208	6.8	96,153	35.9	498,534	186.2
1998	270,248,003	1,533,887	567.6	16,974	6.3	93,144	34.5	447,186	165.5
1999	272,690,813	1,426,044	523.0	15,522	5.7	89,411	32.8	409,371	150.1
2000	281,421,906	1,425,486	506.5	15,586	5.5	90,178	32.0	408,016	145.0
2001[2]	285,317,559	1,439,480	504.5	16,037	5.6	90,863	31.8	423,557	148.5
2002	287,973,924	1,423,677	494.4	16,229	5.6	95,235	33.1	420,806	146.1
2003	290,788,976	1,383,676	475.8	16,528	5.7	93,883	32.3	414,235	142.5
2004	293,656,842	1,360,088	463.2	16,148	5.5	95,089	32.4	401,470	136.7
2005	296,507,061	1,390,745	469.0	16,740	5.6	94,347	31.8	417,438	140.8
2006[3]	298,754,819	1,435,951	480.6	17,318	5.8	94,782	31.7	449,803	150.6
2007[3]	301,290,332	1,421,990	472.0	17,157	5.7	91,874	30.5	447,155	148.4
2008[3]	304,374,846	1,392,629	457.5	16,442	5.4	90,479	29.7	443,574	145.7
2009	307,006,550	1,318,398	429.4	15,241	5.0	88,097	28.7	408,217	133.0

[1] Populations are U.S. Census Bureau provisional estimates as of July 1 for each year except 1990 and 2000, which are decennial census counts.
[2] The murder and nonnegligent homicides that occurred as a result of the events of September 11, 2001 are not included in this table. The crime figures have been adjusted.
[3] The crime figures have been adjusted.

Source: From the FBI Uniform Crime Report, 2009. (http://www2.fbi.gov/ucr/cius2009/data/table_01.html)

▶The Unreported Crime

As will be discussed in much greater detail later in the text, not all victims actually report being assaulted to the police, and rape has often been labeled as the most underreported crime. There are many reasons why victims may choose not to report their victimization, but it is important to acknowledge the number of unreported incidents in order to get a better understanding of the actual number of incidents that take place. One method used to make that determination is through the use of victimization surveys, wherein questions about crime and their victimization are sent to a large number of citizens or to a certain population. The thought process is that the selected respondents would have a chance to report their victimization via a criminal offense which for some reason was never reported to the police nor put through the legal process. One of the more common governmental surveys is the National Crime Victimization Survey (NCVS), compiled by the Bureau of Justice Statistics (BJS). The NCVS was initiated in 1972 to complement the official statistical information on those incidents already reported to police. This allows for the collection of additional information and aids in the determination of the actual prevalence of crime by including those crimes which were never reported. The NCVS is an annual effort completed by about 80,000 persons age 12 and older in approximately 43,000 households twice each year regarding their victimizations from crime. The NCVS collects information on rape and sexual assaults as well as other offenses such as robbery, aggravated assaults, simple assaults, and some property crimes such as burglary and theft.

Other private or nongovernmental surveys have been completed with the intent to uncover unreported incidents, sometimes targeting a specific population group, and again to determine the exact number of incidents and victims or at least identify those which were never reported to the police. One often cited survey was completed by Mary Koss et al.,[11] which was particularly focused on college both male and female students, in an effort to determine the victimization rate and how many of these incidents were unreported to the police. The survey was administered at 32 different universities and colleges across the United States, to a national sample of 6,159 male and female college students who actually participated. The survey questions were designed to determine the actual instances of rape, attempted rape, sexual coercion, or other unwanted sexual contact ranging from age 14. Some of the more important findings that Koss reported included:

- One-quarter of women in college were victims of rape or attempted rape, and the vast majority knew their assailants.
- Fifty-two percent of all the women surveyed have experienced some form of sexual victimization.

---

[11] Koss, M. P., Gidycz, C. A., & Wisniewski, N. (1987, April). The scope of rape: Incidence and prevalence of sexual aggression and victimization in a national sample of higher education students. *Journal of Consulting and Clinical Psychology, 55*(2), 162–170.

- One in every 12 male respondents admitted to having fulfilled the prevailing definition of rape or attempted rape.
- Of the women who were raped, almost three-quarters did not identify their experience as rape.
- Three-quarters of the women raped were between ages 15 and 21; the average age at the time of the rape was 18.
- Forty-seven percent of the rapes were by first or casual dates, or by romantic acquaintances.
- The majority of instances took place off campus with nearly 50% taking place at the males' home or car, or other location.
- One-third of the women had never discussed what happened to them to anyone.
- More than 90% never reported incidents to the police.

These findings sent shockwaves through the country, because this was a potential offense rate far beyond what anyone had ever suspected. Since this study was released many other experts have come forward with criticism of the study, particularly the makeup of its questions, which seem vague and easy to misinterpret. Using terms such as "unwanted sexual contact" were argued as being too ambiguous and unclear to count as an actual forced or coercive sex act of "rape." What is interesting about the study is that it has resulted in more conversation about the design and execution of the study rather than examination of its results, and, like other aspects of rape, the acceptance or criticism of the results depends on which group is considering it. The main important point of this study is to validate that there are many incidents of sexual assault and rape that are not being reported to the police and that many incidents involve much younger victims and offenders than we may have believed. The exact number is not known and the problem of these types of anonymous surveys is that they are based almost exclusively on the self-reporting of an event, without an ability to later verify their accuracy. The survey administrator is absolutely dependent on the information supplied by the respondents. This means the survey is also subject to deliberate falsification of information if the respondent so desired. What percentage is or could be false is really unknown. It is unlikely we will ever know for certain how many more offenses have taken place that are never reported, but it is important to know that there are more incidents that occur than are officially reported.

Further validation that many rapes go unreported comes from studies of incarcerated sex offenders who report being convicted of one or two rapes, but may have admitted to committing many more that were never reported to police. Again, such information is dependent on self-reporting which is subjected to deliberate falsification from the respondent, but such information supplied by an offender is a statement against self-interest and thus may be a little more accurate or believable.

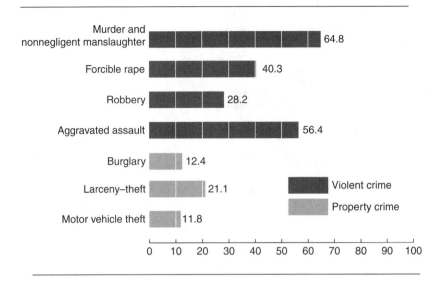

FIGURE 1-2 Percent of crimes cleared by arrest or exceptional means, 2010.

Source: From the FBI Uniform Crime Report, 2010. http://www.fbi.gov/about-us/cjis/ucr/crime-in-the-u.s/2010/crime-in-the-u.s.-2010/clearances-figure

▶ Clearance Rates and Prosecution

The annual FBI UCR also provides statistics for clearance rates for these same crimes and reflects what is also known as the solved rate. For a case to be cleared requires at least one person to have been arrested, charged with the commission of the offense, and turned over to the court for prosecution.[12]

Figures 1-2 and 1-3 were obtained from the 2010 and 2009 UCRs and reflect the overall clearance rates for these same violent crimes. Note there is a slight, insignificant downturn in the clearance rates between 2010 and 2009. Basically, this means that for every 10 rapes reported, the police were able to make an arrest or close the case as resolved in 4 of them. An average clearance rate of 41% for rape is significantly below that of murder, negligent homicide, and aggravated assault, but is significantly higher than robbery, burglary, and other property crimes. The problem is not just clearing the case, but being able to take the case to court and then to get a conviction. Getting the case to court and getting a conviction is, of course, one of our

---

[12] For the purposes of the Uniform Crime Report, a crime index offense is cleared when a law enforcement agency has identified the offender, there is enough evidence to charge him, and he is actually taken into custody. The arrest of one person can clear several crimes, or several persons may be arrested in the process of clearing one crime.

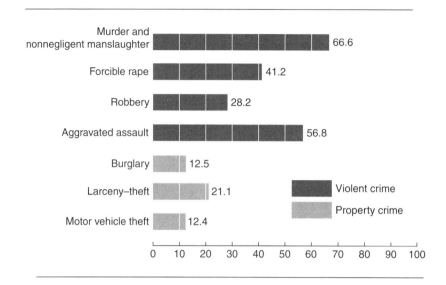

FIGURE 1-3 Percent of crimes cleared by arrest or exceptional means, 2009.

Source: From the FBI Uniform Crime Report, 2009. http://www2.fbi.gov/ucr/cius2009/offenses/clearances/index.html

main goals as detectives. Unfortunately, there are a going to be a great many cases that prosecutors will determine lack any prosecutorial merit and may decide to drop charges against a suspect. This could be based on the lack of evidence, no other witnesses, or even the prosecutor's impression of the victim and his or her complaint.

It is also possible that victims at some time during or following the investigation may elect not to go forward with the investigation or decide to drop charges against the offender. It is also very likely the prosecutor will decide to accept a plea bargain from the offender, which is an offer to plead guilty, but for a lesser offense. Many times this offer allows the offender to plead guilty for a minor crime such as simple assault or some type of property crime such as burglary or unlawful entry in order to avoid pleading guilty to rape or another sex-related crime and thus escaping other control measures such as registering as a sex offender. Even still, when those cases do end up with an arrest and a prosecution, there is always a chance that the jury is not convinced beyond a reasonable doubt of the offender's guilt and the offender is acquitted.

What we have to remember whenever we try to determine how effective we are as police officers in working these cases is that it can be very frustrating. Although we may have cleared or resolved a case, it does not mean it will lead to a prosecution or a conviction; perhaps worse, even when there is a conviction, it may not necessarily mean the offender will end up in prison or, just as likely, he will only receive a suspended sentence or probation.

▶ Conclusion

This chapter identifies several important issues and problems associated with the investigation and prosecution of rape and sex-related crimes. First, these offenses have been long looked at as criminal acts and often deserving the most severe of penalties. However, they have not always been seen as a crime against women themselves, and even more importantly, historical laws and procedures were sometimes designed to inhibit, prohibit, and even discourage a woman from making a false report against a man. As we will see throughout the remaining text, this fear of a false report, whether real or imagined, has an impact on the way that rape is investigated, the way the victim is seen, and the way the case is prosecuted in court. It is also clear that throughout history it was the victim and her background, her morals, and her behavior that were scrutinized more closely than the suspect.

It is also hard to judge whether we as police are having any effect in our efforts to catch offenders and punish them. It becomes difficult to accurately judge police failure or success when it is clear not all offenses are being reported. Although we accept that many victims do not report their assaults, the problem is that we do not know *exactly* how many go unreported because we generally have to depend on self-reporting surveys that may or may not be accurate, depending on the survey questions and motives of the respondents. We also know there are false rape reports or reports we later determined did not occur as alleged. But since there is no standardized method to collect such statistics we also have to depend on studies that examine a few separate police departments and then perhaps extrapolate the results.

These are just a few of the issues that surround the investigation of rape and sex-related crimes; detectives need to be aware of these issues and their impact on individual victims, their communities, and society as a whole.

▶ Further Reading

MacFarlane, B. A. *Historical Development of the Offence of Rape* [Originally published by the Canadian Bar Association in a book commemorating the 100th anniversary of Canada's criminal code, titled: "100 years of the criminal code in Canada; essays commemorating the centenary of the Canadian criminal code", edited by Wood and Peck (1993)]. Retrieved May 14, 2012, from http://www.canadiancriminallaw.com/articles/articles%20pdf/Historical_Development_of_the_Offence_of_Rape.pdf

LeDoux, J. C., & Hazelwood, R. R. (1985). Police attitudes and beliefs towards rape. *Journal of Police Science and Administration, 13*(3).

Raphael, J., & Logan, T. K. *The use (and misuse) of data on rape: Restoring sexual assault to the national agenda*. A white paper prepared for the DePaul University College of Law and the University of Kentucky. Retrieved May 14, 2012, from http://www.counterquo.org/assets/files/reference/The-Use-and-Misuse-of-Data-on-Rape.pdf

CHAPTER TWO

The Female Victim

In order to successfully investigate sex-related crimes, it is vital to understand the potential impact on the victim. Although detectives can sympathize with the victim and become quite familiar with the abuse and trauma victims may have experienced during their assault, most still may not grasp how the whole concept of rape affects females even before any assault actually takes place and continues to affect them long after the event is over. The purpose of this chapter is to explain the effects of these assaults on victims and why they may seem to exhibit unusual or unexpected behavior after they have made their complaint.

▶ Before the Assault

For women, the fear of being assaulted and injured actually begins well before any assault takes place, and the fear of being raped or attacked directly affects women and how they live their lives. For some women, rape is feared more than murder[1] and the best examples of this can be demonstrated in how women react to different situations and their overriding concern for their safety. Examples include small personal safety practices such as an insistence to park closer to the entrance of the mall or department store when going to shop; walking toward their vehicle or house with their keys already in their hand; and looking downward while approaching an unknown man, never making eye-to-eye contact with them. It is not unusual for women to take some type of self-defense classes and then prepare themselves further by carrying some type of personal protection device, such as a firearm, mace or other chemical spray, or a whistle. This fear or wariness of a potential assault also directly affects how concerned men tend to be over their wives, daughters, and other female loved ones. This concept is best explained by a few

---

[1] Warr, M. (1985). Fear of rape among urban women. *Social Problems, 32,* 239–250.

simple questions: Do we treat our daughters differently than we treat our sons? Are there situations or places we might allow our teenage sons to go or participate in some activity but would forbid or discourage our teenage daughters from going by themselves? As parents, we generally demand to meet and evaluate the young men who want to date our daughters, but is there the same insistence or concern to meet the young woman your son is dating? If we meet the young man who wants to date our daughters, is it because we want to make sure we have done all we could to protect them from being assaulted? Women may also decline to participate in certain events because of their fear of being assaulted whereas such concerns are generally not expressed by men. Other examples of women's modified behavior include their manner of dress for certain situations, where they decide to go or not go, and what activities they may participate in.

These examples are simple but recognizable concerns women and men express over the threat of becoming a victim of rape or sexual assault. It is important to recognize how much these behaviors and concerns have become a part of our culture and society. They are so "normal" that we may not even be aware of why we are doing such things and such preventative measures are often subconscious rather than actual conscious thoughts. It is also the reason why we (police) become so suspicious when the actions of the female victim run counter to what we normally expect from them.

▶ During the Assault

During assault, victims suddenly have to deal with the very thing they have feared and tried to protect themselves against their entire lives. Now, unlike their perception of how they would respond if ever confronted, many victims become concerned with only one overriding thing: trying to survive and not get hurt. For many who are attacked in a blitz-style assault, there is no chance to run or escape and their sole defensive action may be to cover up or try to ward off the physical attack. In other cases the event is a complete surprise, such as waking up with a knife to the throat and threats against their children or having someone they thought they could trust suddenly turn on them. This fear of death or injury and their desire to simply survive can lead victims to do whatever is necessary to live through the attack. This often translates into victims freezing and offering no physical resistance to the attacker, which unfortunately, victims typically view after the event with a great sense of guilt or shame as they begin to process what happened to them. When considering the wide range of possibilities victims may be confronted with during a sexual assault, it is not that difficult to understand their fear. Examples of what might happen to a victim include:

- The victim could be kidnapped and taken to another location.
- The victim could be bound, gagged, and physically assaulted.

- The victim could be drugged or otherwise incapacitated and unable to resist.
- The victim could suffer a multitude of possible injuries including cuts, contusions, lacerations, broken bones, bites, or even internal injuries.
- The victim could be forced into degrading or humiliating sex acts.
- The victim could be photographed during the assault.
- The victim could be left naked in a public area.
- The attack could result in pregnancy or sexually transmitted disease (STD).
- The attack could lead to severe long-term psychological trauma.

Although somewhat atypical of what we generally find in rape cases, the following case study effectively demonstrates the whole range of possibilities in sexual assaults.

Case Study 2-1

A female finally broke up with her boyfriend of several years who was becoming too possessive and too demanding. The boyfriend, unable to accept the breakup, began to exhibit stalking behavior toward his ex-girlfriend in order to somehow win her back. The ex-girlfriend, however, was clearly no longer interested and resisted any attempt at reconciliation. One day she was driving her car to go shopping, accompanied by her mother in the front passenger seat and her two children strapped into carseats in the backseat. As she turned onto the on ramp leading to the highway, her ex-boyfriend's vehicle came up from behind and flashed his lights to get her to stop. She pulled over and parked on the side of the on ramp. The ex-boyfriend approached and after a heated argument where the victim again adamantly refused to reestablish their relationship, the boyfriend suddenly pulled a gun and shot the mother three times, killing her instantly. He then forced the woman out of her vehicle and back into his car and drove away, leaving the children crying and strapped into the backseat with the engine still running. As they drove, the ex-boyfriend repeatedly threatened to take her into the woods and kill her and then kill himself. After an extended time driving around and talking, the woman begged the man to go back to the vehicle to retrieve her children and then she would to go with him to a motel. The children were then retrieved and placed into the boyfriend's vehicle. The boyfriend drove them all a short distance to a motel and rented a room. Once inside the room, the woman acquiesced to his sexual demands out of fear for her life and her children's lives. The ex-boyfriend then raped the victim repeatedly as her children watched TV in the same room. During pauses in the sexual assaults, the woman convinced the boyfriend she was ready to get back together with him and begged him not to kill her and children. She managed to come up with an elaborate lie she would tell authorities about the death of her mother and promised not to tell police about what really happened. The boyfriend finally agreed and dropped them off near her house after she promised not to go to the police. As soon as the boyfriend departed, the victim went straight to the police and reported the murder and rape. The boyfriend was quickly arrested, prosecuted, and convicted. This victim then had to deal with the murder of her mother that took place right before her eyes, her own rape and brush with death, and the fact her children were also present for the entire ordeal.

Victims of sex crimes experience what can only be described as an invasion of the most personal part of their body that only they have a right to share. Even during incidents where no real physical injuries or trauma are inflicted, victims still experience the absolute loss of their personal freedom and more importantly the *loss of control* over their very person, and the most intimate aspects of their bodies.

In cases involving drug-facilitated sexual assaults (DFSA) or alcohol-facilitated sexual assaults (AFSA), there are other issues that come into play. In situations in which the victim is rendered unconscious or otherwise unable to resist, the issue of loss of control is even greater. Because these victims have lost control not only of their bodies, but over their consciousness, they may not even be aware something has happened until much later. Even if they become aware of being sexually assaulted, they may not ever fully realize exactly what happened to them while they were in an intoxicated state. It is also common for many victims to be unaware of their sexual victimization until they are contacted by police, who are trying to identify pictures or videos of unconscious women taken by an offender who used alcohol or drugs to disable his victims. As part of their sexual assault, these offenders often photograph or video record the whole event. Imagine the victim who was so drugged she had no idea what had happened to her and only found out about her victimization from the police. Other aspects of DFSA and AFSA are discussed in greater detail later.

Many times these assaults take place not while the victim is out in public and unprotected, but where and when the victim is supposed to feel the safest. Statistics show that more rapes and sexual assaults take place inside the victim's own residence than outside their home.[2] This includes incidents in which the victim allowed an offender into her own residence for whatever reason and is later attacked, and also includes incidents in which the offender makes an illegal entry into the victim's residence during the hours of darkness and accosts the victim, many times while she is asleep.

---

[2] Greenfield, L. A. (1997). *Sex offenses and offenders: An analysis of data on rape and sexual assault.* Washington, DC: Bureau of Justice Statistics.

There are even more difficulties or stressors to the situation when the offender is not some unknown stranger, but someone the victim actually knows. Statistics[3] also show the vast majority of sexual assaults are committed by someone the victim knows. Sometimes these incidents are referred to as *acquaintance rapes*, which simply means that the victim knows or is acquainted with the offender. These *acquaintances* can range from personal friends, coworkers, trusted professionals, family members, to husbands or boyfriends. A great many incidents actually take place during dating situations, resulting in another similar term of *date rape*. There is really just a minor nuance or difference between *acquaintance* and *date rape* situations. Acquaintance implies a general knowledge or relationship, while date rape refers primarily to incidents that take place within those social situations of "dating." These concepts are covered in more detail later in the text.

Regardless of the circumstances, when the offender is someone they know, victims may also have to deal with other personal issues such as possible misplaced trust for the offender. Other emotions include guilt for somehow contributing to their own victimization by sending out mixed signals, wearing the wrong clothing, engaging in consensual kissing and intimate petting with the offender, using alcohol or drugs, and exercising general poor judgment. They may be upset to think they somehow misjudged another, lowered their guard, and allowed someone into their private space only to realize they may have made a huge mistake. These varying emotions are going to play a big part in the way the victim responds and is able to recover after the assault.

▶ After the Assault

Most victims report that their main concern and goal during the actual assault was to survive—to avoid getting hurt or to avoid harm to their children or others. Many times they offer no real resistance and comply with everything the offender demands because they want to avoid getting hurt. This is why victims often may not seem to be as physically traumatized or injured as one might expect during these incidents. But, the emotions resulting from the fear, shame, and guilt will often start to manifest themselves within minutes after the assault and once the offender and victim have separated.

Regardless of the circumstances of the assault and whether or not the victim suffered great physical injury, and regardless of whether the offender was a boyfriend, husband, date, or a total stranger, the victim must now make an important decision: whether or not to report the incident. Based on the circumstances, this is not always an easy decision for victims to make. If victims choose to notify the police, their lives will change completely and often permanently.

---

[3] Extent, nature, and consequences or rape victimization: Findings from the national violence against women survey. U.S. Department of Justice Office of Justice Programs, January, 2006.

Unfortunately, the process of reporting a sex crime is more involved than just picking up the phone and asking for assistance or simply reporting a crime. Once victims call the police they are going to have to expose to others what happened to them and will be forced to deal with the reality of the entire situation. Most victims are also unfamiliar with the entire investigative process and this might be their first real personal contact with the police. Although victims may understand or expect the police are going to ask about what exactly happened to them during the incident, they are probably not aware of the requirement to ask them deeply personal, private, and often intimate questions relating not just to the assault, but to their private life as well. These questions are not designed to injure or further humiliate them, but because of the nature of the event, these questions are often necessary. The victim will be asked about aspects of the assault including the before, during, and after. Other types of questions include but are not necessarily limited to:

- What was the victim made to do or what was forced upon her?
- What sex acts did the offender demand, and what was the victim forced to perform?
- Was the victim drinking alcohol or taking drugs?

Explaining the sex acts that they were forced to perform or that happened to them can be very traumatic for victims, especially when the sex acts went beyond their normal sexual experience or were especially embarrassing or humiliating. Then consider how victims must feel when describing these same events to strangers, often having to repeat what happened to them several times to medical doctors, then to the police, to the prosecutors, and eventually in court.

In some instances, victims must also endure questioning concerning their personal situations and their own sex lives including:

- When was their last consensual sex?
- Where did the last consensual sex act take place?
- Who was their last consensual partner?
- Do they have any STDs?
- When was the last time they douched, showered, or changed clothes?

These questions can obviously be embarrassing but are not designed to be; they are absolutely necessary to evaluate potential physical and forensic evidence at the scene or collected during the victim's medical examination. But it is not hard to imagine the additional embarrassment and guilt from a married victim who has to admit that her most recent consensual partner was not her husband; or the single female who must admit her last consensual partner was a married man; or for a younger female still living at her parents' house to admit she is already sexually active. There is also a very distinct possibility that if the victim does not answer such questions truthfully, these facts will be unearthed by the police during the investigation and thus bring doubt on the original complaint, or even worse, will be brought out and used by the defense in court. So, any effort to protect herself or her consensual partner will often be looked at as an inconsistency, or worse, that the victim is lying about the incident and may very well affect the investigation or prosecution of the offender if uncovered.

Frequently, the various questions being asked and their explanations are happening while the victim is attempting to deal with traumatic shock coupled with a wide range of emotions. Even worse, victims will be evaluated at each step in the process to make sure they are telling the same story in the same manner, and any deviation from their original statement may cause suspicion as to the validity of her complaint. In addition, the victim is asked to undergo an extensive and sometimes invasive medical examination as soon as possible to validate and document any injuries and attempt to collect as much forensic evidence as possible. For a multitude of reasons, the victim is often looked at and treated as little more than a walking "crime scene" during the initial stages of the investigation. This is a necessary part of police protocol because of the fragile nature of the evidence, but it can serve to further traumatize the victim.

While they are undergoing the potentially humiliating medical examination and if the incident took place at their house, it is likely the police are in their home, searching for evidence of the crime. To emphasize the point during training sessions to police, we ask: How many of us right now are ready for the police or any other stranger to come in and see exactly how we live? How many of us want some stranger to be touching our things?

When we fully understand the process of what victims must go through once they report what happened to them, it is not too difficult to understand why so many victims decide not to report their victimization. Even when everything goes as well as possible, it is likely they will still wonder if it would have been better not to have reported their victimization than to go through the subsequent investigation. The combination of the retelling of intimate personal details; the potentially distressing medical examination; the "invasion" of their home, first by the offender and then by the police; and what must seem like the victim's requirement to somehow "prove" she is not lying, is tantamount to what has been termed the *second assault*. The second assault is our criminal justice system (CJS), which provides all of the legal and constitutional guarantees and protections to the suspect, *but provides nothing for the victim*. The victim's protection is supposed to come from the individual components of the CJS—the police, the prosecutor, and the courts. Theoretically, these three components should be working in close harmony with each other to achieve justice for the victim. Unfortunately, this is not always the case; instead, the victim of a sexual assault must also deal with and confront sometimes deeply held institutional prejudices within each component of the CJS.

▶Institutional Prejudices

Institutional prejudices refer to the general mindset or belief systems of individuals, an agency, or a department that may directly influence the response to certain crimes, suspects, or events. These prejudices are not necessarily seen in formal, written departmental policy or protocols, but in the way individual persons react or respond to situations. **Box 2-1** illustrates an example of the institutional prejudices victims have to deal with.

BOX 2-1

In a course on investigating sexual assaults for police detectives, students are shown two photographs of women and told they are both victims of sexual assault. They are then asked to identify the sexual assault victim they would prefer to have come into their office. One photo depicts a victim that has been severely beaten, with visible human bite marks on her arms and back. The other photo shows an attractive younger woman with no visible evidence of trauma who is smiling into the camera and is dressed in a very smart outfit.

Without exception, every group of detectives in every class responds to the question described in Box 2-1 by choosing the victim who clearly shows signs of trauma. Their rationale is that they "feel better" about that victim because they can clearly see signs of trauma and abuse. They almost always observe that the injuries to the victim's back are such that they could not be self-inflicted. Therefore, they all feel better about working that particular case than the other victim's who did not have any visible signs of injuries. These law enforcement professionals were honest in their rationales and responses to the question. While they were more than willing to investigate the crime and give it their all to find an offender, they wanted to be certain the victim was a real victim— meaning the victim was telling the truth about what happened and the detectives would not be wasting their time. This clearly demonstrates the term *institutional prejudices* as it applies to these incidents. This prejudice does not only occur with the police, however, because other similar prejudices exist in each component of the CJS. Various problems and prejudices involving the court and prosecutors are further detailed later in this text. Regardless of where the prejudices arise, they are another issue victims face.

These prejudices are not generally based on sexism, misogynistic thoughts, or some overriding acceptance of the offender's action. Instead, they are developed over a period of time from a combination of many different sources, including inexperience and poor training and bad personal experiences working such cases. Additionally, a great deal of the negative thoughts probably originate from the various rape myths that continue to circulate around the profession and through our society, regardless of their validity. Rape myths are common beliefs about the offense of rape and rape victims that are thoroughly embedded in our society and culture but are not based on facts. Some of the most common myths are listed in **Box 2-2**.

BOX 2-2 Rape Myths

- Women who do not want to be raped can avoid it.
- Women reporting rape without physical injuries are lying.
- Women naturally lie about rape.
- Women secretly fantasize about being rape victims.
- A man can't rape his wife.
- Only "bad" women get raped.
- If the assailant, victim, or both are drunk, the assailant cannot be charged with rape.
- If a person does not "fight back" she/he was not really raped.
- Women who are drunk are willing to engage in any kind of sexual activity.
- Rape and sexual assault are provoked by women who tease.
- Women "cry rape" because they had sex and then changed their minds.
- If it is really rape then the victim will report it immediately.
- Rape only happens to women who are on the streets late at night.

It is the combination of these and other rape myths together with false rape complaints which cause a general suspicion to fall on almost every new victim and perpetuates these institutional prejudices. Unfortunately for all victims, every well-publicized false rape complaint adds to the suspicions of police toward every new victim. Examples of such highly publicized cases are described in **Case Studies 2-2** and **2-3**.

Case Study 2-2

Cathleen Crowell

On July 9, 1977, Cathleen Crowell, then a 16-year-old high school student, was observed by a passing police patrol walking alone in a park at night. She appeared dazed and injured and reported to the police she had had been physically assaulted, abducted by several men in a vehicle, driven around town, and raped in the backseat of the car. She claimed that during the assault the offender used a broken beer bottle to make several cuts across her abdomen. During her medical examination semen was noted in her underwear. During the investigation the police identified a likely suspect and Crowell was shown several mug shot pictures. She identified a likely suspect from the photos and later participated in a physical line up. She was able to identify the same young man in the lineup as her attacker, and the man, later identified as Gary Dotson, was arrested. Dotson had a minor criminal record, but nothing violent or involving sex crimes. Forensic examination of the semen stain found the same blood type as Gary Dotson. Crowell then testified in court, identified Dotson as her attacker, and he was convicted and sentenced to a lengthy prison term. His subsequent appeals were all denied and he was destined to remain in prison for a long time. However, in 1985, some 8 years after her initial report, Crowell (now Webb), now married with children, came forward to her church pastor and confessed to helping send an innocent man to prison by lying about being raped. She insisted that she had made up the entire story because she had been having unprotected sex with a boyfriend and believed she may be pregnant. She believed being pregnant would cause her great problems with her foster family and she could gain acceptance and sympathy if she were seen to have been raped. Unfortunately, although she came forward asking for Dotson's release from prison, neither the prosecutors nor the courts believed her recantation. It still took a considerable amount of work to gain Dotson's eventual release from prison. As a side note for this case, Dotson was actually among the first persons released from prison based on DNA analysis that confirmed the semen found in Cathleen's underwear was from her boyfriend at the time and not Dotson.

Case Study 2-3

Tawana Brawley

On November 28, 1987, an African American female teenager was seen climbing into a plastic garbage bag and then lying down in the muddy ground inside an apartment complex in Wappingers Falls, New York. Witnesses were uncertain what was going on with the female and contacted the police. The girl was later identified as 15-year-old Tawana Brawley and she was found with her clothes torn, cut, and partially burned. Her body and clothing were smeared with feces, and written in charcoal on her chest and torso were the words "KKK," "NIGGER," and "BITCH." Brawley, who had been missing for 4 days, reported she had been abducted by several white men shortly after she got off the bus after school and was taken into the woods and sexually assaulted. She also claimed that at least one of the men was wearing a badge, implying that a police officer was involved in her assault. She reported being held for 4 days and repeatedly sexually assaulted, racially taunted, and physically abused. The case was quickly seized upon by famous civil rights activists who viewed it as a means by which to demonstrate that the police and judicial system were racist and corrupt. It became unimportant that many of the facts and circumstances as reported by Brawley proved to be inaccurate or blatantly false. Forensic tests of her rape kit found no evidence of sexual assault, she had no bruises, contusions, scratches, or other injuries consistent with her story, nor were there any injuries from exposure of bare skin which would be expected if someone was outside when the temperature dropped below freezing at night. There were also several other discrepancies in Brawley's story, as she began telling different versions of what happened to different people.

Other witnesses placed her attending parties in a nearby town during the period when she was supposed to be "missing." More importantly, witnesses observed her, on the morning she was allegedly abducted, entering an empty apartment at the same complex. Other forensic examination indicated the damage done to her clothing had occurred in that same apartment and the animal feces smeared over her body when found were determined to have come from her neighbor's dog. Although all evidence pointed to a false complaint, the civil rights activists persisted in their support of Brawley, and eventually directly accused a number of men from the local police, the county district attorney, and the Governor of New York of being actively engaged in a cover up. After 7 months of investigating the facts, the county grand jury determined that Brawley's charges were false and that her condition when found had been self-inflicted. It was never clearly established why she concocted the false complaint, but it is suspected she did so to avoid getting into trouble for cutting school and staying out with her boyfriend.

The concept of and other problems associated with false complaints are covered in greater detail later in this text, but for this chapter, the importance of false complaints is their contribution to police officers' general suspicions of every new victim that comes into their offices. This suspicion absolutely contributes to the institutional prejudice and unsympathetic, unprofessional, and callous treatment of victims by police; examples of this treatment have been described by several female authors, including Susan Estrich,[4] Robin Warshaw,[5] and Susan Brownmiller.[6]

Contrary to the various rape myths, the facts about rape and sexual assault tell a much different story. The actual facts of rape are that most victims are not assaulted by strangers and not seriously physically injured. The violent attacks in dark alleys or the kidnapping and torture do of course take place, but are actually infrequent. The reality of sexual assault is the vast majority of victims are not physically assaulted and therefore may not display any outward signs of trauma or injuries that we have been programmed to expect. Unfortunately, after the assault so many victims seem to do everything "wrong" in the eyes of the police—meaning they do not to act in the way police believe a victim should act. Examples of victims' behavior that run counter to police expectations include the following:

---

[4] Estrich, S. (1987). *Real rape: How the legal system victimizes women who say no*. Cambridge, MA: Harvard University Press.

[5] Warshaw, R. (1994). *I never called it rape, the MS. Report on recognizing, fighting, and surviving date and acquaintance rape*. New York: Harper Collins.

[6] Brownmiller, S. (1975). *Against our will: Men, women, and rape*. New York: Ballantine Books.

- Victims often shower or douche before calling the police.
- They change clothes, throwing out or washing the clothes they were wearing during the assault.
- If the assault takes place inside their own house, it is not unusual for victims to try to clean up the scene.
- Victims do not immediately call the police to report the crime.
- The delay in reporting can be hours, days, even weeks.
- They report the incident to family or friends but decline to report to the police.
- They are uncooperative with the police.
- They may hesitate to discuss certain aspects of the assault.
- They refuse the medical examination.
- They contact the offender again.

None of these actions negates their victimization, but they do create difficulties for the police and the subsequent investigation. The problem is the dichotomy of a victim reporting the incident to the police and requesting assistance after having hindered the investigation by destroying forensic or physical evidence or refusing to cooperate and provide the necessary information needed to find and capture the offender. What also makes so many cases very difficult to understand is the fact that victims do not always act or respond to the assault in the way we as detectives believe a victim *should* act after such an experience. This includes a wide range of what may be considered as inappropriate emotions and actions such as smiling, laughing, displaying a carefree or seemingly unconcerned attitude, or failing to fully cooperate with the investigation. This "inconsistent behavior" is better described as *counterintuitive victim behavior*, and is covered in more detail in the following section.

▶Counterintuitive Victim Behaviors

Counterintuitive victim behaviors are actions or behaviors by the victim that seem out of place or inconsistent with the event. We see these actions and behaviors both during the actual assault and afterward. Although they may be indicative of a false complaint, they are also very likely part of victims' personal *coping mechanisms* developed to adapt and adjust to their particular situation. Considering the fact that during the assault victims are mostly concerned about surviving and not getting hurt, it is therefore *not* inconsistent when victims do not physically resist or are compliant with the demands of the offender. After the event, victims are not necessarily thinking about such things as evidence, forensics, and having to corroborate their statements. It is very likely that they have never been a victim before and while dealing with the flood emotions and fear of the event, simply return to what they know or what they think they should do. There may also be other background or cultural issues at play with some victims that could also cloud the issue. These responses are not always present in each individual victim, but they are not so unusual as to raise immediate suspicion as to the validity of the complaint. **Case Study 2-4** emphasizes this point.

Case Study 2-4

The police were having difficulty in evaluating a complaint made by a 68-year-old female who reported she was accosted in her bed by a male who had apparently broken into her house in the middle of the night. She was forced to get up and give the intruder money from her purse and afterward was sexually assaulted in the living room, both on the sofa and then on the floor. The man then fled the area. However, the woman did not immediately call the police and instead started to clean her living room, including blood on the carpet originating from her own internal injuries caused during the assault. The police were not called until the next morning when a relative of the woman came to visit and observed the woman in obvious shock, wearing bloody bedclothes, as she was trying to clean her blood from the carpet. It took several minutes for the victim to tell the relative what happened and for the relative to summon the police. Medical examination revealed trauma to her genitals but no semen was noted. The woman was only able to give a minimal description of her assailant and few details about the sexual assault, stating simply, "He just got on top of me and did it," but refusing to provide any further details. With no signs of forced entry to the house, some of the older detectives were seriously beginning to disbelieve the woman's complaint, thinking she might be suffering from some type of dementia and might have actually caused the injuries to herself, perhaps through some sort of self-gratification. They believed this would explain why she was cleaning up the house and never actually made the report to the police herself. However, this was a clear demonstration of counterintuitive victim behavior, and further investigation of the victim and the condition of the remainder of the house revealed the true explanation.

The victim was described as a very likeable, 68-year-old widow, who had lived in the same house in the same small town since she was married at age 18. Her husband had passed away 5 years before, and she had 2 grown children who lived in other small towns nearby. After only a few moments of discussing the case with the detectives, it was clear the woman was not suffering any type of dementia or loss of mental capacity. As described by the police, the woman had poor vision and without her glasses could hardly see anything in focus, which could explain her inability to properly describe the offender in any detail. It was also very likely based on her individual circumstances that her husband was her one and only sexual partner. Her lack of details about the sexual assault, therefore, was likely the result of her own shock, embarrassment, and humiliation over the incident. The victim's descriptions relating to the robbery of money from her purse and events leading up to the assault and events after the assault were very clear and precise—only the details of the sexual assault were limited. In regard to the house, the police reported the entire house was immaculate and very well maintained. It was then easy to explain that cleaning the house was likely the woman's way to emotionally deal with her victimization. Based on her own life experiences this was her way to cope with the situation. It was likely she was not able to grasp or accept what had happened to her at that point, so she simply returned to doing what she would normally do if the house was messy, and she was trying to clean it up. Based on this evaluation, the police then looked at the case from a different perspective and eventually an arrest was made.

As demonstrated in the case study, the victim's response was nothing like police would have expected under those circumstances and their initial response was to doubt the veracity of her initial statement and look for other possible explanations. This is not always the fault of police as many have not received sufficient training to understand and recognize counterintuitive behaviors are part of the victim's coping mechanism to the event. Other examples would include a victim who is questioned about the sexual assault and answers with a slight giggle or smile. This is not the victim laughing at what happened, but most likely feeling embarrassed—a giggle or smile is often just a nervous response.

In 1974 Burgess and Holmstom[7] first coined the term *rape trauma syndrome* (RTS) as a way to explain some of the immediate reactions and long-term effects on victims who have been sexually assaulted. RTS is essentially a form of post-traumatic stress disorder (PTSD). Burgess and Holmstrom described RTS as having two distinct stages. The first is an immediate or acute phase "in which the victim's lifestyle is completely disrupted by the rape crisis." This stage is the one most often confronting the police during the preliminary investigation and their initial interactions with the victim. The effects include physical, emotional, and behavioral stress reactions that result from the person being faced with a life-threatening event. Immediately following the assault the victim may exhibit severe emotional mood swings as the realization of the events begins to sink in. These emotions could include general denial and disbelief over the events, marked by comments such as: "I can't believe he did this. I can't believe this happened to me. Why did this happen?" Then, just as quickly, the victim might display anger and outrage over the incident, making such comments as, "That bastard, he has no right to do

---

[7] Burgess, A. W., & Holmstrom, L. L. (1974). Rape trauma syndrome. *American Journal of Psychiatry, 131*, 981–986.

this to me. Who does he think he is?" It is not uncommon for victims to express fear of the offender or outwardly display fear of any man. It is also not uncommon for victims to alternately express guilt, shame, and embarrassment as they come to terms with what happened.

After some period of time (depending on the victim and the events), victims enter the second phase, known as the *long-term process*, "in which the victim must reorganize their disrupted lifestyle." In this stage the victim must come to terms with what happened to her and eventually decide to continue with life. For many victims this is easier said than done; the long-term effects may last weeks, months, years, or in some cases a lifetime. Some of the many short- and long-term symptoms and reactions to sexual assault are listed in **Box 2-3**.

BOX 2-3

The Acute Phase

Physical reactions: nausea, nervousness, tension

Sleep disturbances

Eating disturbances

Shock, disbelief, denial

Disorientation

Humiliation, guilt, and shame

Feeling dirty, unable to get clean

Emotional outbursts

Withdrawal or detachment from events

Sense of limited future with their life, marriage, or love life

The Long-Term Process: Reorganization

Changes in lifestyle

Continuing nightmares, sleeping disorders, and flashbacks

Development of phobias and hypervigilance

Exaggerated startle response

Avoiding activities that are reminders of the event

Desire to change jobs, housing, or any general disruption of normal events

For women: gynecological problems and changes in menstrual cycle and functioning

Musculoskeletal pain, migraine headaches, genital/urinary difficulties

Problems with normal bowel movements after anal assaults

Continuing general depression

Lack of sexual interest with former consensual partner

Aversion to any sexual activity

Pain during intercourse

Suicidal thoughts

There is no way to predict how any particular victim will respond to her assault and a lot will depend on the victim, the offender, and the dynamics of the event. The victim refers to individual background, life experiences, education, and prior sexual experience. Offenders have their particular typologies as well, along with their interactions with the victims, if they are known or unknown, and also their sexual experiences. The last real unknowns are the dynamics of the event and what exactly happened, how much force was used if the victim was injured, and what sex acts were demanded or were forced on the victim. As we look at the victim and her actions before, during, and after, we have to take all three of these variables into consideration. Dealing with these symptoms or reactions also depends on what support system—such as mental health assistance or a good family support structure—is available to the victim to help her deal with the situation.

Another common finding is that some victims' extreme sensitivity to safety concerns, which is likely to last long after the assault, could lead to compulsive behaviors such as repeatedly checking the windows and doors of their homes and always being hypervigilant about what is going on in their surroundings. This can be exhausting to victims as well as those around them who may not understand the compulsion and hypersensitivity to their security. This can also impact their willingness to leave their comfort zone or engage in normal activities. Some victims may also increase their use of alcohol or illicit or prescription drugs as a way to self-medicate their continued stress, anxiety, or fear. Some may require medication or begin to use alcohol to help them fall asleep. Unfortunately, the use of alcohol and drugs in this respect and for this purpose could lead to other long-term problems, such as dependency. These effects can have an impact on significant others who must also adjust to these changes.

As victims begin to regain control over their lives and come to terms with what happened to them, there is a very real possibility that they may announce to the detective or the prosecutor they no longer want to go forward with the prosecution; even to the point of *recanting* their complaint. In fact, this is so common it is almost an expected event in the course of the investigation on cases that are taking a long time to progress to court. Victims become tired or frustrated with the process and may say they are eager to move on with their lives and forget about the incident. However, it is likely that the victims have not yet come to terms with the issue and attempts to drop the case are a form of denial that anything actually happened to them and a desire to avoid the pain of delving further into the issue. Many detectives misinterpret the victim's request to drop the charges as an attitude of indifference displayed by the victim and as indicative of a false report. Unfortunately, some detectives who do not put forth the effort to find out the cause of the victim's change of heart might not only stop the investigation but also seek to charge the victim with making a false police report. Detectives must take a critical look at all victim recantations first as a sign of a victim's frustration or other efforts to deny anything happened to her. All recantations should be thoroughly checked out and investigated and never taken at face value. They are typically an indication that the victim, regardless of statements to the contrary, still has not come to terms with the events and may need to go to some type of counseling.

Eventually the victims will begin to gain control over their lives and go back to the world they once knew—how long it takes to reach this point is again dependent on the victim, the event itself, and whether or not the victim was able to maintain her support system or was able to obtain mental health counseling. Also important to the recovery is whether the offender was a stranger or someone the victim knew. If the offender was a stranger, victims will likely continue to cope with issues of safety and security and increased awareness, while in cases where victims knew the offender, they will likely contend with trust issues in their future relationships.

▶ Vicarious Victims

Another type of victim that we seldom consider but may be just as victimized by the event are those known as the *vicarious victims*. This term refers to those persons who are also affected by the rape and sexual assault by their association with the victim. This includes parents and spouses, boyfriends, brothers, or any other close friend who, even though they were not threatened or physically harmed, are just as likely to be affected by what happened. Many times they will be suffering from guilt or frustration of not being able to protect their loved one from harm. Some cultures will also suffer from shame, disgrace, or loss of honor due to a child's or wife's victimization. This becomes important because such feelings directly impact their ability to deal with the situation and hinder the long-term recovery of the victims. The vicarious victimization of family members has to be recognized and understood as the case is developed as it could also lead to recantations by the victim who is also being influenced by them. We see this when victims elect not to pursue the investigation or testify in court because of the perceived humiliation or shame that is also felt by their families.

Yet another group of vicarious victims that is seldom considered—in spite of their tremendous impact on the investigative process—is comprised of the police, the medical personnel, and the prosecutors who deal with these cases and victims day in and day out. This victimization can be seen in how these persons treat the victim—how quick they are to disbelieve, how they sometimes only do the minimum work necessary to close the case, and how they try not to get too personally and emotionally involved with the victim or the case. This is one of the ways the *institutional prejudices* are created, not by misogynist police officers, but those who may become burnt out or even numb to the victims and the effects of the crimes on them. It takes a concerted effort not to allow this to happen, because this only serves to further traumatize the victim and allow offenders to go free to offend yet again and create other victims.

One of the ways to combat this situation is to simply adopt and maintain a version of the golden rule: *"I will investigate this case in the same manner as I would want another detective to investigate if my wife or daughter is ever a victim."*

▶ Summary

Deciding to report a rape is going to change a victim's life forever, and no matter how much a woman thinks she is prepared to respond and protect herself, so many times she never has a chance. When assaulted, victims simply decide they want to survive and not get hurt or not allow their children to be hurt. Victims are going to "do everything wrong" as far as the police and prosecutor are concerned and will not act in the manner which we think they should have acted. Unfortunately, we are going to be confronted with many forms and instances of counterintuitive behaviors or actions that just do not make sense to us. But remember, there is no telling how we would respond in a similar situation. Would we remember to do all the right things? Our first meeting with victims and our subsequent treatment of them is going to set the stage for the entire investigation and have a significant impact on their eventual recovery.

CHAPTER THREE

Special Victims

There is no such thing as a typical rape case and victims can be found in any size, shape, color, national origin, age, or sex. This chapter is about the frequently overlooked victims, those that we may not typically think about when we think about sexual assault and rape. These special victims include *males, the elderly, the mentally disabled,* and *the underage* who are all routinely victimized; as with other cases, offenses against these victims are not always reported to authorities and properly investigated. Proper statistics are not always collected to fully document the extent of their victimization.

▶ Male Victims

Historically, the rape of a defeated male enemy was considered the special right of a victorious soldier and was seen as the true symbol of the defeat and total subjugation of the opposing army. This was based on a widespread belief that any male who was sexually penetrated, even if by rape, was considered to have "lost his manhood," and could no longer be a warrior or ruler. Male rape was also considered a particularly cruel form of punishment; it was reserved by the Romans as punishment for adultery and by the Persians as punishment for violation of the sanctity of the harem. Most detectives are well aware of young boys and even teens being targeted and sexually victimized by pedophiles. In fact, boys are much more likely than girls to be sexually abused by strangers or by authority figures in organizations such as schools, churches, or athletic associations. Offenders who target younger males, generally juveniles, are also more likely to have multiple victims compared to those who target and sexually assault younger females. The assailant can be a stranger, an acquaintance, coworker, teammate, family member, or someone the victim knows well and trusts.

The legal definitions of rape and sexual assault against a male can vary between the states. For instance, in some states, the term *rape* is used only to define a forced act of vaginal sexual intercourse while an act of forced anal intercourse is termed *sodomy*. In other states, the crime of sodomy may also include any forced oral sexual act or the sexual use of any foreign object. More and more states are now using more gender-neutral terms to define acts of forced anal, vaginal, or oral intercourse, wherein all forced sex crimes are described as sexual assaults or criminal sexual conduct. The various crimes are then further defined by degrees depending on the use and amount of force or coercion on the part of the assailant.

It is unclear exactly how many males are assaulted in their lifetime, because like other sexual assaults not every crime is reported to the police, but estimates range from 9–20% of all males being sexually assaulted at some time in their lives. Unfortunately, there is a bit of a societal and cultural bias against seriously considering adult males as being victims of sexual assault. This may be attributed to some stereotypical beliefs and rape myths that men do not experience sexual assaults outside the homosexual community or prison setting. In reality it is incorrect to refer to the sexual assault of men by men as "homosexual rape," since such assaults often have nothing to do with the sexual orientation of either the victim or the offender but rather are perpetrated to assert physical dominance over the victim. Like the rape of women, there are also many rape myths pertaining to male victims; some examples are included in **Box 3-1**.

BOX 3-1 Myths Pertaining to Male Victims of Sexual Assault

- Men cannot be sexually assaulted.
- Male rape only happens in prisons.
- Rape in gay relationships or couples does not exist.
- Getting an erection or ejaculating during sexual assault means you "really wanted it."
- Most rapists are strangers.
- Male rape victims do not suffer as badly a female rape victims, because there is no fear of becoming pregnant.
- Men cannot be sexually assaulted by women.
- Only gay men sexually assault other men.
- Only gay men are raped or sexually assaulted.
- Men who rape other men do so for sexual gratification.

As with female victims, the sexual assault of men should be viewed as an act of violence motivated more by aggression, power, anger, or the need to control, and not as an act of sex. Sometimes the assault is an expression of contempt toward someone the offender perceives to be a homosexual. Assaults on men also tend to involve much more physical force, and thus can be more traumatic and brutal, but unless there are serious injuries they are often not reported. Male victims often suffer from a sense of being "different," which can make it more difficult for men to seek help and report the incident to police. They may also be confused when, during an anal assault, they experience an erection a result of stimulation of the prostate gland. This is not an indication of sexual arousal but a physiological response, but it adds to the confusion of the victim who is dealing with the assault and the after effects.

Impact on the Male Victim

Men who have been sexually assaulted may experience the same emotions of shame, guilt, and anger as female victims, along with the same overwhelming sense of a loss of control over their own bodies. Heterosexual male victims may especially doubt their own actions leading up to the assault and be concerned that they somehow gave off "gay signals" that were then acted upon by the offender. It could be similarly damaging for a gay man who has not yet openly admitted his sexual preference in that he was somehow broadcasting his "secret sexual identity" and now may be "outed" because of the assault. Many victims are unable to outwardly express these emotions or feelings, because men are taught that it is *unmanly* to be so emotional. Instead a male victim may show anger more readily, since this is one emotion that is acceptable for men to express. Hostility and aggression are more likely with male victims rather than the tearfulness and expressions of fear commonly expressed by females. All of these factors combine to affect the victim who reports their victimization to the police. Victims typically report two basic long-term concerns because of their victimization: Either they may start to question their own sexual identity and wonder if they are actually homosexual themselves, or they may fear they will become sexual offenders themselves. Neither is the case of course, but both are commonly expressed victim concerns. Other long-term effects can include but are not limited to those found in **Box 3-2**.

BOX 3-2 Long-Terms Effects on Male Victims

- Denial, shame, or humiliation
- Depression
- Fear and a feeling of loss of control
- Loss of self-respect
- More cautious, less self-confident attitude
- Vivid flashbacks to the attack
- Anxiety
- Withdrawal from normal activities
- Revenge fantasies against offender (sometimes extremely violent)
- Nervous or compulsive behavior
- Depression and mood swings
- Hypersensitivity to personal safety
- Increase in alcohol and drug use or abuse
- Changes in sexual activity (both homosexual and heterosexual)
- Self-destructive behavior
- High risk behaviors
- Changes in sleeping patterns
- Intimacy issues
- Questioning of sexual identity
- Development of phobias related to the setting
- Imaginary ailments (hypochondriacal symptoms)

Women can also sexually assault men. Although it is not nearly as common as male-on-male assault, it does happen. Frequently it is seen in marital or other domestic-type relationships and in the workplace where the female is in the role of the superior or supervisor and may force herself onto a male subordinate. Perhaps one of the best examples of this is when female teachers use their age, life experiences, and maturity to manipulate their younger students into having sex with them. When a woman does sexually assault a male, the possible impact on the victim may be downplayed by the police, prosecutors, and the general public, and with the exception of juvenile victims, it may not even be viewed as a crime. Other aspects of females as sexual offenders are covered in greater detail later in the text.

Police Investigation of Male Victims

Most detectives receive extensive training in conducting investigations on children or juvenile victims of sexual assaults, but receive almost nothing by way of training for male-on-male sexual assaults. The exception would be correctional investigators who are very familiar with male-on-male rape since it is common within many correctional facilities. In cases within the correctional setting, rape is more about power, control, and dominance rather than any type of sexual gratification, and many times multiple offenders are involved. The rape itself may be inflicted to intimidate the victim or others within the institution or as retaliation for some institutional cultural offense.

As in other rapes, many of the offenders in male-on-male cases are known to the victim as coworkers, fellow students, or teammates. However, there is likely to be a larger percentage of stranger offenders.

Groth[1] identifies three general styles of attack for these offenders as entrapment, intimidation, and physical force:

- *Entrapment* refers to instances where the victim might first be rendered unable to resist through intoxication or drug usage, and once unconscious, is sexually assaulted. An example is an offender who offers to take the intoxicated victim home, and then along the way stops and makes sexual advances. In this sense the victim is essentially "trapped," and because of his intoxication cannot escape or is unable to resist the offender's advances. Another example is the victim who claims to wake up to the offender performing oral sex on him as he was sleeping or passed out from alcohol intoxication. We often see this with roommates or others who already ready know each other.

- *Intimidation* refers to threats of physical violence or even brandishing a weapon at the victim to overcome resistance and obtain his compliance. We may also see something similar in instances involving superior and

[1] Groth, N. A., & Birnbaum, H. J. (1979). *Men who rape: The psychology of the offender.* New York: Plenum Press.

subordinates wherein the intimidation used may not necessarily be a physical threat, but rather involving current or future employment, duty assignments, and opportunities for promotion.

- *Physical force* is basically a physical assault on the victim which may include simply holding down a victim and removing clothing or could be combinations of punching, kicking, or the use of a weapon until the offender is able to control the victim and overcome any resistance. The amount of physical force may depend on the resistance of the victim or could be part of the offender's need to physically punish the victim.

The sexual assault may take many forms depending on the offender and his ability to control the victim and overcome resistance. Examples include forced anal intercourse on the victim or forcing the victim to perform fellatio on the offender. However, it is also likely the sexual assault may consist of the offender performing fellatio on the nonconsenting victim. There are even instances where the offender has demanded the victim perform anal sex on the offender. Unless the victim was severely traumatized and required emergency medical treatment, many reports of male-on-male assault are delayed sometimes for lengthy periods of time, and in many cases they are never reported at all.

In some cases the victim may visit a medical clinic not necessarily to report a sexual assault, but out of concern about possible exposure to HIV or other sexually transmitted diseases. The medical examination of the victim and collection of forensic evidence is covered in greater detail later in the text. Regardless of how a report was made, as detectives we need to look at each report in the same manner as we would any other complaint, being cognizant that the male victim is going to have many of the same emotional issues as the female victim, including the fear he will not be believed or will be laughed at by authorities. The investigation is carried out in much the same manner as with female victims, including a victimology, a behavior-orientated interview, crime scene investigation (if possible), and forensic medical examination.

Although not as frequently reported as sexual assaults on females, male-on-male rapes and sexual homicides do happen to both homosexual and heterosexual victims. Well-known serial killers such as Randy Kraft, John Wayne Gacy, and Jeffrey Dahmer targeted, raped, tortured, and murdered homosexual and heterosexual males.

▶ Elderly as Victims of Sexual Assault

Elderly victims can be male or female and are defined as being 60 years of age or older, although many people in this age range are fully capable and live normal lives with minor lifestyle differences based on normal aging process. There are others in this same age group who are unable to function normally and are generally dependant on others for their needs. This includes those with physical handicaps, medical conditions, or with some type of cognitive impairment, such as dementia or Alzheimer's. The elderly are considered *special victims* because they are not always able to defend themselves, and therefore may be specifically targeted or seen as targets of opportunity because of their inability to resist or flee and because the older generation may hesitate to discuss sex, even their own victimization, under any circumstances. Thus, when they are victimized, they may be hesitant to make a complaint. Some elderly may be physically unable to communicate their victimization to others—another example of a cohort whose victimization may be much underreported.

Sexual assaults on the elderly can take place at any time or location including inside their own residences and long-term care facilities. Offenders who target the elderly tend to be some type of caregiver, and may include relatives, extended family members, or employees at residential facilities. The motives of offenders who target the elderly are unclear. They may be the result of a deviant sexual attraction to the elderly known as *gerontophilia*, or they could be seen as a way to redirect anger. In the latter case, the anger may not be directed at that particular victim, but the victim may symbolically represent some other elderly person. It is also clear that some offenders may look at the elderly as people who can be easily manipulated and over whom they can exercise power and control. It is also possible for assaults within a facility to be committed by other residents within the facility.

There are three types of approaches used by the typical sexual offender to gain control over a rape victim known as *the con, the blitz,* and *the surprise.* Burgess, Prentky, and Safarik[2] have provided a variation to these three standard methods of approach when dealing with elderly victims:

- *The con* is where the victim may be manipulated or coerced into compliance with the offender. This may be a case of convincing the victim to accompany the offender to some location where the offender can assault the victim in private. Because some victims are totally dependent on others, the con may not be that difficult to establish. Many victims, because of a physical or mental infirmity, are dependent on others and therefore may be naturally trusting toward others.

- *The blitz* is a sudden physical assault used to gain immediate control over the victim. Because of their age and physical limitations, a great deal of physical force may not be needed to obtain control, overcome resistance, and gain compliance. However, because of their frailness, even minor physical assaults can be dangerous to an elderly victim and even the threat of violence may be enough to gain compliance and cease any resistance.

---

[2] Burgess, A. W., Prentky, R. A., & Saffarik, M. (2008). Sex offenders of the elderly. In R. R. Hazelwood & A. W. Burgess (Eds.), *Practical aspects of rape investigation: A multidisciplinary approach* (4th ed.), Boca Raton, FL: CRC Press.

- *Surprise* occurs when victims are assaulted while they are sleeping or under the effects of medication. Touching or fondling victims as they are being moved or while undergoing some form of medical procedure is also possible. Many assaults within residential facilities may take place within the victim's own room even when a roommate is sleeping in the next bed.

Sexual assaults perpetrated against the elderly may include the full range of vaginal, anal, and oral sex, but assaults may also be limited to touching, fondling, or otherwise exposing the victim's genitalia. A major difference between elderly victims and younger adult victims is the amount of physical trauma to their genitalia that results from sexual assault. Many elderly victims may not have engaged in any type of consensual sex for a number of years and the natural aging process may present physiological problems that make intercourse more painful. An example is provided in **Case Study 3-1**.

Case Study 3-1

An 80-year-old female victim reported that in the early evening hours her 50-year-old female caregiver answered a knock on the front door of her residence and was immediately blitz assaulted by a younger man who forcefully entered the house. He then violently attacked the caregiver by repeatedly stabbing her until she was dead. The offender then came further into her house, took the elderly victim out of her wheelchair, carried her back to her bedroom, and laid her on the bed. He then undressed her, removed her adult diaper, and vaginally raped her, causing her great physical pain. Afterward the offender briefly looked around her house and then walked out the front door.

The victim eventually was able to call police and because of her injuries she was admitted to the local hospital. She was very confused and because of the extent of her injuries it was several days later before the police were finally able to talk with her about what happened. During the interview she was very uncomfortable with talking about any aspects of the sexual assault, explaining that her husband was her one and only sex partner during her entire life. He had died some 20 years before, and she said, "I thought I was through with all that." She had a very difficult time describing exactly what happened to her, because as is the case with many elderly people, the subject of sex is seen as very personal and private. The victim may still be embarrassed about discussing the subject with a female detective.

Although the victim in Case Study 3-1 was not physically beaten by the offender, like other elderly postmenopausal victims, she did sustain significant genital trauma in the form of tearing of the vaginal vault during the rape as well as a broken pelvis. The event was so emotionally and physically traumatic she was never was able to fully recover physically or mentally from the assault and died several months later, never leaving the hospital.

There are many investigative difficulties associated with elderly victims. Burgess[3] has identified seven of these factors or barriers that frequently confront the police conducting elder sexual abuse investigations:

- Delay in reporting
- Delay in evidence collection
- Impaired mental/physical functioning
- Assessing intentional bruising and injury
- Sensory defects
- Psychological response of the victim
- Relationship between the victim and offender

All of these factors can be very problematic for police officers and some-times very difficult to overcome. Other barriers, as noted in the case study, include a general hesitancy of some victims to report or even discuss aspects of their sexual assault out of embarrassment. Other victims may suffer from dementia or Alzheimer's disease and may be unable to adequately explain what happened to them and who was involved. Many sexually abused elderly victims may also lack a local support system, such as family and friends they may turn to for assistance. It is also possible in many situations for the victim to have been assaulted on numerous occasions before the abuse is ever reported to the police. This delay may be the result of their fear of the offender or even a result of a long-term care facility trying to limit damages from possible lawsuits by not notifying authorities of any resident complaints or evidence of employee misconduct. Other examples include a general hesitancy of family, friends, or the authorities to believe what an elderly or mentally disabled person may report because of their diminished cognitive abilities; thus, some complaints may be dismissed as being fanciful or delu-sional. Some offenders have come to understand this hesitancy to believe victims and use it to their advantage.

Signs of Abuse

Although elder abuse can take on many forms, there are several common findings that may alert authorities, caregivers, or family members that some type of abuse may be occurring. Some of these findings are listed in **Box 3-3**.

---

[3] Burgess, A. W. (2006). *Elderly victims of sexual abuse and their offenders.* Rockville, MD: National Institute of Justice.

BOX 3-3 Signs of Elder Abuse

- Genital or anal pain, irritation, and/or bleeding
- Bruises on external genitalia or inner thighs
- Abrasions, scratches, or lacerations
- Cigarette burns on a nonsmoker
- Difficulty walking or sitting
- Presence of pressure marks
- Sexually transmitted disease
- Inappropriate relationships between victim and suspect
- Inappropriate response to efforts to undress or bathe the victim

---

Any of these findings, without an adequate explanation, should raise the attention level of caregivers and family members. Although these are some typical injuries we see with sexual assault, it does not mean some of these injuries or findings might not be the result of the normal aging process, an accident, or could otherwise have been self-inflicted.

Some behaviors are also consistent with some type of abuse. Examples include victims' general withdrawal from normal or routine activities and preferring to remain in their bed or in their room. This behavior is even more important when this sudden change in behavior or attitude is directed toward a particular person. Sometimes a little more difficult to see or understand are changes in their financial accounts, altering wills, checks written as loans or gifts, or cash gifts, especially if given to non-family members. This may be a sign of some type of extortion or blackmail—perhaps a victim is paying the offender in order to be left alone. It can also be a sign of the victim being conned out of his or her money by an offender.

Interviewing the Elderly

Interviews of the elderly take a little more time and patience, both to arrange and to conduct. Like other victims, it is important to take some time to get to know elderly victims, develop some trust and rapport, and make them feel comfortable before discussing the events of the assault. It is also important during these initial stages of introductions, polite conversation, and rapport-building to attempt to determine the victims' cognitive and physical ability and their emotional state. This also includes a general assessment of their ability to talk, to hear, and to see with or without glasses. If there are some sensory problems then we want to be able to adjust our methods to make sure we can effectively communicate with them. Caregivers or family members may be able to provide a key to better communicate with the victim, such as the need to speak louder, to interview in a more brightly lit room, or even to allow the victim to write down their answers to your questions on paper.

Victim interviews are covered in greater detail later in the text, but it is important to note that elderly victims may not be able to provide as many offender behavioral details as can younger victims because of the stress of the interview and physical state of the victim. However, some elements to cover in the interview, such as how the offender was able to seize and maintain control of the victim or the victim's nonconsent and efforts to resist, might require less detail. Controlling or obtaining compliance from an elderly person is generally not going to be too difficult. Therefore issues of consent may not be as important as issues of the sexual assault and the strength of the identification of the offender. Evidence is very important if the report is made contemporaneously with the event. However, with the elderly victim a medical examination should also be conducted for treatment and not just documenting possible traumatic injuries. Lastly, we need to be very aware that the same symptoms of rape trauma syndrome are also likely to be present, along with the other emotional issues previously discussed.

Even with a good offender identification and victim testimony, there is often a hesitancy of prosecutors to take elder sexual abuse cases to court because of the difficulties of some cases. Such difficulties include potentially complicated medical issues, a lack of independent witnesses or corroborating evidence, a delay in reporting, conflicting victim statements, and a lack of jury appeal of some victims. Other factors include the frequent lack of physical and forensic evidence because of the delay in reporting, the question of the victim's capacity to testify, and general concerns about the victim's overall victim competency. These include their ability to express what happened to them immediately after the assault or that their capacity to express themselves may diminish in the intervening period between the incident and court date.

▶ Mentally or Physically Disabled Victims

These are victims who are considered to have some type of disability defined as a sensory, physical, mental, or emotional condition lasting 6 months or longer that makes it difficult for a person to perform activities of daily living. Mentally disabled persons also typically have developmental delays in learning, processing information, and possibly an inability to recognize threats or react to threats that makes them highly vulnerable to victimization. Although their mental disabilities may affect their ability to independently care for themselves or adapt to changing conditions, they are increasingly being integrated into the community and away from institutionalized care. The vast majority are able to live successfully within their community, but may be four times more likely than their neighbors to be targets of sexual assault and other violence. For sexual predators, mentally disabled persons are seen as easy victims because they may not understand what is happening to them, and in some cases may actually participate in their own victimization, as shown in **Case Study 3-2**.

Case Study 3-2

The Glen Ridge Case

This well-publicized case occurred on March 1, 1989 and involved a mentally disabled 17-year-old female who was enticed by a group of high school athletes she knew to go with them to the basement of a nearby residence. After initially refusing, she agreed when told one of the popular boys she liked would go on a date with her. A number of high school boys were already in the basement when she arrived. The victim was then convinced to undress herself, and the boys later inserted a broomstick and then a baseball bat into her vagina. The victim said she didn't resist because she thought if she did these things the boys would like her and it was very important to her to be liked. The difficulty in this case was establishing if the victim was able to knowingly give consent to the act. While being interviewed, the victim did not seem to understand what was going on and did not want to get the boys into trouble because she still wanted to be friends with them. Several of the boys were arrested and convicted of the assault.

As shown in this case study, the mentally disabled may be especially prone to sexual abuse based their reliance on others, such as caregivers or other authority figures, to help them out or tell them what to do. There is also likely an ignorance of sex or sexuality, and an underlying need to be accepted by others, especially their peers. As demonstrated in the case, the victim may actually participate in their own victimization if asked to do so as a way to please others or to try to fit in with peers. In other cases such as **Case Study 3-3**, the victim may be especially susceptible to suggestion or following directions of others.

Case Study 3-3

State v. Ortega[4]

S.G. was a 30-year-old woman with an IQ in the 40s who lived with her husband in an "intensive tenant support program" that housed mentally retarded individuals and had staff available 24 hours a day. S.G. had a significant eating disorder that prevented her from knowing when to stop eating, could not live independently, and *suffered from an inability to resist the instructions of others.* A caseworker worked with S.G. and her husband 60 hours a week to ensure they received support and education.

---

[4] *State v. Ortega-Martinez 124 Wn.2d 702 (1994)*

On the evening of December 7, 1990, S.G. took a bus to Mount Vernon where her advocate was supposed to pick her up. Because of a mix up, the advocate did not meet her at the bus stop as planned, and S.G. waited "a long time." At some point while she was waiting, she was approached by the defendant, Alejandro Ortega-Martinez and according to S.G., Ortega-Martinez told her to leave with him and she complied. She testified that after they walked together a long time and got into his pickup truck, Ortega-Martinez threatened to kill her if she did not remove her clothing. She described subsequent events that indicated sexual intercourse occurred between the two. It is undisputed S.G. and Ortega-Martinez remained in the truck the rest of the night and that the next morning Ortega-Martinez walked her back to the bus station where he had found her. With the assistance of the Greyhound terminal manager, S.G. then called her advocate. After being returned home by the advocate, S.G. called her cousin. The cousin came to her house and, upon hearing what had happened, notified the police and took S.G. to the hospital. The doctor who examined S.G. found several small bruises on her neck, a bruise on her leg, and trauma to her vaginal area. The doctor testified the trauma to her vaginal area was consistent with injuries from penetration.

In the Case Study 3-3 the victim was able enough to ride a bus, get married, and live in a residential facility but unable to express nonconsent or actively resist. In this case the victim was not forcefully removed; rather, she was just told to accompany the offender away to a point where he could assault her and she obeyed. As with all sexual assaults, consent of the victim is a very important part of the investigation. The difference with mentally disabled victims is that they may in fact have consented or did not resist the advances of the offender, so the issue is going to be whether or not such a victim was able to give knowing consent or appreciated the concept of consent versus nonconsent. This is demonstrated in **Case Study 3-4**, which is based on a case from Washington state wherein the offender tried to establish the victim's consent to his sexual advances but the evidence presented established the victim was so mentally disabled she was incapable of understanding the full nature of the sex act.

Case Study 3-4

State v. Summers[5]

According to the record of trial, the victim, a 44-year-old mentally ill woman, met the defendant on a public street. After talking to the victim and telling her to follow him, the defendant took her inside a private apartment and

---

[5] *State v. Summers*, 70 Wn.App. 424, 432, 853 P.2d 953, *review denied*, 122 Wn.2d 1026 (1993)

proceeded to have sexual intercourse with her. Testimony at trial established that although the victim knew a baby was a result of a man "put[ting] a wiener in you," but she only spoke in fragmented and confusing sentences, had no knowledge of sexually transmitted diseases, thought a penis was a tail, and did not know how to read. Holding the jury had sufficient evidence from which to conclude the victim did not understand the nature or consequences of sexual intercourse, the court of appeals affirmed the defendant's conviction. It concluded: "The evidence showed that [the victim] had a basic understanding of the mechanical act of sexual intercourse, but this should not be equated with an understanding of its nature and consequences."

These case studies are examples of why there are specific laws enacted to protect victims with any "mental incapacity," defined as: a condition existing at the time of the offense which prevents a person from understanding the nature or consequences of the act of sexual intercourse whether that condition is produced by illness, defect, the influence of a substance, or from some other cause.[6] Mentally disabled victims include those who are permanently mentally disabled or those who are in a temporary state of mental disability due to injury or other medical condition. Some states also have included involuntarily intoxicated individuals into this category of temporarily mentally disabled victims. These protections are seen as society's responsibility to protect individuals from themselves (as in the case of nonforcible sex offenses involving minors), and to protect mentally impaired individuals who may be unable to make judgments for themselves.

Although mistake of fact is not a defense for sexual offenses with a minor, it is a possible defense for a physically helpless or mentally disabled adult victim if the perpetrator can show that he reasonably believed that the victim was not physically helpless or mentally disabled. We try to establish the concept of consent and understanding of the sexual act through coordination with caregivers, doctors, family members, and through the victim's interview.

Interviewing Mentally Disabled Victims

Interviewing mentally disabled victims can be a challenge even to the most talented interviewer, because the interview is not just about gathering information on the criminal complaint; it is also about evaluating victims and their ability to communicate and their understanding of the event. Thus, one of our first steps is to evaluate victims to assess their degree of disability and their ability to explain what happened to them and who was involved. This includes starting out with some basic and neutral warm-up questions to get an overall sense of the victim's vocabulary, attention span, and ability to concentrate.

---

[6] *State v. Summers*, 70 Wn.App. 424, 432, 853 P.2d 953, *review denied*, 122 Wn.2d 1026 (1993)

We also want to make sure that when we start talking about the event, we are not communicating at a so high a level that they do not understand the questions or so low a level that we appear to be condescending. General opening questions could cover such basics as their name, their parents' names, their age, where they live or work, who their best friend is, their favorite TV show or book, or their favorite thing to do. As with small children, in some cases we might want to determine if the victim actually understands the concept of telling the truth and lying. This aspect could be very important in validating the later courtroom testimony of the victim, especially concerning the identification of the offender and the sexual acts. The defense will certainly attack any identification by a mentally disabled person if there is any chance of improper questioning or asking leading questions by the detective. Like child sexual assault victims, a consideration should be made to video or audio record the interview to demonstrate very clearly the ability of the victim to communicate and the way in which they identified the offender. **Case Study 3-5** demonstrates some of the difficulties in interviewing the mentally disabled.

Case Study 3-5

Peters v. Whitley[7]

On February 17, 1982, while Willie Peters sat on the porch talking with a friend, Ramona Washington returned from school and joined them on the porch. Peters was told that Washington was retarded, and Peters whispered to Washington and held her hand. Washington remained on the porch with them until her mother called her in for a bath. After the bath, Washington went outside and disappeared. Washington normally did not venture very far from the house and after a search, Washington's brother-in-law found her on a hill behind the house. Washington had scratches on her knees, elbows, and lower back, and she was nervous and upset. Washington's underwear and sanitary napkin were found hanging on a nearby bush. Washington was incapable of undressing herself, and because of her obesity and lack of coordination, she could not have climbed the hill without assistance. Washington was helped down the hill and taken back to the house where she became increasingly agitated. The police were summoned and Washington and her mother were taken to the police station where Washington identified Peters in a photographic lineup as the man who had harmed her. Washington clapped, laughed, and cried hysterically, as she pointed to Peters's photograph. Washington reacted with similar high emotion when taken back to the scene of the crime. Based on Washington's identification, the police obtained

---

[7] 942 F.2d 937: *Willie Peters, Petitioner-appellant, v. John P. Whitley, Warden, Louisiana State Penitentiary, et al., Respondents-appellees* Sept 24, 1991

a warrant and arrested Peters. That evening, Washington was taken to the hospital for an examination. The emergency room doctor observed the scratches on Washington's body but found no lacerations in her genital area. Although tests for the presence of seminal fluid and spermatozoa in Washington's vagina were inconclusive, their probity was diminished because Washington was menstruating at the time of the incident. Menstrual blood can wash away evidence of a sexual assault. At trial, the officers who investigated the incident and conducted the photographic lineup testified along with Washington, her mother, and others who were present. Washington also identified Peters in court by pointing to him and calling him "Ronnie," and she testified that he stuck his "thing" in her (pointing to the vagina). The judge examined her outside the presence of the jury to determine her competence and questioned her at length to determine whether she could distinguish between the truth and a lie and understood the consequences of lying. Although Washington was not always responsive and her attention wandered easily, she indicated that she knew the difference between truth and falsehood, that she believed in God, that it was wrong to lie, and that she would be punished for lying. After the judge found Washington competent, he put her under oath so that her previous testimony would be sworn. The jury returned a unanimous guilty verdict.

Later in this text when discussing the interviews of other sexual assault victims, it is strongly recommended *not* to conduct a victim interview with family members or close friends present, because of the added pressure on victims not to report certain aspects in front of their parents or friends or because their parents may try to unduly influence them. The mentally disabled may be the exception to this general rule; it may be more helpful to have someone the victim already trusts or is already acquainted with in the room to provide support, or more importantly, to help in the communication with the victim. In Case Study 3-5, the mother and the friend's presence during the police interview of the victim greatly assisted in the interview. Whenever family and friends are used in this manner we want to ensure that they are assisting the victim in the process, but are not answering for the victim. It is also important to note that in all of the presented case studies that had various difficulties in the investigation, particularly regarding the victims' abilities and a lack of forensic evidence, a successful conclusion was still reached; however, it took extra effort to do so.

Offenders

There is no typical sexual offender who targets the mentally disabled; they can be strangers, as described in the previous case studies where victims are targets of opportunity. They can also be persons who are already known and trusted by the victims. They can include family members, personal care attendants, neighbors, schoolmates, or other acquaintances. This may present other problems for detectives, especially when the suspect is a family member, and the rest of the family tries to protect the suspect at the expense of the victim. In some cases it may be important for police and a primary care physician not to totally rely on family members or caretakers to provide an accurate account of the mentally disabled patient's sexual history, ability to communicate, general truthfulness, understanding of sexuality, or ability to consent to a sex act. An independent assessment should be considered by the detective or other forensic experts to confirm his or her ability levels.

▶ Other Status Victims

Although we have concentrated primarily on the mentally disabled, there are other groups of individuals who are equally in danger of being victimized. This includes those persons who are physically helpless—the unconscious, paralyzed, restrained, intoxicated, or drugged—who are incapable of resisting or granting consent to sexual acts. Although not as prevalent, they are still vulnerable because of their overall conditions. The issues of alcohol and drug intoxication and incapacitated victims are covered in greater detail later in the text.

Another common nonforcible sex act is carnal knowledge, or sexual relations with an underage person. In this particular instance the sex act does not have to involve any force and the victim may in fact have consented to the intercourse, but because of the victim's age, the act is a criminal offense. This is another example of what is known as a status offense. A status offense is relative to the victim and assumes based on their status, such as their age and maturity level, they are considered incapable of giving consent to sexual acts.

▶ Conclusion

Special victims can be a challenge for all detectives. First, sex crimes involving the very old and the very young or mentally impaired victims often stir up numerous emotions in everyone involved in the investigation. It takes a concerted effort to remain focused on gathering the facts and evidence, even when it becomes difficult because of the status of the victim. It will also take time and extra effort to gather the necessary information from these victims. But as these last case studies demonstrated, arrests and convictions for these offenses are possible if the extra effort is made by the detective and prosecutors.

▶ Further Reading

Scarce, M. (1997). *Male on male rape: The hidden toll of stigma and shame*. New York: Plenum Publishing.

CHAPTER FOUR

The Victim Interview

The victim interview process described in this text is primarily based on the behavior-orientated interview technique that was first described by Robert Hazelwood and Ann Burgess[1] and used by Hazelwood in his many law enforcement classes given on this subject as well. This technique is centered on a detailed interview with the victim with the goal not just to get the details necessary to establish a criminal offense was committed, but also to provide key identifying data based on the offender's verbal, physical, and sexual behaviors displayed throughout the encounter. Identifying these offender behaviors helps to identify the different personality characteristics exhibited by the offender. Recognizing these characteristics helps to correctly identify the offender type as described later in this text. Once we identify the offender type, we can then use this information to formulate a plan to capture the offender, possibly link cases together, and work with the prosecutor to take the offender to court.

Another benefit of the behavior-orientated interview technique that is extremely important to the investigation of sexual assaults is that it helps deal with the very real problem of false complaints. Using this technique in combination with other techniques described later in this chapter, it is nearly impossible for a false victim to provide the information necessary to continue with their false report. There is simply too much detail required for them to continue. Additional details relating to false complaints are provided elsewhere, and are therefore not covered further in this chapter.

When done correctly, the victim interview can be a very lengthy process, fraught with stress and emotion. So, prior to conducting the victim interview, there are several important things to consider.

---

[1] Hazelwood, R., & Burgess, A. (2004) *The practical aspects of rape investigation: A Multidisciplinary approach* (4th ed.). Boca Raton, FL: CRC Press.

▶Initial Steps

The first step is to evaluate the victims to determine if there is a need to have them examined by medical personnel either because of physical injuries or to look for forensic evidence. This is the first important determination and decision at this stage. If needed, they should be examined and treated as rapidly as possible, before the victim interview is attempted. It is important to stress that such evidence is extremely fragile and needs to be collected as soon as possible. Additionally, if the report is contemporaneous with the event, the victim is going to feel better once they are able to use the restroom, change clothing, and perhaps wash up a little.

The key consideration concerning the medical exam is the time between the event and the report. If the report is made contemporaneous with the event, then the medical examination should be an automatic consideration. If the event took place more than 96 hours prior to the event, then the examination is generally not effective. If the event took place 24–96 hours earlier, then it is strongly advised for the victim to be seen and examined, if not prior to the interview, then immediately thereafter.

Once the medical issues have been addressed, the next decision is whether or not the victim is able to sit through a lengthy interview. This concept runs somewhat counter to what we as police officers generally think about these types of critical interviews. As police officers, we want to get started on the investigation as quickly as possible because we know the best chance of recovering important evidence and solving any case is within the initial stages. For homicides we generally say the best chances of solving a case is within the first 48–72 hours; afterward the chances of solving the case start to diminish. The same is true for most criminal offenses including rape and sexual assaults. But, because the victim statement is so critical for the success of the investigation, when the victim is in no physical or emotional condition to give a good, detailed statement or is too distraught to sit through the lengthy process, then it might be better to delay the interview. We see this in cases where the victim suffered extreme physical trauma or if the assault involved sexual torture. It is also a consideration when the assault took place in the early morning hours, or took place over an extended period of time. If the victim had been drinking alcohol or using drugs, a delay may be necessary if for no other reason than to allow the victim to recover sufficiently enough to render a coherent statement.

The delaying of the victim interview, however, is always a roll of the dice. There are times when the victim returns as agreed upon and is able to give a good account of what happened. There are other times, however, when victims are so overcome by events they elect not to return to the police, or, even worse, they are influenced or threatened by the offender, their family, or a significant other and never return to make their statement. While it is important to get any statement, a rested victim is more likely to give a better statement. We must balance the possibility of getting a better statement with the possibility of the victim deciding not to go forward with their complaint. This is a good example of the cause of some unreported rapes. The greater problem when this happens is that the offender will not be likely to face prosecution and might commit another offense on someone else, or in many situations, with the same victim again. Any delay in taking a statement from the victim is event and victim dependent. If the decision is made to delay the detailed interview for another time, it is recommended that a definite appointment be made before the victim is allowed to go home. This is important because we do want to make certain they come back for their interview at a set time. If the victim interview is delayed, a crime scene examination and medical examination should still be conducted to document and collect any physical or forensic evidence.

Another important initial consideration is who is going to conduct the victim interview and who else is going to participate in the interview process. There are many schools of thought concerning this aspect and many believe a female officer is the best person to conduct the interview. The reasoning is that because of the events, a female may be more understanding or the victim may be more reluctant to discuss embarrassing details with a male. In many cases however, this concept is more likely the result of males being embarrassed and made uncomfortable by the process and subject, thereby suggesting it is better done by females. In reality, with rare exceptions, males can be just as effective as females regardless of what happened during the event. The decision should be based on the victim, including differing cultural and religious considerations. For example, some women would be reluctant to even be in the same room with a man who is not her husband or may be culturally prohibited from expressing to any man what happened. In these situations, common sense dictates that a female officer conduct the interview to avoid any further trauma to the victim. It would also be important to have a female assigned the case or at least be part of the investigation. These situations do not happen often, but they are likely to increase as the number of immigrants increases.

As for who should be present during the interview, there are some basic guidelines and recommendations as well as some definite dos and don'ts. One recommendation is always to have a second person inside the room when you talk to the victim. This second person may be another detective, a female officer, or if available, a rape crisis worker or victim's advocate. This second person is basically present to avoid any possible impropriety complaints made by the victim against the interviewing detective and to provide general support to the victim.

▶ Victim Advocate

The victim's advocate, sometimes referred to as a rape crisis worker, can be an invaluable member of the investigative team and, whenever possible, should be a part of the interview. Their key role is to provide general support to the victims in their time of need. While we as police are generally focused on gaining the facts, establishing evidence, identifying witnesses, and other aspects of the investigation, we frequently forget about the victims themselves. This is another reason for the need for the crisis workers, because it is their function to pay attention to the victims and be able to reach out and offer support during especially embarrassing, emotional, or traumatic moments.

It is also important to coordinate in advance with the rape crisis worker, either in previous mutual training or prior contacts with them. If this is not possible, then it is necessary to sit down and talk with them for a few minutes prior to the interview to make sure they understand their key role in the interview process. Take some time prior to the interview to cover the basic concept and goal of the interview and the potential length of time necessary to gather all of the important details of the event. Brief them on the likelihood of asking the same questions several different times during the course of the interview. This needs to be explained to show that we are neither implying nor insinuating that the victim is not telling the truth or that we do not believe the victim, but that we are trying to get as many details as possible. Experience has shown that many rape crisis workers may not understand the complete interview process and may become defensive and protective of the victim if they think the detective is being unprofessional or does not believe the victim. However, in reality we are trying to capture as many important details as possible, because the more times the victim answers the same basic questions the greater the likelihood we can get additional important details as the victim recalls what happened. The rape crisis worker may not fully understand that point but a short briefing to explain the reasons for our actions will go a long way toward a successful interview. A second important reason to talk with the worker prior to the interview is to advise them not to insert themselves between the detective and the victim by asking questions of their own, answering questions for the victim, or trying to interpret what the victim is saying. Instead, we would like them to basically sit down, hold the victim's hand if necessary, but otherwise remain quiet.

There are two times during the interview when we do want the rape crisis worker to talk or to interrupt. The first is if they believe the victim needs a break because they are becoming emotional or the event is becoming overpowering to them. Remember, this is an emotional event and the last thing we want to do is to inflict additional injury. There are times when short breaks to calm the victim down are in order, and unless there is an overriding reason not to do so it is generally advisable to take a break when requested. The second instance of appropriate interruption is when the victim's advocate may have information they want to provide to the detective—either the victim may have told her something different earlier or perhaps the detective did not fully understand or has misinterpreted something the victim said. In such situations we want the advocate to advise us of this potential error, but not in front of the victim. It is best to take a break, clarify the situation, and then continue with the interview

Other considerations are also important when determining who will be present in the interview with the victim. For instance, it is strongly recommended that family members *should not* be present during the interview with their family member. Rather than helping, family members tend to put considerable additional pressure on the victim and could cause them to hold back critical information out of fear of the possible reaction of the family member. Examples include younger victims who were engaged in voluntary drug or alcohol consumption prior to or during the incident or who were already sexually active prior to the reported crime. Guilt or shame could cause the victim to skip over these important aspects of the event. This may become important when information is obtained later in the investigation that contrasts with the victim's initial statement or where the victim failed to acknowledge. The implication arises that the victim was not telling the truth, which creates problems for the police investigation and the victim who may have to be re-interviewed. Another reason to avoid having family members in the interview is the influence they may have on the process; in many cases the family may even try to take over the interview. Examples of this include encouraging the victim to identify an offender even when they are uncertain, or in some cases, even discouraging a victim from identifying an offender if he is known to the family or is also a family member. We see this particularly with younger and incest victims. Often the adult family member may believe they are helping with the interview by encouraging the juvenile victim, but in most cases they actually are a hindrance and should be excluded.

Husbands, boyfriends, or life partners should also be avoided for the same reason of hindering the victim from telling the complete story and adding additional trauma to the victim. An example would be a victim who out of fear was compliant and offered no resistance to the offender. Although this response is clearly understood by most detectives and police, this may not be understood by a husband who might challenge the victim if present during the interview, as if she could have prevented the assault or willingly participated. Further difficulties arise when the victim must also provide details of some of the offender sexual demands or what she was forced to do. Again, not only does this embarrass the victim but could lead to the additional trauma of having to explain it in front of a husband, boyfriend, or partner. There is also the very real possibility that the victim's partner would become upset at the questioning and insert himself into the process, possibly by defending the victim if questioning is not going the way he expected it to go. There is also a distinct possibility that the husband or boyfriend wants to hear the interview to learn the identity of the offender because he intends to take some action on his own. It is also a consideration that the victim may have been involved in an extramarital affair prior to the assault and would not want to discuss it in front of her spouse. There are many reasons to avoid bringing family members into the interview room and very few advantages; there should therefore be careful consideration before they are allowed to participate or even witness the event.

▶ The Victim's Statement

Another important decision is how to best obtain the victim's official complaint statement, and there are many schools of thought. Traditionally, the victim is interviewed and a written statement is rendered as to what happened. From this statement, the detectives are able to obtain the necessary details and allegations of the various criminal offenses that may have been committed. This is known as locking the victim into their statement, and it is a very important part of the investigation. The advantage to obtaining some type of victim statement is determining the exact allegations and specifics of the event; this statement will then be available for review during the remainder of the investigative process. The disadvantages of a written statement are the potential conflicts that arise from additional information learned later in the investigation that may conflict with the initial statement, or that after time has passed the victim's recollection may change or new information may be remembered. In these situations it may appear as if there is an inconsistency between the initial statement and subsequent investigation or statements. Inconsistent statements are going to be used by the defense as evidence of potential mistakes, misunderstandings, or even allegations of a false report. These potential conflicts are the reason why many prosecutors have instructed police detectives in their jurisdiction *not* to take a written statement from the victim. Instead they are to prepare a written report based on their oral interview with the victim. In this way they believe they can get the basics of what happened, but if there are any conflicts that come up later in the investigation or if the victim's testimony in court varies from the initial report, these inconsistent statements become problematic for the defense who only has a report from the police and not a statement to use against the victim.

There is also a school of thought that promotes video recording a victim's statement in the same manner as child abuse investigations. The concept is allowing the jury to actually see the victim give her statement and see her reactions, as well as capture everything she said during her statement. This offers advantages and disadvantages and must be carefully considered before initiating such a process. The advantage is the video captures everything within the interview. There are many times when certain nuanced points may be lost on the detective as they go through the interview process but then picked up on when they review the interview. Video recording allows the detective to go through and watch the entire process as many times as necessary, and it allows the prosecutor to see the victim and judge how she will respond in court. This process also plays very well to today's reality television culture, since people are used to seeing the process on television. Therefore, it may be very powerful evidence for the jury to be able to see the victim during her initial statement reporting what happened.

Paradoxically, the disadvantage to video recording the victim statement is also the fact it captures everything. In this sense it also will capture those seemingly inappropriate victim behaviors discussed earlier, such as smiling or nervous laughter as they describe what happened. Whereas detectives might be trained to understand these inappropriate behaviors, it may require the prosecutor to locate and use expert witnesses to be able to explain how these behaviors are part of the victim's dealing with the trauma. A video of the victim's interview is liable to be looked at as very powerful evidence for the defense attorney to imply the untruthfulness of the victim's allegation. Therefore, detectives need to understand how seemingly very good evidence can turn into very bad evidence against the case and victim. As long as we as detectives and the prosecutor are aware of the reason for the inappropriate behaviors we can generally overcome any of these problems, but it will frequently take additional experts to fully explain them in court.[2]

One additional step during the course of the interview is to take a few minutes to ask the victim to prepare a rough sketch of the room, house, or area where the sexual assault took place. When the incident is alleged to have occurred at a hotel or at an offender's house the victim's ability to sketch the scene may prove to be powerful corroborative evidence if it matches what is later observed during the scene examination. In some incidents the assault took place inside the victim's own residence and during the course of the assault the offender moved the victim from one location to another. In these situations it is a good idea to have the victim roughly sketch out their residence and then explain on the sketch the path that was taken through the house from location to location. A dotted line maybe used to demonstrate movement in the scene. This will not only aid in the understanding of what happened during the event and perhaps in time sequencing, but it could also spark additional memories of what happened during the event as the victim recreates what exactly happened to her. Later, during the offender interview, the offender will be asked to do the same thing, and this simple sketch may turn out to be important corroboration if the offender also makes a similar sketch. Lastly, this sketch could also prove to be important when conducting the scene examination because we may not know that the offender or victim went into a certain area of the house during the event; this might cause us to take another look at the scene for additional evidence processing. The sketch is an important part of the interview but should not be attempted while the victim is telling their story as it tends to distract them from providing the details of the event. Perhaps the best suggestion is allowing the victim to do the sketch after the basic facts have been obtained but before the written statement is completed.

---

[2] If an agency decides to video record victim or suspect interviews, a policy should be established to ensure that all victim and all suspect interviews are recorded. The problem that arises without such a policy is we are providing a defense attorney with an excuse to cast doubt on the appropriateness or legality of any unrecorded interview. Basically, if the agency routinely records only some of these interviews, the question will become, why wasn't a particular interview recorded? The implication will be that something happened in the course of this interview that police did not want anyone else to see. The solution: If an agency begins to record victim or suspect interviews, then they should record them all.

From the detective's perspective the final consideration prior to the start of the victim interview is to determine the basics of the initial report from the police perspective. We are concerned with the following type of information:

- Who made the report to the police—was it the victim or another person?
- What exactly was reported; what exactly did the victim or other person first report to the police?
- What was the initial observation or examination of the crime scene from responding officers or crime scene technicians?
- What are the initial results from the medical examination, if completed?
- Was there any other contact with any other police officer or detective (to check for consistent statements)?

This basic information is important because we want to determine if there are any conflicts in the victim's initial report, or inconsistent statements by the victim or any witnesses that we want to address and clarify during this first interview. Therefore, whenever possible, we want to speak to every officer or person the victim may have spoken to or interacted with from the time they made the initial report until they arrived for the interview. Such inconsistent statements or conflicts are always better to be addressed up front, rather than later in the investigation, because corroboration of the victim's allegation is such an important aspect of the investigation. We also want to be able to recognize and acknowledge any *consistent* statements from what the victim initially reported, what they reported to other police officers or persons of authority, and then what the victim reports during her initial interview. Consistent statements can be seen as a form of corroboration and can also be very powerful forms of evidence. Conflicts and what appear to be inconsistent statements should be expected and not necessarily looked at as suspicious or as evidence of a false report. Rather this is often the natural result of information being passed from one person to another, to another. What we want to do is reconcile all of these potential conflicts during the first interview. There is an old adage we use when we talk about interviewing child abuse and rape victims. Basically this adage says: *"We interview the victim one time for the prosecution; every other time we interview for the defense."* The meaning of this adage comes from the fact that statements will often change over time and as they are retold. This is actually a natural process as the victim begins to remember more and more of the incident or as memory fades. This however often results in inconsistent statements because the new statements will frequently conflict with what was initially reported. So, every time the victim is re-interviewed we can expect the defense to use this as an example of inconsistent statements or implying that the police somehow influenced the victim to change or add to her story.

The location of the victim interview is also an important consideration, but there are few absolutes as to where an interview must take place. Whereas the preference is generally at the detective's office or an interview room at the police station, we do not want the interview process to take on the trappings of or be confused with an offender interrogation. There are often times when we have to be flexible about the location, and it is not uncommon to conduct the initial interview at a location outside the police station. This may include having to interview the victim in her hospital room if she was severely injured, or at her own residence if the victim is too traumatized to leave her house or unable to find someone to stay with children so she can go to the police station. There may be other cultural problems that have to be addressed prior to the interview so detectives must simply be flexible.

▶ The Interview Process

Establishing rapport and trust with the victim is absolutely vital to a successful interview. Thus, the introductory stages of the actual interview should be devoted to establishing rapport and trust and between the victim and the detective. We can do this by taking a few minutes to explain the interview process. Remember this is likely the first time that the victim has ever had any contact with the police and probably the first them she has been a victim of a crime. Generally victims' only source of reference is what they have seen on television or what others have told them. The process can be overwhelming to someone who has recently gone through an assault. Much like what we did with the victim's advocate, it is a good idea to explain the interview process to the victim, particularly how long it may take and the necessity to repeat certain questions. Again, we want to emphasize this is not because we do not believe them, but rather we want to make certain we capture as many details as possible. We want to give them the option of taking a break when they feel the need. These initial steps are designed to give as much control back to the victim as possible. This is an important consideration because so many victims report that loss of control over their bodies and lives was one of the biggest traumatic experiences of the assault. Taking these few minutes to talk to the victim before we start the actual questioning on the event will go a long way to give control back to the victim as well as establish rapport.

During this initial introductory step is also a good time to gather some basic background information on the victim, which actually accomplishes several important things. First, we will need the background information as part of the victimology assessment that we will be conducting. Such background information includes home addresses, education level, date of birth, marriage status, and their individual family situations. Starting with these basic questions also tends to lower the stress level of both the victim and the detectives who are all engaged in a stressful, highly emotional event. Normal, back-and-forth questions and answers help establish the rapport and lower the stress levels of everyone. The second reason for these basic questions is simply to get the victim used to answering questions—after all, we are subjecting the victims to something they are likely never to have done before.

We do not want this to turn into an interrogation, or a "yes or no"–type question and answer interview, so we are essentially getting the victim used to answering questions in detail. These small steps will pay big dividends in the amount of information obtained during the interview process. This introductory step is almost completely administrative in nature (based on the limited type of personal information) but is a critical step in the interview process and should be looked at as the first step in making a good witness for court and also to aid in the eventual recovery of the victim.

Once the background information has been gathered, it is time to start moving into the core of the interview in which the victim recounts what happened. Remember, nothing happens in a vacuum, so there is always a before, during, and after to every event. Therefore, we want the victims to begin their narration of what happened some hours or in some cases even days before the criminal event took place in an effort to establish the "before" of the event.

What we are looking for is: What was the victim doing, where were they, who were they with, and most importantly, was there any interaction between the victim and the offender leading up to the assault? In cases involving stranger-on-stranger offenses, the *before* we are looking for is what may have brought the offender and victim together or how might the victim have come to the attention of the offender. This concept of what was going on before the incident may also be used to help formulate the victimology assessment as described later in the text. In circumstances where the victim and offender are known to each other, the before of the incident may have to include a much longer period of time than just a few hours. What we are looking for in these cases is the exact relationship between the victim and offender—particularly if they were dating, in a long-term relationship, or married. The before might also have to include details and background relating to their previous relations. How far back and in what detail the 'before' explanation should provide is really victim and event dependent.

The best method for capturing the information concerning the assault is to ask open-ended type questions such as, "Please think about what you were doing or where you were at a few hours before the incident took place. Start there and tell me everything that happened." This is a very open-ended question and what we are looking for is the victim's narration of the entire event. We are looking for and want to encourage the victim to tell her complete story starting from a period hopefully well before the incident, continue through the incident and exactly what happened to them, and then what happened afterward. Using this method the victim is now telling us what she generally remembers of the entire event, and more importantly, she will also tell us what she thinks is important. We also hope to learn whom she had contact with prior to the incident—those who may later prove to be witnesses. Especially important are any witnesses who may have seen the victim prior to the assault and again after the assault to determine if there were any physical or emotional changes noted in the victim. We attempt to learn what the victim was doing at certain times and locations throughout the pre-crime activity, which gives us a chance to identify additional investigative leads for potential interviews with persons she had contact with prior to the assault. We ask the open-ended question and then encourage the victim to continue without interruption through the entire recounting of the assault and its aftermath, including reporting the incident to the police. We want the victim to continue to tell us about the incident until she comes to the end and says something to the effect of, "That's it."

Once the victim has said, "that's it," or words to that effect, she is saying this is the end of her story. Until she comes to that point, the detective's response to any stoppage or hesitancy in the statement should be "please continue," or, "go on," to encourage the victim to continue with her story. As the victim is telling her story we do not want to interrupt or stop the flow of information by asking questions or seeking clarification of statements. When victims are interrupted by questions while telling their story, they often lose their train of thought and valuable evidence may be lost. An example is in the following exchange:

Victim: And then we went to a fast food restaurant, got something to eat, and I said goodbye and walked into the parking lot. I was putting the key into the door lock when I saw a guy getting out of a red...

Detective: So what did you order in the restaurant?

Victim: And I saw he was a—What? Oh, um, a hamburger, I think.

Detective: A hamburger? OK, are you sure?

Victim: Well hamburger or cheeseburger and fries.

Detective: OK, what did everyone else get?

Victim: I don't know. I'm not sure.

Detective: OK, go ahead and continue.

Victim: OK, well then I was pushed to the ground and he started hitting me....

In this case, the victim was about to tell the detective she saw the man parked in a red Mustang next to her car and provide a good physical description of the offender, and even more important, that she had seen him inside the restaurant while she was inside. Unfortunately, the detective interrupted her train of thought, and when she continued she left out that part of her story. This type of incident has occurred many times when the interviewer started asking inconsequential questions that only served to distract the victim. At this stage of the interview, the detective should remain in a strictly listening mode. The victims may be hesitant and halting, or concerned that they are talking too much, so they may need to be encouraged, but the detective's main job at this stage of the interview is to keep the victim talking and telling her story, without interruption. If possible, the lead detective conducting the interview should not even take notes, relying instead on his partner to note the basic facts and identify areas that might require explanation or clarification later in the interview. This allows the victims to continue unhindered with their story.

Not asking questions takes great discipline, because as police officers we deal in facts and evidence. Typically, we want to cut through all of the extraneous information and get to the specifics of the event, and therefore we feel the need to clarify certain statements as they are made. However, when we interrupt the victim, we are interfering with her telling of the story and what *she* believes is important. So, instead of telling us what she thinks is important, she begins to react to our questions and may refocus her story based on our interest or start telling us what she thinks we are really interested in. Once the victim has completed telling her story of the events by announcing, "that's it," or words to that effect, the detectives should take a few moments to review their notes. The victim has now told us the basics of what happened. Because this is the first time she is telling the story, there may be few details pertaining to the event itself, but generally there are a lot more specifics about her actions before and after the event. After reviewing the notes and those areas where additional questioning might be necessary, start again with an open-ended question. This time we want to try to focus a little more on the *during* of the event, or the actual assault, without limiting the events that followed. Therefore, we want to ask something to effect of, "Go back in time to say 15 minutes before the assault took place, and then tell me everything that happened."

Again the victim is allowed to retell her story without interruption from just before the incident, through the incident, and then after. With the second retelling the detectives again are in a strictly listening mode. This second retelling will likely contain increased details particularly during the description of the sexual assault. This increased detail is the result of the victim going through and recalling what happened for a second time. This is normal for anyone recalling a particular event. The narrative should continue until the victim again says, "that's it," or words to that effect. Again, the detectives can take a few moments to review any notes, which at the same time allow the victim to recover and take a break. Then, when ready, the victim will be asked to go back and retell the story with a similar open-ended question to the effect of, "Please go back, just before the actual assault took place, and tell me what happened."

This is the third time the victim has been asked to go over and describe the event; however, by now the focus is more on the assault itself or the *during* of the event and the actual sexual assault than the two previous sessions were. Because this the third time the victim is telling her story there are likely to be even more details of the event, which is normal and expected. The victim continues with her story until she reports, "That's it."

Generally, this point of the interview is a good time for a short break to give the victim a chance to recover. It also allows the detectives to review their notes from the three different questioning periods. There are two key features we want to look at after the initial questioning. The first is whether there are any conflicting or inconsistent statements made between the three times the victim reported what happened. There is likely to be greater detail each time the story is told and there may be insignificant changes both in information added or where certain information may be left out as the story is retold. These examples should not necessarily be considered as a conflict or as inconsistent statements but rather the victim remembering more details or clarifying certain facts. What we are looking for in conflicts or inconsistent statements are those wherein the victim has significantly changed the substance of the events. We are also looking to see where, after retelling the event three times, the victim is still overly vague or appears to be unable to supply any real details of what happened. Another thing we are looking for are any gaps in the sequencing of the event where the victim may have skipped over certain actions. Examples of sequencing gaps are found in **Box 4-1**.

BOX 4-1 Sequencing Gaps

- "I was running along the track and he tackled and raped me and then ran away."
- "We were kissing on the sofa and then suddenly I was naked."
- "I told him no and to stop repeatedly. After he was done he just left me on the bed and walked out."
- "I was fighting him off and then he did it."
- "We were kissing and then my panty hose came off."
- "He was holding me down and I blacked out; when I got up my pants were around my ankles."

There are a few explanations to these gaps including times when victims begin to describe something that happened which made them feel uncomfortable, degraded, or otherwise humiliated. The gap is an area that causes them distress and therefore they attempt to skip over it. There is also a chance that the gaps may be an attempt by victims to avoid having to admit to some participatory conduct, such as their own voluntary use of illegal drugs or alcohol or because they may have initially consented to kissing, petting, or other sexual activity but at some time during the incident they changed their minds. One other possibility is an intentionally false report made by the victim. Gaps appear in this situation because the "victim" is trying to explain what she has never experienced and therefore skips over what we know are important aspects of the event. Both the inconsistent statements and any sequential time gaps need to be addressed, clarified, and explained during the remainder of the interview.

There are also a number of important factors and particular offender behavioral characteristics we should have picked up on as the victim related her story. These factors are important elements of the behavior-orientated interview process and we need to take note of them as they are going to help us determine the type of offender that was involved in the assault through all of his verbal, sexual, and physical behaviors displayed before, during, and after the event. Hazelwood and Burgess have identified these important factors, which are described in greater detail in the following section.[3]

▶The Approach

The approach is basically how the offender first made contact with the victim. The three basic approaches are known as, the *blitz*, the *surprise*, and the *con*.

Blitz

The blitz-style approach is essentially a sudden, unexpected, and unprovoked physical attack on the victim. The purpose is to physically overpower the victim, keeping her from fleeing or from offering any resistance. This approach is typically the one wherein the victim is out jogging and an offender runs out from behind and hits her on the head with a blunt object, then sexually assaults her, and then flees. This approach is not used that often, but it frequently catches the attention of the public because of the violence of the act and the physical trauma inflicted on the victim. Usually there is no doubt an assault has occurred when a victim is attacked in this way.

Surprise

The surprise approach is basically where the victim is literally *surprised* by the unexpected appearance of the offender, who then is able to seize and maintain control over the victim. Generally, a minimal amount of force, verbal threats, or display of a weapon are used in order to get control over the victim and/or overcome resistance. An example of the surprise approach is when an offender hides in the backseat of a vehicle and waits until the victim gets inside and then suddenly appears and takes control. Another example is when an offender enters the victim's house during the hours of darkness and accosts her in her bedroom while she is asleep and unable to flee or resist. In this particular situation, the victim is also almost always unable to resist because the offender is prepared while the victim is not.

Con

The con approach involves employing a ruse or using impersonation as a way to maneuver or lure the victim to a place where the offender can then seize control over the victim, through physical manhandling, through a display of a weapon, or with verbal threats. An example of such a ruse was Ted Bundy's

---

[3] Hazelwood, R. R., & Burgess, A. W. (2008). *Practical aspects of rape investigation: A multidisciplinary approach (Practical aspects of criminal & forensic investigations)*. Boca Raton, FL: CRC Press.

favorite method of capturing his victims: He would walk through a college campus while wearing a cast on his arm and carrying a large number of books. Then he would struggle and appear helpless with the books as a potential victim approached. Bundy was waiting for the coed to do the natural thing—offer to help carrying the books to his car which was prepared at a secluded spot in a nearby parking lot. Once the coed reached the spot and Ted saw the coast was clear, he would strike the coed with a blunt object that he had already secreted nearby. He would then throw her into the car and drive away. Other examples of ruses include strangers' requests to enter the home of a potential victim under the guise of needing to use the telephone or restroom or requesting a drink of water, or they might impersonate a repairman, salesman, or police or security officer.

It is not necessary to ask the victim about the approach the offender used because in listening to the victim talk about the incident, it should become clear which approach the offender used to get access or gain control over the victim. This approach needs to be noted as it is going to be an important aspect of identifying the offender type as described later in the text.

▶ Control

The next topic we need to focus on and recognize is control; that is, how the offender was able to establish and then maintain control over the victim, ensure victim compliance, overcome any resistance, and prevent her escape. When conducting the victim interview the detective should not ask, "How were you controlled?" Rather, through the victim's statement we should be able to understand the method used as she talks about the incident itself. Perhaps a better question to ask at some point to clarify the situation would be: "What do you think would have happened if you tried to get away?" This may help the detective understand how the offender was able to maintain control over the victim and why the victim may not have given any resistance to the offender. There are four generally accepted means to control the victim: *mere presence, verbal threats, display of a weapon,* and *physical force.*

Mere Presence

Because the offender is generally larger in size and stature and stronger than the victim, the victim can be intimidated by the size difference between the offender and the victim and therefore does not resist out of fear of injury. Remember that rape or sexual assault has been feared by many women their entire lives and now suddenly it is occurring. For most victims, escaping the incident without being murdered or seriously injured is their main goal. This is why the vast majority of victims will report being so surprised and fearful they did not try to escape or actively resist. This aspect may cause a considerable amount of shame and self-doubt as they struggle with the fact they did not try to do anything to get away from the offender. Many offenders will be able to use their size and strength to maintain control over the victim and never have to resort to other means. If this fails or the victim is not intimidated enough, then the amount of force and control may escalate.

Verbal Threats

Verbal threats to cause physical harm or death, often delivered by the offender with emotion and anger (coupled with the offender's larger size), are generally enough to stop the victim from actively resisting. It is important to note whether the threats were used immediately upon contact with the victim in order to seize and maintain control, or whether they were used during an escalation when the offender's mere presence was not enough to gain or maintain control. Verbal threats may be used by the offender throughout their contact with the victim and may include not just threats against the victim's own safety but also threats toward other family members, especially children who may also be present at the scene. Verbal threats against the victim are extremely important because they are a form of the offender's *verbal behavior*; therefore, the exact threats and the manner in which they were made, such as the tone of the offender's voice, need to be well documented in the statement as they will be very important later on when trying to identify the type of offender.

Display of Weapon

Display of a weapon does not mean it was actually used, but rather the offender showed it to the victim and indicated his willingness to use it if the victim did not comply with his demands, stop resisting, and/or to prevent her escape. This can be any weapon of the offender's choice, but typically it is some type of a sharp weapon. However, a fist raised at the victim in a threatening manner can be seen as a display of a weapon as well. The implication is if the victim does not stop resisting, then she will be struck by a fist. As with verbal behavior we want to determine if the display of weapon occurred during the offender's initial contact with the victim, or if it was made as a result of escalation: Is this an incident where mere presence and verbal threats did not work and the situation escalated to the level that the offender displayed a weapon as an additional threat? This is also an important example of the offender's physical behavior, so the manner in which the weapon was displayed is very important to document. Additionally, the display of a weapon is often coupled with additional threats as a means to make the victim understand what is about to happen to her if she continues to resist. Therefore, any additional verbal behavior is important to capture.

Physical Force

This is the application of some type of physical force against the victim. The use of physical force is extremely important and, as with verbal threats or display of weapon, we want to establish whether the physical force was used immediately by the offender or if it was used as the result of escalation of his efforts to overcome resistance and establish control over the victim. The use of physical force is an extremely important escalation and again helps us to identify the type of offender involved in the incident. The use of force is so important that it is the next area we should concentrate on in the victim interview.

▶ Use of Physical Force

If physical force was used against the victim, it is important to note when exactly it was used, when it stopped, and the extent of the force applied.[4] As previously stated, the application of physical force is extremely important offender behavior, because from an investigative perspective, there is a great difference in offender types from one who does not use any force to another who uses more force than is needed to overcome resistance. This aspect will be covered in greater detail later on in the text when we attempt to identify the offender type through these types of behaviors. Although by definition all rapes and sexual assault involve force, what we are looking to do is clarify its extent by answering some of the following general questions (note that we are interested in when the force was applied and when it stopped):

- Was force used during the offender's initial approach in the form of a blitz assault? If so, did the application of force stop once the victim was under control and stopped resisting, or did it continue?
- Was physical force used *only* to establish control after other means had failed?
- Was the force used equal to the victim's resistance efforts or was it far beyond what was necessary to control the victim and overcome resistance?
- Was physical force applied even when there was no need to do so? For example, during the sexual assault itself or after the sexual assault was over but prior to the offender's departure?

---

[4] Physical force in this context refers to punching, kicking, slapping, or use of a weapon directly against the victim—whether to intimidate or to cause physical harm. It does not refer to aspects of physical torture or injury inflicted against the victim as part of the sexual assault. Those aspects are covered later during the interview.

Just as important, we want to determine the specific extent or level of force that was applied to the victim. In this context we note there are four levels of violence or force: *minimal, moderate, excessive,* and *brutal.*[5]

Minimal Force

This is on the low end of the scale of force and is generally limited to things like shaking the victim, light face slapping, or holding the victim down to prevent her from escaping. Force in this case is used more to intimidate, control, and seek compliance of the victim rather than to cause injury. Some verbal threats may be used, but typically are not very profane and may only be a warning to stop struggling and resisting the offender.

Moderate Force

With moderate force the offender becomes more abusive and thus the violence is increased. Examples include the victim's hands or arms being forcefully held down, the victim being thrown or pushed to the ground or onto a bed, or repeatedly slapped with the palm or back of the hand. Such application of force is related to the victim's continued struggling or resisting, and although the slaps are much harder and administered in a painful manner there is no intent to cause physical harm. At this level of force we also expect the offender's verbal behavior to be more profane and with anger being displayed.

Excessive Force

With excessive force, we see an increasing level of force and violence being applied, even when the victim is not resisting or has stopped resisting. Force may also include the violent ripping and tearing off of clothing or the beating of a victim who is trying to comply with directions of the offender but is not doing exactly what the offender demands. In this case the victim is likely to be beaten on all parts of the body, but particularly the face, with fists, feet, or some type of blunt-force objects. The offender in this case clearly wants to inflict trauma onto the victim and visible injuries such as lacerations, contusions, or abrasions are likely to result. Defensive wounds are also likely to be present on the victim. The verbal behavior likely to be present tends to be very profane and personally derogatory toward the victim. Expect the

---

[5] It is important to note that the level of force used is a subjective determination by the detective, not based on a victim's impression. A victim whom has never experienced any type of physical assault may report a slap in the face or being pushed down as being *brutalized.* In reality such force is more consistent with the lower end of the violence scale rather than the upper limits. So we listen to the victim's description of events and then subjectively place the violence level into one of the four levels of force.

verbal exclamations by the offender to accompany the punches or kicks delivered to the victim.

Brutal Force

There is generally no doubt when a victim has been exposed to brutal force because the victim is likely to have suffered extreme injuries. It is also not uncommon for these victims to be killed during the assault. In brutal force cases, there is intentional infliction of injuries on the victim even when there is no resistance. Brutal force may continue and may become part of the sexual assault such as through insertion of foreign objects into the genitalia of the victim. Verbal behavior is also likely, but may take on a different form, tending to be less profane and becoming more sexual in nature.

▶Consent

The next important area to cover is the concept of consent, because it is a major element in all sexual assaults. Essentially we are looking at what the victim may have said or done to clearly communicate her nonconsent to the sexual act to the offender. This is important because if the victim consented to the act, then no criminal offense was committed. It is also why consent is one of the leading defenses offered by so many offenders. The issue of consent is especially important because if the victim acquiesces or simply goes along with the offender and never outwardly expresses her nonconsent and there were no threats made by the offender, then a criminal offense might not be established. Expressions of nonconsent do not have to take on any particular form and a clear, unambiguous, "No" or "Stop," stated by the victim to the offender is generally enough to transmit nonconsent. The problem is when the victim gives unclear or conflicting statements to the offender. For example, a victim might say, "No," but continue with intimate petting or seem to favorably respond to the offender's continued petting. We often see this with younger victims and younger offenders where the victim may even acknowledge she vacillated between yes and no. Therefore, it is important during the victim interview to note exactly what the victim may have done to transmit her nonconsent to the offender. In certain cases it may require additional questioning to determine how the victim communicated her nonconsent.

There are at least two instances when *nonconsent* can be assumed. These cases include when the victim is intoxicated through alcohol or drugs, or is otherwise physically or mentally incapacitated. Examples would also include persons who are unconscious for whatever reason or other persons who are incapable of consenting because of a mental disability. Essentially, an unconscious victim cannot give knowing consent to the sexual act. The second instance is when physical force is used on the victim, a weapon is displayed in a threatening manner, or when other verbal threats of physical violence are introduced. The law does not require the victim to suffer injury in order to resist the assault, and in these cases it is assumed that the victim did not consent.

Several other instances occur from time to time where issues of consent are important. These include instances where the victim is coerced into having sex with the offender not through physical force or threats, but threats to her continued employment by a employer or supervisor; other similar circumstances would be in the military, where the offender is a superior and demands sex from a subordinate with promises of promotion and good assignments or implications of receiving dangerous or unpleasant duty if he or she declines. One last instance is where the victim has sex with an offender because she thinks the offender is someone else. For example, a wife who is awoken in the night by a man she assumes is her husband wanting to have sex might willingly participate in the act. Although the victim may have consented to the act, it was done through trickery because she thought the offender was someone else. Therefore, this should be treated as any other nonconsensual sexual assault.

It is important to note that nonconsent does not have to be verbal; it can also be seen in the actions of the victim toward the offender during the assault. One of the ways to show nonconsent is through resistance.

▶ Resistance

Resistance is a key focus area of the victim interview and should been seen and documented as evidence of nonconsent. If the victim consented to the act, then it stands to reason that the victim would not resist. It is also important to remember that the vast majority of victims do not actually resist in the manner which we might expect; that is, through some type of *physical* resistance. This is because so many victims are confronted by an offender of superior physical stature, are threatened with a weapon or threats against themselves or others, are somehow physically incapacitated, or have submitted to the assault in order to avoid any serious injuries. The victim may offer resistance in other ways that we can document based on her statement. Resistance can be expressed by the victim in three different ways: *passively*, *verbally*, and *physically*.

Passive Resistance

Passive resistance is basically the victim's noncompliance with the instructions or demands of the offender. For example, the offender demands the victim take her clothes off and the victim does not respond. Basically, when the victim does not do what the offender demands, this should be seen as a means of resistance. If the victim was not resisting, then she would have complied with the request or demand.

Verbal Resistance

Verbal resistance is anything the victim may have said to the offender to delay, reason, or avoid the assault. This not only includes the "No" or "Stop" type of statements but also includes any efforts to distract the offender or engage him into conversation. For example: "I asked him why he was doing this. What would your mother say about this? I don't want to do this. Please let me go, don't hurt me. Would you want someone to do this to your daughter?"

Physical Resistance

Physical resistance includes those actions in which the victim uses some physical means to try to resist, stop, or escape the assault. This includes hitting, scratching, or kicking the offender; or use of a whistle, chemical spray, weapon, or some other personal protection device. But, it also includes efforts to deflect the offender's attempts to inappropriately touch or otherwise assault the victim. In the case of acquaintance or date situations, the offender might attempt to initiate sexual contact through intimate petting and touching of the victim's legs, breasts, or groin, but the victim simply blocks or removes his hand—this is still an example of physical resistance.

As resistance can be powerful evidence of nonconsent, during the victim interview one of the things we want to try to emphasize is the number of times and instances where the victim offered resistance to the offender. As stated earlier, resistance should be seen and pointed out to the prosecutor and jury as evidence of nonconsent transmitted to the offender throughout the incident. **Box 4-2** contains examples from victims' statements where they have described the various types of resistance they offered toward the offender. Note that in some cases the victim may have employed multiple means or ways of resistance. Looking at each statement we should be able to identify whether passive, verbal, and/or physical resistance was offered by the victim during the assault.

BOX 4-2 Signs of Passive, Verbal, and Physical Resistance

- "He told me to take my clothes off, but I just stood there."
- "He started to kiss me. I said, 'no don't,' and then moved my head from side to side to keep from kissing him. He then held my head where I couldn't move it and tried to kiss me again so I bit his lip."
- "He started to kiss me and touched my breasts. I stopped kissing and pushed him back and told him it wasn't going to do him any good because I wasn't sleeping with him."
- "He put my hand on his penis and I took it away."
- "He started to touch me down there so I crossed my legs."
- "He tried to put it in my butt, but I told him it hurt and begged him to please stop. I then started to cry."
- "He put his hand on my breast and I said to stop and removed his hand."

Each of the statements in the box detail different efforts by victims to resist their offenders. Each of the victims' actions should be seen as an example of nonconsent to the offenders' actions. This becomes particularly important when dealing with the so-called "he said, she said" cases found many times in acquaintance or date rape situations. In these cases we are frequently dealing with no other forensic or testimonial evidence to back up the victim's claim of assault.

Offender Reaction to Resistance

Generally, when resistance is offered by the victim, this will trigger some type of response from the offender. The offender's response or reaction to the victim demonstrates significant behavior we can use to identify the particular offender type. Therefore, when victims describe their efforts of resisting we want to carefully note all of the behaviors and reactions of the offender. This is particularly important when the victim says she actively or physically resisted, because an active physical resistance generally results in more offender behavior, and how an offender responds to victim resistance is extremely important. The offender generally responds to victim resistance in one of the following five ways:

- *Ceasing the demand.* This occurs when the offender makes a demand or request, but when the victim resists, the offender stops the demand and instead moves on to another demand. In this case the offender does whatever the victim will allow him to do but does not press the issue.
- *Compromising or negotiating.* A compromise occurs when the offender makes a demand for a certain act or for the victim to do something but when the victim offers resistance, they may agree to do something else. An example frequently seen is a demand or an attempt by the offender at anal sex, but the victim protests or resists and instead offers to perform oral sex or vaginal sex in order to avoid it. The offender may accept one of these other acts instead. What we are looking for is a demand for one thing, but the offender settling for something else.
- *Fleeing.* Fleeing typically occurs when the offender meets unexpected resistance from the victim and instead of forcing the issue or attempting to negotiate, he breaks off the attack and flees the scene. We typically see this occurring in the very early stages of the assault when the offender is unable to exert any control over the victim and simply aborts the attack.
- *Use of threats.* Verbal or physical threats such as the display of a weapon are important to note because they are essentially verbal exchanges with the victim. It is important to capture exactly what the threats were and how they were made, including the tone of the offender's voice. Threats generally include displays of anger, emotion, or frustration, which are also important to document. Not all threats are necessarily directed against the victim herself; many times the offender includes threats to

harm the victim's children or other members of the family who may be in the house.

- *Use of force.* The last offender reaction is again the application of physical force, and always, if force is used, it is very important to note and document it. The key factor we are looking for is whether the force used was limited to what was needed to overcome the victim's resistance or if the force was beyond what was needed to overcome resistance. An offender using his hands to grasp his victim's hands to keep her from hitting him, using his superior size and weight to hold his victim down, or forcefully removing the victim's clothing are examples of using force that is necessary to overcome resistance. However, the offender who immediately resorts to a punishing physical attack that includes punches to the victim's head and face or kicking the victim is displaying quite different behavior. Even more important to note is the offender who continues the physical assault long after the victim ceases to offer resistance. It is also important to note whether the physical resistance of the victim causes the offender to become *sexually stimulated* or *aroused*. This type of offender is stimulated by forcing the victim and overcoming the victim's resistance.

During some assaults the offender might suddenly and unexpectedly turn violent and may begin to use physical force; this is known as a *change in attitude* of the offender. If there was an attitude change, then we want to explore with the victim to determine what happened to cause or precipitate the change. This could result from something the victim did or said, or it could be the result of some sexual dysfunction of the offender. When the victim reports a sudden attack for seemingly no reason, additional questions are needed to clarify what happened immediately before this attack or attitude change. This is an important aspect of the assault because it may indicate a particular sensitive area to the offender. Often with the application of force, the offender may also become frustrated or angrier with the victim. This may result in an additional verbal exchange by the offender with the victim, perhaps in the form of profanity or additional threats. Again, these are important exchanges and should be documented in detail as accurately as possible.

▶ Type and Sequence of Sex Acts

This aspect of the assault is likely to cause the most problems during the interview because this is typically the most traumatic and embarrassing part of the incident. It can be especially stressful for the victim whenever the sexual acts they were subjected to or forced to perform went beyond their normal sexual experiences. This part of the interview is extremely important for a number of reasons. First, it is needed to determine exactly what offenses were committed and to establish the necessary legal elements of proof for those offenses.

Remember, there are many instances where the victim is not just subjected to vaginal rape; some of the more common examples of other sexual offenses include cunnilingus, fellatio, masturbation, or insertion of foreign objects. The sequence of the various sexual acts demanded and completed are also important because it may identify potential sexual dysfunctions experienced by the offender.

The importance of the sequence of sex acts is demonstrated in the following examples. The offender demands to be touched, then demands oral sex to become aroused and erect, and then engages in vaginal sex. In another example, the offender engages in forced anal sex and then immediately demands oral sex. In this case, there is not just a sexual dimension but also a humiliation and degradation of the victim. How many times the offender was able to engage in sexual intercourse and achieve gratification is also an important behavior. The typical expectation is that the offender attacks the victim and engages in some type of sexual assault, then reaches climax and departs the scene. Other offenders may engage in repeated sexual assaults with the same victim, during the same incident, but over a much longer period of time. Thus, we should not get locked into the concept of quick encounters in which the victim escapes or the offender flees the scene. Again, it is the total sexual behavior which is important to note and will go a long way in identifying the type of offender.

Based on each particular offender's sexual preference, he might demand that the victim say or do certain things. Each of these demands or preferences are important to help identify the various criminal acts, but also to provide an understanding of the sexual behavior of the offender. This sexual behavior can tell us a great deal about the offender. Often during the recollection of the sexual assault the previously described "gaps" in the victim's story tend to occur. These gaps are likely to be at the time the humiliating and degrading sexual acts may have taken place. Therefore, this is one of the parts of the interview that may need to be repeated several times in order to get all of the necessary details of the event. This is both to fully understand all of the offenses that were committed during the act and because this is perhaps the only time during the incident when the offender displays their sexual behavior.

▶ Scripting

When the offender requests or demands that the victim say or repeat certain phrases during the assault, this is what we call *scripting*. It can take on many forms depending on the offender's particular fantasy or needs; the offender might need to hear the victim say these things in order to become aroused, to perform, or to achieve gratification. What the victim is demanded to repeat can tell us a lot about the offender, so it is important to note this behavior.

Some of the more common examples of scripting demands on the victim include:

- "Tell me you love me."
- "Tell me you like it and it feels good."
- "Tell me I'm better than your husband."
- "Tell me you want me."

As is apparent from these statements, many of the scripting demands seem to reinforce the offender's fantasy that the event is a consensual incident, rather than one of coercion and force. It does not matter that the offender is demanding the victim to repeat these phrases, having the victim actually say them may be important to the offender for their gratification. Scripting is different from the question-and-answer type conversations between the offender and victim that might take place before, during, and after the assault; it is a specific demand to repeat or say certain phrases.

Scripting is not always on victim's part; some offenders, particularly sexual sadists may also employ scripting toward the victim. They might need to say particular things to the victim, rather than need or require the victim to repeat things back to them. Scripting in this case is more about the offender and the offender's own fantasy, and it tends to be much more threatening, profane, and sexual in nature. The main goal of the offender is to cause fear and discomfort in the victim as this is part of his fantasy. Many victims of sexual sadists report being bound and blindfolded and that the offender then began talking to them prior to their assault, making such statements as:

- "I'm going to fuck you!"
- "I'm going to cut your tits off."
- "You're going to suck my dick and like it."
- "You're going to be subjected to the most severe physical pain and torture possible."
- "I'm never letting you go. You're going to be my sex slave and do what I tell you to do or I will kill you."

Offender scripting may be a lot more detailed than just a few sentences uttered in a threatening manner prior to the assault. Some victims have reported that the offender actually seemed to be reading something to them; others have reported the offender played a recording of a scripted and prepared statement to them prior to initiating the assault and torture. We see these examples of scripting with sexual sadists and their main goal is not just to inflict pain onto the victim, but rather to watch the victim suffer and to gain absolute control over the suffering. With these statements, the offender is trying to induce the fear and dread in the victim prior to the sexual assault. It is therefore important when discussing the verbal behavior displayed by the offender that we capture exactly what is said and at what point in the assault (before, during, and/or after) the behavior occurred. Later in the text we will see how different offender types would be expected to exhibit different verbal behaviors toward the victim and during the incident.

▶ Sexual Dysfunction

When reviewing the sexual assault in detail we are also interested in determining if the offender may have experienced any type of sexual dysfunction during the incident. Examples of sexual dysfunction include *erectile dysfunction, premature ejaculation, retarded ejaculation,* and *conditional ejaculation.* Sexual dysfunctions may cause general frustration, embarrassment, an emotional outburst, or a violent anger reaction often directed at the victim. This may also result in more verbal, physical, or sexual behavior as the offender attempts to deal with the dysfunction.

Erectile Dysfunction

The inability for the offender to obtain or maintain an erection is one of the more common dysfunctions experienced. The victim may not understand that the offender who was not erect or was unable to get erect and complete the sexual assault was experiencing a sexual dysfunction. It is instead described as the offender being unable to penetrate the victim or a demand for the victim to do something to arouse the offender such as touching, masturbating, or performing oral sex. It may also include efforts by the offender to engage in some type of foreplay with the victim.

Premature Ejaculation

Premature ejaculation is essentially the offender achieving gratification and ejaculating almost immediately upon insertion or in a relatively short period of time. It is also not unusual for an offender to ejaculate prior to insertion of the penis. This is also likely to cause an emotional reaction or response by the offender, which may result in additional verbal, physical, or sexual behaviors.

Retarded Ejaculation

Retarded ejaculation refers to the offender's *inability* to achieve final gratification or orgasm. Victims may not understand the term and may report that the incident lasted an exceptionally long period of time, or felt like it would never end. This is not a case of the offender tying to stimulate or please the victim or showing concern for the victim's sexual gratification. Instead it is the offender's inability to climax. This condition frequently results in the offender becoming frustrated and angry and may require additional effort such as a demand for other sex acts, a change in sexual positions, or other demands of the victim. It is not unusual for the offender never to be able to achieve gratification and simply give up or stop the assault. It is also likely that the offender will somehow blame his inability to achieve gratification on the victim and take it out on her through additional verbal or physical abuse.

Conditional Ejaculation

Condition ejaculation is basically where the offender must do or requires the victim to do something in order to achieve gratification. If that condition is not met, then the offender may not be able to perform or achieve orgasm. These conditions could include anything from the victim repeating certain phrases, being required to wear certain items of clothing, or performing certain sex acts, or the offender insisting on certain sexual positions or anything else that he has determined is necessary to be present in order for gratification. Conditional ejaculation often revolves around fetishes and deviant sexual behaviors. Conditional ejaculation is not something the victim or even many detectives might be aware of or understand. Therefore, it may only become apparent and relevant during a serial rape investigation where the same offender has repeated the same actions with each of his victims in order complete the sex act. This is very strong evidence we can use to link cases together, because it tends to be unique to a particular offender.

All aspects of sexual dysfunctions are an important part of the offender's sexual behavior and we are looking not only to address or identify them, but also for the offender's reaction to experiencing them. Frequently, sexual dysfunction results in frustration, anger, or other emotional outbursts causing the display of behavior such as a demand for other sex acts to be performed by the victim or an expression of increased anger through verbal or physical abuse of the victim. It is also important to note what the offender did to overcome his dysfunction because again this tends to be unique to particular offenders. The victim may have to be guided on this point because during the actual sexual assault she was probably thinking of her own safety, trying to deal with her own emotions and wellbeing, and may not necessarily be aware of any problems experienced by the offender.

We can gather information concerning these dysfunctions or problems through the victims' description of event. Examples include:

- "He put my hand on his penis, but it was not erect at all. He told me to make him hard. So I moved my hand up and down on the shaft a few times until he got erect."
- "He tried to put it into me but he couldn't and then forced me to suck his penis until he got hard."

▶Departure from the Scene

The length of the entire event and the assault itself generally depends on the offender, and for most offenders assaults tend to be of short duration; however, some offenders will perform multiple assaults. If the victim is especially compliant and there is little chance of being interrupted, the assault could last much longer. After the assaults have ended we are then looking for the circumstances relating to the offender's departure from the scene and victim. This is the start of the *after* of the event. Frequently, at the departure or after the sexual assault there may be additional offender behaviors. These include additional verbal behavior ranging from apologetic comments, to threats if she calls the police, to special instructions for what the victim should do after the offender leaves, such as count to 100 or wait 5 minutes. It could also include additional threats against the victim to return and assault her again or threats of physical harm against her family if she reports to the police. The exact wording of these threats is very important as it often is part of the offender's modus operandi (MO) and is likely to be repeated from victim to victim.

One offender type may actually apologize to the victim and ask for forgiveness for what he did to her; he may also ask the victim's permission to come back and see her again, or even ask the victim for a date. This is covered in more detail in later in the text, but these statements or requests to see the victim again need to be taken seriously because the offender may in fact attempt to recontact the victim. In this offender's fantasy, the sexual assault was a consensual experience and not the result of force. At the conclusion of the interview some instructions should be provided to the victim in case the offender does attempt to recontact her so the victim knows what to do.

Other offender actions relate to efforts not to leave any evidence behind. These actions include making the victim bathe, douche, or even demanding the victim shave off her pubic hair in the shower.[6] This could also expand to forcing the victim after the assault to strip the bed and wash and bleach the sheets, blankets, and clothing, or to clean up anything else the offender may have touched. This is very important behavior because it is an indication of an intelligent and perhaps more experienced offender who understands the importance of forensic evidence.

Other possibilities include the offender committing another criminal offense by demanding money, valuables, or property that belong to

---

[6] The demand for the victim to shave her pubic hair in the shower after the assault was initially believed by the police to be part of the sexual assault as a way to further stimulate the offender or as a way to humiliate the victim. Instead, it was the offender trying to eliminate or destroy potential trace and biological evidence by forcing its removal from the victim. Efforts to clean the victim could also include forcing the victim to get into her swimming pool, using a garden hose outside to wash herself off, or forcing her to wipe with a towel and the offender then taking the towel when he left.

the victim. Again, depending on the victim, it is not unusual for the offender to demand money or valuables after the assault before they agree to leave.

▶ Trophies or Souvenirs

The taking of small personal items belonging to the victim or an item from the scene is common and may have great value and importance to the offender. These items are not always of monetary value and may be no more than a photo; small items of jewelry such as earrings, a watch, ring, or necklace; a driver's license; keychain; or an item of intimate apparel such as a bra or panties. In some instances even a sanitary napkin or tampon may be taken from the victim. What is taken from the scene or victim is dependent on the offender.

These items are known as *trophies* or *souvenirs* and are used by the offender as a symbol of triumph or victory over the victim, in the same sense as a hunter who mounts and places the head of a prized deer he killed on the wall. It also serves as a remembrance of what happened in the same sense as any other souvenir purchased or collected in our normal travels. The value the individual places on the items depends on the offender. Some items are taken and retained for a period of time and then disposed of when they no longer serve their purpose; other items are collected and retained, have great value to the offender, and are used to relive the incident or as masturbatory aids in between victims. Some are also likely to be retained by the offender regardless of how incriminatory they will be if they are found by the police. A good example of this behavior was exhibited by the infamous serial killer John Wayne Gacy, who was well aware the police were looking at him as a suspect regarding the disappearance of young males. Even though he was aware of the likelihood of the police coming into his home and conducting a search for evidence, he still retained many of the souvenirs he had collected from his many victims. These items had such significance to him he could not get rid of them despite how incriminating they were. These items were found during a police search of his house and were used against him. Therefore, it is important to determine from the victim if such small items are missing. If not noted by the victim during the interview, then it is suggested she go back and look through her purse, wallet, or if the incident took place inside her residence, throughout the house to determine if any items are missing.

▶ Description of the Offender

One of the last things to cover during the interview is getting as much detailed descriptive information about the offender as possible. This description should include the obvious general identifiers such as race, height, weight, eye and hair color, and hairstyle. Next is the particular clothing the offender was wearing at the time. Clothing description should include not just the outer visible clothing but should also include any undershirt and underwear that was worn. For males the type of underwear worn by the offender is probably the same type they wear normally and may prove to be another piece of victim corroboration if the offender is ever identified. Other important data we need to capture includes tattoos, body piercings, and other physical features such as the presence or absence of body hair. This is may be particularly important if the offender has significant head, arm, chest, or back hair. In one serial rape investigation, one of the physical features of the offender noted by all victims was the presence of a very hairy chest and back. It became somewhat easier when dealing with potential suspects to simply determine if they had such body hair. When the suspect was eventually located he was found to have excessive body hair on his chest and back.

Other important factors include the condition of the offender's teeth, breath, or body odor or other unusual smells such as gas, oil, chemicals, tobacco, alcohol, or the presence of aftershave, deodorant, or cologne.

▶Overall Nature of the Offense

Throughout the course of the interview we are also trying to evaluate other actions of the offender that may not necessarily come out through the typical questions and answers, but that from the general responses we can deduce. One of the more important aspects of offender behavior concerns the amount of preparation undertaken by the offender to commit the offense. More obvious signs of preparedness include efforts to hide his appearance such as wearing a mask, other attempts to hide his facial features, or placing something over the victim's head to keep her from observing him. Other signs could also include efforts to avoid leaving trace or forensic evidence behind such as wearing gloves or using a condom.

Some offenders will even prepare and bring with them a "rape kit," which is a collection of items they believe they might need in order to commit the sexual assault. The collection of items contained in the rape kit depends on the individual offender and his intelligence, experience, or fantasy. Many such kits are made up of common items such as rope or line, tape, condoms, gloves, and a mask. Others may be much more advanced, containing police radios, sex toys, burglary tools, camera or video equipment, knives, or other weapons. It is not unusual for the offender to spend a great deal of time before an assault organizing and selecting the type of items to place into his rape kit because preparing the kit can be seen as another way to continue the fantasy about committing the rape. **Case Study 4-1** presents an example of the effort an offender put into preparing his rape kit, which indicates the level of preparation involved prior to committing the crime.

Case Study 4-1

A college coed was kidnapped at dusk in the parking lot of her dormitory as she was getting out of her car. She was forced back into the car, pushed over to the passenger side, and forced down toward the floorboards; a pillow case or something similar was placed over her head. The offender got inside and drove her vehicle a short distance away and then forced her out of her car and into the offender's vehicle. Again, she was forced onto the floor, her head still covered. He then drove a short distance and stopped the car. The victim was allowed to sit in the seat and then the pillowcase was taken off, but it was already dark and the victim could not make out the offender's physical features. The offender then opened a small bag and pulled out a screwdriver—the victim became alarmed because she sensed that it was going to be used as a weapon. Instead, the offender took her hands, then from the handle of the screwdriver removed a small strip of previously prepared masking or duct tape from the handle, and then individually wrapped each of her fingers tips with tape. The victim was then subjected to several sexual assaults including vaginal rape and being forced to perform oral sex on the offender both in the vehicle and then outside on the hood of his car. The victim claimed he used a condom prior to vaginal sex and afterward placed the used condom into a paper bag he also had in the small bag. After the offender was done, he allowed the victim to redress, and then removed the tape from her fingers and placed them into the paper bag with the condom. He then drove the victim a short distance away and allowed her to get out of the car and directed her where to go to get help. The victim reported the incident and the police launched their investigation but questioned the victim's report concerning the tape on her fingers. However, less than 10 days later, a second coed at another university some distance away was kidnapped in almost the exact fashion—including the kidnapping, placement of tape on each of her fingers, changing vehicles, and similar sexual assaults in a secluded outdoor area. The second victim was released a short distance from a convenience store. However, this time the offender placed the tape on the victim's fingers inside her vehicle, before they moved to his vehicle. The offender had accidentally dropped the screwdriver onto the floorboards of the victim's car and it was later recovered, validating the victim's statement.

This case study demonstrates the amount of time and preparation some offenders may go through in order to commit the crime. This is in direct opposition with certain other offenders who seem to spend very little time in preparation and take no precautions to hide their faces or appear concerned about leaving forensic evidence behind. This type of offender tends to use whatever materials happen to be present at the scene to help commit the crime. Instead of bringing duct tape or some ligature to tie up the victim, the offender might use a telephone or electrical cord he obtains at the scene.

It is important to note one final type of preparation—whether the victim appears to have been selected or specifically targeted by the offender. We can see this in a number of examples including the low risk assessment based on the victimology, recent thefts of small laundry items from the victim, recent residential break-ins without property loss, reports of peeping toms, recent nuisance or threatening emails, hangups or obscene phone calls, or feelings of being stalked or observed by unknown persons.

▶ Summary

The interview of the victim is a critical step of the investigative process that is more than just sitting down and asking a few questions or having the victim write in her own words what happened to her. We usually have one time to interview the victim and need to be prepared to get as much information as we can and clear up any potential inconsistencies or explain any problem areas such as a delay in reporting. The Hazelwood and Burgess behavior-orientated interview technique is relatively easy to use but takes discipline and sometimes great effort from detectives to listen to the victim and not interrupt her. It offers the best opportunity to gather many details and information about the offender, identify investigative leads, and establish victim corroboration.

▶ Further Reading

Carney, T. P. (2004). *Practical investigation of sex crimes: A strategic and operational approach*. Boca Raton, FL: CRC Press.

Hazelwood, R. & Burgess, A. W. (2008). *Practical aspects of rape investigation: A multidisciplinary approach* (4th ed.). Boca Raton, FL: CRC Press.

Napier, M. R. (2010). *Behavior, truth, and deception: Applying profiling and analysis to the interview process*. Boca Raton, FL: CRC Press.

CHAPTER FIVE

Victimology[1]

"Tell me about your victim, and I'll tell you about the offender." With this simple statement, Roy Hazelwood[2], in his many training classes, sums up just about everything there is to know about the importance and necessity of victimology. Prior to the 1980s the background and personality characteristics of the sexual assault or murder victims were largely ignored or considered as a relatively minor part of the overall investigative effort. If the victim's background was deemed important by detectives, it was typically because they were suspicious of the validity of the victim's complaint or the particular victim was some type of celebrity. Therefore, the police effort to obtain background information more often amounted to a cursory criminal history check or a collection of tidbits of information provided by witnesses. Due to this lack of thorough effort, it is not surprising that the value of a victimology was not understood or appreciated at the time.

This has begun to change with the increasing development and use of what we refer to as a *victimology assessment*. This is the study of victims, through their background and personality characteristics, in order to understand how they came to be victims of crime or why they were selected by the offender in the first place. It is also designed to provide insight into the victim and identify any risk factors, personality characteristics, or behaviors that may have contributed to their victimization or that may have attracted an offender. While the victimology assessment is based on the victim's background and personality characteristics, it is used to tell us about the offender. Therefore, a victimology assessment should be viewed not just as a basic requirement, but a critical phase in all homicide and sex crime investigations, particularly in stranger-on-stranger type of incidents. To provide an understanding of the importance of the victimology assessment, this chapter covers some of the basics of the assessment, starting

---

[1] Much of this chapter is taken from: Adcock, J. M. & Chancellor, A. S. (2013). *Death investigation*. Burlington, MA: Jones & Bartlett Learning.

[2] Robert R. Hazelwood was one of the original members of the FBI Behavioral Science Unit.

with the "risk factors" for becoming a victim and how these are used to begin to understand the offender.

▶Risk Factors

Risk factors are those intentional or unintentional parts of our lives that may influence how we live or why we do certain things. For instance, if someone's workplace is a great distance away from home and they must travel on a highly congested interstate for an extended period of time in the mornings and again in the evenings, he would be at greater risk for getting involved in an accident than someone who lives a short distance away from work and only briefly has to deal with a small amount of traffic. In another example, if a person lives in a high crime area where lots of residential burglaries are occurring, he should expect to eventually become a victim of such a crime—not necessarily because he is doing anything wrong, but because he lives in an area that experiences a higher probability of burglaries. In these examples there are no negative implications as to the first person's driving abilities or the second person's involvement with criminal activity; rather the routine circumstances of their lives place them in situations where there is a greater chance of becoming particular types of victims. **Box 5-1** lists a few common examples of what we now refer to as risk factors and upon which we will base much of the victimology assessment.

BOX 5-1 Risk Factors

- Personal use/abuse of alcohol or drugs
- Involvement in criminal activity
- Working where there is cash/money around
- Multiple short-term sexual partners
- Hitchhiking
- Working within the public view (nurse, waitress, cashier)
- Living an alternative lifestyle
- Associating with known criminals
- Participating in criminal activities
- Living in a high-crime area
- Participation in Internet dating

The assessment and information collected consists of both factual and subjective criteria about the victim. Although we are using the assessment primarily on homicide and sex crimes it can also be used for other investigations as well, with the type of information sought for the assessment changed or adapted depending on the type of crime or the type of victim. For instance, we want most of the same basic information on every victim, but we may adapt or include in our assessment other factors based on the specific individual victim and the individual crime. Specific information sought based on the type of victim and crime would include but is not necessarily limited to the following examples:

- *Females*: Dating history and marital status; current and past employment; outgoing personality or shy and withdrawn; confident or uncertain. How do they dress—sexy, alluring, revealing, conservative, or casual? Questions may also have to include their sexual history and sexual interests. Heterosexual, homosexual, or bisexual? Are they conservative or promiscuous? Other similar questions would have to be based on the specifics of the particular crime.
- *Males*: Employment, current and past; alcohol and drug involvement; military experience; marital status and dating history. Any history of extramarital affairs? Are there any problems at home, work, or personal life? What is their socioeconomic status and financial situation? What is their physical stature, manner of dress, and sexual orientation? If homosexual, are they aggressive or passive? How would they respond to challenges or threats? Would they be considered as aggressive or nonaggressive?
- *Young children*: Is their personality type dependent or independent? Are they outgoing and warm to strangers, or shy and fearful? Do they easily make friends and playmates or have difficulty establishing peer relationships with children their own age? Living conditions—single parent (which one) or both parents in home; is child's parent living with an unmarried partner or multiple nonmarried partners? Are there other children in the home? What is the child's family's economic situation? Is there any use of drugs or alcohol in house by parents? Could the child be easily manipulated by an adult?
- *Teenagers*: Teens are somewhat different because they are at the stage in life where they are more mature than children, but do not yet have the life experiences of adults. Therefore, their victimology is more complicated than for adults and may require additional questions, such as: What is their maturity level and is it age appropriate? Do they have a dependent or independent personality? Are they outgoing or shy? Do they have age-appropriate friends or generally older friends? Do they actively engage in online social networking? Do they have cell phones with texting abilities? Do they participate in school activities, and what are their grades/success in school? Are there disciplinary or attendance problems? What is their current dating status? Do they have boyfriends or girlfriends or any "romance" problems? Any other problems at school? "Teenage" problems at home or with other siblings? What were some recent events in their lives? Do they have plans for the future? Do they engage in high-risk behaviors such as drug and alcohol abuse?

  With teens, two particular areas require special attention. The first is understanding how friends of the victim may be able to apply peer pressure to get the victim to do something he or she would not normally do.

Because teens are younger and less mature they are therefore more easily influenced by others and more likely to participate in certain things because they want to belong. The second is their use or experience with the Internet, participation in the social media, and texting. It is not unusual for teenagers to be actively involved in exchanging much personal information, even sharing sexual photographs of themselves with others they only know through the Internet via email, or sharing these with friends or acquaintances via cell phone in what has become known as *sexting*. This is high-risk behavior that many parents may be unaware of.

These various facts and personality characteristics relating to the victim, together with the crime scene examination, are used to paint a picture of the individual victim. As stated earlier, the victimology assessment is based on both factual and subjective criteria and the general guideline is there is no unimportant piece of information relative to the victim.

▶ Factual Information

Examples of the type of factual information to be included (but not limited to) in the victimology assessment are listed in **Box 5-2.**

BOX 5-2 Examples of Factual Information

- Age and sex
- Physical features or traits (hair or eye color, height, weight)
- Basic family structure (mother, father, siblings)
- Marital status
- Education level
- Basic employment history (occupation history)
- Criminal history
- Medical history
- Disabilities and other physical attributes
- Mental disabilities or impairment

As noted earlier, facts are information about the victim at the time of the incident that is essentially undisputed. These facts are what they are and cannot be changed.

▶ Subjective Criteria

Subjective criteria are somewhat different from facts; they relate to different aspects, circumstances, or conditions of victims' lives that may or may not have contributed to their victimization or elevated risk factors. Some of these subjective criteria depend on the age and sex of the victim and include but are not limited to the information listed in **Box 5-3**.

BOX 5-3 Subjective Criteria

- Use of alcohol or drugs
- Socioeconomic level
- Type of employment (especially public jobs, e.g., waitress, convenience store clerk, nurse, salesman)
- Sexual preference/orientation (heterosexual, homosexual, bisexual)
- Sexual history, multiple partners, extramarital affairs, or particular sexual interests
- Marital status (how many)
- Children (how many)
- Normal manner of dress
- Hobbies
- Free-time activities
- Social activities
- Family interpersonal relationships
- Friends and acquaintances and support system
- Last known activity
- Participation in religious events/activities
- Participation in high-risk activities (e.g., hitchhiking, drug usage, multiple sex partners)
- Has the person been a victim of crime before?
- Use of the Internet social networks or dating sites

Information concerning the victim's *residence* or *living situation* may also prove to be important because this provides additional personal information about the victim and how he or she was living at the time. Such information would include but not necessarily be limited to that listed in **Box 5-4.**

BOX 5-4 Information About Victim's Residence

- Does the victim live in a house or apartment?
- Does the victim own or rent his/her residence?
- Does the victim live alone, with family, or with roommates?
- Is the victim living with a spouse or significant other?
- Is the victim living with children?
- How long has the victim lived in his/her residence?
- How long has the victim lived in the same town?
- What is the location of the victim's residence (inner city, suburbs, rural)?
- Is the victim's residence located in a high-crime area?
- Does the victim have established roots in the area?

Other subjective criteria are more focused on aspects of the individual's *personality* and *emotional maturity*. Examples include but are not limited to those listed in **Box 5-5.**

BOX 5-5 Examples of Personality and Emotional Maturity Level

- Personal aggressiveness, anger, or anxiousness
- Temperament: cool and calm or prone to emotional outbursts
- Personality: impulsive or reflective
- Self-esteem or self-worth; feelings of confidence or uncertainty
- Normal manner of dress, personal hygiene, and overall appearance
- Open and friendly to strangers or shy, nonconfrontational, and passive
- Athletic or nonathletic
- Normal response to confrontation
- What was the victim's likely reaction to the assault (submissive or resistant)?
- What was the victim's last known activity; what was he/she doing prior to the assault?

All of the facts in Boxes 5-3 and 5-4 are considered subjective because of the amount of weight or consideration given to them is based on each individual victim and the event dynamics of what happened. One factor, such as church attendance, may prove to be relatively important in the lifestyle or personality characteristics of one victim, but play no role in another. These examples of factual information and subjective criteria are not all inclusive but are a representative sample of the type of information about the victim that may prove useful and necessary to complete the assessment.

▶Victimology Information

Information concerning the victim the can be gathered through a wide variety of sources including official school, medical, or work records such as interviews or supervisory evaluations of their work performance. Much of the needed information can be gained through interviews of family and friends, coworkers, neighbors, or others who have routinely interacted with the victim. Canvass-type questions to family members and friends are also extremely important and should include not only the basic questions concerning knowledge about the event itself but should also contain personal questions relevant to the victim that might not be readily apparent based on the initial crime scene evaluation.

There is a wide range of canvass-type questions we want to ask as we conduct the investigation. In many instances these questions are going to revolve around the reliability and general truthfulness of the victim. The reason for this is the need to establish credibility of the victim. *Credibility* should be looked at as another form of corroboration and can be found in the victim's background if we look for it. When looking for the general reliability and truthfulness of the victim we might also want to ask the types of questions listed in **Box 5-6.**

BOX 5-6 Credibility of the Victim

- Did the victim have any physical or mental disabilities?
- Did the victim have any fears, anxieties, or phobias?
- Tell me about the victim—what type of a person is he/she?
- Is the victim generally honest and dependable?
- How would you generally describe the victim?
- What is the victim's reputation among her friends?
- What was the victim's general lifestyle?
- Tell me about the victim's interpersonal relationships, boyfriends/girlfriends/spouses.
- Did the victim recently start dating or recently end a relationship?
- Tell me about the interpersonal relationships within the victim's family.
- What is the victim's best and worse personality characteristic?
- Does the victim have any particular routine?
- Does the victim take or abuse drugs? If so what type?
- How would the victim respond to a threat or a confrontation?
- How would the victim respond to strangers?
- Does the victim engage in high-risk sports or activities?
- Is the victim a risk-taker or conservative by nature?

Not everyone who knows the victim will be able to answer all or any of the questions from Boxes 5-4, 5-5, and 5-6, nor is it necessary to ask every one of them in every single sexual assault investigation. However, they are especially helpful in the so-called "he said, she said" type of investigations, where the case is based on the word of the victim against the word of the offender. In these situations, establishing the victim's background and credibility is critical. These types of questions are designed to be asked in an open-ended manner, eliciting more than a simple yes-or-no answer. This allows the interviewee to expand his or her answer and focus on what he or she believes is important about the victim. Some witnesses may feel obligated out of friendship and loyalty to paint the victim in a better light or to avoid any negative statements. The purpose of these questions is not to criticize or somehow degrade the victim, but to understand who she is and if her personality, lifestyle, or other aspects of her life played any role in what happened to her. Extra effort may be needed to explain the importance of these background questions in order to obtain an accurate assessment.

During investigation of stranger-on-stranger incidents, it is also important to ask during these canvass-type interviews whether or not the victim ever made any statements or relayed any concerns about their own personal safety or of unwanted sexual attention from a specific individual such as a coworker or supervisor. Frequently, victims will have discussed problems with close friends and family but declined for many reasons to make a formal complaint to their employer or the police, believing they could have deflected the inappropriate attention on their own. If such a problem or issue existed, it might not be found in the police department's database, but would be revealed during the canvass interviews of family and friends. Specific questions to probe such issues include but are not necessarily limited to those listed in **Box 5-7**.

BOX 5-7 Has the victim ever:

- Discussed any unwanted sexual advances from employers, coworkers, or other associates?
- Mentioned any obscene phone calls or other forms of harassment?
- Mentioned being followed or being watched by anyone?
- Expressed fear of an ex-boyfriend, girlfriend, or date?
- Believed someone had been inside her house when she wasn't home?
- Noticed any loss of personal effects from her house or laundry (e.g., underwear, intimate attire, or other personal effects)?

The importance of this type of information can be demonstrated in **Case Study 5-1**. It is based on a sex-related homicide but the same principles described earlier are highlighted and demonstrated.

Case Study 5-1

College Coed Found Brutally Murdered

A female in her mid-20s was found brutally murdered and raped in her apartment. She had been stabbed and her throat was cut while she was on her bed; she was then left naked, sexually posed, and propped up against the wall. There were indications of forced entry through the kitchen window, but no suspects were immediately identified. During the victimology canvass interviews of her friends, several reported the victim's comments about a certain male neighbor who lived in the apartment building next door, who would stand out on the balcony of his second-floor apartment smoking cigarettes at night and looking down into her ground-floor apartment as she was washing dishes or cooking. Friends reported that his actions gave her the creeps but he had never approached her nor they ever had any face-to-face contact. Based on this information the police turned their focus to the neighbor, and eventually through their investigation and later DNA analysis, he was connected to the scene and was convicted of the homicide.

The victim in this case study had never reported her feelings or concern to any authorities, and the only way the detectives became aware was by asking about any concerns expressed by the victim to her friends or family members. This highlights the importance of conducting canvass interviews as part of the victimology assessment. Canvassing is important to the investigation of sex crimes because, as shown in the case study, the victim may have confided in friends about encounters or inappropriate contact with the offender that made the victim feel uneasy or the victim may have rebuffed the offender's sexual advances or attempts at establishing a relationship. Such information can be used to validate statements made by the victim. For instance, prior to the sexual assault, the victim might have told friends or coworkers about the offender's unwelcome advances or other inappropriate and unwanted sexual conduct. This would be consistent with the victim's claim after the incident that such advances or conduct by the offender were nonconsensual. These consistent statements can be seen as an example of corroboration and are especially vital to investigations of acquaintance rape–type situations.

The victimology canvass-style interviews also are important for another reason. In cases where the incident involves coworkers or employer–employee or supervisor–worker relationships, it is not uncommon to identify similar behavior from the offender toward others. Frequently, as canvass interviews are conducted about the victim, the detective finds additional witnesses or victims who may have experienced the same unwanted advances or conduct from the offender.

Employment history is another aspect of the victimology assessment. Employment is important because the workplace is typically where victims spend approximately one-third of their days and work plays an important part in people's daily lives. Employment is often either the source of pleasure and satisfaction or a source of stress and frustration. The type of work and victims' satisfaction with their current employment situation can help determine what was going on in their lives at the time of the incident. For sexual assault investigations, we want to focus in particular on any job where the victim is routinely exposed to the public, such as a nurse, waiter/waitress, receptionist at a business, salesperson, cashier, or bartender. All of these are examples of *public jobs*, meaning they deal or interact with the public as opposed to someone who works on an assembly line or works in a small cubicle out of the sight of the general public. Public jobs, especially those involving money, food, and/or alcohol, tend to expose the victim to the public eye and therefore increase the likelihood of her having caught the attention of an offender. Employment becomes more important when dealing with stranger-on-stranger incidents than some type of acquaintance situation.

▶ Investigative Use of Victimology

As mentioned in the first paragraph of this chapter, while the victimology assessment is all about the victims and their particular background and individual personality characteristics, it is actually used to tell us about the offender. The victimology assessment essentially is an effort to look at the victim through the eyes of the offender and perhaps determine why the victim was chosen. It may also be able to assist in the narrowing of the pool of possible suspects through identification of certain offender characteristics through the victimology. Once the background information is collected, the various identified "risk factors" and individual personality characteristics pertaining to the victim are identified and evaluated. The victim is then placed into one of three risk categories—high, moderate, or low. The risk categories simply refer to the likelihood of the victim to have become a victim of a crime. The higher the risk category, the more likely the victim is to have come into contact with an offender and thus become a victim. This is not designed to imply anything bad or unsavory about the victim, but rather we are looking at the victim to learn about the offender.

High-Risk Victims

High-risk victims are almost expected to have become victims of crime based on their residence, employment, or general lifestyle. Examples include but are not limited to: runaways, homeless persons, drug abusers, criminals, and prostitutes. These are obvious potential crime victims, because they routinely put themselves into contact with a criminal element, operate within a high crime area, or interact with other criminals. Generally, it is only a matter of time before they are eventually victimized. Engaging in almost any criminal conduct should place the victim almost automatically into a high-risk category, because those who are engaged in criminal conduct often associate themselves with others involved in criminal conduct.

Some not so obvious high-risk individuals who are just as likely to become victims of crime are those persons (discussed earlier in this chapter) engaged in some type of public type of employment, including convenience store workers, bank tellers, waitresses, and nurses. They may be normal, law-abiding, and hard-working citizens with no criminal background or other deviant type lifestyles, but because of their employment in the public, it places them at an increased chance of contact with potential criminals on a routine basis; therefore, they may be considered to be in the high-risk category. It is common sense that the more time you spend in a high-crime area, the more likely you are to come into contact with the criminal element and thus become a victim of some crime. In certain situations, the elderly may be considered as high risk because of their inability to defend themselves regardless of where they live or frequent. Some elderly persons are intentionally sought after by certain muggers and burglars because they generally will offer very little resistance.

Moderate- or Medium-Risk Victims

Moving down the scale are *moderate-risk* individuals; these are generally persons who would probably be placed in a low-risk category and thus very unlikely to come into contact with a criminal element; but something they were engaged at the time may have placed them into a higher risk category. For instance, a housewife whose car breaks down on the highway after dark is at higher risk; although she may not normally be a high-risk individual, her situation increases her risk factor. Another example would be a traveler who takes a wrong turn off the interstate and finds herself lost and driving around in a high-crime area in an unfamiliar city. Her normal lifestyle would not place her into such a position, but through circumstance her risk factors were elevated.

Low-Risk Victims

Low-risk victims, based on their lifestyle and personality characteristics, are unlikely ever to become victims of crime, primarily because they are not engaged in the typical high-risk behaviors or are they are seldom in the public enough to come into more than happenstance contact with a *stranger offender*. An example of a typical low-risk victim would be a stay-at-home mother and wife, with a stable marriage, who has no outside employment, does not abuse drugs or alcohol, is not involved in any extramarital affairs, and lives in a safe residential neighborhood.

Placement of the victim into one of these categories is another subjective determination based on all of the facts and circumstances and the individual victim. Therefore, different detectives using the same criteria, even on the same case may, feel it best to place victims under similar circumstances into a different categories based on their own judgment. This happens frequently, particularly when the concept is first being introduced and until the detectives gain experience in making these assessments. The key to success, however, is to apply the same logic and criteria for each case in the same manner as every other case. As an example of how a victimology assessment is used to categorize the victim, compare the facts of two basic victim assessments in **Table 5-1** and assign their risk factors and risk category based on the limited information provided.

TABLE 5-1

Victim 1	Victim 2
35-year-old, married housewife	21-year-old college student
Married 12 years	Single with multiple short-term sexual relationships
Mother of two children, age 9 and 7	Works as a waitress and as an exotic dancer
College degree	Few college friends
No outside employment	Recently moved into town
No history of alcohol or drug abuse	Abuses alcohol and drugs

(continues)

TABLE 5-1 *(continued)*

Victim 1	Victim 2
Attends church regularly	Does not attend church
No criminal history	No criminal history
Lives in middle-class neighborhood	Lives in an apartment off campus
Knows all of her neighbors	Unknown to any neighbors

Victim 1 would be the typical low-risk victim. There are several key factors that make this assessment relatively easy. First, the factual information includes her age, marital status, children, and socioeconomic status. Subjective factors include church attendance, known to her neighbors, and lives in a middle-class neighborhood. The subjective criteria here are used to provide a flavor of who the victims are. All factors for this victim are indicative, at least on the surface, of an emotionally mature and responsible person. Can a victim with these factors still be irresponsible and immature? Of course; but all things being equal we can assume that she is somewhat responsible and at a low risk for becoming a victim during the routine course of her life.

Conversely, Victim 2 is a classic example of a high-risk victim. Factual information, including her age, marital status, drug and alcohol abuse, and multiple short-term sexual relationships, are all indicative of her being a high-risk victim because persons of this age and similar living conditions tend to engage in higher-risk behaviors than older, more mature and experienced persons. Although Victim 2 does not necessarily engage in prostitution or other criminal acts, her job as an exotic dancer increases her chances of coming into contact with offenders who may frequent those types of establishments. Her recent arrival to the town, nonattendance in church, and the fact that she is unknown to her neighbors are all examples of subjective criteria that can be used to round out the victim's assessment.

When comparing the two victims, it is clear that Victim 2 is more likely to eventually become a victim of a crime. However, it is also important to note that Victim 1 may actually be more susceptible to an offender's con approach. Again, this is based on her overall general assessment that would indicate that although she is older, more mature, and more responsible, she may also be more naïve in the ways of the criminal world and therefore more trusting of people including strangers. She may fall for an offender's polite request to come into her house to use the phone, get a drink of water, or willingly follow the directions of someone impersonating an official. However, Victim 2, through her jobs, has probably heard every story and pickup line, has likely had to routinely confront unruly or drunk customers, and is likely more attuned to a con or a pickup line and more suspicious and self-aware regarding the potential dangers of strangers.

Victimology assessment can also aid in other aspects of the investigation, particularly in serial crimes when an offender's modus operandi (MO) or signature might be identified through similar types of victims. This can be a good investigative starting point in linking together what appear to be similar crimes or even linking together crimes that on the surface appear to be dissimilar. An example is provided in the **Case Study 5-2**.

Case Study 5-2

Series of Six Early Morning Home Invasions

There was series of six early morning burglaries/home invasions in a rural county. After gaining entrance into the homes, the offender accosted the elderly female victims who were all living alone and sleeping in their beds. In five of these cases the offender entered the residences through a window, and after gaining control over the victims raped them and in several cases inserted foreign objects into their vaginas or anuses, but the sexual assaults were relatively short in duration. Afterward, he walked the victims through their houses demanding to see their purses, then robbed them of whatever cash or valuables they had and then left. However, there was some question if the sixth case involved the same offender or a new offender. In the sixth case, the offender did not enter through an open window and instead jimmied the rear door. He then accosted the sleeping victim and repeatedly sexually assaulted the female both vaginally and anally. He also demanded and received oral sex, but he did not insert any foreign objects into the victim or attempt to rob the victim. This appeared to be a significant deviation from the established MO of the other incidents, and there was serious concern that a second offender was engaging a similar type of criminal act against elderly females. However, upon a detailed look at the victimology of the sixth victim and comparing it to the other five victims, it was noted that victim number six reported that she was so afraid for her safety that she had offered no resistance at all and was completely compliant with all of the offender's demands. The other victims all reportedly resisted in some way, either verbally or physically, and some victims were actually struck by the offender for their resistance. It was clear that because the sixth victim was so compliant, the offender was basically free to do whatever he wanted to do and therefore he did more sexually to that victim than any other victim. The method of entry was also different, but victim six insisted that all of her windows were locked from the inside. The other five victims all reported they were uncertain if their windows were locked or not.

In this case the victimology comparison helped link the sixth case to the same suspect, and explained the change in MO or offender behavior. Once the offender was arrested, he confirmed that he stayed longer with the last victim because she was so cooperative and never said or did anything to resist him as the others had. Therefore, especially in serial offenses, it is important to not only look at each individual victim but also to be able to compare them with each other for any similarities that may provide a clue as to the goal or motive of the offender.

There are also victimology assessment applications when dealing specifically with sexual assault where the victims may have unintentionally contributed to their victimization. The following case study demonstrates this concept.

Case Study 5-3

School Dorm Environment

In a school dorm environment the victim and her friend came into a common room to watch a movie playing on the television. There was an open seat on a sofa next to another male student they knew, but had no previous social contact or interaction with other than to say hello in passing. The lights in the room were lowered for the movie, and shortly after their arrival the friend got up and moved to another seat to talk on her cell phone and not bother the others. Within just a few minutes the male student, without ever talking to the victim, reached over, placed his hands over her groin, and began to rub her vaginal area over her clothing. The victim was both shocked and stunned. She removed his hand and tried to move away on the sofa. The male, however, reached over and pulled her back toward him. The victim stated she was so in shock she didn't know what to do; she called out to her friend to come back and sit with her, but her friend did not understand the request and did not return. The victim again tried to move away and was again pulled back by the male, who then started to put his hands into her sweatpants to fondle her vaginal area. The victim later reported that she was almost frozen with fear and started to mentally withdraw from the situation. The victim explained that as a child she had been sexually victimized from age 7 to 12 by an older male relative. She started to feel the same fear, dread, and helplessness she had felt before, and could not escape what was happening to her. Instead, she reverted to what she had done before which was to remain quiet not resist. The offender was forced to stop when others came into the room unexpectedly and the lights were turned on. The victim then snapped out of it, stood up, and immediately left the room and reported the incident the following day.

In this case study the prosecutor was hesitant to take any action at all, because he could not understand why the victim did not she say or do anything to stop the act if she was not consenting to it. It was only after the police were able to explain her background and victimology that the prosecutor was able to understand the dynamic that was involved. The victim had mentally retreated to her previous victimization and her lack of resistance was not consent; it was the way she had dealt with this situation in her past. The victim's friend had also acknowledged she was asked repeatedly to come back to sit with the victim but she had misunderstood the reason for the request and did not do so. The victimology assessment in this case was used to help explain some *counterintuitive behavior* of the victim.

▶Offender Risk

One of the last considerations about the victimology assessment deals with the offender and other facts of the case. As stated earlier, the victimology assessment is based on the victim, but we use it to tell us about the offender. Remember, offenders do not typically strike victims by chance—instead they are often looking for particular types of victims. These might be victims who are distracted or otherwise not aware of their surroundings. They might be looking for victims who are unlikely to offer resistance and who they believe they can control either through physical intimidation, through physical force, or through threats against the victim or against a small child or other family member.

Looking at both the victimology and other aspects of the assault such as time and location, we now want to assess the amount of *offender risk* that was involved in the commission of the crime. That is, how much risk or chance was the offender was willing to take in order to commit this particular offense, at this particular time, at this particular location, and with this particular victim. The offender risk is essentially the chance of being interrupted, identified, or arrested during or after the commission of the crime. From an investigative standpoint, we note that the higher the risk factor of the victim, the lower the risk that the offender must take to commit the crime. Conversely, the lower the risk factor of the victim, the higher the risk the offender must take to complete the offense. Serial murderers are generally so successful because they tend to seek out higher risk victims such as street prostitutes or hitchhikers. Most of these high-risk victims are selected as a matter of pure chance, such as when the prostitute plying her trade on the street comes into contact with an offender who is looking for an easy victim. Prostitutes are a good example of highly sought after or popular targets of offenders because of their high-risk victim behaviors. In **Box 5-8**

BOX 5-8 Prostitute High-Risk Victims

Who will the prostitute go with?	Just about anyone
What will the prostitute do?	Just about anything
When will they do it?	Just about anytime
Where will they go?	Just about anywhere
Why will they do it?	Because they think they will get paid
How will the police and public respond to their rape or death?	Without a lot of sympathy or concern

---

Hazelwood demonstrates the problem of prostitutes as high-risk victims using the standard who, what, when, where, why, and how questions.[3]

With typical high-risk victims there is not a lot of public outcry for the police to do anything until there are several victims or the offender makes a mistake and assaults one of the more traditional low-risk victims.

Low-risk victims are more often specifically targeted by the offender. In these cases, the offender may have some amount of prior knowledge of the victim and has specifically planned to assault that particular victim, as opposed to another victim they contact by chance. This does not mean that the offender actually knew the victim personally; it may be a case of the victim being observed at some prior time by the offender who returned at a later time to commit the assault when it was to their advantage to do so. This is not an absolute rule, but with all things being equal and no other evidence pointing to another direction, it is a good course of action and assumption until additional evidence can be developed.

This is not to say that offenders will not take high risks and target a low-risk victim, because they do. However, offenders who take high risks to complete a crime tend to be either very *impulsive,* and therefore act without a lot of forethought and planning or they are very *ritualistic* and act with more premeditation.[4] Later in the text, aspects of impulsive and ritualistic offender behaviors are discussed in greater detail. We can use those offender behaviors in combination with the victimology to tell us the offender type we are dealing with.

▶ Criminal Investigative Analysis (CIA) and Sexual Homicides

A victimology assessment is also an integral part of any criminal investigative analysis (CIA), or the more familiar term, *offender profile.* If a profile or crime analysis is ever requested, the analyst is going to spend a great deal

---

[3] Hazelwood, R., & Michaud, S. G. (2001). *Dark dreams: Sexual violence, homicide, and the criminal mind.* New York: St Martin's Press.

[4] The terms impulsive and ritualistic were coined by Hazelwood and Dr. Janet Warren as part of their effort to identify certain offender typologies. They translate loosely to the traditional organized and disorganized offenders. Hazelwood, R., & Michaud, S. G. (2001). *Dark dreams: Sexual violence, homicide, and the criminal mind.* New York: St Martin's Press.

of time reviewing the victimology so they can get a sense of the victim—who she was, what would make her susceptible to an offender, and what would make the offender think she was vulnerable to assault. A victimology assessment is a very important tool in the detective's toolbox. By obtaining a good picture of the victim, we can identify several potential witnesses and evidence through her background. Victimology assessments and CIAs are also extremely helpful in serial offender cases when attempting to identify any commonalities between each incident, such as victim selection. A CIA or offender profile does not identify a particular offender, but rather identifies the type of offender who may be involved in the incident and may help to narrow the potential offender pool to that type of offender.

The victimology assessment and CIA are also extremely important in cases of sexual homicide, where the victim is not just attacked and sexually assaulted or raped, but is also murdered during the course of the incident. Sexual homicides are defined by Geberth[5] as: "when there is evidence of sexual activity observed at the crime scene or upon the body." This evidence includes the victim's lack of clothing, being sexually posed, or having their body, particularly the genitalia, mutilated. Sexual homicides are best seen, evaluated, and investigated through the lens of a sexual offender. In this case there may be additional lines of questioning that may be important when constructing the victimology. This particular line of questioning is typically reserved for the very close personal friends and may take additional coaxing or convincing before obtaining an answer. The line of questioning revolves around: *"What do you know about the victim that no one else knows?"*

This particular question is important because typically we all have three sides to our lives and personality.[6] There is a *public side;* this is what we normally present day to day. It is what most people will use to describe us and our lives and personalities because they see us mostly in public settings and situations. It is the way we typically interact with others and how we handle the normal stresses of work, marriage, family, interacting with our children, and all of life's other responsibilities and obligations.

The second side is known as the *private side* to our lives. This side is typically shared only with our closest relatives or intimates such as husbands, wives, boyfriends/girlfriends, lovers, or best friends. This private side shared with others may include our personal fears, phobias, concerns, likes or dislikes, past personal history, any interpersonal conflicts, future plans and goals, personal or romantic relationships, sexual interests and/or sexual history, or other important things going on in our private lives. Typically, a victim's private side relates to these types of interpersonal situations and problems that may affect the victim but may not be well known to others outside his or her closest inner

---

[5] Geberth, V. J. (2006). *Practical homicide investigation: Tactics, procedures, and forensic techniques* (4th ed.). Boca Raton, FL: CRC Press.

[6] This concept is based on a quote attributed to Gabriel Garcia Marquez. "Everyone has three lives: A public life, a private life, and a secret life." Marquez was a well known Latin American novelist of the 20th century.

circle of family and friends. In a normal victimology assessment, we use the public and private side of the victim to form our assessment and generally that will suffice to get our understanding of the victim.

In cases of sexual homicide we also want to explore what is known as the *secret side* of victims' lives. This is the side that few, if any, are ever aware of existing, yet we all have one to some extent in our own lives. Our own family and closest friends, or in some cases even spouses, might not know about this secret side, because we typically reserve this aspect of our lives to an extremely limited number of people. This "secret life" may be no more than a brief Internet search for pornography when no one else is around or an email or telephonic correspondence with someone outside a marriage or other personal relationship. It may also be as simple as cheating on income taxes or stealing from a job. But, the secret life of a person may consist of things no one else would believe possible; examples include: housewives or teenagers engaging in prostitution, a husband or wife involved in a secret homosexual relationship, involvement in an extramarital affair, participation in criminal conduct, or participation in some type of dangerous deviant sexual practices such as autoeroticism. The possibilities of what people may be experiencing in their lives are limitless. **Case Studies 5-4 and 5-5** are examples of the secret life and how it could affect the course of the investigation.

Case Study 5-4

Police in Small Town Mystified

Police of a small town were mystified when a young and attractive high school teacher was found brutally murdered in her apartment, the offender leaving her nude and sexually posed at the scene. She had been strangled, stabbed, and anally and vaginally raped. The teacher was generally known as coming from a "good" local family, was active in her local church, and considered to be a dedicated and talented teacher, with no criminal background at all. There were no signs of forced entry into her apartment and the police were stymied about identifying any potential suspects. During background investigation of the victim, however, the police learned some shocking facts. The victim routinely smoked marijuana and a small amount was found in her apartment; they learned she frequented numerous bars and nightclubs in neighboring towns including gay establishments. They learned she was also very sexually promiscuous, engaging in multiple short-term heterosexual and homosexual affairs. Many times her sexual partners were married men and were taken back to her own apartment where they engaged in sexual intercourse. None of these facts were known or suspected by her family or her closest friends. These revelations caused the investigation to turn in a completely different direction.

Case Study 5-5

Death Investigation of a Senior Corporate Manager

This death investigation involved a very well respected, married, female senior corporate manager and mother of two children, who would have under normal circumstances been rated as a low-risk victim. However, based on aspects of the victim's secret life the investigation became somewhat complicated when it was discovered she had engaged in considerable Internet interaction with other females, including often taking on a male persona during chat sessions with other females. She was also collecting some pornography over the Internet and had shared it with others. On multiple occasions she had traveled to meet with females she had communicated with online and had also engaged in homosexual sexual relations with them. Her conduct was completely unknown by others in her immediate family. Her actions of meeting strangers and engaging in multiple extramarital sexual affairs with persons she met over the Internet contributed greatly to the elevation of her risk factors and added a new and unexpected dimension to the investigation.

Although delving into this personal type of material may seem like an invasion of privacy, it may provide the critical information in the formulation of a motive or provide a rationale/explanation as to what may have happened and provide a direction in locating a suspect. We should always exercise caution and be sensitive when going down the path of a victim's secret life, because bringing it to light may interfere with our ability to continue working with the surviving family. After all, no one wants to see a family member dragged through the mud or have their memories tarnished, and not all aspects of the secret life are germane to the motive behind the death. What we are essentially trying to do with the victimology is determine as much about the event as possible and how the victim was seen by the offender. This information combined with the other events of the assault, is used to give us additional insight into the background of the offender.

Social networks, online dating sites, and Internet chatting has given everyone old enough to use a computer the chance to have an active secret life because on the Internet, *you can be anyone you want to be*. It provides a chance for people to chat with others, flirt, and even explore their own particular fantasies or interests. The real physical danger of the Internet is when people decide to meet with someone they only know from chatting or emails. This is not only individual high-risk behavior, but can turn out to be a very significant part of a person's secret life.

▶ Conclusions

In a perfect world, it would be beneficial to assign a detective during at least the preliminary stages of the investigation to focus exclusively on the victim in order to conduct a proper victimology assessment. This is a basic step when conducting a homicide investigation, but it is also extremely important to sex crime investigations, especially when dealing with a stranger-on-stranger type of incident or in cases of "he said, she said" situations. However, due to manpower constraints of many agencies this is not an option, so it becomes an additional responsibility for the assigned case detective. When completed correctly, much information can be developed concerning the offender in addition to identifying aspects of credibility and corroboration of the victim.

▶ Further Reading

Gebreth, V. J. (2006). *Practical aspects of homicide investigation: Tactics, procedures, and forensic techniques* (4th ed.). Boca Raton, FL: CRC Press.

Hazelwood, R. B., & Burgess, A. W. (2008). *Practical aspects of rape investigation: A multidisciplinary approach* (4th ed,). Boca Raton, FL: CRC Press.

Ressler, R. K., Burgess, A. W., & Douglas, J. E. (1988). *Sexual homicide: Patterns and motives.* Lexington, MA: Lexington Books.

Schlesinger, L. B. (2004). *Sexual murder: Catathymic and compulsive homicides.* Boca Raton, FL: CRC Press.

CHAPTER SIX

Human Sexuality

One of the first important concepts relating to sexual offenders is that there are no data or research that establish that sexual offenders are somehow predestined to commit sexual offenses because of their DNA, their education, their own victimization, their family situation, their socioeconomic level, or where they live. Research has shown that no one suddenly wakes up one morning and decides to commit a rape or become a sex offender. Instead, sexual offenders are individually created and developed through their own particular set of life experiences. This chapter provides an overview of human sexuality and its impact on our lives, but we cannot hope to cover all aspects of human sexuality in a single chapter. This is complex subject matter and there are already countless texts written by professional practitioners that are fully devoted to this theme. Instead, the intent of this chapter is to cover some basic concepts of human sexuality to understand how sexual offenders develop over the course of their lives and how their sexuality influences their actions and offenses. It also discusses some aspects of deviant sexual practices.

Regardless of who we are, where we live, our country of origin, our racial background, whether we are male or female, or whether we are young or old, *human sexuality* plays a very important role in our lives. It helps make up a great part of who we are, what we do, and how we express ourselves as sexual beings. To some extent it can also play a part in other aspects of our lives including our cultural, political, ethical, moral, and religious beliefs. Human sexuality is a complex combination of our cognitive, emotional, sensual, and behavioral elements that is based on our internal fantasies and desires. All of this forms our individual patterns of experience. Although there are "normal" ranges of acceptable public conduct, for the most part, our personal sexuality and interests are private aspects of our lives. When the sexuality and interests of mutually consenting adults remain within what society has determined to be the acceptable range, they present no problem to the community and therefore seldom come to the attention of the police. Generally, this personal behavior only becomes a police or governmental problem when the sexual behaviors and interests go beyond mutually consensual acts and involve coercion, force, or the exploitation of others.

What exactly a society or community considers acceptable and what it considers as unacceptable activity are primarily based on several divergent factors including: *culture, religious beliefs, our own individual, personal, and therefore subjective thoughts,*[1] *and societal norms.*

Cultural considerations take in a wide spectrum of possibilities and include our traditional taboos such as general prohibitions against some sex acts. For instance, we have determined culturally that sex between family members should be prohibited and it is a fairly well established taboo across nearly all cultures in the world. Another such cultural belief is the age of consent, or the age a person can give knowing consent for sex; those under-age are protected by law in the United States (the age of consent varies among the states). This is how we as a culture protect young people from making immature mistakes. There is no real criminal reason for these protections, especially when most of the interactions appear to be consensual, but we have traditionally established there is a need for the prohibition to protect certain members of our society.

Societal decisions are what we as a society or community have established as our norms and thus what is acceptable. Examples include prohibitions against acts of prostitution, public nudity, or certain elements of pornography. Theoretically, if these acts are consensual and do not involve force, the real criminality of these acts is based upon the perceived offense to the community or violations of particular societal norms. It is important to note these same consensual acts are not always illegal in other countries or even in some states. There are certain countries where voluntary prostitution is completely legal and even sanctioned; public nudity on beaches or at public swimming pools is considered perfectly acceptable; and there are even locations in the world where hardcore adult pornography and child pornography are made and distributed.

Religion may also play an important part in the moral aspects of what conduct we might consider acceptable or unacceptable. Examples include prohibitions against or efforts to limit premarital sex, incest, homosexual conduct, or the use of contraception. Each religion essentially accepts or discounts certain activities based on its moral precepts and teachings.

The final contributing factor to what sexual conduct is considered acceptable are our own *personal or individual thoughts*. These include what turns us on or what we find sexually stimulating. Our thoughts on the concept are based on our personal life experiences as well as outside influences that have formed our belief system and add to the individuality aspect of the acceptable conduct.

---

[1] Aggrawal, A. (2008). *Forensic and medico-legal aspects of sexual crimes and unusual sexual practices.* Boca Raton, FL: CRC Press.

▶The Human Sex Drive

The human sex drive is among the strongest physical and emotional bonds we experience as human beings. Perhaps only our need for sleep, food, and desire for shelter is stronger; one only has to look around our modern society to see the impact of human sexuality and sex drive on our daily lives. Sex and sexuality are depicted in various forms and fashions in nearly every movie or television show, they are flaunted in our commercials or product advertisements, and are increasingly emphasized in our clothing styles. It is important to note that the sex drive not only includes the natural desire or instinct to reproduce, but it also appeals to the emotional and psychological need to enjoy physical contact and interaction with other human beings. There are three basic components that combine to form to the human sex drive: *biological, physiological,* and *psychosexual.*[2]

Biological

We share some of the biological components of our sex drives with other animals of the world; that is, we have the same natural and instinctive desire to couple together and have sexual intercourse for reproductive purposes. The difference is that animals are essentially doing so out of the basic need to reproduce and are responding to nature's signals to males that the female of the species is ready to receive them and produce offspring. Humans have the physical ability to have sex whenever they want (or are able) just for the sheer pleasure derived from the act. This biological aspect affects our sexual orientation and our sexual impulses, but does not necessarily impact the individual form through which it is expressed. The biological component makes up only about 10% of the human sex drive and therefore has very limited relevance to investigations of sex crimes.

Physiological

The physiological component is what we refer to as the physical desire to experience the sex act as a release. It is the physical urge to engage in sexual relations and achieve sexual gratification; it is activated as the body begins to respond to external stimuli and becomes aroused. The pattern of arousal and reaction to the stimuli depends on the individual and what he or she considers to be sexually attractive. Interest and intensity vary from person to person, so what is stimulating or arousing to one may not be for another. This same pattern may also be interrupted by any number of sexual dysfunctions that are physiological in nature. In some instances, a physiological response

---

[2] Hazelwood, R. R., & Burgess, A. W. (2008). *Practical aspects of rape investigation: A multidisciplinary approach* (4th ed.). Boca Raton, FL: CRC Press.

is possible even during a forced incident, such as a male that experiences an erection while being sexually assaulted or a female victim who may actually experience an orgasm while being raped. Neither example reflects actual sexual interest or voluntary arousal but simply reflects the physiological response to stimuli. The physiological component makes up about 20% of the human sex drive and has little relevance to the investigation of sex crimes.

Psychosexual

The psychosexual component is basically the *emotional component* of the drive or what is in "the mind" and constitutes the most variable and individualistic aspect of the human sexual experience. The psychosexual aspect combines with the various other aspects of personal experience to reflect unique behaviors or stimuli that are sexually arousing to individuals. The psychosexual component is emotional and mental, yet it makes up about 70% of the human sex drive. Thus, we consider the brain to be the primary and largest sex organ of the body, because the sex act typically begins in the brain and is manifested into a physiological response of the body through arousal of the sexual organs, and the desire to complete the act. It is also the mind that exerts the most control over males' ability to "perform" and females' ability to "enjoy the sex act."

What an individual considers arousing or sexually stimulating is referred to as an *erotic mold* or *lovemap*[3] and is as individual as our other personality characteristics. An illustration would be a couple with a steady or permanent consensual sexual partnership in which they learn over time what is sexually stimulating to their partner and how they can arouse each other. This might include a particular physical attribute; some "special" location; a particular touch; the type of sex acts suggested, offered, or implied; along with any of the other sensory factors such as smell, taste, touch, or sound. Consensual partners use this erotic mold or love map of their partner to arouse or otherwise signal them that they are interested in sex. Human sexuality is a sensory-based act, meaning it is controlled and enjoyed through the senses. While all humans employ their senses to some extent to enhance their sexual arousal and performance, the sensory response is generally different between males and females. For males, sight or the visual stimuli creates the greatest arousal; while for females the sense of touch generally creates the greatest arousal. The other senses also play a part in providing stimuli. Examples include anything from wearing perfume to speaking a certain phrase or making a particular sound which the other recognizes from experience as a "signal" of the other's interest in sex. So, how are these erotic molds or love maps formed? Basically, our own sexual behavior and what we are exposed to or what we focus on as being important create the key to our sexual gratification.

---

[3] Money, J. (1989). *Lovemaps: Sexual/erotic health and pathology, paraphilia, and gender transposition in childhood, adolescence, and maturity.* Amherst, NY: Prometheus Books.

If normal persons use these sensory acts for arousal or stimulation, then it is important to remember that sexual offenders will also engage in some form of stimulation or arousal. This can explain why certain offenders may engage in exhibitionism, make obscene phone calls, or demand their victims do certain things, or repeat certain words or phrases as they are being assaulted—anything that may help them to become and remain aroused or stimulated. What exactly sexual offenders might consider stimulating tends to be more centered around deviant sexual acts.

▶ Sexual Behavior

Sexual behavior is made up of four basic components identified as *fantasy, symbolism, ritual,* and *compulsion*.[4] The extent or influence of any of these separate components is dependent upon the individual and/or other factors.

Fantasy

According to *Merriam-Webster's Dictionary*,[5] *fantasy* is defined as "the power or process of creating especially unrealistic or improbable mental images in response to psychological need; *also*: a mental image or a series of mental images (as a daydream)." All humans engage in or have engaged in fantasy to some extent. As an example, we see children fantasizing roles for their playtime activities, or in some cases inventing "imaginary friends." As adults we are no different and may fantasize about such things as a winning lottery ticket and how we would spend the money; we might also imagine aspects of a new job, a new girlfriend/boyfriend, future plans for children, or any number of other life plans. For the most part fantasy is normal, harmless, and generally no cause for concern.

Fantasies are generally pleasant and short lived and do not always involve sex; they do not always contain a lot of specific details and may have a vague continuity based on some unfulfilled desire or activity. Sexual fantasies can also take place in our normal lives. Although everyone engages in some type of sexual fantasy from time to time, males tend to engage in sexual fantasy much more often than females.[6] For most of us, sexual fantasy—whether it is achieved through a mental image of a particular act or through cooperation and participation of a consenting partner—can be enough to satisfy certain psychosexual needs. Therefore, it is not necessary to seek other outlets or to have to employ coercion or force on a nonconsenting partner. One of the more

---

[4] Holmes, S. T. & Holmes, R. M. (2008). *Sex crimes: Patterns and behavior* (3rd ed.). Thousand Oaks, CA: Sage Publications, Inc.

[5] *Merriam-Webster*. (2012). Retrieved from http://www.merriam-webster.com/dictionary/fantasy

[6] Leitenberg, H., & Henning, K. (1995). Sexual fantasy. *Psychological Bulletin*, 7(3), 469–496.

modern examples of fantasy is the concept of *cybersex* wherein two or more persons exchange a series of instant messages or texts describing a mutual sexual act they are imagining performing for or to each other—conducted perhaps thousands of miles apart via the Internet.

For others, particularly sexual offenders and serial killers, the mental fantasy or having a consenting partner is simply not enough. They have an overwhelming desire to fulfill their particular fantasy in reality. Because of their particular fantasy or sexual interests, a consensual partner is not available or one cannot be found (or is not desired), and offenders might seek out a nonconsenting partner and use force or coercion to complete the act. Once coercion and nonconsent are interjected into the act, the fantasy has become a criminal act. Understanding the fantasy component is an extremely important concept when dealing with sexual offenders and can be seen as the basis for later deviant behavior. A core sexual fantasy typically begins to take root at about age 16 when the basic theme or desire is created, and it is then continually developed as a person matures and begins to engage in gradual or partial elements of the fantasy. The fantasy itself is also reinforced through masturbation or with available consenting partners, including wives, girlfriends, or prostitutes. Fantasies may also be tested or enhanced through use of inanimate objects such as dolls, drawing, photographs, pornography, or articles of clothing. It can take a number of years for a fantasy to begin to emerge as criminal conduct as offenders begin to emerge from masturbation to forcefully acting out their fantasy with a nonconsenting person.

Fantasy can be looked at as a play that is acted out in the mind of the person that requires a set, script, actors, many times props, and a director.[7] Because each person creates their own script and directs the images, a person's sexual fantasy is always perfect; that is, every actor plays their part correctly and it turns out exactly the way the person wants. However, reality is not perfect and the outcome of a coerced or forced act never matches the fantasy of the offender, so after the sexual assault he then edits the fantasy based on what he has learned from the experience and then seeks out another victim to try again. Fantasy is also seen as the rehearsal for reality and many offenders will take fantasy to the edge to try it out. For instance, Edmund Kemper III, also known as "the Co-ed Killer" from Santa Cruz, California, was a well-known serial killer who—before he started murdering college co-eds—picked up several young women who were hitchhiking and took them where they wanted to go and let them out of the car without incident. Kemper used these instances as rehearsals for when he began killing and to heighten his fantasies because of the thrill he got from having the power of life and death over the passengers since he could kill them or let them go as he desired. After several rehearsals he finally felt confident enough to start acting on his fantasy and began to kidnap, rape, kill, and mutilate his victims.

---

[7] Hazelwood, R. R. & Burgess, A. W. (2008). *Practical aspects of rape investigation: A multidisciplinary approach* (4th ed.). Boca Raton, FL: CRC press.

According to Hazelwood and Burgess,[8] the ability to fantasize is based on the general intelligence of the offender, so a person with a less-than-average intelligence level typically lives in a less complicated internal world. Therefore, his fantasies tend to be very basic and generalized rather than very specific and detailed. If we were to use an analogy of art to describe the detail of these offender fantasies, we would say their drawings or paintings would be of stick figures. They are also less likely to carry out the more complicated crimes or fantasy scenarios. However, a more intelligent person typically lives in a much more demanding world and can handle more complicated matters. These offenders are able to develop much more complex scenarios, even involving multiple players. They would be constantly editing and improving them. If using the same analogy of art to describe their fantasies, they would be Rembrandts: very detailed and well thought out.

Symbolism

This is the practice of injecting something with a *symbolic* meaning or expressing one's innermost feelings through a visual or sensual representation, and may translate to fetishes and partialisms.

Fetishes

The most common fetish objects are underpants, bras, stockings, shoes, boots, or other intimate apparel. We see this many times when someone will ask their consenting sexual partner to wear a similar object as part of their normal consensual encounters. Others may masturbate while holding, rubbing, or smelling the fetish object; or it may be sufficient simply to hold or otherwise use the object; and again as long as there is no force or coercion involved, there is no real harm involved. These sexual fetishes can become highly compulsive, however, because a person associates a normally neutral object with sexual excitement and for some it becomes so powerful that normal sexual gratification without the object becomes difficult or impossible. Although everyone can develop a fetish, it is more commonly practiced by males than by females. Men may also commit a larceny in connection with obtaining these fetish objects. Examples are thefts of intimate female apparel from clotheslines, from washing machines, or many times men may actually commit a burglary in order to steal such items from a dresser drawer or the laundry basket of a particular female.

Partialisms

Partialism is where someone has attached a sexual interest or feelings onto certain parts of the body such as breasts, buttocks, or legs. Some body parts may be culturally driven, such as the back of the neck for some Asian cultures.

---

[8] Hazelwood, R. R. & Burgess, A. W. (2008). *Practical aspects of rape investigation: A multidisciplinary approach* (4th ed.), Boca Raton, FL: CRC press.

The feet are also another very popular part of the body. This could also include hair, eyes, or hands. Women and men may have partialisms, but it is primarily a male-driven aspect.

Both fetishes and partialisms are normal and provided they are used within consensual context and no other crime is committed, there is generally no problem. However, problems arise when persons have achieved an unhealthy attraction to a particular symbol that becomes so important that it *must* be present in order for them to be sexually aroused or they force them upon an unwilling partner.

Some crimes may spark a sexual symbolism to offenders. Burglary is said to be very symbolic of sex, and many burglars report having erections and even experiencing orgasms upon first entering someone's home. The strong sexual attachment to burglary comes from illegally entering the home of another which symbolizes the offender's exertion of absolute control and dominion over another. This sense of control comes from the ability to go to a place no one else is allowed to go and touching and taking the private property of another without anyone stopping them.

Ritualism

Couples that have been together over a period of time almost intuitively know when their partner is sexually interested and receptive to sex through the use of certain words, phrases, or gestures that carry their personal sexual message. Through repetition these become known and understood between the two and thus become "a ritual." This concept can be the basis for some couples to seek something different to spice up their lives perhaps because their consensual sex life has become routine. This ritual between consensual partners can be changed or kept the same depending on the couple. Problems result for certain persons who, in order to achieve arousal and gratification, must perform their established ritual in the same manner, and possibly in the same sequence of events. This may include using certain words or phrases, certain sex acts, certain sexual positions, or even wearing certain clothing. If the ritual is not performed or "scripted" in the same manner each time, they may not become aroused, and the act must be restarted or abandoned. In a sexual crime the ritual may become a part of an offender's "signature" that is repeated during each offense and can be used to link cases together.

Compulsion

Compulsion is not the same as coercion or being forced to do something; rather, it is basically the desire to repeat the sexual process in a particular manner every time and has both a physiological and a biological basis. The problem occurs when the particular compulsion to complete the sex act in a particular way becomes so overwhelming that the normal emotions and caring for the partner are missing. Many offenders describe an overwhelming "compulsion" or need to satisfy themselves via sexual assault or murder.

Many sexual offenders may also suffer from *hypersexuality*, or the insatiable need for sex. This is not a need for the intimacy of the sexual experience but rather the physical act, and the gratification becomes most important. A good example of this was Albert DeSalvo, also known as the "Boston Strangler," who reportedly demanded sex from his wife an average of five to six times per day, every day; in between the consensual sex acts he would often masturbate. Jon Barry Simonis was a prolific serial rapist claiming to have raped more than 75 women during his crime spree; he described his sex drive as "trying to fill a bottomless pit with buckets of sand."[9] These examples are the exception rather than the rule for sexual offenders and are extreme examples of the compulsion aspect.

▶ Paraphilia

The term paraphilia was first introduced by the German psychiatrist Richard von Krafft-Ebing in 1886 in his famous *Psychopathia Sexualis* (*Sexual Pathology*), though it was not widely used until 1980 when it was adopted into the third edition of the *Diagnostics and Statistical Manual of Mental Disorders*, commonly known as the *DSM-III* (the *DSM-IV* is the most current version). These types of activities or interests were generally considered to be distasteful, abnormal, or perverted. They were collectively referred to in various studies as examples of sexual deviation, sexual anomalies, or sexual perversions. In earlier versions of the *DSM* (editions *I* and *II*), homosexuality was also considered a deviant sexual act.

According to the current *DSM-IV*, paraphilias are characterized by recurring, intense, sexually arousing fantasies, sexual urges, or other behaviors generally revolving around:

- Nonhuman objects
- The suffering or humiliation of oneself or one's partner
- Children
- Other nonconsenting persons

These involve an overwhelming desire or preoccupation with some object, person, or behavior to the point where it is required for arousal or complete gratification. The practitioner may become so dependent on that particular object or activity that when it is not present, they may not be stimulated enough to perform or be able to achieve gratification.

More than 500 different paraphilias or paraphilic behaviors have been identified; although there are some females that may have interest in or

---

[9] This comment was made during a videotaped interview of Simonis by Roy Hazelwood and Ken Lanning at Angola State Prison in the late 1970s. This was one of a series of interviews conducted by the original members of the FBI's Behavioral Science Unit of Serial Offenders.

voluntarily engage in some forms of these acts, they are overwhelmingly practiced by males. These paraphilias typically begin to develop in individuals during early puberty and are fairly established as part of their normal sexual repertoire by their early to mid-20s; once they are established they tend to remain consistent over time. This is because these sexual practices are maintained by offenders through their sexual fantasies and are continually reinforced through masturbation or through consensual acts with a consenting partner.

The paraphilia continues to be reinforced by the association of sexual gratification with that particular fantasy. So many offenders re-offend after they are released from prison because they have kept the fantasy of their sexual acts alive through masturbation. Once released they then seek to put these same fantasies into practice through coercion or force on another victim. Paraphilic activity is seldom limited to single interests or activities, and it is not uncommon for sexual offenders to engage or have interest in multiple paraphilias at the same time. This is known as "clustering," and most sex offenders exhibit two to three different paraphilias during their sexual assaults, which can be detected if we study their contact with the victim. For instance, Dennis Rader, the "BTK killer," routinely engaged in a number of paraphilic behaviors both during his crimes, as evidenced by his crime scenes, as well as practicing some activity in between his offenses. His paraphilias during his crimes included sadism and bondage, which were demonstrated at his crime scenes where he bound, raped, and murdered his victims. He also engaged in autoeroticism and transvestism in between his murders.

Offenders may have a passing interest in several different paraphilias before settling in on those that really stimulate or excite them. In his taped interview with Hazelwood and Lanning, Simonis described how he first started offending by making obscene telephone calls, which progressed to window peeping (voyeurism), and eventually began to expose himself to women. He tried each paraphilia for a while and then moved on until he was able to begin raping women and committing burglaries.

The following is a compilation of some of the most common of the approximately 500 known paraphilias.

Anal Eroticism

Anal eroticism is the localization of libido in the anal zone, or erotic activity focusing on the anus and sometimes the rectum. This can be pleasurable due to the abundance of nerve endings in the anus. This activity is marked by the insertion of objects into the anus during sexual intercourse or during masturbatory activity. Objects range from typical sex toys, such as dildos and vibrators, to 'everyday' objects that would not be considered sex related. These objects may include various vegetables, a summer sausage, a soft drink bottle, screwdrivers, wrenches, and any number of other objects. It is not unusual for a practitioner to put objects into their anus and then be unable to remove them. One example used during training courses is a man who was brought to the emergency room to remove a potato and jar of strawberry jelly that he had inserted into his anus but could not remove.

Anthropophagi

Anthropophagi involves eating the victim's flesh; flesh is either bitten from the body (e.g., nipples that are bitten off) or sliced from the body (eating slices of flesh).

Autoeroticism

Autoeroticism comprises sexual feelings, arousal, or gratification achieved through anoxia, or depleting the oxygen supply to the brain; it is also known as the *breathless orgasm*.[10] Cutting off the oxygen to the brain by use of ligatures, by hanging, or a plastic bag over the head is an extremely dangerous practice, so practitioners generally plan these events with safety mechanisms in place to prevent accidental deaths. However, many times the safety mechanisms fail which leads to the accidental death of the practitioners, known as *autoerotic misadventures*. We know a lot of what goes on not from practitioners who have provided their insight into the practice but through video made by the victims for later use as masturbatory aids; such videos have been found at death scenes where victims had unwittingly recorded their death. There are often a number of paraphilias used in combination with autoeroticism such as *transvestism, sadomasochism and bondage, anorectal eroticism,* and *pornography.* It is important to note that *autoeroticism* is a *solitary event* and instances where two or more persons are found to be engaging in this activity of self-hanging or asphyxiation are better known as sadism.

Auto-Sadism

This is sexual gratification through self-inflicted pain.

Bestiality

Bestiality involves arousal from and sexual contact with an animal and/or the animal is a *preferred* sexual partner no matter what other forms of sexual outlet are available.

Cannibalism

This is a form of anthropophagi deriving pleasure from eating human flesh.

---

[10] Money, J., Wainwright, G., Hingsburger, D. (1991). *The breathless orgasm: A lovemap biography of asphyxiophilia.* Amherst, NY: Prometheus Books.

Coprolalia

This is the use of obscene language as a form of sexual stimulation.

Coprolagnia

This is sexual arousal or excitement through feces related to coprophilia (see below), but it is based on the feces themselves rather than the physical act of defecation.

Coprophilia

This is sexual gratification associated with the act of defecation or through contact with feces. This activity is also included within the sadomasochism (S&M) activities repertoire (see "sadism," defined later). This activity may include eating, smelling, or handling human excrement or other filth. It is related to "coprolagnia." (See **Case Study 6-1**.)

Case Study 6-1

The state police were called to a roadside rest stop where travelers reported a man inside the Porta Potty. Police responded and found the particular Porta Potty did not have plumbing; the toilet was placed over a large tank, which contained the human waste material. They found a man inside the holding tank, covered with feces and urine. He was removed and admitted he had taken off his clothing, and was able to lower himself from the toilet into the tank where he remained for a length of time observing both males and females using the toilet, because he was sexually excited by the process. He was found out when he attempted to climb out of the tank but his body weight caused the metal casing supporting the toilet seat to collapse and he could no longer get out. Nearby, he had other clothing in a plastic bag which he intended to change into after he was "finished." The man admitted to engaging in this activity previously at other locations.

Erotophonophilia

This is sometimes known as lust murder, and is one of the more extreme types of paraphilia. This is where sexual excitement and gratification of the offender are experienced through the murder and mutilation of the victim. This is marked by mutilation of the victim, especially directed against the genitals, and may include removal of the breasts, vagina, or penis.

Exhibitionism

The act is commonly known as "flashing," where the exhibitor exposes their genitalia for the purpose of sexual gratification. The sexual gratification is not necessarily from showing their genitalia, but comes from the reaction, shock, and fear of the person who was flashed. As the victim reacts, the offender achieves momentary power and control by causing the reaction. Activity is reinforced through masturbation. Interestingly, the act rarely takes place in a setting that would be conducive to having *sexual relations*. It is frequently linked with a *compulsive* pattern of behavior wherein the *display* occurs in the *same place and time*. This is more prevalent among males; however, females may also engage in a form of exhibitionism by arranging themselves to be seen undressed or nude by others, for the purpose of causing a reaction of others. The thrill or excitement comes not from exposing themselves, but from the reaction of the other person.

Fisting

Fisting is a sexual activity that involves inserting the whole hand into the vagina or rectum. Once insertion is complete, the fingers either naturally clench into a fist or remain straight. In more vigorous forms of fisting, such as "punching," a fully clenched fist may be inserted and withdrawn slowly. This is another example of anal eroticism where the hand, rather than a foreign object, is used on a consenting partner.

Flagellation

This is sexual gratification associated with whipping or being whipped; it can be sadistic or masochistic.

Frotteurism

This is sexual arousal or excitement through rubbing up against another person in a crowd. This is basically rubbing against another person, even through clothing, and there is no need for bare skin contact.

Gerontophilia

Gerontophilia is sexual interest in elderly persons, generally of the opposite sex. This could include victims in their 70s, 80s, or even 90s. The type offenders who commit sex crimes against elders are thought to harbor deep-seated resentment and hatred for the elderly.

Infantophilia

This is the sexual attraction to infants.

Infibulations

This is self-torture involving piercing the nipples, labia, clitoris, or penis with sharp objects. These piercings can be permanent with a stud and post or temporarily used during sexual acts.

Klismaphilia

This is sexual arousal or excitement from enemas or through introducing liquids into the rectum and colon via the anus.

Masochism

The essential feature of masochism is the sexual arousal or excitement resulting from receiving pain, suffering, or humiliation. The pain, suffering, or humiliation is very real and can be physical or psychological in nature. Some of the better known forms of masochism include bondage, discipline, whipping or spanking, some torture, and various domination punishments. The amount of pain involved can vary from ritual humiliation with little violence to severe whipping and torture of the genitalia. Various other role-playing forms are seen as master–slave, rapist–victim, police–suspect, and many other forms of superior–victim types of relationship. This can also be male as giver and female receiver or female as giver and male as receiver. Some role playing and sexual torture can be extensive and may include a great number of props such as uniforms, special clothing, various items of bondage, and various torture devices such as clamps, vibrators, or dildos.

Mysophilia

This is arousal or excitement from general unclean or dirty surroundings.

Necrophilia

Necrophilia is arousal or excitement from contact, including sexual intercourse, with the dead and is viewed as one of the more serious and dangerous deviant practices, especially because some offenders may kill a person in order to have sex with them. There are at least three distinct types of practitioners/offenders of necrophilia: *pseudonecrophilia, regular necrophilia,* and *homicidal necrophilia.*

Pseudonecrophile

Pseudonecrophiles are those who fantasize about having sex with a dead person, and, although they have a general transient attraction to a corpse, a living person is still their choice for a sexual partner. Some practitioners may not be able to have normal interaction or sexual relations with a living person and they rely on fantasy to escape the need for such interaction. This fantasy is often acted out by consensual partners or prostitutes who will "play dead" while their partner has sex with them. It is not uncommon that the consensual partner will take a cold shower or bath prior to sex to add to the effect of "being dead."

Regular Necrophile

The "regular necrophile" engages in sex with the dead but does not engage in the murder of the victim. These practitioners may seek employment at funeral homes where they can interact with the dead and have a chance to have sex with the bodies. Others may resort to grave robbing and then having sex with the victim. One of the better known examples of this is Ed Gein, who was known to remove bodies from cemeteries and to bring them back to his home where he interacted with them.

Homicidal Necrophile

Homicidal necrophiles are the most dangerous of the offenders because they may kill their victims in order to have sex with them; there are numerous examples of serial killers who have engaged in this deviant act.

Case Study 6-2

Some of the most famous and prolific serial killers such as Ted Bundy, Edmund Kemper ("the Co-ed Killer"), and Gary Ridgway ("the Green River Killer") all engaged in necrophilia with their deceased victims. Bundy and Kemper actually decapitated their victims and brought the heads back to their residences where they had oral sex with them later. Gary Ridgway also returned to his victims to have sex with them days after he murdered them and left them in the woods. Ridgway placed stones into the vaginal tract of his victims he left in the woods, and when the bodies were found it was believed that the stones were perhaps symbolically placed into the victims because they were prostitutes. Ridgway, however, clarified his actions by saying he merely wanted to limit possible insect infestation of the vaginal tract as he returned to have sex with them.

Necrofetishism

This is a fetish for dead bodies. One famous example of a practitioner of this is Jeffrey Dahmer, who kept bodies in his house where he slept with them in bed, posed them, and photographed them in different positions.

Pedophilia

This is arousal or sexual attraction to younger children. Pedophiles prefer children as sexual partners even when adults are available. There are two types of pedophiles: *situational* and *preferential*.

Situational Pedophiles

This offender is not an actual pedophile in the sense that he only seeks out children, because the situational offender may prefer an adult as a sexual partner but will offend against children if no adults are available. Situational offenders may only offend against a single child over the course of their lives or may do so sporadically in those instances when they want to engage in sex and no adult is available.

Preferential Pedophiles

These offenders choose children over adults, even when consensual adult partners are available. These offenders will usually have a particular sex and age group that they are attracted to and prefer.

Piquerism

This is arousal or excitement through infliction of small, nonlethal cuts or stabs on their victims.

Pornography

Pornography is arousal or excitement through viewing of obscene pictures or other materials. Because men are more visually aroused than females, pornography typically appeals more to men than to women. Pornography is a multibillion-dollar industry and there is pornography for every fetish or paraphilia imaginable. Standard monthly men's magazines such as *Playboy*, *Penthouse*, and *Hustler* that show naked pictures of voluntary models posing in sexually provocative positions are not a legal problem. This does not mean they do not ever cause problems based on religious, moral, and exploitatative grounds, but those are other issues that do not affect law enforcement. Law enforcement comes into play in pornography when the models depicted are underage, especially younger children, or if they were drugged, forced, or coerced into participation. A second problem involves the depiction of sexual violence such as torture or even murder of a victim, such as in so-called snuff films. Although this type of material may not necessarily be a legal problem because of the first amendment, it is what some offenders are looking at. Offenders might use this type of material to refine their fantasies and reinforce the belief that their deviant conduct is normal. For each kind of paraphilia mentioned within this chapter there is some form of pornography available for practitioners to view.

Pygmalionism

This is arousal or sexual excitement associated with female statues or dolls. Lifelike, full-sized, and anatomically correct dolls are a big part of the pornography industry and fulfill this paraphilia interest.

Pyromania

This is arousal or excitement generated through setting off fires and may include smaller nuisance-type fires or an arson, such as the burning of a large structure.

Sadism

Sexual sadism refers to sexual pleasure derived from the infliction of pain, suffering, and/or humiliation upon another person. The pain and suffering of the victim is pivotal to the sexual arousal and pleasure of the sadist. When used in a consensual circumstance it is known as *sadomasochism* (referred to as S&M), because one partner is willing to be punished or humiliated for their sexual gratification and one partner administers the humiliation or punishment for their gratification. There are a number of S&M acts that generally include some form of flagellation, bondage, or noninjurious torture. It often includes combining the physical elements into fantasy play scenarios such as, master and slave, severe boss and "naughty" secretary, queen and manly slaves, police arrest, or military training. Other aspects of S&M activity involving humiliation of the victim through other paraphilias are covered elsewhere in this chapter. From a law enforcement perspective, S&M activity between consenting adults seldom poses any problems. However, for a sexual sadist, the victim is not a consenting adult and generally is subjected to severe torture and injury and thus becomes a law enforcement problem.

Scatophilia

This is the sexual attraction to making obscene telephone calls. This is similar to exhibitionism, wherein the offender is looking to cause a reaction in the victim. He is looking to express his power as the victim is shocked, disgusted, horrified, or scared. He is depending upon this reaction for his erotic stimulation. Some offenders may start with this type of nuisance offense and then, as they become more confident or they need increased stimulation, progress to other offenses.

Scoptophilia

With scoptophilia the practitioner receives sexual gratification by peeping through windows to watch people in their homes. This could range from observing normal activities to watching private sexual behavior between couples. The excitement comes from the power of being able to watch someone without that person's knowledge. This is another name for what we more commonly know as *voyeurism*. Many sexual offenders may start out engaging in this activity before moving on to other acts.

Transvestism

This is arousal or excitement centered on wearing the clothes of or imitating the opposite sex. Although it can be practiced by both sexes, it is more commonly associated with males. Interestingly, most practitioners are heterosexual males who are aroused by wearing female attire. This is frequently found during the practice of autoeroticism where the victim is also dressed in female attire.

Troilism

This is arousal or excitement generated through engaging in sex acts with several partners at the same time or in front of others. This can also be a form of exhibitionism and voyeurism wherein another person realizes sexual pleasure from observing others and/or themselves in some sexual act.

Case Study 6-3

Serial murders Fred and Rose West, from England, were practitioners of troilism. Rose, with the knowledge and permission of her husband, would engage in prostitution and bring her customers to their house and perform sexual intercourse with the customer while her husband would watch them from a hidden place. He would become sexually aroused by observing the act.

Urolagnia

This is arousal or excitement through contact with urine or involving the act of urination. The offender achieves sexual arousal or gratification by the sight, odor, or contact with urine, or they may drink their own urine or urine obtained from another. The term *golden shower* is often associated with this paraphilia and refers to the acts of having someone urinate onto another person or themselves. This activity is also included in the long list within the S&M repertoire involving humiliation through the use of human urine.

Voyeurism

See also "scoptophilia." Receiving sexual gratification by peering through windows to watch people, ranging from watching normal activities to watching private behavior. Many sexual offenders may start out engaging in this activity before moving on to other acts.

▶ Summary

As described in this chapter, human sexuality is a complex combination of cognitive, emotional, sensual, and behavioral elements. Every person has his or her own particular lovemap or erotic mold based on what is sexually stimulating or arousing to them. No one wakes up one day and decides to engage in deviate sexual activity or commit a rape; it is a process developed over years with many outside influences as well as an individual's own personal life experiences and is developed further through *fantasy, symbolism, ritual,* and *compulsion*. These four components help us to understand the sexual offender and other aspects of deviate sexual activity. One of the key factors we can use to identify offenders' sexual behavior comes from their sexual parapahilias that are frequently exhibited during their sexual assaults.

Paraphilias are not always associated with sexual assaults or sexual offenders. The only real problem with most of the sexual paraphilias is the very real possibility of causing harm to oneself or to one's partner during the act, or when the paraphilias are coerced or unwanted by one of the participants. There are some notable exceptions such as erotophonophilia, infantophilia, necrophilia, and pedophilia, which are of course all criminal acts. From an investigative perspective, it is important for detectives to have a basic understanding of deviate sexual practices as outlined in this chapter and be able to identify them during the victim interview. Without such basic knowledge it can be very easy to discount a victim's statement of what happened to her as untrue or made up. Understanding the various aspects of deviate sexual activity and being able to identify the various paraphilias when they are employed by a sexual offender are also very good means to link seemingly unrelated cases.

▶ References

Aggrawal, A. (2009). *Forensic and medico-legal aspects of sexual crimes and unusual sexual practices.* Boca Raton, FL: CRC Press.

Hazelwood, R. R., & Burgess, A. W. (2009). *Practical aspects of rape investigation: A multidisciplinary approach* (4th ed.). Boca Raton, FL: CRC Press.

von Krafft-Ebing, R. (1998). *Psychopathia sexualis.* New York: Arcade Publishing.

CHAPTER SEVEN

Offender Typology

There are several important misconceptions about sexual offenders and the crimes of rape or forced sexual assault. One of the biggest misconceptions about the sexual offender is that the offender is essentially a frustrated male, who searches for and assaults a female victim because he is seeking a sexual release. Continuing with this thought process, the offender's behavior is understood to be guided or influenced by his sexual desire.[1] This is not correct, and what is surprising to most laymen is the fact that the vast majority of sexual offenders may already be involved in a consensual sexual relationship at the time of their crimes. Many are married, have girlfriends, or have other available consensual partners. Therefore, rape is not about seeking a sexual release. In fact, many offenders report that the sex resulting from their assaults is not very satisfying at all.

In reality, the crime of rape is not about sex. It's about the offender using sex as a weapon and expression of other nonsexual needs such as power and anger.[2] Both power and anger produce emotions and cause what we know as verbal, physical, and sexual behaviors on the part of the offender. Understanding and recognizing these behaviors helps to identify certain personality characteristics of the offender. Recognizing these personality characteristics helps us to categorize the type of offender, and if we can identify the offender type, then we can understand much about his basic motivations and goals behind the assault. This in turn can often tell us about some of his expected pre- and post-crime behaviors, and many times a lot about the background of the offender.

---

[1] One of the key arguments for legalized prostitution is the belief it will lower the incidence of rape because offenders will be able to have a legal outlet for their sexual demands or needs through use of a prostitute, and therefore it would not be necessary to assault a nonconsenting victim. This is not true since prostitution already exists, particularly in larger U.S. cities, and prostitutes are readily available. Even in Nevada where prostitution is legal in several counties, rapes still occur.

[2] Groth, A. N. (1979). *Men who rape: The psychology of the offender*. New York: Plenum Press; p. 5.

It is essentially possible to paint a portrait of an offender whom we may never have seen, but whom we recognize by his behaviors. This information is also invaluable in determining if the offender may be involved in other incidents, is likely to reoffend in the future, and most importantly, if the violence level is likely to increase.[3]

▶ Rapist Typology

There is a wide range of offenders with a wide range of individual motivations. A rapist typology is a way to recognize similar behaviors and categorize them into different types of offenders. It is important to remember while trying to place these offenders into particular categories that no one offender is going to fit perfectly into any particular category. Instead, there is what Hazelwood[4] calls a *blending* or *mixture* of the offender types, also commonly know as *bleed over,* meaning some offenders may share some characteristics of other offender types. For example, after reviewing the basic facts of a particular case, we can identify 10 different characteristics from a particular offender. It is not uncommon for these characteristics to be split among different categories of offenders. As an example, two or three characteristics may belong to one type and seven or eight characteristics to another type. Even though bleed over occurs frequently, there is generally enough information available to properly place the offender into the correct offender category. It is at this stage of the investigation when the behavior orientated interview technique and the detailed victim statement becomes so important.

One of the first things we want to look at is the victim's statement and other case facts to determine whether or not the offender displayed *selfish* or *unselfish behaviors.*[5] This does not mean to look at an offender with some level of kindness or understanding, or attempt to portray him in a more favorable light. Rather, this is the first of the subjective determinations regarding the offender's overall actions based on the verbal, physical, and sexual behaviors exhibited during the incident as described by the victim.

Unselfish Behaviors

When we talk about being unselfish in general terms we think about such things as giving, sharing, caring, and expressing or showing concern, which are centered on the wellbeing or feelings of another. For sexual offenders,

---

[3] Ainsworth, P. B. (2001). *Offender profiling and crime analysis.* Portland, OR: Willan Publishing; p. 108.

[4] Hazelwood, R. R. & Burgess, A. W. (2008). *Practical aspects of rape investigation: A multidisciplinary approach* (3rd ed.). Boca Raton, FL: CRC press.

[5] Hazelwood, R. R. & Burgess, A. W. (2008). *Practical aspects of rape investigation: A multidisciplinary approach* (4th ed.). Boca Raton, FL: CRC press.

displaying unselfish behavior results from two motivations: 1) They have no real interest in causing any actual physical harm to the victim; and 2) They believe their expression or showing concern for the victim might actually "win the victim over" to them or change the victim's opinion of the offender. Many act in this manner because of their sexual fantasy of wishing the experience to resemble or perhaps turn into a consensual relationship with the victim. There are several examples of unselfish verbal, physical, and sexual behavior that are fairly easy to recognize.

Unselfish Verbal Behaviors

One of the first recognizable characteristics of the unselfish offender is his verbal behavior or communication toward the victim. Typically, it is not very profane or harsh and will be similar to normal conversations that may be held between close friends or intimate partners. It may also consist of questions posed to the victim concerning her background or family history, or of other unsolicited comments made by the offender during the assault. This is why it is so important to document any verbal comments, questions, or conversations by the offender, because it can be very revealing as to his motivation. This verbal behavior may take on many forms depending upon the offender and the victim and could range from voluntary statements or comments addressed to the victim to questions about the victim's personal life. These comments should be seen as an effort to reassure or calm the victim and hopefully lower her fear or concern for her safety, or may appear to be complementary and flattering toward the victim; examples of verbal behavior could include statements, comments, or questions such as those listed in **Box 7-1.**

BOX 7-1 Examples of Unselfish Verbal Behavior

"Don't worry, I won't hurt you."   "Don't be afraid."

"If you do what I say, you won't get hurt."   "You're so beautiful."

"Your husband is a lucky man."   "You have a sexy body."

"Are you comfortable?"   "Does it hurt?"

"Should I stop?"   "This is not your fault."

"Does it feel good for you?"   "Do you do this with your husband?"

"How long have you been married?"   "Where do you work?"

"Where are you from?"   "I hope you can forgive me."

"Can I see you again?"

These types of statements may seem somewhat out of place when you consider the context and circumstance in which they are said, but for this type of offender they are not unusual. Therefore, it becomes very important during the victim interview to ask about any statements made by the offender, because the victim may also not consider these statements as important. There is often a resemblance to a casual conversation between the victim and offender.

In some circumstances, it may resemble the intimate personal conversations of spouses or lovers, commonly called "pillow talk," wherein the offender seems to be acting and treating the victim more as a lover than as a victim of a crime.

It is also not uncommon for the offender during the course of his conversations with the victim to make unsolicited, but very important and many times accurate statements about his own personal life, such as those listed in **Box 7-2**. To the uninformed, these types of statements seem odd and out of place based on the circumstances. However, they are a good example of unselfish verbal behavior toward the victim.

BOX 7-2 Examples of Offenders' Statements About Their Personal Lives

"I'm headed back to prison after this."

"I don't know why I keep doing this."

"I have a beautiful wife and kid at home."

"This is not how I wanted this to go."

"You would never look at me in the daylight."

"Don't worry, you're not to blame for this."

"I'm sorry this had to happen to someone like you."

"You didn't deserve this."

Unselfish Physical Behaviors

One of the first things we will note with unselfish physical behavior is the lack of physical violence used against the victim. If force is used, it is probably applied to gain and maintain control over a resisting victim, rather than to punish or harm the victim. Any weapon that is used would be more likely to be used to intimidate rather than to inflict any injuries or become part of the sexual assault. This is important behavior, because it is an indication that the offender does not want to harm the victim. An example of such behavior is noted in **Case Study 7-1**.

Case Study 7-1

As she entered her house, a victim was surprised by an intruder who was waiting behind the front door for her entry into the house. Immediately upon her entering the house the attacker moved to seize her and get her under control. But to the offender's surprise, the victim savagely fought back. This caught the attacker by surprise, and he began using more force to try and subdue her and began to stab her in the back with a small penknife he had brought with him. The two struggled all over the living room until the victim was exhausted by the ordeal and literally collapsed onto the floor. She had been stabbed more than a dozen times in the back, sustaining mostly shallow wounds but several were relatively deep and she was bleeding profusely.

As she was fighting back, the victim also reported the offender kept repeating, "Stop. Please stop," as she was struggling to defend herself or escape. When the victim finally stopped struggling and collapsed onto the floor exhausted, in pain, and trying to catch her breath, the offender stopped fighting as well. He then moved the victim onto her side, knelt down beside her, and brushed her hair from her face as if to help her breathe. The victim then quite calmly asked for a drink of water. The offender almost immediately stood up and walked into the kitchen and got a glass of water and brought it back for her. She drank the water and then sat up on the floor. Although she was still bleeding from the many wounds, she asked for a washcloth to wipe the sweat from her face and try to cool down. The offender stood back up and walked to the kitchen to search for a washcloth in the kitchen. He found a towel and put it into the sink to wet it. While he was doing that, the victim managed to get to her feet, open the front door, and flee from the house.

The offender described in this case study fled the scene. Despite the violent nature of the event, the offender actually displayed unselfish behavior. Examination of all of the case facts determined the injuries were inflicted not out of an attempt to harm the victim, but almost out of "self-defense" after the victim put up such a strong and unexpected physical resistance. There was no indication that the injuries were inflicted to harm or kill the victim, and although numerous wounds were inflicted on her back and shoulders, none were life threatening or very deep, and the use of force stopped after the victim stopped resisting. Additional examples of unselfish behavior can be seen by the concern expressed by the offender toward the victim in several ways. The first was the brushing of the hair back from the victim's face to help her breathe; the second was the offender getting the glass of water when the victim asked for one; and third, he got up and looked for a towel in the kitchen so he could soak it with water to help her cool down, again based on her request. Lastly, there never was a sexual assault, although that is clearly what was intended. Instead, after the victim was injured, the offender made efforts to make her comfortable rather than continue with his sexual assault.

It is also not uncommon for offenders, in an effort to calm and reassure victims they will not be harmed, to give their weapons to the victims. The purpose is to show they mean them no harm so the victims will not be afraid. What becomes difficult for many to understand is when the victim returns the weapon to the offender. Victims sometimes report they did not know how to use the weapon or thought the offender was only setting them up to be hurt if they tried to use the weapon.

Unselfish Sexual Behaviors

The unselfish offender may attempt to involve the victim in the sexual act as much as possible, such as by requesting or demanding the victim take her own clothes off or getting the victim to ask to take the offender's clothes off.

This plays into the offender's fantasy that this is not a forced sexual assault, but a consensual love-making experience. Therefore, the unselfish offender does not always force the victim, and rather relies on her compliance. If the victim complies, then the offender continues. But if the victim declines or passively resists in some way, the offender may move on to other demands and find what the victim is willing to do. The offender displaying unselfish sexual behavior may also be an attempt to stimulate or arouse the victim, much like a consensual partner. Offender actions could include kissing, fondling or sucking the breasts, or digitally manipulating the other genitalia. Some offenders may actually attempt to perform oral sex on their victims as a way to arouse them or get them interested in having sex with the offender. The thought process continues back to the concept of unselfish behavior—that if the offender is "nice" or "does the right thing" to the victim, the victim might begin to enjoy the incident and then want to actively participate and that the incident, which is clearly forced and unwanted, will somehow become a consensual experience.

Selfish Behavior

There is a distinct and easily recognizable difference between the unselfish and the selfish offender. The selfish offender has no interest to involve or otherwise show concern toward the victim, and the assault is not about the victim; it is about the offender and what he wants to do. Instead of being the object of concern, the victim is treated much like a prop or something to be used, abused, and/or discarded after the offender is done.

Selfish Verbal Behavior

Verbal behavior for the selfish offender is generally marked by harsh, abusive, threatening, and often profane language that is usually directed towards the victim. The language and statements are often loud, demeaning, humiliating, and demanding. Comments, when made, tend to be very nonpersonal, meaning they are not about the victim; they are about the offender and also tend to be more sexually orientated. Examples include but are not limited to those listed in **Box 7-3.**

BOX 7-3 Examples of Selfish Verbal Behavior

"Get them clothes off or I'll rip them off."   "You better move that ass."
"You're a stupid bitch."   "You better do what I say."
"You stupid fat whale."   "You disgust me, you whore."
"You're giving me that pussy right now."   "Shut your mouth, bitch."
"You're going to do me right now."   "You slut."
"I ought to beat the crap out of you."   "I'll cut your throat, bitch."
"I'm going to do you and you're going to like it."   "Shut up no one asked you."

With the selfish offender, it becomes clear the offender is not interested in taking or having a conversation with the victim; instead they talk "at the victim," sometimes in a derogatory, demeaning, and profane manner.

Selfish Physical Behavior

Passive, verbal, or physical resistance offered by the victim will have no effect on the selfish type of offender, and he will overcome any resistance with whatever force is necessary. These offenders are not interested in victims' fear and may in fact become more excited or aroused by their fear and resistance. The victims and their feelings will be of little concern to these offenders. The application of all levels of force (i.e., minimum, moderate, excessive, or brutal) is likely at any time during the assault, including the force used to capture and maintain control over the victim, to overcome resistance, and during the sexual assault itself. In some circumstances we see the application of force against the victim even when no resistance is offered. It is also not unlikely for the offender to physically assault the victim after the sexual assault is over but before the offender and victim separate. The use of weapons to threaten or injure the victim is also likely with selfish offenders. Although any weapons might be used depending on the offender, blunt-force and sharp-force instruments tend to be preferred types of weapons.

Selfish Sexual Behaviors

Selfish offenders have no interest in trying to arouse the victim; instead, their concern is for the victim to arouse them. They are only interested in their own gratification or the victim's humiliation. Since they have no feeling toward the victim, they could not care less whether the victim is aroused or interested in the sex act at all. Instead of caressing the victim to arouse or stimulate her, the selfish offender is more likely to pinch her, bite her, and twist her breasts or genitalia. Forced oral, vaginal, and anal intercourse are all likely and may be committed in any combination or order. Whether offenders cause pain or injury to the victim is not their concern, and for some offenders, causing pain is what makes the assault more gratifying for them.

Other Evaluations

When evaluating crime scenes, we frequently refer to certain offender actions as being *organized* or *disorganized*. We are looking for certain recognizable offender characteristics or behaviors displayed at the scene or during his interaction with the victim to find signs of criminal sophistication or experience, maturity level, and intelligence level. Examples include the amount of preparation or planning displayed by the offender or if the offender made any efforts to hide his identity or otherwise hinder his identification, such as by wearing a mask to hide his face or wearing gloves in order not to leave fingerprints. Other examples include whether the offender brought the necessary tools or equipment needed to complete the crime with him or whether he relied on what was available at the scene. We also try and determine if the offender seemed to be concerned or unconcerned about leaving evidence behind that could later be used against him.

Ritualistic Offender

For sex crimes, other terms are used to describe the overall offender behavior, known as *ritualistic* or *impulsive*.[6] A *ritualistic* offender roughly but not exactly corresponds to what is better known as an *organized* offender. The typical organized offender appears to be more in control of the victim and the events, displays more preplanning or premeditation, and generally implies a more experienced or intelligent offender. For sexual offenders, their conduct exhibits more *ritualistic* behavior because of the amount of prior planning and preparation involved to commit the crime, especially the amount and type of precrime fantasizing. These types of offender may seek out particular victims or are seeking a certain type of victim to fulfill their particular fantasy, and thus they tend to strike when they are ready to offend, make efforts to hide their appearance, or limit the amount of evidence left behind, and therefore are more likely to escape being caught.

Impulsive Offender

An *impulsive offender* roughly but not exactly corresponds to what is known as a *disorganized offender*. The disorganized offender typically exhibits a general lack of control over the victim and the events, with little evidence of preparation and preplanning. Therefore, impulsive offender assaults are much more spontaneous than ritualistic offender assaults. This type of offender generally reacts to circumstances as they occur and tends to act less on fantasy. For example, these offenders may strike as they come into contact with a victim, wherever they happen to be at the time. Because these crimes are so spontaneous, there is not always an effort to hide their appearance or concern about leaving physical or forensic evidence behind.

Fantasy

Since fantasy plays such an important part in sexual crimes, we can use that to understand the difference between the two types of offender activity. For the impulsive offender, fantasy does not play as much of a part in the incident. It may be there to a certain extent, but it tends to more basic and may lack any specific themes or real direction. So, it is not always seen as part of impulsive offender assaults or apparent from offenders' interactions with their victims. For ritualistic offenders, however, fantasy is extremely important and often is well developed into very specific themes. We see their fantasies and in some cases their paraphilias displayed or played out during their assaults or their interactions with their victims. For these offenders, their fantasies play

---

[6] Hazelwood, R. R., & Burgess, A. W. (2009). *Practical aspects of rape investigation: A multidisciplinary approach* (4th ed.). Boca Raton, FL: CRC Press.

a major role in their sexual assaults. Understanding the overall basics of *selfish* and *unselfish*, and *impulsive* and *ritualistic* behaviors, we can now start to move to identify the individual offender types.[7]

▶ Rapist Typology

There are six distinct types of offenders; four are the primary types of offenders, which are commonly known as *power reassurance, power assertive, anger retaliatory,* and *anger excitation.* The other two types are more atypical offenders known as *opportunistic* and *gang/multiple rapists.*

The four primary offender types all have distinct personality characteristics that help us to differentiate between the categories. The different characteristics within each offender type are not always absolutes; therefore, when describing these general traits and personality characteristics, note that words such as "typically," "likely," "generally," "seldom," or "usually" are used instead of absolute terms such as "always" or "never." This takes into consideration that not all offenders are the same and there may be some minor fluctuation and preferences between individual offenders. For example, if a characteristic of a particular offender type is a preference for victims who are taller, left-handed, red-headed females, this does not mean there are not some offenders within same category who actually prefer victims who are shorter, right-handed, and with blonde or brunette hair.

Power Reassurance

Power reassurance is the most common type of sexual offender and makes up approximately 81% of all sexual assaults. Because these offenders are so numerous, we tend to know a lot about their particular personality characteristics because we see them demonstrated time and time again. This offender type includes some distinct personality characteristics and physical attributes that make them somewhat easy to recognize. Perhaps the biggest one of these personality characteristics is their low self-esteem and lack of concern for their personal appearance. This can also translate to generally poor personal hygiene. It can also be seen in their clothing, which may be dirty and in poor condition, and their general living conditions would likely mirror the same lack of concern for their personal appearance. They typically have poor interpersonal skills and do not have a wide range of friends. They tend to engage more in individual or

---

[7] Groth, N., Burgess, A. W., & Holmstrom, L. L. (1977). Rape: Power, anger and sexuality. *American Journal of Psychiatry, 134*(11), 1239–1243 first developed the concept of rapist typology and Hazelwood, R. R. & Burgess, A. W. (2008). *Practical aspects of rape investigation: A multidisciplinary approach* (4th ed.), Boca Raton, FL: CRC Press further defined the rapist typology as used in this text. There are other terms used by other experts to describe and categorize sexual offenders, but these are the most recognizable and understandable.

solitary pursuits rather than joining in with others. They would be described by those who know them as loners who are gentle, shy, quiet, or passive, and certainly nonconfrontational when dealing with others. They are typically underachievers in school and in life and would seek out some type of menial employment where they do not have to routinely engage with the public. One would be unlikely to find them in the military, but if they are or were in the service, they have probably been unsuccessful and would likely not complete their term of enlistment or would leave after their first enlistment. They are generally unsuccessful in the service because they are typically nonathletic and would not be interested in the physical fitness and sometimes Spartan concepts of the selfless service and sacrifice of military life. They would also have difficulties in adjusting to the discipline, uniformity, teamwork, and responsibility encouraged and demanded by military service.

This offender type is generally more nocturnal, meaning they feel more alive and awake in the nighttime than the daytime. Again, during nighttime there are fewer opportunities or requirements to engage with others. It is not unusual for this offender type to be out walking or riding a bicycle at nighttime around residential neighborhoods as part of their precrime activity. This is actually the offender conducting surveillance to locate and select targets prior to the assault. If he sees a potential victim, he will identify any potential vulnerability he can use to complete his assault, such as small children living at home or the victim living alone. It is not uncommon for these offenders to engage in window peeping or to sit nearby and watch the residence as they conduct a surveillance of the area or the particular residence. So, searches outside the residence may be very beneficial for footwear impressions, cigarette butts, or even latent prints on the window. Most residential burglars (not just these particular offenders) typically enter through unlocked doors or windows rather than forced entry. There are a couple of reasons for this. First, it is not always necessary to force entry, because so many residences are not properly secured, frequently with unlocked doors or windows. If a residence is secured, they may simply move to another house. Second, the offender does not want a premature confrontation with the victim that might be caused if the offender wakes the victim up by forcing entry. Instead, the offender wants to be in a position to immediately seize and maintain control over the victim and limit his or her resistance. This offender typically strikes when the victim is alone or has small children within the residence. Small children present in the house offers the offender the chance to make threats against the children in order to gain compliance and limit the resistance of the victim.

Because these are ritualistic offenders, they generally have an established pattern or modus operandi (MO) and tend to repeat that general theme throughout their assaults. They typically have located and targeted several victims in advance, and when they set out to commit their assaults they simply go find whatever victim is available. If the offender shows up at his first victim's house and she is not home or he cannot easily gain entrance, he is likely to simply move to the next victim he has already identified. If the offender gains entrance but the victim manages to resist, the offender is likely to break off the attack and flee the residence, but it is not unusual for him to go straight to the residence of another preselected victim and attempt to assault her instead. This means that as police are responding to the first victim, the offender is already on the way to assault the next victim.

The typical victim is within 4 years (+/−) of the power reassurance offender's age, although some offenders may intentionally seek out older or somewhat younger victims. This type of offender is seeking to resolve his issues of self-doubt by asserting his masculinity. In fact he generally feels inadequate around women, particularly those around his same age. So, if he is in a personal relationship with a woman, she is typically younger and less mature. Although these offenders are typically nonviolent, they tend to appreciate even the momentary sense of power and control they hold over the victim, even though it is limited to that particular incident. They generally have no intention or desire to injure the victim and are therefore considered the least violent of all of the sexual offender types. In fact, this offender may actually dislike what he does and be concerned that he may hurt someone. This is the only offender who typically displays *unselfish behavior*. So, when we read a victim's statement and we recognize the displayed unselfish verbal, physical, and sexual behaviors, then it is almost certain to be this offender type.

This offender type would also likely engage in other low-level and basically nonconfrontational crimes. Examples include window peeping, thefts of clothing from clotheslines or laundromats, or residential burglaries, and the offender will likely have a police record for these types of offenses. This offender type has an active interest in pornography and therefore may be an adult bookstore patron, visit or subscribe to pornographic sites on the Internet, or call the "1-900" telephone sex lines. Although they may view and collect pornography, it tends to lack any specific themes, such as sadomasochism (S&M), bondage, or child pornography.

Their generalized fantasy revolves around the assault being a consensual experience or their somehow being able to turn the assault into a consensual or romantic sexual relationship with the victim. We see this when offender attempt to engage the victim in the activity as much as possible, such as by asking victims to undress themselves, asking them to change sexual positions, or engaging in conversation with them. They may also ask or demand that the victim say or repeat certain phrases or comments to them during the assault. This demand to repeat certain words or phrases is known as *scripting* and it is one of the elements that will be present in offenders' assaults and may be used to link assaults together. What they want the victim to say to them depends upon the offender and his particular fantasy and could include the following demands:

- "Tell me you love me."
- "Tell me you need me."
- "Tell me how you like this."

- "Say you want to make love to me."
- "Tell me to make love to you."
- "Tell me this feels good."

Scripting is an example of the senses being used to arouse or stimulate. In the case of scripting, the sense of hearing is used to stimulate or arouse the offender and thus adds to his fantasy.

This offender type typically uses a minimal amount of force and generally only enough to seize and maintain control over the victim. These offenders may make certain demands of the victim, but are then likely to negotiate[8] or drop the demand rather than force the issue. Part of this is because of their general insecurity dealing with women and partly because of their fantasy that the assault is really a consensual experience and one doesn't force a consensual partner. The assault itself typically does not last long, but since this offender essentially does what the victim allows, the more passive the victim, the more they will demand and the longer they might spend with victim. As they gain more experience and confidence through repeated assaults, they will tend to demand more activity from the victim, and may become more forceful and less likely to negotiate in their assaults. See **Case Study 7-2** for an example of such behavior.

Case Study 7-2

An offender was linked to a number of sexual assaults in several police jurisdictions that took place in single-family houses and in apartments. The offender would enter the residence late at night or in the early morning and confront the victims while they slept. During one case, the victim was actually up using the restroom and surprised the offender as he moved through the house toward her bedroom. In each case the victim had younger children and the offender assured the victim that neither she nor her children would be harmed if she did what she was told. In one case, the victim was sleeping with her young child and the offender allowed her to put the child to sleep in another bedroom and then returned her to her bedroom and raped her. This offender assaulted some victims inside their own rooms in their beds, but he brought those victims who were especially compliant into the living room, and on one occasion took a victim outside onto the patio to rape her. Some assaults were rather quick, but there were several that lasted quite

---

[8] Negotiation with the victim essentially occurs when the offender demands a certain sex act or that the victim do something, but the victim resists by offering to do something else instead. For instance, if the offender demands anal sex and the victim refuses or continues to resist but agrees to perform oral or vaginal sex instead. This is an example of the victim negotiating with the offender. This does not in any way imply the victim's consent to the act; rather, the victim is trying to limit her victimization.

a while, including multiple assaults from various positions, and demands of oral and anal sex. In these incidents the offender sat down and talked to the victim while smoking a cigarette. During these conversations the offender asked personal questions about the victims and volunteered that he was also married and the father of a younger daughter, and on one occasion indicated that he had been a victim of a sexual assault when he was younger. Although the assaults were similar, some police agencies questioned whether all of the assaults were related to only one offender due to the differences in the sexual assaults and his interactions with the victims. However, it was clear when looking at each individual victim that he simply spent more time and had more interactions with the more compliant victims.

Two other things are fairly unique to this type of offender. First, it would not be unexpected for the offender to apologize to the victim for forcing her to go through the assault. Remember, these offenders are not particularly proud of what they are doing and are concerned that they may in fact injure someone in the process. Therefore, an apology for their contact is not so difficult to accept when we consider that they generally demonstrate unselfish-type behavior. The second rather unique thing about this particular offender type is the very real possibility that they will try to contact the victim again at a later time. This is an example of their basic fantasy that the assault was actually a consensual experience. Efforts may include sending mail, telephone calls, or even emails with requests or an expression of interest to see the victim again. It is not uncommon for an offender to return any valuable items he may have taken during the incident as a way of showing he is "not really a bad person."

This becomes important when the offender specifically asks the victim during or after the assault if he can come back or says he is interested in seeing the victim again. He says this because he is probably thinking about this possibility, and he may in fact return if the victim appears agreeable. **Case Study 7-3** demonstrates this.

Case Study 7-3

I went with a few friends to a local bar but I didn't stay long because I was tired. I only had a few drinks and then returned alone to my apartment. I got ready for bed, set my alarm for the next morning, and went to sleep. I was awakened from a deep sleep by the presence of a body lying in bed next to me. He was on my left side. I was startled and said, "Who are you? Get out." The man then turned onto his right shoulder and put his left hand over my mouth. He then whispered, telling me "not to say anything and to be quiet." He then told me to take my hand away from his wrist. I had grabbed it when he put his hand over my mouth. I was having a hard time breathing and I told him I couldn't breathe, so he eased off and took his hand away. He then put his hands under my shirt and felt my breasts for a few minutes and then put his hand into my panties and felt around down there. He then removed my panties down to my ankles and told me to spread my legs, but I couldn't spread them because my panties were around my ankles. So he bent down and took my panties all the way off. I didn't know what to do so I just lay there not wanting to make him mad. He then told me to open my legs and I did. He then got on top of me and then put his penis inside of my vagina. He had intercourse with me for about 2 minutes. As he was moving in and out of me was asking me, "Doesn't that feel good?" I didn't really answer and he finished in just a few minutes. He then removed himself from inside of me and lay on top of me for a moment. He then asked in a whisper if I wanted him to come back tomorrow. I was afraid and didn't answer so he asked again and I said yes, but it was just to get him to leave. He then got off of me and pulled up his pants and then left the room. I stayed for a minute, and when I was sure he was gone, I got up, locked the door, and then called the police.

In this particular case study we can see examples of several different characteristics of the power reassurance type of offender. He used the surprise approach, there was a clear lack of physical force other than maintaining control over the victim, his instruction not to say anything was a request rather than an implied threat, there were some limited attempts at "foreplay" to arouse the victim, and the offender did express interest in whether she was enjoying the experience. All of these are examples of unselfish behaviors. Lastly, the offender asked if he could come back. What is important to note is this was a request and not a threat to come back. As a follow up to this incident, the police set up surveillance at the same apartment the next night, and at around 10:00 PM the suspect did return and was arrested as he attempted to reenter the building.[9] Therefore, it is an important consideration for detectives to identify the offender's particular characteristics and advise the victim of the importance of contacting the police should the offender attempt any type of further contact with her.

After the assault, a power reassurance offender would be expected to take something from the victim or the scene as a souvenir that he would use to relive the incident later on. It is also likely he was keeping a record of his activities. In the past, such records would consist of some type of handwritten journals or notebooks. In more modern times, it is more likely such offenders keep records using a computer or other electronic devices such as cellular phones to record their activities.

---

[9] In this case the offender was actually very surprised that the police were waiting for him and said that he believed the victim had really consented to his advances and invited him back for another sexual liaison. Whether he really believed it or it was just part of his fantasy is unknown; however, he maintained his story all the way through his trial. He was convicted and sentenced to 15 years for Rape and Burglary.

This offender's pre-crime behavior may include participation in other low-level, nonconfrontational crimes including window peeking and theft of clothing from clothing lines or residences. It is not uncommon for offenders to commit residential burglary without committing any other crime—meaning they may break into a house, but do not steal anything inside the house. The thrill of being where they are not supposed to be, the power of exercising control over someone else's personal life, and the power from their success after the escape are most important to these offenders.

Offenders of this type typically operate within their comfort zone and may even attack within their own residential neighborhood. The concept of a comfort zone, however, is a relative term is and does not specifically imply the comfort zone is their residential area. It could also include the area where they live, where they used to live, where they frequently visit, where they go to school, or where they work. All of these could be looked at as a comfort zone because the offender feels comfortable in that particular area.

Post-Crime Behavior

Although power reassurance offenders may feel guilt for committing an offense, it will dissipate over time, and since the fantasy does not go away, they will eventually reoffend. Since fantasy never equals reality, these offenders may go back and edit their fantasy to incorporate what worked and change what did not work and thus try to improve or perfect the act for the next time. Other expected post-crime behavior would include an increase in alcohol or drug intake. There is also likely to be an increase in offenders' anxiety levels, which may be noticeable for those close to them, especially immediately following the incident. Because they are so anxious afterward, it is not uncommon for offenders to miss work or school in the 2–3 days following the incident. This aspect may prove to be an important investigative step once an offender is identified to go back and check the offender's employment records compared to the dates of each incident to see if there are correlations between them. This does not always happen since it depends upon the individual offender, but it happens enough to be worth the effort to check.

Investigative Summary

Power reassurance offenders are the most prolific of the offender types, meaning they commit more offenses than any of the other types. Once they get started, you can expect an assault every couple of weeks until they are caught. One difficulty police have is that not all of the victims of this offender type call the police to report their victimization. So, we have to bear in mind if we have 10 reports of sexual assault over a period of 6 months, there is a good possibility there are double that number because some assaults were not reported by the victims. It is also likely that some reports are of burglaries or attempted burglaries but not sexual offenses, and thus are not being considered part of the offender's actual activity. This is demonstrated in **Case Study 7-4**.

Case Study 7-4

A married couple came home late at night and discovered an unknown male sleeping inside the second bedroom of their house. He had apparently gained entrance into the house through an open window. The husband roused the man and ushered him out of the house. The man apologized profusely and claimed he mistakenly entered their house thinking it was the home of a friend. This event was never reported to the police and only came to the attention of detectives when conducting a canvass of neighbors from another reported rape in the immediate area. Interestingly, the couple reported that the husband had only just returned from an extended business trip that day. The couple was later able to identify the man they found in their house through a photo lineup by the police. The suspect was a serial offender and police suspected he had gone to the residence thinking the victim was living alone and when she was not there, he decided to wait for her return, and was surprised himself when the husband had returned.

Another reason for a lower number of reports is the likelihood that the offender might be striking in neighboring cities, and we have failed to link him to those cases we have thus far identified.

Power Assertive

Power assertive is the second-most prevalent offender type, and these offenders commit about 12% of the total sexual assaults. There are several recognizable personality characteristics of this type of offender that make him fairly easy to identify. These offenders are very concerned with their physical appearance and personal image and it is very important to them how they are seen by others. They are typically very well groomed, well dressed, and have exceptional personal hygiene. These offenders are generally in good physical condition and would likely exercise frequently in order to stay so. They may be quite athletic and may have participated in sports or still be engaged in such activities. However, it is interesting to note many offenders' preference for individual events rather than team sports. Wrestling, boxing, tennis, or other individual sports would be more to their liking, primarily because they are somewhat self-centered and selfish. Thus, the concept of team play, personal sacrifice, and working with others is somewhat difficult for them.

In keeping with their personal image of a "macho man," these offenders are likely to continue this theme in all parts of their personal lives, such as their choice of car, their manner of dress, and their employment. For instance, this offender is likely to be attracted to things that would gain respect or envy from other males or impress females, such as owning a big truck or a sports car. They would typically engage in what they would also consider to be macho activities, including spending time at bars where they would drink "manly" drinks. They tend to be openly hostile to homosexuals and homosexuality, and display this through their verbal behavior and actions toward the subject or individuals. **Case Study 7-5** is a good example of the impulsive and violent nature of this offender type.

Case Study 7-5

During the course of a background investigation on a serial offender, investigators learned that the offender's vehicle, a bright red Camaro convertible, was purchased through his credit union. When checking his credit files, investigators found several interesting notations made by loan officers in the file that spoke a lot about this offender. The offender had insisted on buying this particular vehicle, but his credit was such that any vehicle purchased would need to be financed at a very high interest rate. The offender said that he wanted the vehicle enough that he was willing to make payments up to $800 per month in order to get it. He did eventually get the loan and was paying a little over $700 per month, while the rent on his apartment was $650 per month. The vehicle and the image it provided for him were so important that he was willing to spend more on it than his residence every month in order to drive it. This same vehicle was used to pick up his many victims who reported he was very clean, very well dressed, and driving a "flashy" sports car.

The power assertive offender's choice of employment tends to be centered on blue-collar type jobs that would be considered macho; examples include employment in heavy construction, law enforcement, or the military. They would especially like law enforcement and the military because they would not only have a manly uniform to wear but would also have the ability to control others and tell them what to do. Being in uniform, armed, and being able to tell others what to do is the ultimate symbol of machismo as far as these offenders are concerned. These types of offenders are frequently seen in the military where they can use their rank or position of authority to gain control over other soldiers and victimize them. Through his assaults, the power assertive offender proves or validates his virility as a man and tends to live and operate out of some sense of personal entitlement via his position. Other examples include politicians and sports figures who believe they can do whatever they want, break any rule, and never be held accountable for their actions.

This offender is quite able to socially interact with people, including males and females, without any difficulty. In fact, he can be quite charming toward females and capable of using the con approach to give victims a sense of wellbeing and safety—until he is ready for sex, when he can become demanding and will not take no for an answer. Basically, this offender is not always out seeking a victim; rather his victims may be those who are unfortunate enough to come into contact with him in social settings or in dating situations. These offenders are also prevalent in many of the alcohol-related incidents described in more detail later in this text, and we see them quite often in marital rape situations.

In dating situations, it is not uncommon for victims to report that up until the sexual assault began, they were actually enjoying the date and the attention of the offender. Many others report that in all likelihood they might have engaged in consensual sex with the offender at a later time, but he insisted on having sex before the victim was ready. Unfortunately, this type of offender generally lacks the patience to wait for a consensual situation and instead demands sex on the first date or even the first time he and the victim meet, regardless of the victim's interest or lack thereof. This type of offender simply does not take no for an answer. In his interactions with the victim, the offender does not request that the victim do something; he demands it. For example, if the victim refuses to undress as told, the offender is likely to tear her clothes off or remove them forcefully. **Case Study 7-6** presents a an example of this type of behavior for this offender type.

Case Study 7-6

Victim #1 needed to go home from a teen gathering and accepted the offer of a ride home from the offender when her other friends declined to help. He was from another local high school, and although Victim #1 did not know him personally, she did know who he was. As they were driving, not even speaking to each other, the offender slowed down and unexpectedly stopped the car, leaned over, and tried to kiss her. Victim #1 rebuffed his attempt, insisted she wasn't interested, and asked him to just take her home. He stopped trying to kiss the victim and started the vehicle, but instead of driving toward her house, he sped up and drove to a secluded spot where he again stopped the car and then turned his full attention toward her. The victim struggled to keep the offender's hands off of her, and kept saying, "No, stop—what are you doing?" The offender met her resistance with more force and began to make verbal threats that if she continued resisting he was going to kill her. He managed to push her into the backseat of the vehicle and then ripped at her clothes. The victim, overcome with fear and exhausted from the struggle, ceased to resist, and the offender vaginally raped her. Afterward he got dressed and drove her back to her house. Before she got out of the car, he threatened to do it all over again if she went to the police. The victim was so traumatized she refused to make a criminal complaint, but did agree to a limited sexual assault examination.

Just a short time later, the offender was present at another gathering of high school students where Victim #2, a high school teen, went outside to await her ride home. The offender offered to take her home but she declined as a ride was on the way to pick her up, but she did ask if she could sit in his car while she smoked a cigarette because it was cold outside. He agreed and when she got into the car, he drove off. Victim #2 protested but was told to "Shut up." The offender drove to a secluded spot and as in the previous incident, began to aggressively assault the victim. Using force to overcome the victim's resistance, he managed to push her into the backseat where he tore at her clothes and threatened her. The offender then vaginally raped the victim. Instead of leaving after he was complete, he delayed for a few minutes and then forced the victim over onto her stomach and sodomized her. Afterward he drove the victim back and threatened her if she went to the police.

Case Analysis

As additional background, the offender was very handsome, well groomed, and outwardly concerned about his appearance. He came from an affluent local family, was athletic, and a star on his high school wrestling team. In both cases, we see examples of the offender deciding he wanted sex and refusing to take "no" for an answer, even from girls he did not know well. His verbal, physical, and sexual behavior were selfish, with little concern expressed over the victim, and clearly the assaults were about his particular wants and needs. Although he did use physical force, he only used what was needed to overcome victim resistance, and once the victim's resistance was overcome, the force stopped. In these two examples, we can also see fairly clearly how an offender may develop a particular MO. Although not exact, they are similar enough to perhaps link his conduct to each case and certainly something to look at in other incidents before or after these were reported.

For this particular offender type, sex is simply expected and he justifies his actions as his right as a man to have sex whenever, wherever, and with whomever he wants. If resistance is met, he will overcome the resistance as needed, including with the application of force. However, if force is used, it is generally limited to a moderate level and used to maintain control over the victim and overcome any resistance, but is not used as a part of the sexual assault itself. Basically, we would expect victim resistance to be met with threats, profane language, or slaps. Once the resistance stops, so does the application of physical force, and if the victim does not actively resist, such force is not needed and thus not used. An interesting thing about this offender type is that if they are lucky to meet someone who is willing to have sex with them consensually on the first date, they seldom return for a second date or elect to pursue a further relationship with them.

This offender typically engages in selfish sex wherein any sexual gratification revolves around the offender and not the victim. If the victim or consensual partner is able to achieve sexual pleasure that is not a problem for the offender, but it is not necessarily his concern one way or another. After the assault the offender will express little concern for or interest in the victim. Once he has achieved sexual gratification he is ready to leave. If he has any guilty feelings at all over what he did, they are short lived; as far as he is concerned, anything that happened to the victim was because she did not cooperate or do what she was told. Additionally, the offender may believe the victim should be grateful for the attention he gave her. If the assault took place in a vehicle and the victim had initially resisted, it is not uncommon for this offender to show his displeasure for her actions by pushing her out of the car in a secluded area afterward, even leaving her naked to fend for herself.

Weapons are generally not used, although they may be displayed as a way to communicate threats or to emphasize the seriousness of the offender's demands. If these offenders use a weapon it is probably something they carry with them normally, such as a pocketknife or their own fists.

Power assertive offenders tend to have multiple marriages and are often in conflict with their wives. They are highly critical of others, but because they are so self-centered and selfish, they do not allow themselves to be criticized by anyone. This leads to confrontation. If we were to study their background, it is likely their fathers reacted in the same way.

This is a low to moderately impulsive offender type and the sexual fantasies of these offenders only play a minor role. Their interests are more related to themselves, their sexual gratification, and impressing others. They may have a passing interest in pornography, but it will not be well defined or involve any specific themes. For this particular offender type, multiple sex acts are likely to be demanded and performed, including anal assault. In this case, anal assault is used to show their domination over the victim, and women in general.

Post-Crime Behavior

There may be limited post-offense behavior changes, including an increase in alcohol and drug use. There may be some anxiety for a few days following the incident that could result in missing work or school. But, if there are any guilty feelings they will not last long. More likely, the power assertive offender will contact his friends to brag or talk about his latest triumph with the victim. Generally, he will leave out details involving force, instead claiming it was a successful consensual experience. With this offender there will be no attempts to recontact or desire to ever see the victim again. As far as he is concerned, he got what he wanted and he is done with the victim. It is not uncommon for the offender to discount the sexual experience as "a bum lay" or unworthy of a second attempt on his part. The exception to recontacting the victim is if the offender is in a serious dating or marital situation. In these cases, the offender may not understand that he did anything wrong in the first place or would assume his conduct was OK with his partner. In either case, these offenders are not concerned with their partner's response or reaction in the first place.

Investigative Summary

These offenders have a particular weakness police should exploit when investigation centers on them: their inability to remain silent about the crimes they commit. For this type of offender, it is not enough that he triumphs in his dealings with females or any other crime he may be involved in; he also gains his self-worth through the admiration, respect, or fear from those he knows. Therefore, power assertive offenders tend to be braggarts, especially to their friends "down at the bar" or other similar social settings. What is surprising is the amount of information these offenders will share or what they may do in order to impress others and validate their "macho image."

This offender type is not as prolific as the power reassurance offender. Because they are slightly impulsive, they are able to delay their assaults for longer periods of time and strike only when the need is there or there is an available female. They typically pick their victims at bars and nightclubs, or within some dating situations. Again, they can do so because they have the ability to socially interact with victims and the public.

Anger Retaliatory

Anger retaliatory offenders make up only about 5% of all offenders; therefore, we rarely come into contact with them, but the public usually hears about their attacks because of the violent nature of the crimes they commit. These are the offenders who perpetrate the incidents we read so much about in newspapers or learn about on TV reports: Typically, the victims are innocently out jogging, riding a bike, returning to their vehicle from shopping, or otherwise unexpectedly come into contact with the offender and are suddenly and savagely assaulted in a blitz-style attack and then sexually assaulted. There are several recognizable personality characteristics of this type of offender that make him fairly easy to identify. Perhaps the most apparent personality characteristic of this offender is his quick and violent temper. This will be seen in his sexual assaults and in his personal life as well.

The real motivation of these offenders is to degrade and humiliate women in general. Their anger is not necessarily targeted against any particular victim, but their victims may symbolically represent a particular person. In their assaults, sex is used as a weapon to punish their victims for some real or perceived injustices to the offenders, perpetrated by women. When we come into contact with the victims of this offender type, there is usually no doubt they that the victims been assaulted because physical injuries are generally present along with other signs of physical trauma. Physical assault is going to be a large part of any of this offender type's sexual assaults.

These are highly impulsive offenders whose spontaneous and emotional attacks are brought on not by sexual desire or frustration, but by their individual life stressors. These life stressors may include financial problems, some precipitating event, or recent interpersonal conflict with a wife, girlfriend, or mother. These events may send them into a rage and the attack on the victim is seen as a way to relieve the stress. Therefore, they have no real timeframe or geographical preference for their assaults, and it is not unusual for them to attack within their own neighborhood or comfort zone. Offenders of this type engage in the least amount of sexual fantasy and have the least interest in pornography of any offender type. Because they are so impulsive, their assaults generally do not involve much preplanning or a search for particular victims. Instead, their victims are typically those who are unfortunate enough to come into contact with them when they are enraged and looking for a victim.

Normally, their preferred victims are within the same age range or slightly older than the offender, but are generally not the elderly. Children are also possible victims, but they are not preferred if adults are available.

Anger retaliatory sexual assaults are often marked by violence and profanity directed against the victim. Therefore, force plays a major part of their assault and tends to be used in excessive amounts because anger is the true driving force behind these assaults. It is also possible that the offenders derive some amount of pleasure from their ability to degrade their victims. Therefore, the force is generally beyond what is needed to overcome resistance and maintain control over the victim. It is not unusual for victims displaying even passive resistance to receive multiple punches from the offender for their lack of cooperation. Their violence against the victim does not include sadistic torture, however, as they are not sexually aroused or stimulated by observing the results of their actions or watching the victim suffer.

This offender has a difficult time dealing with females and therefore is seldom able to use a con or a surprise-type of approach. So, there tends to be very little interaction between the offender and victim prior to a blitz-style attack, which is used more by the anger retaliatory offender than any other type of offender. This sudden, violent attack leaves the victim little chance of escape and tends to limit the amount of further resistance. Physical assault may also include ripping or tearing of clothing rather than demanding or allowing the victim to undress herself. Physical assault may occur before, during, and after the sexual assault. Typically, these offenders use their fists but may also kick, bite, or use some other type of blunt object as their weapon of choice, and facial trauma can often be excessive.

Anger retaliatory offenders themselves are also marked by violence and may include very rough handling of their victims, indicating no interest in arousing the victim or seeking their participation in any way. Forced anal sodomy would be expected from these offenders and would be used as a way to humiliate and express their control and domination over their victims. Sexual experimentation such as foreign object insertions are also likely, but other examples of paraphilic behavior are not generally present. They typically spend a relatively short period of time with victims, but they are often humiliating and degrading, exemplified by forcing anal sodomy onto victims immediately followed by a demand of oral sex from them.[10]

It is also very possible that these offenders commit no actual rape in the sense we might expect. In fact, their actions may consist of the physical assault, ripping or tearing victims' clothing, and then standing over their victims while masturbating, ejaculating onto their victims' faces or bodies, or even urinating on them. This is seen as another way to degrade and humiliate the victim, basically by saying, "I didn't even want to have sex with you." These offenders tend to be less educated and could be considered as underachievers in life; they

---

[10] This is an aspect of the assault that many victims may balk at describing or admitting they were forced to do because of the humiliation and degradation they feel.

tend to be alcohol and drug abusers and may have used alcohol prior to the offense to lower their inhibitions and fuel their anger.

These offenders generally prefer some type action-orientated job that would keep them stimulated, and would not be suited for sedentary jobs such as office work or any job involving public interaction or dealing with people. These offenders would probably not be successful in the military. If they have military service, it will likely be as an enlisted man and it is unlikely for them to complete their full term or service contract, primarily because they would object to the discipline and the control exercised over them and would have difficulty in taking orders—especially showing respect to and taking orders from women. They would be attracted to free-time activities involving contact sports or activities.

Post-Crime Behaviors

Post-crime behaviors for anger retaliatory offenders include an increase in alcohol and drug usage and a slightly elevated anxiety level. However, they may actually feel better because of the stress relief from their assault. They will make no effort to recontact the victim and they may not feel guilty for what they did to the victim. They are unlikely to take a souvenir or trophy from the victim to remember the incident, mainly because this offender engages in less fantasy than any other offender type, so it would not have the same meaning as it might to others. **Case Study 7-7** is a good example of the impulsive and violent nature of this offender type.

Case Study 7-7

As I was walking to work early in the morning I could see a tall black man walking on the other side of the street. I saw he was crossing the road and started to walk in my direction. I began walking a bit faster but I could hear him approaching from behind. He then suddenly came up to me and put his arm around my shoulders, like a drunk would do, you know, to hold onto someone. I didn't stop walking but I took his arm off me, and called out to him, "Don't do that in Jesus' name." I think this took him by surprise and he stopped for a second and then he suddenly he jumped out in front of me. He was bent down slightly and bared his teeth and started growling like a wolf or animal. His hands were up in front of him and his fingers were stretched out and moving like they were claws. I called out again, "Stop that, in Jesus' name." It took him by surprise because he straightened up, and I walked around him. He called out to me as I passed by, "Where are you going?" I said I was going to say my morning prayers. Then, suddenly I was tackled from behind and rolled down off the roadway toward the bottom of a small ditch. I managed to stop and tried to get up, but he pulled me back down toward the bottom of the ditch. He managed to straddle me and I couldn't move because he was on top of me. I tried to resist but he grabbed both of my hands and held them to the ground, and then called out in a very harsh voice, "I'm in control, you cannot do anything to me but I can hurt you." He then added very sternly and seriously, "I could kill you now and wouldn't care." I tried to reason with him and said, "I'm a minister and I'm on my way to morning prayers." I tried to calm him down and said that perhaps we could meet later on and talk and could be friends. This made him mad and he snapped back at me, "Shut the fuck up, I'll kill you." I was then trying to push him off with my hand, but he slammed it back onto the ground and threatened to break my hand. I kept struggling and he leaned down and put his forearm across my throat and said if I didn't stop he would break my neck or smother me. He then rose up slightly and started pushing my nose and face down with his open right hand. I don't know if he was trying to smother me or not, but it was hard to breathe. Then he rose up and turned me onto my stomach and pulled my right arm behind my back. I thought he was going to jerk it out of the socket it hurt so badly. He then leaned down and said into my ear, "I'm a man and you're a woman and I want some pussy." He then reached down and put his hand under my shirt and felt my breasts and said, "Just the right size." He then stopped and started biting my neck. He was really biting hard and it hurt. I called out to him to stop and he said if I didn't stop he was going to rip my throat out. He then stopped and told me he was going to rip my throat out if I didn't get my pants off. He rose up slightly and I decided I had to do it or I was going to get hurt. But even after I had my pants off and was in the grass he continued to bite my neck and then the side of my face. He pushed me onto my back again and got in between my legs. He unzipped his pants and pulled out his penis and put it inside me, but it didn't go in very far. I started repeating over and over again, "In Jesus' name, in Jesus' name," over and over. He then bit my face again very hard and told me to shut up and suck him. I hesitated and he bit me again and said if I didn't suck him he was going to bite my face off. He then moved up to where his groin was close to my face and he put his penis into my mouth. But my mouth was dry and I was so scared. This made him very irritated and when he moved to get between my legs again I tried to get up and almost made it to my feet when he knocked me down and said if I did that again he was going to kill me. He then got in between my legs again and inserted his penis into me and started moving in and out. I could hear the birds chirping in the trees above me, and I said, "Listen to the birds, this morning it sounds so pretty." I think this distracted him because he stopped and got off of me and stood up. I managed to get to my feet and was about to run, but as I looked up I could see a police car parked just a little ways down the road. The officer was looking into a car parked along the highway with his flashlight and I called out to him and waved for help. He saw me and shined his flashlight and the suspect then took off running.[11]

---

[11] As an interesting side light to this particular case, as the offender pulled his pants up and tried to get away, his wallet with all of his personal identification fell out of his pants pocket onto the ground. He was arrested within 30 minutes by the police.

Case Analysis

The offender described in this case was identified as an anger retaliatory type based on several easily identified personality characteristics. First, and most apparent, this was an impulsive type of offense. The victim was walking down the street while the offender was walking in the opposite direction but changed direction in order to approach her. This offender appears to be somewhat atypical, because of his initial approach of putting his arm around the victim's shoulders. When that failed, he then attempted to scare the victim by jumping in front of her and growling like a wild animal. However, it is clear he was thrown off his game or distracted by the victim who responded by calling to Jesus rather than responding directly the potential threat posed by the offender.[12] When he was unsuccessful, he then reverted to the blitz assault by tackling the victim and throwing her down on to the ground.

We also see several examples of selfish verbal behavior in this case:[13]

- "If you don't stop, I'll break your neck."
- "Shut the fuck up."
- "Just the right size." (Referring to her breasts as he groped her)
- "I'm a man and you're a woman, and I want some pussy."
- "I'm in control, you cannot do anything to me but I can hurt you."
- "I could kill you now and I wouldn't care."
- "If you don't suck me I'm going to rip your face off."
- "If you don't get your pants off I'll rip out your throat."

There are also other examples of selfish physical behavior in the form of repeatedly biting, pinning the victim down, and pulling her arm behind her back in a painful manner. Other selfish sexual behaviors included forcing the victim to perform or submit to different sexual acts, including forced intercourse. Note also that although the victim attempted to resist verbally and physically, the offender overcame her resistance, but even after the victim stopped resisting, the force continued to be applied. With this type of offender, we would generally expect more of a physical assault, but it is clear the offender was thrown off guard or was distracted by the response and verbal behavior of the victim. Also, since this particular assault was interrupted by the unforeseen arrival of the police, it is uncertain what may have happened if the offender was able to complete the act. This victim did have scratches on her back and buttocks from contact with the ground and several bite marks were present on the back and front of her neck, and along her jaw. In the later question and answer portion of the her statement, the victim said

---

[12] This is an example of when victimology comes into play and we see how the victim's reaction to the threat can influence how the offender interacts with the victim.

[13] Some offender statements in the case study have been changed from 3rd person to first person for easier understanding by the reader.

she could smell alcohol on the offender's breath as he talked to her and bit her, and he also had a strong body odor like he had not taken a shower in while. Note also that there was no attempt to hide his facial features nor was he concerned with leaving behind forensic evidence.

Investigative Summary

For anger retaliatory offenders, *anger* is the driving force behind their assaults; therefore, force is often used far beyond what is needed to overcome any resistance or maintain control. Even passive resistance displayed by a victim may result in severe physical assaults, accented by profanity and very harsh, demeaning, and derogatory language directed toward the victim.

The offenders' anger toward women expressed during their assaults may also be reflected in their normal life as well, in the way they act around or treat women. Although they may not be assaultive toward every female, they are likely to be disrespectful toward or show a general contempt for women. If married, they are likely to engage in extramarital affairs and may be involved in reports of domestic abuse; they are also likely to have been married multiple times. Therefore, locating their ex-wives and girlfriends may be beneficial to understanding these offenders if they are ever identified. They are probably known to law enforcement from previous incidents such as fighting, assaults, or domestic disturbances. It is possible that these offenders have already been through some type of court-directed anger management counseling. Because they have no set pattern or fantasy and typically are responding to their individual stressors, a significant time period may go by in between assaults.

Anger Excitation (Sexual Sadist)

The last of the major offender types is the *anger excitation offender*, also commonly known as the *sexual sadist*. These offenders only make up only about 2% of all offenders so we rarely come into contact with them, but when we do they are unlike any other offender we may routinely investigate. These are the most dangerous and violent of all sexual offenders. Roy Hazelwood has described them as "Great White Sharks"[14] because they are constantly on the prowl for additional victims. What makes these offenders so different from other types is their purpose or goal is achieving sexual gratification not just from the infliction of pain onto another person, but from *observing the suffering of the victim afterward*. Perhaps the best description of this comes from the personal writings of one of the more prolific and dangerous serial sexual offenders, James Mitchell DeBardeleben, which were recovered after his arrest[15] (see **Box 7-4**).

---

[14] This is a term coined and used during Roy Hazelwood's various training courses to describe this type of offender.

[15] Michaud, S. G. (2007). *Beyond cruel*. New York, NY: St. Martin's Paperback. (Previously published as Lethal show. Authorlink Press: Dallas, TX).

BOX 7-4 Sadism

"Sadism: The wish to inflict pain on others is not the essence of sadism." According to DeBardeleben[15], it is not the actual infliction of pain that is so exciting and sexually stimulating; it is being able to dominate, humiliate, and exercise complete control over another person and "do with her as one pleases," without the victim being able to do anything to resist or to defend themselves that provides the satisfaction to the sadist. In his own words, "The pleasure in the complete domination over another person is the very essence of the sadistic drive."

These offenders are stimulated through their complete sexual, physical, emotional, and/or psychological domination over another person. Therefore, their assaults are not the quick and violent incidents with limited contact with the victim that we see with other offender types; these offender assaults may include kidnapping and holding the victim for hours, days, or even weeks, and may include the murder of the victim. Although this is the smallest offender category, these offenders are perhaps the most well known of all sexual offenders in the United States and make up the vast majority of the sexual serial killers identified over the last few decades. Examples of these famous offenders include Ted Bundy, Gary L. Ridgway (The Green River Killer), Angelo Buono and Kenneth Bianchi (The Hillside Stranglers), and Dennis Rader (The "BTK" or "Bind, Torture, and Kill" serial killer). These are only a few of the more well-known serial killers.

There are several recognizable personality characteristics of these offenders that make them fairly easy to identify. These offenders tend to be a little older, generally beginning their forced criminal acts around 30 years old. Although they exist in all races and may include some females, they tend to be white males with an above-average IQ, are typically married with children, and seldom have had contact with the police before they began to offend. These are extremely ritualistic offenders whose assaults are typically premeditated acts completed with great planning and preparation. Their actions are sometimes fueled by intricate, well-developed fantasies and are influenced by a multitude of paraphilic behaviors.

Anger excitation offenders engage in fantasies more than any other offender type and it is often unbelievable how much time, energy, effort, and money offenders will invest to enact their particular fantasies. These offenders also tend to have a great interest in pornography and unlike other offenders, may collect material on specific themes they are interested in, including bondage and S&M-type magazines that are used to fuel their sexual fantasies.

Because of the amount of effort put into their fantasies, these offenders are generally very well prepared and tend to plan and rehearse their crimes prior to assaulting their victims. This would include preparing and using a rape kit. The kit's exact contents are based on the individual offender but typically include weapons of choice, some type of blindfold, condoms, police radios, gloves, duct tape, or precut ligatures. The rape kit may be very extensive and elaborate, more so than that of any other offender type. The preparation of the rape kit may actually become part of their precrime fantasy because as it is assembled or prepared they are thinking about how the various items are going to be used against a victim. It is also not unusual for an offender to alter his vehicle in a manner to assist him in the capture or transportation of a victim, or in the torture of the victim. During police training classes a comparison is made to explain the amount of time and effort expended by an offender to create his rape kit or alter his vehicle. The general comparison is to a fly fisherman who may spend hours carefully constructing a special fly to be used in his hobby of fishing. In the same manner, a sexual sadist may spend countless hours putting together his rape kit or altering his vehicle for his particular sexual interest. These offenders are only limited by time and money. One of the better examples is Ted Bundy, who removed the passenger seat of his Volkswagen Beetle when he went looking for a victim. Removing the seat allowed him to place the victim down on the floorboards and be covered up so no one could see her as he drove her away.

These offenders are able to find employment in white-collar jobs and are able to deal with the public and are often described by coworkers as confident, outgoing, and well liked, but somewhat compulsive. These offenders would actually do well in the military service. Although they would internally object to the military culture of teamwork, accepting responsibility, and selfless service, they are usually manipulative enough to use all of these soldierly traits of others to their advantage—meaning they would likely be able to manipulate others into selfless service, but would not participate themselves. They would probably enjoy the military because they would enjoy the power and control they may exercise over others through their superior rank and would take advantage of every opportunity to use their position or status for their own benefit. These offenders are typically married, displaying a public veneer of "average Joe" and that of a happily married family man with children; they typically drive a well-maintained family car or van. They are unlikely to have any previous arrest record or any history of mental health care. If they own a dog it would typically be a larger, "manly" breed such as a German Shepherd or a Doberman Pinscher. However, because these offenders share many of the same characteristics of criminal psychopaths, their outward average Joe appearance is just a facade presented to the public that hides a very selfish, hedonistic, and narcissistic personality. They also lack the ability to feel empathy, sympathy, or remorse for anyone other than themselves and tend to relate to others in terms of power and control rather than love and affection. This is why their wives tend to be dominated in a slave-like relationship, wherein the wife is supposed to service her husband by doing whatever pleases him whenever he wants it.

It is interesting to note that while wives are generally treated in this manner, this is not the case in dating situations. In fact, while dating, anger excitation offenders are likely to behave in an almost perfect manner, such that the future wife may feel very fortunate to have found such a man. However, once they are married the offender starts behaving far differently and begins making an effort to change and manipulate his new wife into becoming his "slave." **Case Study 7-8** is somewhat atypical in that the offender is much younger than others of this offender type, and he is beginning his grooming process with his girlfriend before they are married.

Case Study 7-8

My boyfriend Hank came to my house and into my bedroom where I was sitting. He came right up to me and asked why I was smoking and defying what he told me. I was lying in bed and suddenly he was on top of me. He told me to take my clothes off or he would rip them off of me. I took my clothes off and he made me orally please him, then he pushed me away and threw me back and got on top of me and penetrated me. All the while he was holding me down by my arms. He then told me to turn over and I said, "No." He then forced me to roll over onto my stomach and I knew what he was going to do and I said, "no, no, no." He then anally sodomized me. I kept telling him no and to stop, but he did not listen and he started to choke me while he was sodomizing me at the same time. Then he then pushed himself off and rolled me back over onto my back and told me to "suck his dick." I said no and started dry heaving from the thought of it but he grabbed my head and forced me over to his groin and then put his penis into my mouth and told me to "suck it." This lasted about 5 minutes and then he pushed me back down onto my back and started having vaginal sex with me again. As he was doing it he bit me hard on my left breast and it made me cry in pain. He just told me to "take the pain" and "I deserved it." After he climaxed inside of me, he then told me he had just "hate fucked me," and I got what I deserved. He then said he owned me and he could do anything he wanted to me and there was nothing I could do about it. I fear him and I didn't really scream or call out because I didn't want it to get any worse. After he raped me we slept until the next morning. I had to go and get my hair cut. When I got back from getting my haircut he demanded that we have sex again. He then made me take a shower with him and we went for breakfast with his brother and mom. We then went home and everything seemed to be going OK. I stopped over at my brother's house to show my new haircut and have a cigarette. A while later my nephew told me Hank was looking for me. I was scared because I was not allowed to smoke so I put some toothpaste into my mouth to cover up the smoke. I went outside and he just said, "Get back to your apartment." I was afraid and I knew I was in trouble, but I drove back to my apartment. When we went inside he said to me, "You know you fucked up right?" I said, "Yeah," and he then threatened to shave my head and break my fingers because I was told not to smoke. He then picked me up off the floor and then slammed me onto the dining room floor and he started kicking me all over—my leg, my side, and my head. He then made me stand up, and he picked me up by my hair and took me into the living room and shoved me onto the couch. He was pacing back and forth and I stood up, and he then kicked me in the belly and I started to dry heave. He went into the kitchen and pulled out some scissors and forced me into the bathroom and showed me the mirror and wrote "do not lie" in lipstick. I looked around and saw my entire bag of makeup was all over the bathroom floor, so I guess he had gone to my apartment when I was gone. He then took the scissors and started to cut my hair, saying, "I told you not to smoke and you disobeyed me and now are going to pay for it." He then got mad and shoved me into the wall a few times. He then walked into the kitchen and came back with a knife and shoved me into the bathroom and stood before the mirror and then started to cut my hair with a knife. It hurt because it was pulling the hair, not cutting it. He then yelled at me and asked why he shouldn't just shave my head. I was crying and begged him to stop because it hurt. He then shoved me into the bedroom onto the bed and got on the bed and then bit my right arm hard. It hurt and he told me to "take the pain." He intended to scare me so I would remember to do as he said. He then took off my engagement ring and said he still loved me and if I was good for a month he would give it back to me. He then made me promise I would not leave my apartment for any reason other than going to work. He made me promise not to leave him. He then said he was going to make sure the telephone was fixed so the only person I could call was him. Just before he left he said that if I told anyone about what happened that he would come back and kill me and my parents and brother. But then he kept telling me how much he loved me and *wanted to turn me into a good woman.* I later talked to my mother and she called the police. This was not the only time this happened but it was about the worst.

Case Analysis

Although only a small portion of this particular case study is related to a sexual assault, the totality of the case study leaves little doubt as to what type of offender this represents. The offender's verbal, physical, and sexual behavior is extremely selfish and are all related to control and punishment. However, the punishment inflicted was not for the generic reason of being angry at all women; it was inflicted as punishment because the victim did not do what the offender had ordered or demanded. Making the victim promise not to go anywhere other than to work and to drop all contact with her family or anyone else are examples of how the sadistic offender isolates his wife and victim from any other support structure. This case is somewhat atypical because the age of the offender is mid-twenties, when typically this offender is much older, and because of the amount of force used to establish control over the victim before they are married. Generally girlfriends are treated much better and are manipulated or coerced into compliance with the offender rather than being physically forced. Like other examples of domestic abuse, the victim in this case study later elected to drop the criminal complaint against her boyfriend and the police investigation was dropped. It is unknown what may have happened to the victim later.

Because they are more socially adept and confident, these offenders have no problems committing crimes that are often a long way from their home or out of their comfort zones. In fact, these offenders love to drive, and enjoy the stimulation of the passing scenery and movement. It gives them the feeling of freedom while they cruise around, constantly on the hunt. Some offenders understand the value of crossing jurisdictional lines, committing one crime or two crimes in one jurisdiction and then moving to commit their next crime in another jurisdiction. The purpose is to confuse and hinder the police investigation. They are generally somewhat older and very adept at manipulation, thus enabling them to employ the con approach moreso then any other offender. Like other criminals they learn from each experience what works, what does not work, and how they can improve. Therefore they are constantly learning, adapting, and improving aspects of their MO and their fantasy. Since fantasy never equals reality, they keep on trying to get it right.

These offenders' offenders typically have a general concept of or ideal type of victim that fits their particular fantasy. This ideal victim may be someone who resembles a particular person or someone with certain physical features they find attractive. It could also be someone with a particular occupation such a nurse, waitress, or professional woman. In these instances, when they are unsuccessful in locating their particular victim type they may actually postpone their assaults until they can find someone who fits their particular interest. For instance, famous serial killer Ted Bundy was not interested in high-risk prostitutes or runaways. Instead, he sought out those who he described as "worthy victims." In his case they were young, attractive college coeds who "had something going for them," whom someone would miss if they were gone. Other offenders simply look for the high-risk victim types such as runaways, drug abusers, or prostitutes. These are preferred victims because their disappearance may never be reported. Even more important, if these victims do survive the assault and make a report, the police may not spend a lot time looking for the offender, thinking the report is likely a dispute over nonpayment for services, rather than a sexual assault.

Anger excitation offenders' assaults tend to be *episodic attacks* wherein based on life experiences and stressors they feel the need to assault or wherein they wait until the "time is right" to attack. So, there is no identifiable frequency or pattern to their assaults. Because so many of these offenders are married or have a significant other and because the nature of their crimes requires isolation and privacy, many of their assaults are planned for when they will have sufficient time and total control over a particular place or when they are able to bring their victims to their own homes. It is not unusual for the offender to have a special room and equipment prepared for his victims. This is likely a place in the house where no one else is allowed to enter.

By spending so much time with the victim, the offender will generally display a variety of verbal, physical, and sexual behaviors. This offender typically uses commanding and degrading language in an effort to demonstrate and maintain control. Some victims report they were forced to listen to the offender talk to them while they were restrained or unable to escape. In these situations the offender's speech patterns seemed unemotional, instructional, and practiced, as if he were reading from something he had previously written down. This is another example of scripting, but in this case, it is designed to instill or heighten the fear and thereby the suffering of the victim by telling her, sometimes in excruciating detail, what she is going to experience. This offender is typically interested in aspects of bondage; therefore, restraints are likely employed to either control the victim or as part of the sexual torture. Many times the bindings and knots are very intricate.

Investigative Summary

This offender, unlike the others, is likely to be very interested in the police investigation and may follow progress of the investigation. It would not be unusual to have him collect newspaper, magazine, or Internet articles about his case or keep video recordings of any television reports. Since this type of offender follows the police investigation, he is likely to change or alter his MO based on newspaper reports, but retain his basic theme or fantasy. If the offender is involved in the murder of a victim, there are other things to be taken under consideration. For instance, it would not be unusual for the offender to return to the body dump site to check on the police progress and determine if the body has been found, but also to relive his victory and excitement over the event; some offenders return for the chance to have sex with the deceased victim again.

There are some other important investigative considerations when dealing with this type of offender. First, because this offender's fantasy often includes kidnapping, torture, and murder, there is a very real possibility of multiple crime scenes. This would include the abduction site, any vehicle used to transport the victim, the torture site, and if the assault results in murder, the body dump site as well. Second, this offender is likely to engage in sex with the victim before, during, and even after death of the victim. The focus of the offender's physical attacks and torture is often centered on the sexual organs, which includes the cutting, stabbing, biting, and/or twisting of the breasts or buttocks and insertion of foreign objects. This offender is anally fixated and anal assaults are therefore very likely. Examination of the victim tends to establish evidence of forced oral, vaginal, and anal rape of the victim. This offender is also very likely to take a souvenir or trophy from the victim to maintain the fantasy. It is also not unusual for this offender to photograph, audio record, or video record his assaults. These images and recordings would be used later for masturbation and to help him edit his fantasies. These items should be looked at in the same general vein as a souvenir; it is very likely offenders will keep and safeguard these images and recordings regard-less of how incriminating they may be. When the victim's death does result from the assault, the cause of death is frequently from asphyxia through ligature, manual strangulation, hanging, or suffocation. Ligature marks from restraints are common findings on the wrists, ankles, and neck of the victim.

Success will make the offender grow bolder as he becomes more self-confident with each victim. This tends to bring about his downfall as he grows so confident that he begins to take chances.

Unfortunately, many of the victims of a sexual sadist are eventually murdered once he has tired of them. If a victim does survive an assault by a sexual sadist, there is going to be little doubt as to the physical and sexual trauma inflicted upon her.

Opportunistic

Opportunistic offenders are atypical sexual offenders because they usually only commit their crimes when an opportunity to rape presents itself during the course of another crime. A common example would be a burglar who conducts residential burglaries and after breaking into a house, discovers a vulnerable female and decides to rape her. Another classic example is a robber who plans to rob a convenience store but discovers a vulnerable female and decides to rape her as well as rob the store. In each of the examples, the offenders were intent on one crime, but because of the opportunity or circumstances, they changed their habits slightly and offended in a different way. When investigating rapes that take place in conjunction with other offenses, we need to identify the dominant crime—what was the *initial* intent of the offender? We need to determine whether we looking for a rapist who burglarizes a house as part of his MO, or if we are looking for a burglar by profession who also happens to commit a rape.

This is an important determination because when we set out to look for these offenders, we have to look at them based on the dominant crime. Meaning, if our offender is a burglar, then we have to look for him in the same way as we would look for any other burglar and not look for him as we would a sex offender. This is because it is likely that if the opportunity does not present itself again, the offender may never commit another rape or sex crime, but it is very likely that he would commit other burglaries or robberies or whatever criminal act he normally engages in.

One other example of an opportunistic type of offender is discussed in greater detail later in the text when dealing with drug and alcohol facilitated sexual assaults, wherein the offender sees and takes advantage of an incapacitated victim. This may or may not be what we would consider as a typical sexual offender, but someone who offended because the *opportunity* and victim was presented to him.

Gang or Multiple Offenders

The other atypical offender type is *gang/multiple offenders*. This is an atypical offender because contrary to many beliefs and television depictions, rape and sexual assaults are most often individual events; there is generally only one victim and one offender involved in the actual assault. There are many reasons behind this, but generally it is because the rapist's ego would not support or tolerate a second person who he would have to "compete against." Most are also too selfish to have anyone else present to share in their pleasure or arousal. This does not mean, however, that there are not "partner" or multiple offenders who do work together and are involved in committing rapes and sexual assaults. The difference with these offenders is that they are typically a subtype of the anger excitation or sexual sadist, and torture and the murder of the victim is the eventual goal.

There have been several well-publicized examples of multiple offenders or partners who were actively engaged in sexual offending together. A few examples of these offender partnerships include:

- **Lawrence Bittaker and Roy Norris:** Two offenders who met in prison and verbally fantasized about kidnapping and sexually torturing their victims. Bittaker once boasted he planned to be "bigger than Manson." Once they were both released from prison, they got together and to fulfill their fantasies bought a silver 1977 GMC cargo van and remodeled the interior. They called it the *Murder Mack* and used it to kidnap teenage girls and then rape, torture, and eventually kill them. As part of their torture, they liked to use vice-grip pliers on the breasts and nipples of their victims, and then recorded their screams. These recordings were used later to relive the incident and to aid in masturbation.

- **Angelo Buono and Kenneth Bianchi, "the Hillside Stranglers":** These offenders were cousins who together kidnapped females and brought them to Buono's house where they raped, sexually tortured, and then murdered the victims. They then intentionally publicly displayed victims' naked bodies in neighborhoods or on various hillsides. This was one last effort to show their power and control over the victims and over the police who were unable to stop them.

- **Gerald and Charlene Gallego:** This was a married couple who kidnapped and killed 10 people, mostly teenage girls. The victims were usually lured by Charlene to where Gerald waited for them, and they were then repeatedly raped by Gerald and often Charlene would also participate. Their ultimate fantasy was to have a steady procession of disposable "love slaves." Once captured, Charlene claimed she was forced under threat of personal harm to find victims for her husband. Gerald, however, insisted she had willingly taken part, claiming they both had the same sexual fantasy and then carried it out.

- **Charles Ng and Leonard Lake:** These two kidnapped, raped, tortured, and murdered an estimated 25 persons before they were discovered. They created a "bunker" located on Lake's property where they would take their victims to rape and sexually torture them. We know a lot about these particular offenders and their interaction with the victims because they had videotaped many of their crimes and victim assaults. Leonard Lake also created a lengthy video where he explained his intention to create sexual slaves from the women he and Ng had kidnapped.

These examples are but a few of the more well-known offenders who have operated together. Note that these offenders are all examples of sexual sadists who also kidnapped their victims, took them to another location, and then engaged not only rape and sexual assaults but in also in the sexual torture of their victims. Note that for these particular offenders, murder was the eventual goal once they had tired of their torture of the victim.

Investigative Considerations

There is an important investigative consideration when dealing with the so-called "partner" offenders. There is a unique dynamic wherein these partners are not necessarily "equal" partners. Instead, one will assume the role of a leader who tends to be more intelligent and ritualistic, and the other will assume the role of a follower. The follower tends to be of lower intelligence and more impulsive. Partners can create a confusing crime scene where signs of preplanning are present along with signs of improvising and spontaneity. The two different personality types are not generally found together in one person, but are very likely when dealing with two offenders involved in the same crime. Typically, one offender will be more ritualistic, intelligent, with a more dominating personality, while the other partner tends to be less intelligence, more impulsive, and a more subservient personality. Understanding these personality characteristics is very important to aspects of the offender interrogation, discussed later in the text.

Group or Gang Rapes

As mentioned earlier in the text, rape and sexual assaults have been used as terror tactics for thousands of years as a way to completely humiliate and subjugate a population. In modern times we still see this employed as a means of political terror by certain governments or political groups. Gang rape and sexual assaults are also used by certain criminal gangs and groups as a means to control certain populations, particularly in certain Asian communities, such as Cambodian, Vietnamese, or Laotian groups; gang rapes or the threat of gang rapes against wives or daughters are used to terrorize and threaten their own ethnic groups. It is important to remember that in these situations, the concept of rape is not based on sexual gratification; it is another example of sex being used for nonsexual purposes. In these incidents we cannot track the offenders as we would most other sexual offenders, but rather in the same manner as the opportunistic offenders—by concentrating on the dominant crime.

Other incidents involving multiple offenders, better known as a *group* or *gang rapes,* are also possible but they are actually fairly rare. When they do happen they traditionally are much more violent, not necessarily though the sadistic torture but through victims being subjected to much more physical trauma.

Part of the increased physical trauma results from the offenders being unknown to the victim and "anonymity breeding bad conduct."[16] Because the victim may not know the members of the group, this may give group members the idea that they can do more than they might do if they were all known by the victim.

This concept is readily apparent during the so-called group or gang rapes, and some interesting phenomena develop during the course of the incident. The first thing we expect to see is called the "pee pee contest," where each of the participants in the sexual assault may attempt to impress or show off for the other members, thus increasing his standing within the group. This is why in these offenses we see the victim being far more physically traumatized than with most single offenders.

The second phenomenon we see in these cases, which is based on group dynamics, is the development of a leader. This is the offender who will stand out within the group and typically acts as the main catalyst for the assault and may direct the activities of the remainder of the group. This may be the person who either commits the majority of the sexual assault, or could be the one who stands back and directs others to do so. Another part of the group dynamics of these events is the emergence of the person known as the *reluctant participant*. This is the person within the group who is not as enthusiastic and may not want to participate in the assault. It is also likely this person may even speak out against the group's intention or action, or try to intercede to limit the physical trauma to the victim.

Many times the reluctant participant may refuse to fully participate in the assault or may be forced through peer pressure or other threats against his own wellbeing to participate as a way to prevent his report to the police. It is also important to note that many multiple offender incidents do not start out as rape or sexual assaults but escalate into these crimes through the course of events. Examples would include younger participants such as college fraternities, college athletes, or young soldiers. Generally, these groups are engaged in "partying" fueled with alcohol, drugs, or both and then "things begin to happen."

The statement of "things begin to happen" is no attempt whatsoever to legitimize, discount, or excuse what happened. Rather, it indicates that many times these group actions do not necessarily start out with the intent to seek out a victim and sexually assault her, but someone in the group may begin to interact with the victim or victims and the previously described phenomena begin to show. As the situation develops, a leader emerges and begins to takes charge, and the idea or concept to rape or "have fun with" the victim is imitated. In some instances, particularly at parties, the victim may have

---

[16] We see examples of this same concept during protests, political demonstrations, or even during riots. People will respond and become more unruly and destructive when they are part of a crowd and there is no ability to identify them within the crowd. This is why we teach that the best way to calm a crowd and defuse a situation is to bring out a video camera and start to film the crowd. Once the crowd sees they are being documented and possibly identified for later prosecution, they tend to calm down.

consumed a quantity of alcohol and may no longer be able to defend herself or is intoxicated to the point of losing consciousness. When this happens, it is not unusual for males to simply take advantage of her condition and engage in sex. In these cases, there may be no physical trauma inflicted on the victim because she was not able to resist. In other cases the victim may actually have consented to sex with one offender, but not with the other members of the group. In these instances, the *pee pee contests* may start, with each offender doing more and more to the victim to show off to the others.

Investigative Considerations

When conducting our investigation into group events we want to concentrate on identifying two persons. First, we want to focus on the leader because this is the person that is likely the most culpable through his participation or leadership of the event. The second person is the reluctant participant. It is especially important to identify this offender because he has probably already demonstrated that he knows the group was doing something wrong and is the most likely person to come forward as a witness against the other members of the group. Then, we concentrate as best as we can on the exact participation of each member of the group.

Because of the *pee pee contest* and anonymity of the participants, there is likely to be much more physical trauma and injury to the victim, and thus the victim will likely be much more traumatized afterward.

▶ Conclusions

Being able to identify the offender type will go a long way in preparing the investigative plan, identifying potential pre- and post-crime behaviors and activities, as well as formulating an interrogation strategy as suggested later in the text. Understanding offender typology is also very helpful when issues of possible false complaints come up, as a false victim may describe particular verbal, physical, and sexual behaviors that appear to come from a mixture of offender types that are unlikely to have occurred. Understanding the characteristics of the various offender types is going to be very beneficial. It does take experience to be able to recognize the various personality characteristics of each offender, but it is well worth the time and effort to learn them.

▶ References

Ainsworth, P. B. (2001). *Offender profiling and crime analysis*. Portland, OR: Willan Publishing.

Canter, D. (2000). *Criminal shadow: The inner narratives of evil*. Irving TX: Authorlink Press. (Originally published by Harper Collins, UK, 1994.)

De River, J. P. (1956). *The sexual criminal: A psychoanalytical study* (2nd ed.). Springfield, IL: Charles C. Thomas.

Groth, N. A., & Birnbaum, J. H. (1979). *Men who rape: The psychology of the offender.* New York: Plenum Press.

Hazelwood, R. R., & Burgess, A. W. (2009). *Practical aspects of rape investigation: A multidisciplinary approach* (4th ed.). Boca Raton, FL: CRC Press.

Stevens, Dennis J. (2001). *Inside the mind of sexual offenders: Predatory rapists, pedophiles, and criminal profiles.* New York: Authors Choice Press.

CHAPTER EIGHT

Special Offenders

Like special victims, there are also special offenders that do not quite fit squarely into the offender types previously identified. These are the offenders that we do not always think about, but are present nevertheless. These special offenders include but are not necessarily limited to: *date and acquaintance rapists, juvenile offenders, female offenders, and pedophiles.*

▶ Acquaintance Rape

As previously discussed, the vast majority of sexual assaults involve offenders and victims who know each other, and are therefore referred to as acquaintance rapes. Because the victim and offender know each other, the identification of the offender is not always the major difficulty in the investigation; rather it is the *relationship* between them which leads to difficulties. We have previously discussed the concept of marital rape and how the relationship between the victim and offender can influence the reporting, investigation, and prosecution of those offenses. Many of these same difficulties are found in acquaintance situations as well. We are also dealing with offenders who do not attack their victims without warning, do not leap out of the woods, wait for victims in parked cars, or break into homes to surprise their victims in bed. Instead, they generally have a much more subtle approach that does not always involve physical force or injuries to the victim, and may actually leave the victim uncertain if she was victimized or not; she may worry her conduct somehow contributed to the situation, and is therefore equally at fault for what happened.[1] The result is that freqently these assaults are never reported to the police, never investigated, and never prosecuted, leaving the

---

[1] A good reference for better understanding the concept of acquaintance rape is: *I Never Called It Rape*, by Robin Warshaw, Harper and Row Publishers, New York. It is cited several times in this chapter and provides a good overview of how these assaults affect the victim.

offender free to continue his actions. Because so many of our investigations fall into this category, it is imperative that we understand some of the underlying conditions that may have influenced the offender to commit the assault or the reluctance of the victim to report the assault. We want to also look at this issue from an investigative perspective so we can identify these offenders, develop our evidence, and bring them to justice. Although we are talking about an acquaintance rapist, this does not mean we are creating a separate offender typology; rather, we are talking about one of the other offender types using his relationship with the victim to gain access for the assault.

Since there is not a separate offender typology, what makes the offender in these circumstances so different from the others we have already discussed? When discussing offender typology we noted that sex was not necessarily the goal or the motivation of the offender; rather, the issue was power and control over the victim, and sex was being used as a weapon to achieve that goal. We will see that this is not always the case in many of the acquaintance situations, where clearly the motivation and goal is having sexual intercourse with the victim, and offenders may believe their actions are the result of seduction rather than force or coercion.

Valliere[2] identified two main motivations for the nonstranger rapists. First, there is a sexual deviance on the part of these offenders that allows them to continue their assaults even on a drugged or intoxicated victim and maintain their assaults in spite of a victim's crying, pleading, active resistance, or getting sick or passing out. The second motivation stems from their personality characteristics; they have a generally narcissistic and selfish outlook that lacks internal controls such as guilt, remorse, empathy, or compassion toward others. For some offenders, it is all about their pleasure and satisfaction; they are not concerned with others, and what society and criminal law would define as rape, they may look at as a "sexual conquest." They may actually believe that the concept of societal rules does not apply to them and their actions can be seen as examples of the sense of entitlement so many of them feel.

Box 8-1 outlines the differences between the basic goals and motivations that exemplify the differences between stranger and acquaintance situations. Looking at Box 8-1, several factors stand out and will become very important when trying to understand these offenders. In both circumstances the motivation is all about the offenders; they are typically selfish, hedonistic, and have little regard for the victim's feelings. The differences are especially apparent within the interaction between the offender and the victim in acquaintance rapes; although force may be involved, it does not always include physical trauma or threats. Many times the force may be limited to the offender who simply does not take "no" for an answer or uses some type of coercion rather than threats and physical force. The resistance of the victim is interpreted as the victim playing hard to get or being coy, rather than as nonconsent and resistance.

---

[2] Valliere, V. N. Understanding the non-stranger rapist. America Prosecutors Research Institute. *The Voice*, 1(14), 1–6.

BOX 8-1 Differences Between Acquaintance Rapes and Stranger Rapes

Stranger Rapes

Sex is not the goal; sex is used to service the offender's nonsexual needs such as:

- Power and control
- Expressing anger at the victim or women in general
- Validating their own masculinity
- Their ego, their needs, their desires
- Humiliation and subjugation over the victim
- Intentional infliction of pain and suffering on victim
- They know they have committed a crime, but do not care

Acquaintance Rapes

Sexual gratification is offenders' primary motivation and goal:

- There are some issues of power and control
- It is mostly about *getting laid, getting lucky, or scoring*
- They look at their actions as *seduction*, not rape
- They operate out of a sense of entitlement
- It is about their ego, their needs, their desires
- Some may not even recognize they have done something wrong
- Many are surprised when they are arrested or confronted

Although conceivably all of the offender types can be found in acquaintance rape situations, it is the *power assertive* type of offender that is more frequently found in this type of situation than any of the other offender types. The power assertive offenders operates with a general sense of entitlement, considers sex to be his right as a man, and sees his encounters not as rape but as seduction.

We often inaccurately think of this type of rape or sexual assault as only associated with dating or social situations and many times the "assault" is explained as the result of a misunderstanding or confusion between the victim and offender, rather than an intentional sexual assault. In reality, these *acquaintance* offenses take place in a wide range of situations including professional relationships such as a counselor, therapist, religious official, or even a medical doctor, who may use their official position to gain access and then take advantage of or sexually assault their victims. Similarly, we see these incidents in the workplace where an offender tries to use his or her position as a supervisor to coerce the victim into having sex or to overcome resistance through offers of reward or threats concerning the victim's continued employment. There are other circumstances when offenders may use their age, experiences, and maturity to coerce their victims into having sex. This is seen particularly with younger victims, such as between a high school freshman and a high school senior, or a high school student and a college student. Generally, we are looking at an age and maturity level of more than 4 years difference. There is also a perceived social status that may be used by offenders to coerce or otherwise force themselves onto their victims. The perceived social status may include coming from wealthy, powerful, or well-known families and would also apply to star athletes from high school, college, or professional teams. Athletes are perhaps the best example of the concept of *entitlement*, which is displayed in their conduct and lives. Athletes often believe they are somehow entitled or privileged to do whatever they want to whomever they want because they can deliver a performance on the court or on the playing field. We see this in action when athletes are defended by their professional teams or their universities in order to protect the institution's investment and keep the athletes playing. This is translated to offenders as another example of their continued exceptional athletic performance allowing them to do whatever they want without any fear of being held accountable.

Other general characteristics of this offender type include their general beliefs and attitudes toward women, ranging from aggression or anger in their intimate relationships, to using violence as part of their problem-solving skills, to being excessively demanding toward their own wives, girlfriends, or partners. It would be very likely for them to boast or brag to other male friends about their sexual exploits and conquests. Their stories, however, would not likely include elements of coercion, force, or the victim's resistance and non-compliance, but rather on their overall sexual performance. What is missing with many of these offenders and adds to the prosecution's difficulties is their general lack of other criminal behaviors or involvement in any other criminal activity. In fact, it is not unlikely to have many otherwise upstanding members of the community or even famous persons accused of such conduct. They often use their reputation or good standing as a way to argue how unnecessary it is for them to have forced themselves onto someone or committed rape when they have the ability to find consensual partners. Instead, the offenders typically use their relationship or legitimate contact with the victim to give them access. Examples of this access include but are not limited to:

- Being married to or in a long-term relationship (e.g., living together) with the victim
- Being in a superior–subordinate relationship wherein aspects of either rewards or punishments for sexual favors are implied (this could also include teachers and students, soldiers and their officers, or employee and employer)
- Times when the offender and victim are alone or isolated and thus the offender feels comfortable enough to make overtures toward the victim (e.g., when working late at night or on weekends and offering to drive the victim home, or for military this could include deployment)
- During a professional setting such as a doctor's appointment, counseling or therapy sessions, or other similar situations
- During other social settings, such as parties

In some of these situations, it may be the case that the victim and offender may have only just met and do not fit into what we many of us think of as acquaintance-type situations. In some situations it is almost a case of pseudo-acquaintance because the offender and victim may know each other's names, but they do not "really know each other," and therefore are not fully acquainted. An example is provided in **Case Study 8-1**.

Case Study 8-1

A local neighborhood party involved a lot of drinking and "good times." At around 9:00 PM a female was clearly drunk and was taken back to her house by her husband to go to sleep. The woman was put to bed and the husband returned to the nearby party. At about 11:00 PM the woman was awakened by a man she recognized as "Mark," who was in bed with her and was initiating sexual intercourse with her. Mark was a friend of her neighbor, but she had only met him that evening and they had only exchanged a few words throughout the night. The woman actively resisted and called out to her husband, but he was still at the party. Mark continued his assault and after he climaxed, he got dressed, left the residence, and returned to his residence. The wife got up after he left, found her husband, and reported the rape. During his subsequent police interview, Mark steadfastly maintained the sex was consensual based on the *relationship* they had established that evening and that he had been invited to her house specifically for sex.

No information developed during this case study indicated there was any type of relationship established between the victim and offender prior to the assault. Every witness at the party confirmed the victim was not being flirtatious with anyone and had actually spent most of the time talking with a group of the neighborhood wives. However, the prosecutor in this case was initially hesitant to prosecute based on his concept of acquaintance rape and the intoxication of the offender and victim. It took some convincing to show the prosecutor there was no acquaintance or prior relationship between the offender and the victim, and the fact that the victim could readily identify the offender had no bearing on the incident. The offender was later prosecuted and convicted of burglary and rape.

As demonstrated in this case study, the term *acquaintance* is a relative term and therefore covers a wide range of possibilities. The offender and victim in the case would fit better into the category of *pseudo-acquaintance*; that is, they knew each other, but other than a few casual words over the course of a few hours; they had had no other contact. Other examples of the pseudo-acquaintance include a convenience store worker where the victim buys her morning coffee or fills her car with gas, a doorman or security guard at work, or a bus driver on a regular route. The victim and offender may know or recognize each other, but there is no real relationship between the two.

▶ Date Rape

The term *date rape* is frequently used interchangeably with acquaintance rape. It essentially refers to the fact that the incident may have occurred during the course of a date or other similar social setting. This adds some difficulties to the investigation because many times there is alcohol involvement, and because there are many rape myths and beliefs that are firmly established in the mindset of our society and culture related to dating. **Box 8-2** lists some of the more prevalent myths that apply to dating situations.

BOX 8-2 Prevalent Myths About Date Rape

- A woman who gets raped "asks for it" when she goes into a man's house or "parks" in a car with him in an isolated area.
- A woman implies sex is expected when she invites a man to her own house or apartment.
- If a man pays for dinner, drinks, and so on, then sex is expected and "owed" to him because of his "investment."
- Intimate kissing or sexual petting is tacit proof of a woman's interest in sexual intercourse.
- Once a man reaches a certain point of arousal, he cannot just stop.
- Most women lie about rape because they have regrets after consensual sex.
- Women who say "no" really mean "yes," and you can tell by their dress and actions what they are really thinking.
- Certain behaviors such as drinking or dressing in a sexually appealing way make rape a woman's responsibility.

As with many of the other rape myths, note in the examples listed in Box 8-2 the general theme of blaming the victim and her actions for contributing to her victimization. These myths perpetuate the idea that the offender was simply unable to control himself, was acting in accordance with cultural expectations, or that it was the victim's own failure to make her nonconsent known that caused the problem. Warshaw[3] identifies this concept as "justifiable rape," wherein the victim's own behavior is seen as being responsible for triggering the man's actions, and although this is not a legal concept, it does influence the opinions of the police, the jury, and even the victim's family. Even though we know how misguided these myths are, when a victim comes to the police station to report a sexual assault and she is dressed in a provocative manner, is not physically injured, and has been drinking, her report will likely be initially viewed with some doubt and suspicion as if to say, "Well, you dressed like that and you were drinking alcohol, what did you expect would happen?" This is not just an indictment of the police, because we most genuinely believe our duty and responsibility is to protect and serve. What it reflects is the frustration and realization that regardless of the amount of time and effort spent on the investigation, these cases seldom find their way to court.

Physical force is seldom found in these situations since most of the offenders in acquaintance and date rape cases have used the con approach to lure the victim to a location where they can take control and the victim unable to resist. They are generally able to socially interact with others and can initially be quite charming, but may turn demanding, insistent, and even abusive in order to have sex with the victim. This almost sounds like an example of a Dr. Jekyll and Mr. Hyde personality change. These situations are the typical "he said, she said"

---

[3] Warshaw, R. (1988). *I never called it rape*. New York, NY: Harper and Row; page 42.

cases in which the victim reports her version of what happened and the offender reports his version of what happened, and without any other evidence or corroboration they are unlikely to result in arrest or prosecution. The difficulty in many of these cases is that no one wants to believe that an otherwise good, upstanding, and popular guy would do something like this, or that a man with a lot of money and sex appeal would not be able to find plenty of consensual partners and thus would have to resort to rape. Later in the text we discuss conducting these types of investigations in greater detail.

▶ Juvenile Sexual Offenders

Another special offender that we come into contact with is the juvenile sex offender; that is, those offenders who generally range in age from 12–17. Although they are thought to be uncommon, we still see them enough that we need to be aware of them. It is unknown how many juvenile offenders are actively engaged in sexual offending, because many of their crimes are committed with their peers, often in dating situations, and many of their victims, like so many others, never report their victimization. Frequently, the victim is also a juvenile and may not understand that she was victimized in the first place. There is no specific victim of choice for these offenders, so the victim chosen generally varies with the individual offender's age, maturity level, experience, and fantasy. Perhaps more important for this type of offender is the general availability of victims, because juvenile offenders do not always have the ability to search for victims outside of their own neighborhood or comfort zone. Their victims of choice tend to be situational through coming into contact with the offender through normal circumstances or because they happen to live within the same general area as the offender.

Because of their education level, maturity, and limited criminal and sexual experience, this group of offenders displays a wide variety of different patterns of offending and preferred victims. Victims could include younger children, peers, adults, and the elderly. Many juvenile offenders may also be developing and experimenting with their sexual interests and therefore start out offending with whomever happens to be available to them. Then, as they gain more experience, they may move onto other victims.

Younger Children as Victims

With younger victims, the offender is most likely known to them. In many instances the offender maybe a babysitter, an older sibling, or another relative such as a cousin who, because of his family relationship, is in close contact with the victim. Commonly in family situations, the offender is placed in a responsible or authoritative position over the victim or other younger children, such as an older sibling used as a babysitter for his younger siblings. Generally, the juvenile offender who targets younger children is limited to victims within his own comfort zone. Therefore, it is not unexpected that the majority of these type offenses may occur at the victim's or offender's residence and take place over a long period of time with multiple assaults possible.

The sexual assaults may be very intrusive and possibilities include vaginal and anal assaults, with both heterosexual and homosexual assaults possible. Even with younger children, sexual experimentation such as foreign object insertion is possible. We often see sexual experimentation with the victims because the offender may be sexually inexperienced and the assaults are more about "learning opportunities" than sexual gratification. Some incidents may consist of no more than encouraging younger children in the offender's care or with whom he has contact with to get undressed for the offender to view or to direct the children to engage in "mutual exploration" while the offender simply observes. An example of such juvenile offender activity is noted in **Case Study 8-2**.

Case Study 8-2

Police were called to the scene of a residence where the parents returned home to find their babysitter, a 14 year old, in the back bedroom with their 3-year-old daughter and 4-year-old son. The babysitter was sitting in a chair watching the naked children playing with each other on the bed. It was later learned that the babysitter never touched either victim himself, but instead encouraged the children to touch each other and got them to pose in different positions with each other.

Other acts can be more intrusive but are not necessarily physically "violent" as we see in adult incidents. Instead of physical force there is more likely to be intimidation, coercion, and threats used to maintain control, overcome any resistance, and ensure compliance. Threats to some younger victims may include damaging or taking away a favored stuffed animal or toy. In older children the threat may be to injure the child, another sibling, a pet, or the child's parents. These threats are not just used to obtain compliance, but also to prevent reporting the incident to the victim's parents or another adult authority. Although these threats are unlikely to be carried out, they will seem real to the younger victims and are usually successful. Because of their youth and stature, any physical resistance by victims is generally limited and easy to overcome.

Unfortunately, parents may unwittingly assist in the assault of younger children because it is not unusual for the parents, prior to their departure from the house, to instruct the younger children, "Behave and do what 'Johnny' says." Of course, nothing in that statement should imply parental concurrence or acceptance of their children's victimization, but it could be used by the offender as a way to overcome any resistance or insure compliance of the victims. Therefore, the offender is able to use his status as the "responsible" older child.

Juvenile offenders can be very prolific and will often reoffend with the same victim(s) over and over if not reported. In these incidents what might start out as general exploration may continue on to touching or sexual assaults as the offender gains experience and the victim's natural reluctance is overcome. If no physical assault takes place and no force is ever used against the victim, the victims may never come forward to make a complaint. However, these assaults are frequently uncovered when victims begin to sexually act out at other locations, and this behavior is brought to the attention of the parents.

Peers as Victims

Peers are victims who are within the same general age group as the offender and may be known or unknown to them. Examples include classmates, others from the same neighborhood, or someone the offender met elsewhere, such as the mall or a dance. Most of the offenses committed against peers are against those the offender already knows and would fall into the same acquaintance rape circumstances described earlier. If the offender knows the victim, the con approach and efforts at "seduction," as in a dating or other social setting may be tried first, including the use of alcohol or drugs to help lower the inhibitions of the offender and to intoxicate the victim. "Seduction" does not always work based on the sexual inexperience of both offender and victim. In these situations, typically limited or no force is used, and the victim may initially consent and participate in kissing and mutual petting, but maintain limits on how far she is willing to go. Like other acquaintance-type situations, many of these events may start out as consensual but turn criminal when the offender refuses to take "no" for an answer and continues. Although generally nonviolent, if the victim is noncompliant or continues to resist, the offender may use force to establish and maintain control and/or to overcome resistance. Part of the problem with this offender is the lack of maturity and lack of experience in using other means to control the victim, which causes frustration in the offender, leading him to overcome resistance through force.

Because of their age, the offender and victim often live within the same neighborhood, it is not unusual for the setting of the assaults to be the victim's or offender's house while their parents or other family members are away. Peer victims are also assaulted in public areas such as parks, playgrounds, or in schools; incidents involving strangers tend to be more situational and impulsive in nature and the result of the victim being in the wrong place at the wrong time. The stranger-on-stranger situations may also involve more physical violence since concern about being identified to the police is diminished and caution about injuring the victim to avoid getting into trouble may not be present. The sexual assaults may include both vaginal and anal assaults, depending upon the sexual experience of the offender. Genital trauma to the victim may be possible based on age and sexual inexperience of the victim or offender and the resistance or compliance of the victim. The sexual assault tends to be relatively short in duration, and the entire contact with the victim may be influenced by the location of the assault and the general compliance of the victim. The less resistant and more compliant the victim, the longer the offender may stay with her.

One feature of juvenile peer offenses is the number of instances involving multiple offenders participating in the assault. Some offenders will gain strength and confidence from the presence of others. **Case Studies 8-3 and 8-4** are examples of juvenile assaults involving multiple suspects and targeting the mentally disabled.

Case Study 8-3

Three male high school students ranging in age from 16–18 years old were out driving when they came upon a 16-year-old female special education student they knew from school. She was walking home and they offered her a ride, which she accepted. However, the students took her to another house where over the course of several hours they sexually assaulted her. They compelled her to perform oral sex on them and then vaginally assaulted her using a broomstick.

Case Study 8-4

Five youths, including three juveniles, were arrested for raping and sexually assaulting a mentally disabled woman. Much of the assault was videotaped by one of the participants. The victim, who reportedly had an IQ of 70 and the social skills of a 5 year old, was invited to the movies by the teens. Instead of going to the movies, they took her to an apartment and held her for 2 days. While there, she was made to perform oral sex on some of them and have intercourse with others. Later, the teens inserted a broomstick into her vagina, all the while filming their activities. The victim said she had cooperated because she wanted to go home and thought they would let her go.

In both of these case studies the arrests of all of the youths shocked their local communities. Although they are atypical of most sexual assaults, they are good examples of how juvenile sexual assaults may take place, both in the targeting of victims who are unlikely to resist and unlikely to tell others and the presence of multiple offenders during the act.

Adult Victims

Adult victims are also targets of juvenile offenders, but typically it is the older juveniles who will attempt to assault adult victims. The victim generally resides within the offender's comfort zone, and although the victim may not know the offender, it is likely the offender is aware of the victim in some manner such as living in the same neighborhood or apartment complex. As well as being a little older, offenders who target adults tend to be more criminally experienced, confident, mature, and typically much larger in size. The ability to approach, seize, and maintain control over an adult says a lot about an offender's confidence level and is very important behavior to note. Violence tends to increase with the age of the victim, and the older the victim the more likely violence will be used. Primarily because younger offenders lack the confidence or physical stature to control their victims with mere presence, they may use more physical force and violence in order to seize and maintain control or overcome resistance from an older victim. Blitz assaults or a surprise approach are much more likely for juvenile offenders who may not be mature or confident enough to use a con approach, especially on strangers. Because of the increased level of violence, victims are more likely to suffer injuries from both physical assaults and sexual experimentation by the offender.

Elderly

Elderly victims are seen as easy victims for most crimes, but especially for sexual assaults because it is not difficult to control them or overcome their resistance. Most victims are found within the offender's comfort zone, and assaults on the elderly are also typically initiated by a blitz or surprise assault. Physical injury and trauma are likely because of the frail physical nature of most victims and their inability to defend themselves. Vaginal assaults and sexual experimentation are also likely, again because the victims may be unable to adequately resist or defend themselves. Other criminal acts such as burglary or theft are also likely since the opportunity to commit these other acts is present, and the victim is likely to cooperate out of self-preservation.

Investigative Considerations

It is very difficult to identify any specific or typical personality characteristics in juvenile offenders that enable us to place them into one of the four general categories of offenders. This is because the offender is often immature and his life, sexual, and criminal experience is also limited and may change as he gains additional experience through more assaults or through consensual acts. Juvenile offenders are more likely to experiment as they progress until they find what exactly excites them, and only then do they settle into one of the four established categories.

One of the difficulties with juvenile offenders is that they are not often brought to attention of the police until they have offended numerous times on numerous victims. Therefore, expect that an offender may have been engaging in sexual offending for a considerable length of time. Frequently, these types of offenders may be already developing certain antisocial characteristics such as selfishness, a lack of empathy or sympathy, and the ability to manipulate others.

They may also come from an exceptionally protective family system whose members will go out of their way to protect the child. This plays into offenders' sense of entitlement discussed earlier.

▶ Female Sexual Offenders (FSOs)

The concept that women, who are so traditionally thought of as the victims of physical, emotional, and sexual violence, can also be sex offenders is unfathomable to some. In our culture and society women are seen as being the heart of the family; they are supposed to be caring, loving, gentle, and protective of children. Besides, there are any number of rape myths relating to females that help perpetuate these thoughts. Elliot[4] provides some interesting myths surrounding female sexual offenders (FSOs), which are listed in **Box 8-3**.

BOX 8-3 Myths About FSOs

- Females do not sexually abuse, they are the victims.
- Females who sexually abuse children are all mentally ill.
- If females sexually abuse, it is done out of love.
- Females only abuse boys never girls.
- If you were assaulted by a female, you are either a lesbian or gay.
- It is worse to be sexually abused by a man than a woman.
- Males who report sexual abuse by women are fantasizing.
- Males who report their mothers' sexual assaults are having incestuous fantasies.
- If a woman has incestuous relations with an older male son, it is just sex between consenting adults and not sexual abuse.
- If a 30-year-old woman seduces a 14-year-old boy it would not be sexual abuse; if a 30-year-old man had sex with a 14-year-old girl it would be sexual abuse.

It is interesting to note that even when women are the alleged perpetrators, how many myths are out there that blame the victim and not the offender. As a society we have generally resisted acknowledging the existence of females as offenders and the potential harm they may cause to their victims. Although women represent the minority of sex offenders, more and more are beginning to be recognized as sexual offenders and are receiving much more attention. In fact, much of the contemporary research in this area shows that female sex offenders are much more common than previously realized, and the myth that females only offend as a minor participant with a superior male partner has also been shattered. Although the vast majority of attention on sex crimes focuses on men as the offenders, an increased awareness of females as sex offenders has surfaced in recent years. Highly publicized cases involving

---

[4] Elliot, M. (1994). *Female sexual abuse of children.* New York, NY: The Guilford Press.

inappropriate and illegal sexual contact between female high school teachers and their male students are a primary source of this growing attention. These cases are not representative of the full nature or scope of sexual abuse committed by females; however, and they have the potential to promote myths and misperceptions about the broader issue of female-perpetrated sex crimes.

Female sexual offenders are somewhat different from male perpetrators. For instance, they are not as predatory, do not always have a specific "victim age preference," do not actively seek stranger victims, and seldom have more than one victim at a time. FSOs also tend to take fewer risks in offending by targeting their own children or others they exercise control over such as through caregiving, teaching, or babysitting. Their victims may be either male or female, depending on the offender's preferences and motivations and goals for committing their offenses. For example, men assaulting children will view their crimes as acts of sex; even if they try to temper their acts through internalized minimization statements like, "I was just trying to teach her how to be careful; I wanted to show that I loved them." They may deny what they did was a crime, but they understand what they did involved sex. Conversely, FSOs will often deny their acts had anything to do with sex, stating their actions were really about love, romance, and genuine feelings for the victim or may justify their actions as a type of disciplinary measure to the victim for some infraction.

The sexual acts committed during their assaults are also different. Men are more likely to engage in full vaginal intercourse, anal, and oral sex. FSOs are likely to engage in a number of acts including vaginal intercourse, oral sex, fondling, mutual masturbation, showing pornography, and playing various sex games. FSOs are also more likely to use foreign objects as part of the sexual act. Rarely does a female offender "just" sexually abuse a child, and often the incident involves a combination of psychological humiliation, degradation, and physical and verbal abuse.

Characteristics and Typologies

Research on female sexual offenders has identified several common risk factors and personality characteristics of these offenders. These characteristics and risk factors are not present in all FSOs but they are common enough to be able to help identify and document them. Examples are included in the **Box 8-4**.

Based on their motivations and personality characteristics, female offenders can also be grouped into some general categories in the same manner as male offenders. Warren and Hislop[5] have identified these general categories as *the facilitator, the forbidden lover, the instigator,* and *the psychotic.*

---

[5] Warren, J., & Hislop, J. (2007). Patterns of female sexual offending and their investigatory significance to law enforcement and child protective services. In R. R., Hazelwood & A. W. Burgess (Eds.), *Practical aspects of rape investigation: A multidisciplinary approach* (4th ed., pp. 429–443). Boca Raton, FL: Taylor & Francis.

BOX 8-4 Risk Factors for Adult FSOs

Low self-esteem and passiveness
Depression
Feelings of isolation
History of self-injury or suicide attempts
Victimization (especially incest) during their own childhood and/or adulthood is likely
Poor social and anger management skills
Difficulties in their current or past intimate relationships
Fear of rejection and easily manipulated
May be promiscuous
May offend within family or with someone they exercise control over
May offend in conjunction with male
May have history of mental health issues and personality disorders
Alcohol and substance abuse likely
May feel powerless in their adult personal relationships

The Facilitator

The facilitator assists in the procurement of victims in order for her husband or intimate partner to act out his sexual fantasies on a younger child victim, engage in child pornography, or some other form of child prostitution. Although the facilitator may understand that what she is doing is wrong, she may be so dependent on the male and so fearful of abandonment that it overcomes her sense of right and wrong. Some offenders may actively partake in the sexual assault, but most do not or only take part in a limited role. It is also likely that these offenders may seek out other victims in order to protect their own children or themselves from sexual or physical assaults. They generally have low self-esteem, tend to be passive, have a history of mental problems, and are likely to be alcohol and drug abusers.

The Instigator

The instigator initiates sexual abuse, often choosing her own children or other children she may have control over. These offenders tend to experience deviant sexual fantasies. They may insist that their male partner locate and bring them a child or younger victim and then join them in the sexual assault. It is also possible for this offender to have another female join with her in the sexual assaults. These incidents tend to be much more violent and based on anger toward the victim and could result in injury to the victim. Assaults may include elements of sexual torture, vaginal rape, foreign object insertion, and in some instances, gang rape involving multiple offenders. In addition to sexual assaults, the victims are frequently subject to neglect and other forms of mental, emotional, and physical abuse. The offenders are marked by low self-esteem, depression, and practice of self-injury, and may express or show suicidal idealization. It is very likely these offenders were also victimized when they were younger and are continuing the abuse.

The Forbidden Lover

The forbidden lover is the offender type we are probably more familiar with than any other female offenders because of the number of recent media reports of teachers sexually involved with their students. These offenders direct their sexual interest toward a particular adolescent (male or female) they have routine contact with and act toward them in the same manner as they would in an adult affair, engaging in all the romance, intimacy, and implied consent. There is an important difference in these offenders, because they elevate their victims to the status of adults and may actually feel they are in love with their victims and describe themselves as a couple and/or soul mates. Having a younger lover increases the offender's self-esteem, because she feels as if she is admired and even sexually desired by her younger victims. Because no physical force or coercion are used, these offenders may not see their actions as being criminal, and even more importantly, they may not even accept that they have caused any harm to their victims. However, because of their positions as caregivers, teachers, or other authority figures, they can exercise control over their victims and noncompliant or resistant victims could receive punishment or be extorted to comply. Examples include withholding toys, early bed time, or taking away some favorite thing for younger children; for older adolescents examples include awarding or withholding good grades or other factors which could influence victims' academic standing in school. There are instances when adolescents who attempted to break off their relationship with their teachers were threatened with poor grades, which could impact their ability to get a scholarship to college. Some FSOs may use the same forms of abuse or coercion that they themselves once experienced.

Most FSOs tend to be immature, overly dependent, and overly concerned about rejection and abandonment and may be struggling in their own adult lives and adult relationships. So, they gravitate toward younger, less mature adolescents where the risk of rejection is less likely and they can exercise more control over their lives. They generally do not consider what might be at risk or the long-term consequences of their actions; rather they are only focused on themselves and on some immediate gain or reward.

Case Study 8-5

Mary Kay Letourneau is perhaps the epitome of this type of offender and is one of the most publicized cases. Letourneau was a 34-year-old, married mother of four children, working as an elementary school teacher. She met a student at her school and thought his dark Samoan features were exotic, and over the course of a few years became quite attracted to him. When he turned

12 and was in the 6th grade, she then initiated contact with him, offering him rewards for good grades including taking him to a restaurant. During one such dinner she grew bold and Letourneau slid her foot under the table and played "footsie" with him. After the meal, they returned to her car and began kissing in the parking lot and had sexual intercourse. Shortly thereafter they engaged in sexual intercourse in many locations including her vehicle. Letourneau became pregnant and decided she wanted to keep the child, but since she was already married, and based on her victim's different race, it would not be difficult for her husband to see that this child was not his. Her actions eventually came to the attention of the police and she was arrested. Letourneau eventually pled guilty to two counts of second-degree statutory rape and was sentenced to 89 months in prison. Most of the incarceration was suspended based on a promise to attend a sex offenders treatment group and take medication for some mental problems. After 5 months, she returned to her family and almost immediately renewed her relationship with the boy, and soon became pregnant again. She was eventually rearrested, and this time was sent to prison for 7 years. After her release, she almost immediately recontacted the boy, who was an adult by that time, and they eventually married in 2005.

Like other FSOs, Letourneau claimed romance and love as her motivations, but she did not seem to show concern for any possible long-term problems for her juvenile victim and instead was primarily concerned with her own needs. Even violating a court order and a subsequent prison sentence did nothing to interfere with her fantasy to be with the young boy. Letourneau, like other FSOs, is still reluctant to admit any wrongfulness in her sexual interaction with adolescent males. There are very many other examples of FSOs with cases similar to Letourneau's (see **Case Study 8-6**).

Case Study 8-6

A teacher enticed a number of juvenile boys between the ages of 15 and 17 to party and drink alcohol with her. Once they were intoxicated, they went to her house where she stripped off her clothes for them and had sex with several boys, and another took nude photos of her. Once the event came to the attention of parents and police, the pictures were produced as evidence. Several of the boys indicated this was not the first time, and that the teacher had initiated similar incidents several times before she was caught.

Case Studies 8-7 and 8-8, however, are far different from many other offenses by this offender type. They deal with much more than just sexual relations with juveniles but also deal with manipulating their juvenile victims into doing things against their own self-interest in order to keep their relationships with the FSOs going.

Case Study 8-7

A 25-year-old girls' basketball coach and 6th grade math teacher became enamored with a 13-year-old boy in the 8th grade. Eventually, her contact with the boy came to the attention of the police. Her school computer was seized and numerous personal emails between the teacher and student were discovered. The emails clearly established they were engaged in a sexual relationship. The boy's family reported to the police that they had become concerned as the teacher and boy began spending an increasing amount of time together, and she had become obsessive and even gave the boy a cell phone so they could talk to each other. The case grew more intense when the teacher and boy left the area and began to drive to Mexico where the boy had relatives. The teacher and student were recorded as they passed over the border, and she then faced federal charges of transporting a minor over state lines for sex, and into foreign territory. A short time later the boy phoned a relative from a shopping mall to ask for money. The family alerted authorities instead, who eventually found them, arrested the teacher, and took the boy into protective custody. Interestingly, the boy told police that they had intended to keep driving into Mexico and that eventually they would find a place and set up a life together. But there was no specific plan, no ability to earn a living, and they only had about $400 left of the money the teacher originally brought with them.

Case Study 8-7 is an example of FSOs who often do not plan or put forethought into what they will do once they seduce their target, how they will maintain their secret, or how they are going to react if they are ever discovered. They seem to be too immersed in their romantic fantasy to understand the ramifications of their actions or what may lie ahead for them. As noted in the case study, the FSO simply took her victim and drove across the country with a general idea or fantasy of living in a foreign country, with no means of support or income, and somehow being able to live with an underage male. There was no information if she even spoke Spanish.

The following case study is also a well-publicized event that captured national attention for several months in the early 1990s. The event is atypical of this type of offender but it clearly demonstrates how manipulative these offenders can be and how they can take advantage of their younger, more immature and naïve victims.

Case Study 8-8

Pamela Ann Smart was a very attractive young woman who was working as a media coordinator at a local high school. Smart established a relationship with a 15-year-old boy and despite an 8-year difference between them, Smart engaged in sexual relations with the juvenile and developed romantic feelings for him. At the same time this relationship was developing, she was also having some difficulties in her marriage. Eventually she began talking to her victim about helping her get rid of her husband, eventually threatening to leave him and stop having sex with him if he did not kill her husband. Without a great deal of enthusiasm, he agreed to it and then enlisted the help of three other friends. On May 1, 1990, Smart's husband was murdered as he came home, and the scene was staged to resemble an interrupted burglary. The scheme was quickly unraveled by the police and the juvenile lover, his three friends, and Smart were all arrested. The prosecutor alleged that Smart had seduced the young teen in order to convince him to murder her husband so she could avoid an expensive divorce and to collect a $140,000 insurance policy. Smart acknowledged in her testimony that she had had an affair with the teenager, but the murder was actually the result of her attempt to break up with the boy and try to reconcile her marriage. All were eventually convicted and sentenced to varying prison terms.

One of the notable features of FSO incidents is the nonviolent nature of the assaults, which typically involve "seduction" or coercion rather than physical force. This also translates into the legal systems treating female and male sex offenders quite differently. Whereas even a "consensual" sexual relationship between an adult male and an adolescent female is viewed as abusive, criminal, and worthy of severe punishments, the same is not said of FSOs and their sanctions for essentially the same acts. Instead, they tend to be handled far less severely, as our society appears to consider these incidents as not damaging to the victims. This may be one of the reasons why so many of these cases are underreported.

Psychotic

The last type of FSO is known as the psychotic, who is genuinely mentally ill and offends in the context of her illness. The major difference with these offenders is the very real possibility that serious injuries and death may result from their assaults. There are instances where their attacks appear to be the result of some sadistic torture or other ritualistic circumstances. However, when the offender is interviewed, it is clear the assault has nothing to do with sexual gratification but rather is a direct result of mental illness. This particular group makes up the smallest number of FSOs, but when cases involving this type of offender occur, they tend to be reported extensively because of the brutal nature of the assault and death may have resulted.

Co-Offending Women Versus Solo Female Offenders

Particularly unique to FSOs is the likelihood that there is a male co-offender or participant in the sexual abuse, particularly with children. There are some important differences between solo-acting FSOs and co-offending FSOs, such as their victim and modus operandi (MO). For instance, co-offending FSOs are more likely to have multiple young victims and may have both female and male victims rather than just male victims. Co-offending FSOs are also more likely to target their own family members and are more likely to have been charged with other nonsexual crimes such as child neglect or child abuse.

Katherine Ramsland[6] has identified many similarities between the male pedophiles and some FSOs, including their MOs, motivations, sexual interests, behaviors, and personality characteristics. **Box 8-5** identifies some of the very same characteristics between what may seem to be opposite offender types.

BOX 8-5 Characteristics of FSOs and Male Pedophiles

- Frequently married, often with children
- May relate to or feel more comfortable with children than adults
- May have a victim age and sex preference
- May seek employment or activities that allow them to be near children in their preferred age group (including employment as teachers, coaches, or caregivers)
- May volunteer with youth organizations
- May exhibit grooming behaviors toward their victims
- May furnish narcotics or alcohol to the child or adolescent to lower inhibitions
- May go to great lengths to conceal their activity
- Are usually intelligent enough to recognize they have a problem but can rationalize, justify, or excuse their illicit activities
- Believe their actions do not harm the victim
- Target children who seem troubled and in need of attention or affection
- May justify their acts by emphasizing the positive impact on the victim
- Talk about children and adolescents in the same manner one would use to talk about adult lovers
- Usually nonviolent and have few other problems or contacts with the law
- Interested in children ultimately for sexual purposes
- May view or show pornography to victims to lower inhibitions as part of grooming
- May provide pictures of themselves to their lovers
- May go out of their way to win the trust of parents
- May seek opportunities to be alone with the victim (e.g., camping trips, sports, or other activities)
- May volunteer to spend extra time with victims to help in school or sports

---

[6] Ramsland, K. *Female sex offender*. Crime Library. www.trutv.com

Female Juvenile Sex Offenders

Another group of offenders that we hear about even less than FSOs are *female juvenile sex offenders*. This group has only recently come to the attention of the police and clinicians as a genuine problem. The female juvenile offender constitutes only a very small proportion of all juvenile offenders, and as with very many other juvenile offenders, their activity may go unreported for a long time, if ever reported. Juvenile offenders also share many of the same behavioral and personal characteristics as the adult FSO, as listed in **Box 8-6**.

BOX 8-6 Characteristics of Female Juvenile Sex Offenders

- Sexual and physical victimization usually takes place at home (victim's or offender's)
- May live in a dysfunctional family with difficulties in parent–child relationships
- Likely to have been sexually victimized
- May have experienced early and frequent premarital sex (consensual or nonconsensual)
- Likely to be more immature than peers
- Poor school records (underachiever/attendance)
- Experience early onset of puberty
- May fear rejection and abandonment
- Typically have a passive personality type
- May offend within the context of caregiving activities
- May target victims of either gender
- Generally act alone
- History of mental health issues which may including post-traumatic stress disorder (PTSD)
- Alcohol and substance abuse likely

There are several different subtypes of juvenile offenders who are recognizable based on their behavior and intent. As an example, some juvenile female offenders may not necessarily be seeking sexual gratification from their assaults, but instead are relatively inexperienced, naïve, and somewhat fearful with respect to sexual matters. Their motivation appears to be primarily curiosity and their sexual acts are more likely to be the result of experimentation rather than sexual gratification. Frequently, these offenders may target a nonrelated child within the context of babysitting or other similar activities. This type of offender does not always have histories of maltreatment, family dysfunction, or some of the other psychological difficulties that other subtypes have. Another general subtype includes adolescent females who may have experienced some emotional, physical, and sexual abuse themselves. Their assaults therefore appear to be much more sexually aggressive and may resemble what they themselves have experienced. For these offenders, their assaults are not necessarily about experimentation or learning about sex as much as the sex acts themselves. The last subtype includes adolescent females who have experienced much greater levels of emotional, physical, and sexual victimization in their own lives. Many may have been forced into more extensive and repetitive sex offending behaviors at an early age. This has likely contributed to other difficulties within their personal and family life. These offenders also tend to be very sexually aggressive and demanding toward their victims and again may mimic the same types of abuse they suffered themselves. They are more likely to target younger children rather than their own peers because they are likely unable to exert as much control over peers. The offenders would not be interested in pleasing their victim but rather want to satisfy their own needs. It is also likely for many juvenile offenders to continue to progress and to initiate such acts upon their own children in the future as they grow into adulthood.

Juvenile offenders are very likely to have been victims themselves, and this should be a consideration when these incidents come to the attention of the police. It is not inconceivable that the investigation starts on the actions of the offender, but as the case develops a second case will be initiated for her parents or another adult.

▶Pedophiles and Child Molesters

The term pedophilia comes from the Greek words of phillia (love) and pedeiktos (child) and it has come to be associated with child molestation and the sexual exploitation of children. It is perhaps the most hated and repugnant of all sexual crimes because the victim is a child.[7] Even in prison, convicted child molesters are at the bottom of the prisoner hierarchy and must often be housed separately from other offenders to keep them from being assaulted by other prisoners. There are also a great number of myths surrounding pedophiles and child molesters as identified by Groth[8] in **Box 8-7**.

BOX 8-7 Myths About Pedophiles and Child Molesters

The child molester is a "dirty old man"
The offender is a stranger to his own victim
The child molester is retarded or insane
The child molester is a sexually frustrated person
The child molester progresses over time to increasingly violent acts
Children are at greater risk from homosexual then heterosexual offenders

---

Like other myths about victims and offenders, these are of course not accurate and many times the myth is directly contrary to reality. There is still confusion, even among professionals, with regard to the terms child molester

---

[7] Aggrawal, A. (2008). *Forensic and medico-legal aspects of sexual crimes and unusual sexual practices.* Boca Raton, FL: CRC Press.

[8] Groth, N. A., & Birnbaum, J. (2001). *Men who rape: The psychology of the offender.* New York, NY: Plenum Press.

and pedophile. For many the terms have become synonymous and the word pedophile is looked at as just a fancy term for a child molester. The terms are often used interchangeably to refer to all those who sexually victimize children as pedophiles.[9]

Is important to note that there is actually a technical difference between a pedophile and a child molester. Lanning defines *child molesters* simply as significantly older individuals who engage in illegal sexual activity with children. What "significantly older" means is somewhat dependent on the facts and dynamics of the event, but generally speaking we are looking at five or more years age difference between offender and victim. However, a pedophile is someone who engages in pedophilia,[10] defined as: fantasies, urges, or behaviors that are recurrent, intense, and sexually arousing and involve prepubescent children, generally age 13 or younger. At one time the term pedophile was almost exclusively used by mental health professionals to describe those persons engaged in the deviate sexual practice of pedophilia. However, the term has come to mean much more in today's society and nearly everyone routinely refers to those who sexually abuse children as pedophiles. This includes many child abuse professionals, law enforcement, and prosecutors. Increasingly in professional literature and common usage both terms are being replaced by the term predators.[11] The basic difference between the two terms is a child molester is someone who has actually sexually molested a child but may not necessarily be a pedophile because he does not fantasize or have an urge to molest a child, and if an adult consensual partner is present he may have no interest in the child as a sex partner; a pedophile is someone who has a sexual interest in and attraction to children and desires children as sexual partners even when adults are present, but may not necessarily ever act on those impulses or desires. Simply said, a child molester is not necessarily a pedophile and a pedophile is not necessarily a child molester.[12]

Lanning[13] has identified two types of pedophiles or child molesters, which he has termed *situational* and *preferential*. The situational offender is essentially someone who will sexually assault a child victim out of curiosity or when he is interested in sex and there is no adult consensual partner available. The situational offender may offend against a child from time to time but is not necessarily sexually attracted to them. Typically, this offender does not spend

---

[9] Lanning, K.V. (2010). *Child molesters: A behavioral analysis.* (5th ed.). National Center for Missing & Exploited Children.

[10] Pedophilia is one of the deviate sexual paraphilias covered earlier in the text.

[11] Hazelwood, R. R., & Burgess, A. W. (2008). *Practical aspects of rape investigation: A multidisciplinary approach* (4th ed.). Boca Raton, FL: CRC Press.

[12] Because the term pedophile is better recognized by the public and law enforcement, it is used throughout this text to refer to an offender who is sexually attracted to and actually molests children.

[13] Lanning, K. V. (2010). *Child molesters: A behavioral analysis.* (5th ed.). National Center for Missing & Exploited Children.

a great deal of time selecting a victim or make a great investment in securing the victim's cooperation and may use force or coercion in order to obtain compliance from the victim. The preferential offender, however, is what we think of as the typical pedophile who is sexually attracted to and prefers sex with a child even when there is a consenting adult present or available. This particular offender will invest the time, money, and energy to select a victim and use a form of seduction to obtain the compliance of the victim rather than force. The idea is to produce a complianct victim so he or she can be assaulted repeatedly rather than just once.

The "Ideal" Victim

Pedophiles generally have their own concept of the ideal victim based on the sex and age group of the child they are sexually attracted to and will go through a great deal of effort to select a particular victim that matches that sex and age group who they believe can be groomed or seduced into becoming their victim. There are certain general characteristics that offenders are looking for when they select their victim and offenders are especially attuned to look for the child who is going to respond positively to their efforts to manipulate and seduce. A good example of how a pedophile goes about selecting a victim is noted by Groth,[14] who quotes one offender:

> "I can look at the kids in a school yard and tell you who is an easy mark. It will be the child alone and off by himself, the one who appears lonely and has no friends. The quiet kid—the one that no one is paying attention to—that is the one who'll respond to some attention."

The "dirty old man" stalking a playground or driving through a neighborhood with a bag of candy or a box of puppies looking to lure children away to molest them does happen; but as with other sexual offenders, many child molesters are known to the child and usually to the parents as well. The pedophile comes into contact with the child and parents through employment or activities that place him into contact with children, such as teaching, volunteer work with children, counseling, coaching, scout leadership, babysitting, or other such positions where he has the opportunity to spend unsupervised time with a child. The pedophile is looking for those children that may not have the family support structure at home that provides them the attention, affection, and positive influences they need and are easily led by adults. Most importantly, pedophiles seek out a child with one additional characteristic that is critical for them: the ability to keep a secret; meaning, what happens between the offender and victim will stay with them and no one else. In order to

---

[14] Groth, N. A., & Birnbaum, J. Men who rape: The psychology of the offender. Plenum Press, NY.

manipulate the victim and be able to sexually abuse him or her, the pedophile goes through a process known as grooming.

Lanning[15] identifies five stages to the grooming process: identifying a possible victim, collecting information about the intended victim, filling a need, lowering inhibitions, and initiating the abuse. Once the victim has been selected offenders can begin their grooming and seduction process, not just on the victim but also the victim's family. Once trust has been established with the parents and child, the offender begins to fill the need of the victim, sometimes with nothing more than giving him or her time and attention. Eventually the child begins to spend more and more time with the offender and less and less with family and friends. Once the friendship and trust are developed along with the extra attention, they can then be used against the victim when he or she resists any advances of the offender with the threat he or she will have to go home or will not get the same level of attention if he or she does not do what the offender desires. During this same process the offender begins to lower the victim's inhibitions through many different techniques including accidentally touching the child through his or her clothes to see what kind of reaction he receives, arranging for the victim to accidentally see him undressing or naked, or leaving out pornography or sex toys to be found by the victim so the subject of sex can be discussed. Pornography can be especially effective and the offender will use it to show the victim pictures of other children engaged in similar activities, thus giving the impression that such conduct is acceptable and normal. Eventually the offender will suggest that he and the victim also engage in some of the activity as well. The ultimate goal for the offender is not to engage in a single incident of child molestation, but to be able to sexually abuse the child for a period of time and ensure the child remains silent about the abuse.

Offenders

Many offenders have convinced themselves that what they are doing is not wrong and that having sex with a child is actually "healthy" for the child. More so than other offenders, pedophiles frequently associate themselves with other pedophiles to both exchange various types of sexually explicit material (generally child porn) as well as mutual support for their deviate sexual interests and views. Their association may be informal through special Internet sites, based on the age and sex group they are sexually attracted to, or other types of deviate behaviors. One example of a more formal group association is NAMBLA (North American Man Boy Love Association) whose stated purpose is to "end the extreme oppression of men and boys in mutually consensual relationships."[16] Basically this group believes that sex between adult males and male children should not be criminalized. Many offenders look to these

---

[15] Lanning, K. V. (2010). *Child molesters: A behavioral analysis.* (5th ed.). National Center for Missing & Exploited Children.
[16] Taken from the NAMBLA website.

informal and formal groups as a way to validate their own beliefs that their actions are just misunderstood by society and, like interracial marriages in the past, eventually society will come around to realize these sexual acts are not harmful to the victims and should not be illegal.

Cyber Pedophiles

New technology has also been used by offenders as a way to gain access to victims without ever leaving their home. The home computer, the Internet, and children who are not closely supervised have proved to be a boon for pedophiles because with just a few keystrokes, they can have access to literally hundreds of potential victims across the country. The majority of victims of the cyber pedophile are adolescents and teens (ages 12–17) because this age group generally has unhindered access to computers and the Internet. The grooming techniques involved are very similar, including giving the child positive attention and reinforcement that he or she may not be getting in his or her home. The teen years are very difficult for many, so an older man interested in the child and showing attention to him or her can do much for the child's confidence. In some cases it is even easier for an offender to entice victims because over the Internet an offender can be anyone he wants to be, and because so many are older, they can use their age, experience, and maturity level to manipulate victims into doing what they want, including sending offendres sometimes even nude or sexually provocative photos, or meeting offenders and having sex with them. It is sometimes difficult to imagine that teenagers would be willing to send sexually provocative photos to someone they do not know over the Internet, but it happens with great frequency. It is also important to note that the cyber predator can be heterosexual as well as homosexual.

Almost all pedophiles have some type of pornography or other related items including detailed writings or photographs of their contact with a victim. Many offenders also collect "souvenirs" from their victims, which may include small personal items such as a small toy or clothing. One offender was known to collect his victim's underwear and wrote the victim's name and the date the underwear was taken on the elastic band. Almost two dozen pairs were found in a small cardboard box after the offender was arrested and his house searched. These souvenirs and any child porn are generally considered to be highly valued items and are seldom discarded or destroyed. Instead they will be protected at all costs. These items are part of what is known as collateral material and are covered in greater detail later in the text.

Victims

It is not unusual to have victims who were repeatedly assaulted over the course of months and sometimes years who have never have told anyone about their sexual abuse. Because of the grooming process it is also not unusual for the victim to have actively participated in his or her own victimization because he or she was too young to understand what he or she was doing or in the case of older children, he or she was given alcohol, drugs, or other items to obtain compliance.

It is not unusual for some victims to have actually enjoyed the intimacy or the physical sexual acts. Police and parents must realize that part of the grooming process was designed to get the victim to comply with his or her own victimization as much as possible. Thus gifts, money, special treats, privileges, drugs or alcohol are all used as a way to get that compliance. It has nothing to do with the victim's actual voluntary participation. Since each offender has a certain age group of children that he is attracted to, it is not unusual for the offender to assault a victim for a number of years until he or she gets older and leaves that certain age group and is simply replaced by younger children and the cycle of grooming starts over again.

Investigative Conclusions

Experienced pedophiles have their grooming process almost perfected and if any child resists or cannot be manipulated, they are frequently dropped by the offender who then will seek out another victim and start the process all over again. It is not unusual for older, experienced offenders to have literally hundreds of victims over the course of their lives. It is also likely that they have justified their actions in their own minds because to them, they never actually harmed the victim and in fact may have actually voluntarily partici- pated in their own victimization. If a pedophile has been identified, any other child in contact with the offender should be interviewed to determine if he or she was also victimized.

▶ Conclusion

These special offenders can and do present some extra problems for detectives. The main key to these cases, however, is first to recognize and accept that each of these special offenders does exist. Although we do not see them often, we are liable to see an increasing number in the coming years as more and more victims are starting to come forward, not from an increasing number of these types of offenders, but rather from a concerted effort to have victims come forward and report their victimization.

▶ References

Benedict, J. R., (1998). *Athletes and acquaintance rape*. Thousand Oaks, CA: Sage Publications.

Elliot, M. (1994). *Female sexual abuse of children*. New York, NY: The Guildford Press.

Scarce, M. (1997). *Male on male rape: The hidden toll of stigma and shame*. Cambridge, MA: Perseus Publishing..

Warshaw, R. (1994). *I never called it rape*. New York, NY: Harper Perennial.

CHAPTER NINE

Offender Interview

Interrogation is not a skill; it is an art that is developed over time and is one of the most important tools a detective can use to resolve cases. The offender's admission or confession to participation in a crime is one of the main goals of an interrogation because it allows the prosecutor to use his own words against him. Regardless of the advancing sophistication of forensic techniques, there is still no more powerful evidence of an offender's guilt than his or her own admission of having committed the crime in question.

Courts and juries throughout the world and throughout history have looked at legally obtained confessions or other voluntary statements made against self-interest as perhaps the strongest evidence of guilt. Because of the powerful nature of the confession, courts and governments have tried to balance the need of police to capture this evidence with the accused's rights and safety. This balance is seen in various laws forbidding use of torture or other physical means to obtain a confession, and there are other legal safeguards against police abuse of a suspect or offender. This is one of the reasons why the U.S. Constitution contains a number of specific citizen rights and specific prohibitions against maltreatment of suspected criminals. Although they are a valued investigative technique, suspect interrogations have become a major weakness of the entire investigative process. The main problem is not necessarily with any legal violations or use of coercive techniques, but simply with the overreliance on either forensic evidence or a suspect's confession in order to resolve the investigation.

Because of this overreliance on forensics and the confession, detectives have no other tools in their toolbox. If the forensic evidence is available or the offender confesses, they are successful; but when the offender does not confess, the detective is frequently lost, with no idea what to do next, and many times the case is unresolved.[1] Sadly, the overreliance on the confession may

---

[1] This is seen many times when teaching law enforcement classes and discussing aspects of the complete investigative process. Often, detectives will boast of an exaggerated ability to obtain

also lead to false confessions because of the continued insistence to gain a confession from the suspect. Regardless of the crime, confessions are a vital piece of evidence, but in the complete context of a criminal investigation, a confession should be considered as the dessert rather than the main course. In other words, confessions are good to have and we want to make every effort to legally obtain them, but the wisest course of action is to assume at the conclusion of an interrogation that we will have no confession or admissions and should proceed accordingly with that in mind. Another major problem with offender interviews is the somewhat cavalier attitude and approach that so many detectives have about the interview or interrogation process. No suspect interview or interrogation should ever be attempted without first having a clear understanding of the allegations against the suspect and the information being sought. Being unprepared and trying to conduct any suspect interview without such information is inexcusable and more often leads to coercive tactics or an unsuccessful interview.

For sex-related crimes, both the victim and offender interviews are extremely important because so many times, the event involves only two persons, the offender and the victim. Consequently, the victim and offender interviews are more critical to resolving these types of cases than almost any other. There are already number of well-written texts that detail the various legal requirements and other more basic and technical aspects of the interview or interrogation process. This text is focused strictly on the various techniques of conducting an interview and interrogation of a sex offender. Therefore, as the basis for this chapter, it is assumed that the offender has been properly identified, advised of his or her legal and constitutional rights, and has waived those rights and agreed to be interviewed.

▶ Preparation

Being properly prepared is a necessity before attempting *any* suspect or offender interview or interrogation and as such, detectives need to be familiar with the general and specific facts of the crime and a have a clear understanding of what information they are attempting to gain during the interview. This includes not just the various legal elements of the crime, efforts to seek admissions, or a confession, but also to determine if the offender has an alternate version of events or can provide other evidence as to what may have happened. From an ethical standpoint, it should be our goal to establish the

---

confessions from offenders and therefore they see no need to understand any of the other aspects of the investigative process. This is actually not the mark of a talented detective, but the mark of a lazy detective, and although he may have a high confession rate, he is just as likely to have a high unsolved cases rate. An apt analogy is that for the longest time, Babe Ruth held the record for the most home runs in a career, but he also had more strikeouts than he did home runs.

truth of the allegation, whether it validates or invalidates the complaint, and not be solely concerned with obtaining a confession.

Prior to any suspect interview there are some specific pieces of information that should be reviewed by the detective. This is to ensure that the detective has a clear understanding of exactly what the victim is alleging and what criminal offenses may have been committed. Some of the information that should be reviewed is listed in **Box 9-1**.

BOX 9-1 Information to Review Before a Suspect Interview

Victim's general statement of events
First contact between victim and offender—time, date, and location
Identify the various sexual acts demanded and performed
Description of any force, threats, or coercion used by the offender
Any efforts to destroy or eliminate evidence or intimidate victim or witnesses
Description of the offender including physical, scars, marks, and tattoos
Offender behaviors (verbal, physical, or sexual)
How the offender left the victim/scene
Results of crime scene examination
Results of any other witness interviews that have been conducted
Results of medical examination of victim
Results of any forensic analysis if available
Any basic background information on the victim (criminal history)
Any basic background information on the offender (criminal history)

It is especially helpful if we are also able to identify the type of offender that may have been involved in the incident, because this would enable us to tailor the interrogation and the tactics used toward that particular offender type. It is nearly impossible to conduct an offender interview/interrogation without the basic information found in Box 9-1. Without such prior information, the detective does not know which offender statements are consistent or inconsistent with the victim or other factors. Unfortunately, there are some detectives who believe their interrogation skills are such that they are able to interrogate the suspect without even knowing all of the facts and circumstances of the event or anything about the offender. In preparation for the offender interview we should try to know as much about the offender as possible. Although this is true for every crime and for every suspect we interview, it is even more important when we are interviewing sexual offenders. This includes a thorough criminal history check, especially to find out if they have previously been arrested or accused of any other sexual crimes. Offenders' past criminal experience becomes very important, because, like other offenders, they tend to follow a behavioral pattern, especially in their response to interrogation techniques.

Also, if possible, conduct additional interviews with those who know the offender best, such as current or former wives, girlfriends, or lovers.[2] The ultimate goal is to identify the offender's strengths and weaknesses and be able to take advantage of that information. This information is extremely helpful because it will give the detective an idea of how to properly approach the offender in the manner that makes him or her feel most comfortable and therefore more likely to talk and give information and hopefully confess. This is also important from an investigative standpoint because we want to know about the offender's sexual activity and desires, fantasies, and paraphilias. Many times what we see perpetrated or forced on victims may have been previously attempted with previous or current consensual partners. This could also include aspects of the offender's sexual dysfunction and what was needed to overcome that dysfunction. But, from the interrogation standpoint, we want to know information about the offender that only someone who has spent a lot of time talking to or in close contact with the offender will know. Such important information includes but is not limited to:

- Who and what does the offender respect?
- Who or what does the offender not respect?
- What are the offender's weaknesses?
- Did the person being interrogated experience anything similar to the incident under investigation?

From the perspective of the interrogator, one of the most important question to ask is how we know if the offender is lying. What is his "tell?" A tell is the subconscious reaction to stress or emotion and is often associated with card players that subconsciously do something to signal they are bluffing or holding good cards. Recognizing the tell allows the other card players to know when to fold or when they are dealing with an effort to bluff. It is the same concept with lying; that is, for many people there are subconscious signals whenever they lie that they may send out that can be recognized by someone else as signaling a lie. Adults and parents may see the same in children when they begin to lie. If we are able to spot the offender's tell when he begins to lie, then we can gain a huge advantage.

Based on the dynamics of a particular event and the subsequent investigation, this detailed background information is not always possible or practical to obtain prior to the offender interview, but it is worth the effort to obtain it. There are many other aspects of the offender's background that have great

---

[2] Interviewing current or former girlfriends, wives, or lovers is not always practical or possible in every case and it can be very time consuming, but there are certain serious cases in which the extra time and effort will be worth expending. Thus, this concept or technique should be considered as appropriate, not only to obtain extra information about the offender, but also because when the offender realizes you have made the effort, this may change the dynamic in how he or she views you and your investigative effort.

investigative value; these aspects are covered in greater detail later in this text. Part of the preparation on the detective's part comes from not just understanding the basic facts of the crime, but also from recognizing the type of offender that is involved, because each offender type responds to police questioning in different ways. Understanding how the various offender types will respond gives detectives a great advantage, often moreso than for other crimes involving other offenders. As noted later in this chapter, each individual offender type has a specific interview technique that has proven to be very effective. This is one of the reasons behind spending so much time and effort to identify the offender type involved in the incident.

Another major problem with offender interrogation comes from detectives who are not willing to invest enough time and effort into the interview or interrogation. Again, this is another example of the overreliance on the confession and the impatience of some detectives. These interrogations may take hours to overcome the offender's resistance to admitting or confessing to the crime. Therefore, we have to be flexible with the amount of time we may have to expend to successfully complete the interview. Sexual offenders perhaps understand and respect the concept of power and control because they deal and operate under those concepts during not just their sexual assaults, but also in their lives. Therefore, they already understand the power of the police, giving us a great advantage over the offenders. These offenders are only likely to confess when they believe that it is in their best interest to do so, such as when they are convinced the police already have enough evidence to prosecute.[3] Being thoroughly prepared and willing to expend the necessary time and effort on these interviews would be expected, and for some offenders, actually appreciated. The preparation and planning for the eventual offender interview begins with the detailed interview of the victim and continues on with an appropriate offender background investigation.

▶ General Interrogation

There are several important concepts in conducting a suspect interview or interrogation. First, there is a difference between an interview and an interrogation. An interview is typically nonconfrontational, and although we are seeking possible incriminating evidence, it is designed to elicit information from the interviewee in a free-flowing type of exchange. It is conducted when the guilt or culpability of the interviewee is unknown or uncertain and allows for the offender to provide his side of the story as to what happened. Examples of the information we are looking for or expect to obtain is found in **Box 9-2**.

---

[3] Kebbell, M., Alison, L. Hurren, E., & Mazerolle, P. (2010). How sex offenders think the police should interview to elicit confessions from sex offenders. *Psychology, Crime and Law, 16*(7), 567–584.

BOX 9-2 Information to Obtain in a Suspect Interview

If the suspect has an alibi

Identity of any witnesses the suspect can provide to substantiate his alibi or explanation of events

If the suspect has a weapon previously described by the victim

If the suspect knew the victim or was present with the victim before, during, or after the incident

If the suspect has a vehicle, clothing, or tattoos as described by the victim

Explanation as to the victim's complaint: Why would she make the complaint against him?

Explanation of any evidence found at the scene

Explanation of evidence the suspect has to explain his side of the story

Whether the suspect agrees that intercourse or another sex act took place (even if consensual)

During an interview, relatively few direct questions should be asked of the suspect, and 80–90% of talking should be done by the offender and 10–20% of the talking is by the detective. In this stage the detective is asking more open-ended types of questions and then allowing the suspect to fully explain his side of the events; the detective exerts very little control over the process except to keep the suspect from wandering too far away from the main issue.

In contrast, an interrogation is undertaken when the culpability of the offender is fairly certain. In circumstances such as an offender "caught in the act" or immediately thereafter and taken into immediate custody, the police may actually start out with a direct confrontation as to his participation in the event. In this instance, there is little reason not to proceed directly into an interrogation of the suspect. But generally, interrogations are more successful when they start out as interviews and then move into an interrogation to gain further information. Interrogations are both strategic and goal oriented. The strategy comes from knowing the proper technique to use for the particular offender and the main goal is to obtain admissions of guilt from the suspect.

An interrogation once begun is much more direct, accusatory, and controlled. Thus, in contrast to the suspect interview, 80–90% of the talking is by the detective with only 10–20% by the offender. The increased talking by the detective is designed to overcome offender resistance to acknowledging his participation in an event. Although we are using direct confrontation-type questioning, we still want to avoid harsh inflammatory terms such as *rape, force, trauma, assault, beat up,* or *sodomize.* Use of those terms is likely to result in an increase in the suspect's fear of the legal retribution for his acts; therefore, it is better to use softer terms like *sexual intercourse, having sex, making love,* or *oral sex* to describe the events with the victim.

The offender must generally be convinced that he is in a hopeless situation and the only way to save himself is through his confession and that the detective is willing to listen to what happened and get the offender's side of the story. The detective's expression of compassion and sympathy toward the suspect will go a long way to overcome the suspect's resistance. Focus should be on factors leading up to the incident, rather than on the possible punishments or any negative aspects of his conduct. Once the offender has begun to make admissions or finally says, "I did it," the interrogation may revert back to the interview style of the detective asking more open-ended questions and the suspect doing most of the talking. Once the offender has begun to make admissions or confess, it is not unusual for him to hesitate or begin to resist again, resulting in the detective returning to the interrogation style to overcome that remaining resistance.

Another general concept is centered on the sexual offenders themselves. Whereas most criminals tend to operate with a different thought process that justifies their criminal acts, sexual offenders tend to operate out of a sense of entitlement and their actions revolve around anger, power, and control. They are typically self-centered, egotistical, and often master manipulators. Therefore, detectives should approach these interviews much more carefully and better prepared then perhaps they would for more traditional criminals. There is no standard approach or technique for conducting these interrogations; rather, each offender type will respond better to certain settings and approaches. Thinking the standard interrogation approach that may be effective for other common criminals will have the same result for sexual offenders is simply inaccurate. One last general concept for interrogations is the expected outcome. Regardless of the crime, there are three possible outcomes from every suspect interrogation; we refer to them as *admissions, denials,* or *confessions,* and all three can be used as very powerful evidence during the criminal investigation.

▶ Admissions

An admission is an agreement by the offender with some of the basic facts of the incident, but not necessarily a total confession. Many times the offender may admit to certain parts of the incident but then deny any actual criminal activity. For instance, the offender may agree to knowing, meeting, or even having consensual sex with the victim, but would deny any force or coercion in the act. From an investigative perspective, an agreement or admission of even consensual sex with the victim is very important, because one of the main issues we will have to prove is penetration. If the offender admits to performing consensual sexual intercourse with the victim, then we can establish through him that there was actual penetration. At the same time, if the offender admits to performing or having the victim perform consensual oral or anal sex during the incident, then again this can even be seen as an element of corroboration with the victim's statement. The only dispute between the victim and offender may be the element of force or coercion, and we may be able to get this aspect from other sources.

Many offenders will mix as much truth into their statements as possible in order to keep their story straight and believable. Therefore, we need to use this to our advantage as much as possible to identify and corroborate as many of the basic facts as we can. Admissions should be seen as the best opportunity to corroborate aspects of the victim's statement. Any agreement by an offender to the victim statement, regardless of how insignificant, should be seen as further corroborating the victim's statement. Therefore, even minor admissions such as where they met, where they went, what they did, and who they saw or talked to prior to the assault, and the same type of account of what happened afterward, can be extremely important if they are in agreement with the victim's statement.

▶ Denials

A denial is the offender's basic disagreement of involvement in any way with the victim or the incident. This may include denying consensual sexual intercourse taking place with the victim. Denials are more likely than admissions during at least the initial stages of the interrogation. Even at the conclusion of the interview when the offender has stuck to his denials, detectives should pay attention to his statements because of their importance later. Denials are beneficial from an investigative standpoint because as the investigation develops and various denials are found to be lies, they are going to count as examples of guilt by the offender and as a form of corroboration of the victim. An example is the offender who attempts to establish an alibi or denies even knowing the victim and then later we establish that the alibi was false or that he did in fact know the victim; in this case, the denials and lies would become very important. The more the offender's denials are later found to be lies, the stronger the victim's complaint. This is especially important when we are dealing with the "he said, she said" type of investigations in which *credibility* becomes so important.

It is important for the interviewer to take the time to get a good, detailed statement from the offender, especially by asking specific questions about relevant facts of the incident. Each denial offered by the offender is also going to be an additional investigative lead that must be checked out and verified. The reason for this is very simple. Although the offender seems to be denying certain facts about the incident, it does not necessarily mean he is lying. It could very well be that the offender or suspect is telling the truth, and the victim or other witnesses are mistaken or lying themselves. Our job therefore must be to take these conflicting statements from both suspect and victim and then determine what the truth is. To be considered investigatively significant, the denial or lie must be relevant to the incident itself. For instance, if we know that the offense in question took place at 10:00 PM on a Tuesday night, and several weeks later the offender talks about the incident having occurred at midnight on a Wednesday, it may not necessarily be a lie but a mistake in fact. This does occur and these mistakes should not be considered lies unless we are certain the offender specifically intended to lie about some aspect.

What appears to be a mistake requires clarification by the offender and subsequent investigative effort to establish what really happened.

▶Confessions

A confession is the complete, or more often, the partial agreement with the basic facts of the offense as alleged by the victim or determined by the physical evidence. A confession has always been considered one of the strongest pieces of evidence in any criminal investigation and trial, because a confession is a statement made against self-interest by admitting to committing a crime. Like other crimes, full, complete confessions to all aspects of the event are few and far between. More likely are partial confessions where the offender will admit to committing certain crimes or admit to certain acts but will deny or refuse to acknowledge participating in other acts.

Many times this hesitancy is related to the offender who decides it might be better for him to admit to those crimes they are certain the police can prove but refuse to admit to other elements of the crime or to other crimes when evidence of their guilt is not as strong. It is also possible that the offender may not be willing to make a full confession because he perceives the particular crime will make him appear to be a sexual deviant or the particular crimes are so repugnant that he cannot bring himself to admit participating in them.

What frequently happens during an offender interview is a combination of these three possibilities, wherein the offender admits to certain elements, denies other aspects, and/or makes a partial but not a complete confession of some element or criminal act.

▶The Interview Basics

The interview or interrogation of an offender has other important uses besides being an opportunity to gain possible incriminating statements. This is a chance for the suspect to tell his side of the events. As a caution to all detectives, regardless of the evidence or information we may have collected, we must still keep an open mind and be prepared to expend the time and effort to validate any claim made by the offender during his interview. This means any counter claim or explanation should also be thoroughly examined, validated, or corroborated in the same manner as we did with the victim's statement. This is very important because if the offender's statement and offer of other evidence is validated, then we may have to take a closer look at the victim's allegations and other evidence. If the offender's claims can be discounted or proved to be untrue through other investigative activity, then we should look at this as additional evidence of offender guilt and additional victim corroboration.

The offender interview or interrogation is also used as means to identify other investigative leads and other persons who may need to be interviewed such as those the offender identified as potential witnesses or identified as an alibi. But, in addition to these persons related to the incident, we also want to use this opportunity to conduct a background check and identify those other persons who the offender may interact with on a daily basis. Therefore, we are also interested in their current and past wives, girlfriends, lovers, or significant others. As stated earlier, these are extremely important interviews to obtain because of the type of personal information on the offender these close personal or intimate associates can provide. Obtaining this background information may also provide additional witnesses such as friends and employers, as well as prior living addresses. Changes of residence should be noted and a check made with the local police from previous areas to determine if there are any similar cases reported but unresolved, or if they have any information on the offender which may have been developed during other investigations.

Regardless of what may have happened during the event, the detective must take the time and make an effort to remain professional, neutral, and detached, and develop a rapport with the offender. This is not always easy because of the circumstances in some of these cases, but it is imperative to be successful. These offenders are very keen on what others think of them, and if they believe the detective is looking down on them or they are being treated as a deviant, it may turn them off from wanting to talk about the incident at all. As we will see later in this chapter, each offender type responds differently to the police, so efforts to establish a rapport will be different for each offender type. Detectives simply need to be more flexible in their approaches because with these types of offenders, one size does not fit all. Like the victim interview, direct, "yes or no" questions should be avoided. Instead, the same open-ended questioning technique is most effective in gaining as much information as possible. As stated earlier, nothing happens in a vacuum, so there is a before, during, and after to every event. In this case, the offender is providing what he thinks is important to his side of event.

The open-ended questions allow for the free flow of information from the offender, and, as with questioning the victim, offenders should not be interrupted until they have a chance to relate their side story. In the same manner, it is advisable to have the offender repeat his story multiple times. What we are looking for is the offender to clearly establish what he says happened and his exact involvement in the incident. By repeating the process the offender is essentially locking himself into his statement, which makes it difficult for him to change his story once the interrogation process begins. These open-ended questions are also designed to determine the location and actions of the suspect before the incident, during the incident, and after the incident. This is especially important when we are attempting to establish the suspect's alibi or where he was when the offense was committed.

It is easy to lie or misrepresent where you were at a certain or specific time when asked something like, "Where were you at midnight?" However, when asked to relate where you were at from 6:00 PM until 6:00 AM, for instance, if you want to establish a false alibi you must also establish a false reality as to where you were before, during, and after the incident. It becomes fairly obvious that there is a problem with an alibi when details become sketchy around the time of the event.

To effectively interrogate a sexual assault suspect, the investigator must also understand that most offenders will not necessarily admit to committing a crime, but more likely will to try to justify or excuse the crime in some way. Gaining insight into the suspect's distorted perception of his crime is central to the interrogation process. These offender excuses are known as defense mechanisms and we see this in almost all interrogations, regardless of the crime. There are three basic defense mechanisms resulting from any suspect interview or interrogation: *rationalization, projection,* and *minimization.* These are also known as ego-defense mechanisms because they allow the offender an opportunity to offer an explanation of the event or tell his side of the story in the most favorable light to himself. These are also very effective approaches or themes a detective may use to overcome the offender's natural reluctance, resistance, and fear of arrest, prosecution, and punishment.

Rationalization

Rationalization is basically a face-saving effort by the offender, and the detective can allow him to offer excuses to justify his actions. The process of rationalization allows the transference of guilt from the offender onto someone or something else or to downplay his own involvement. The rationalization used by the offender or offered by the detective does not have to make sense to anyone other than the offender. Some of the best examples of rationalization come from pedophiles who often maintain that having sex with children does not actually cause any harm to the victims; or, they claim they just want to educate the child in understanding the joys and benefits of healthy sex. Other rationalizations include general assertions that the sex act with the victim was not forced, but the result of the victim's own desire to have "rough sex," or the knife the victim says was present at the scene was merely a knife the offender always carried and he simply removed it so they would not be accidentally injured. The concept of a sexually aroused man not being able to control himself or not being able to stop once things get started is another example of a rationalization.

Projection

Projection is basically allowing the offender to excuse his own misconduct by projecting the blame or fault onto someone or something else. In this case the offender or the detective may offer attempts to blame the victim for the incident, claiming for instance that the victim has a poor reputation, was leading him on, was wearing alluring or sexy clothing, or was intentionally teasing him. It is also likely for the offender to claim the rape complaint was really about getting him into trouble, the result of a broken relationship, or the result of a wife who has failed to provide the suspect with adequate sexual fulfillment. Alcohol or drug usage is a very popular excuse for a suspect's conduct, because he is able to blame "bad" judgment to be a result of the intoxicant, which caused him to do something totally out of character. In some extreme cases offenders may also offer excuses such as any number of mental or psychological disorders. This can be effective in drawing out information and admissions because so many offenders believe that others also share their same belief system. In the case of multiple offenders it is almost automatic for them to blame each other for committing the criminal act, while each claims he was only present but did not participate. In any case, the offender attempts to frame his story around his innocence and another's guilt.

Minimization

Minimization basically allows the detective or the offender to minimize criminal actions or guilt by playing down the seriousness of the crime and the offender's culpability. Examples would include suggestions such as, "at least the victim was not seriously hurt," or that the offender "did not intend to go so far" or "did not actually hurt the victim." This offers a chance for the offender to claim the incident was a misunderstanding; for example, that if the victim did not want to have sex she would have physically resisted more, would not have gone to the offender's house, or would not have invited the offender inside her house. Other themes include things "getting out of hand" or "going too far," or that the offender's actions were just a momentary, spur-of-the-moment lapse, and not some premeditated act or pattern of behavior.

Minimization is basically an attempt or offer to the offender of some moral relief over his actions by implying many other people have done the same thing he did or others have done far worse. An example would be offering a statement that almost every other guy has used some amount of force during sex and most women just accept that; after all, 99 out of 100 women would never have made a report in the first place. This theme offers a situation where the offender was simply unlucky the victim was so sensitive rather than implying he actually did something wrong.

Remember, if any of these themes are initially presented by the offender or by the detective, they are being used as a way to explain what happened, or to make the offender feel better over what he has done rather than admit to any actual criminal act. Once these themes are accepted, they should be expanded upon and will eventually lead to admissions and hopefully full confessions. All three of these defense mechanisms may be used in the course of the inter-rogation; many times the detective may have to change to different themes if the offender does not appear to be accepting the defense mechanism, depending upon the offender's reaction to them. These themes present the detective with a golden opportunity to develop a rapport and, in some cases, build trust with the offender by appearing as if he is agreeing, supporting, or looking out for the offender or is trying to understand the offender's side of the incident. By focusing on the resolution of the situation and his future rather than punishment or consequences, the offender is often more willing to accept that it is in his best interest to confess to the crime. Which theme is going to be successful is dependent upon several factors including the type of offender, his age, intelligence, maturity, criminal experience, and the exact criminal acts committed. **Case Study 9-1** is a good example of developing these themes.

Case Study 9-1

A college student reported being asleep in his dorm room bed and waking up to find his roommate performing oral sex on him. The victim became alarmed and proceeded to physically assault the roommate and then notified police. The suspect steadfastly denied the accusation and insisted instead he had been assaulted by the victim without warning or provocation and wanted to file assault charges against the victim. The suspect was offered a chance to take a polygraph examination to test the validity of his denial and counter claim, which he accepted and subsequently failed. During the posttest interrogation, the polygraph examiner began constructing a theme or possible explanation for the suspect that would allow him to confess or at least make admissions as to what had actually happened.

Examiner: I think what we are looking at here is a simple misunderstanding of what really happened. I mean you say you were out drinking and were coming into the room late at night. It was dark and you didn't want to turn the light on to wake your roommate? Isn't that right?

Suspect: (Slumping in his chair but nodding in agreement)

Examiner: Then you said earlier your roommate always sleeps in the nude, right?

Suspect: (Nodding in agreement)

Examiner: Well we all know that men when they sleep often will have an erection—it is normal and it happens to us all right? I mean I'm a man and it happens to me, you're a man and it happens to you too, right?

Suspect: (Again, only nodding in agreement)

Examiner: Well, if your roommate was sleeping, had an erection and the covers were not over him, he would be exposed, right? If you then came into the room and it was dark, and you had been drinking, isn't it possible for you to have stumbled over something on the floor and fell? And as you fell that you found yourself right over your roommate and as you fell his penis went into your mouth?

Suspect: (Nodding in agreement and straightening up in his chair)

Examiner: Then your roommate wakes up and thinks you're trying to have oral sex with him? But it is really an accident and unintended? Right? I mean it could have happened that way, right?

Suspect: Yeah, exactly. It was more like an accident.

Examiner: Yeah, so then when your roommate woke up you did have his penis in your mouth, right?

Suspect: Yeah, because I tripped and fell and then it went into my mouth by accident.

Examiner: Then when he wakes up he is surprised to find his penis in your mouth and he jumps to conclusions right?

Suspect: Yeah, he just started yelling and screaming and punching me.

Examiner: See, there you go. And you were just too embarrassed to say anything, right? And you just made up the story about being attacked for no reason?

Suspect: Yeah, because you know what this makes me look like?

Examiner: Exactly.

The case study above is a good example of theme development while offering the chance for the offender to justify or explain his actions, minimizing his own participation, projecting blame against someone or something else, and rationalizing or offering an alternate explanation of what may have happened. Of course the theme and explanation offered to the suspect does not have to make sense to anyone other than the offender. After obtaining the minor admission that the roommate's penis was in his mouth, the examiner continued with the interrogation, concentrating on the unlikelihood of such an accident actually taking place as the examiner himself had first suggested. The suspect eventually made a full confession to performing oral sodomy on his roommate without his consent or knowledge.

Sympathy and Empathy

A successful theme used in non-sex-related crimes is the concept of *sympathy* or *empathy* toward the victim, wherein the criminal is essentially made to feel bad or guilty over his actions against the victim. Whereas this is often successful in other crimes, detectives will note when dealing with sexual offenders, using sympathy or empathy toward the victim or trying to use the concept of right and wrong with their actions is not going to be very effective. This is because sexual offenders typically have no sympathy or empathy for anyone other than themselves. So, the concept that they should somehow feel bad over what they have done to the victim is not going to resonate with them; the only sympathy or empathy they will really respond to is when it is directed toward themselves. They will all generally respond to the detective who appears to be willing to hear their side of the story and hints that he does not believe the victim.

▶ Interrogation Techniques

Each of the offenders will respond most favorably to a particular set and setting of the interviews that are established by the detective. The set and setting refer to where the interview takes place, the conditions, and the particular approach that is used. There is a major reason why we spend so much time and effort to identify the offender type involved in the incident. It plays an important role in the interview and interrogation of the offender. Because we understand the various personality characteristics of each offender type, we also know how they will likely respond to various interview approaches and what techniques are successful for each offender type. Employing these tactics and techniques gives us an advantage we may not have when interviewing other criminals. Each offender type has certain approaches or techniques that tend to be very effective in eliciting information from them. These are not absolutes because not every offender will respond to these particular approaches in the exact manner outlined as follows, but experience has shown these approaches are the most effective for these offenders.

Regardless of the offender type or the interview technique we use, the goal is always to gain more information from the offender rather than give information to them. We do this by asking the offender questions and not answering questions or providing all of the facts and evidence we have against the offender inappropriately.

Power Reassurance

Power reassurance offenders will respond better when the interview takes place in an unstructured environment. Although it may be difficult to make an interview room more "friendly," this setting can be created by detectives who are dressed more casually, such as by wearing slacks and a polo shirt instead of more formal business wear like a suit and tie. The interview should be as nonconfrontational as possible, with no visible signs of authority such as uniforms, badges, or guns being present or visible. It is going to take a little more time to develop a rapport with them because they will tend to be uncomfortable and suspicious around police and are on the alert for tricks or insincerity.

As noted in earlier, these offenders have a poor self-image, are socially inadequate, and are uncertain about their own masculinity. They will be underachievers, but they are not necessarily slow or of low intelligence and most are fairly streetwise. An empathetic approach that builds up the offender is going to be more effective than an approach that is demeaning, direct, or overly aggressive. This is the one offender type for whom using sympathy and empathy toward the victim may be successful, because this is the only offender that had no real intention to harm the victim and may feel guilty for committing the offense. Using the theme of *minimization* and highlighting such facts as the victim(s) was not really harmed during the attack or was not treated very badly can be effective. Since the offender prefers to get the victim involved in the act by asking them to undress or to do certain things, this could be a way to imply that the victim was actually consenting to the act, again trying to minimize the culpability of the offender. This tactic can be successful when you comment to the offender that during his background investigation, friends described him as gentle, quiet, and passive, and how out-of-character this allegation appears to be.

Once the offender has begun to talk, we need to remember that this is a prolific and ritualistic offender, and therefore a lot of time and attention may have gone into victim selection. So, it is important to cover as much about his pre- and post-crime behavior as his account of the assault itself. Since this offender is known to walk around at night or ride a bike through neighborhoods looking for victims, it is important to determine how often he did so, as well as the specific areas he went through. It is likely the offender may have taken souvenirs or trophies and may have kept personal records such as a diary, handwritten notes, charts, or other computer records. Therefore, if the offender ever confesses, it is important to determine if he also has these items. As detectives we would of course want to get these records not just because of possible evidence of a particular incident, but as potential evidence of other crimes we are investigating or for crimes that are thus far unreported.

There are likely other victims or the offender has likely committed other crimes such as burglary, breaking and entering, or small thefts that will have to be covered at some point in the interview. Focus first on the incident with the strongest links and evidence leading to the offender; if the offender has confessed to the incident(s) in question, a statement has been completed. Once this is completed, it is important to then expand the interview and attempt to determine if there are any other crimes that are either reported but not linked to the offender or are so far unreported to the police. Female officers can be effective in interviewing this type of offender because he is seeking favorable contact with females. It is important, however, that the female keep proper and professional boundaries, and it is suggested that a male officer should also be present in the room for officer safety and to keep the offender from making any claims against the female officer.

Caution

These offenders are likely to shut down or be unresponsive if they are brow beaten, intimidated, talked down to, or otherwise humiliated during the interview process. They already have a poor self-image and one of their reasons for committing sexual assaults in the first place was to reestablish their masculinity with the victim, so anything that lowers their image further may lead them to stop the interview or refuse to cooperate.

Power Assertive

Power assertive type offenders are more likely to respond when the interview takes place in a more structured environment, such as the police station or detective's office. These offenders see themselves as macho and hold a very high opinion of themselves; therefore, they are focused on image and would appreciate and respect the concept of power and control. They tend to respond favorably to recognizable symbols of police power, such as uniforms, badges, handcuffs, and guns. For this offender, the detective should be dressed more professionally such as in a suit and tie, perhaps with a badge openly displayed on his belt, and should display an attitude of confidence and authority. This authority can be expressed in small ways such as introducing himself to the offender as "Detective," or if appropriate, using his higher rank such as, "Detective Sergeant" or "Detective Lieutenant," or even "Special Agent." Because these offenders have such a high opinion of themselves, they would respond to the superior rank and to any special attention they may receive from a senior police officer. Control is especially important to this type of offender, and even subtle control works. Examples include making the offender initially wait a few minutes in a waiting room before the detective greets him to bring him into the interview room. The room should have two chairs for the offender to sit in, and the detective might tell the offender to sit down, and regardless of which chair he chooses, ask him to sit in the other. Both of these examples are subtle, and for most people, if this were to occur, it would likely be shrugged off or go unnoted. But for these offenders, it clearly demonstrates the control the detective has over the entire process and thus the offender.

This particular offender would also be impressed by certain props that may be used as part of the interview process. Props would include a thick case file on the desk in front of the detective who is conducting the interview. The thick case file implies the amount of work that had gone into the investigation and how much time was spent or invested. The amount of work coupled with comments on how much time, effort, and how many detectives were involved would again help with the offender's ego, implying how important he must be to have all this attention on him. Another simple tactic that is commonly used to increase the perceived importance or rank of the detective is when the offender is being walked to an interview room inside the station, another detective approaches and asks the case detective a question, to sign for something, or addresses him in conversation as "sir," implying the detective has a higher rank than others. For this offender, this would be another boost to his ego that someone of a high rank would be in charge of his case.

The key weakness of these offenders is the fact that they have almost an overwhelming need to brag to their friends about what they have done—not in the sense that they have raped someone, but rather in their success at seduction or their prowess as a lover. In fact, for these offenders, the criminal act is "not worth committing unless someone else knows about it."[4] **Case Study 9-2** is about a serial killer who demonstrates the need to brag of his exploits to others in order to feel successful.

---

[4] Personal communication with Mr. Richard Walter, a criminal profiler and one of the founding members of the Vidocq Society.

Case Study 9-2

A power assertive-type serial killer was known to pick up street prostitutes and take them to various friends' houses where he would "show off" by verbally taunting, degrading, and threatening them. Many times the offender would begin a physical assault on the prostitutes while others were present and watching. On many of these occasions, he was forced to leave by the others at the scene because they did not want to become involved as potential witnesses to the assault. The offender would then leave with the prostitute, and later he would openly boast to this same group of friends about taking the prostitute out to the woods and killing her. On at least three occasions, he took friends out to the woods and showed them the body of a female he claimed to have murdered. It was not enough for the offender to have simply killed his victim; his reward was showing off and bragging to his friends so they would both respect and fear him. Eventually, the remains of four females were found in this same general area.

This offender will likely respond to two general themes. The first is the *projection* of blame onto the victim or onto someone or something other than the offender. Since the offender operates with a sense of entitlement, he will believe he was in the right to demand sex from the victim in the first place. The second theme the offender would likely accept is sympathy or empathy—not directed toward the victim because that would be totally rejected—but offered as support to the offender. An example of the sympathetic approach is the implication that the interview is more of a formality based on departmental policy and perhaps based on pressure from women's groups rather than the detective's belief that the offender was involved in any criminal offense. This offender is more likely to provide some minor admissions rather than a complete confession, mainly because he will not likely have any guilty feelings and his personality characteristics may not allow him to accept that he has done anything wrong.

Caution

One thing to avoid with this type of offender is anything that would seemingly diminish his self-image of a macho man; his ego is very fragile and does not take criticism well. Therefore, we want to avoid any inference that whatever happened is somehow deviant, unsavory, weird, or perverse. Any approach that tends to diminish his self-image is going to be rejected out of hand and may cause him to halt the interview. Therefore, any unsavory aspects of the incident such as an elderly or younger victim or a particularly deviant sexual act forced onto the victim should be downplayed and not accented during the course of the interview. Because of their sensitivity, these offenders will likely key in on the reaction of the detective to judge how they are being perceived. Hence, the body language, tone of voice, and attitude of the detective need to be controlled, regardless of the circumstances.

Since this offender has little respect for females and will attempt to continue maintaining his macho image, female detectives may have a difficult time with this offender.

Anger Retaliatory

Anger retaliatory-type offenders are also best interviewed in a more structured and controlled environment such as the police station, with the detectives presenting themselves in a more formal and professional manner in order to maintain control. The combination of the offender's impulsivity and violent temper makes him the most difficult to interview of all the offender types, and officer safety considerations should be paramount as the interview is planned. These offenders' assaults are more episodic, meaning that something has happened in their life to create stress, and the attack on the victim is seen as a way to relieve the stress.

Sexual fantasy plays the smallest role for these offenders, and their victims may symbolically represent a particular person who has injured them in the past or just represent women in general. Thus, their assaults are based much more on anger expressed toward the victim than sexual fantasy, and sex is used as a weapon against the victim and not for their own gratification. This offender has a difficult time interacting with others and may be lacking in social skills; therefore he uses the blitz-type approach more than any other offender. Because anger is such a part of his assaults, attempts to use empathy or sympathy toward the victim or other emotional types of approaches would be unsuccessful. Instead, this offender will focus more on logic and his self-preservation so the use of *minimization* toward the victim's injuries and the *projection* of guilt and blame onto the victim are going to be much more successful. Once a general rapport has been established, allow the offender to go through his version of events in the same uninterrupted manner used for the other offenders. This offender type is not likely to be as talkative as other offenders and the detective may have to prompt him with more questions in order to keep the interview going and get his full version of events. Conflicts or inconsistencies need not be addressed at this point, as it is more important to get him talking and hopefully locked into a basic statement before any confrontation takes place. This initial questioning will hopefully establish some minor admissions such as knowing or being with the victim, being in the area at the time of the assault, or even admitting to consensual sex acts with the victim. Using projection and *rationalization* can be effective to establish some of these admissions.

Once the detective is satisfied the offender is locked into his story, then the detective can shift to a more direct and confrontational "in your face" type approach. In this manner, the offender can be directly confronted with any inconsistencies between the victim's and the offender's statement.

Earlier attempts to rationalize his actions or project blame onto someone else must now be shown to be unbelievable or inconsistent with the evidence and other witness statements. Emphasis at this stage is on whatever evidence is available, and the use of false evidence or a bluff can be most effective for this offender, because he generally has not taken the time to consider problems such as being identified or leaving physical or forensic evidence behind prior to committing the offense. Regardless, the offender must be reminded of the futility of his continued resistance. This direct approach is likely to produce an emotional response from the offender and may lead to quick, unscripted, and incriminating statements as he becomes angry or agitated. His emotions and anger will prevent him from thinking clearly and he will make mistakes. Euripides[5] described this weakness best: "Whom the Gods would destroy, they first made mad."

Caution

The detective must be careful to always keep the upper hand with this offender and not allow him to become too emotional and angry and lash out at the detective. Because of his deep-seated and often open hatred of women, it will be very difficult for a female detective to interview this type of offender. This offender requires a more controlled and formal setting; this is both to set the stage so that the offender is not necessarily comfortable but also for the safety of detectives. This offender is the most impulsive of all offenders and typically has a quick and violent temper and may react violently if he perceives a weakness in the detective.

Anger Excitation or Sadistic

"Sexual sadists are masters of manipulation; therefore, the investigator must be well prepared before conducting the interview."[6] Preparation for this interview is more important than for an interview with any other offender type; it should also be conducted in a more formal setting, such as at the police station. The detective should be dressed professionally in a suit and tie, and when possible, should be as old as or older than the suspect and of a superior physical stature. Using rank or position such as "Detective Sergeant Jones" or "Special Agent Jones" is also an important image to establish as this offender is likely respond to the higher authority. This offender is extremely manipulative, a fairly good judge of character, and is generally able to size up a person very quickly. Therefore, the detective must always appear confident, in total control of the situation, and must conduct the interrogation in a more formal manner. If the detective ever allows the interrogation to devolve into a casual conversation or tries to befriend the suspect, the results will prove to

---

[5] A Greek dramatist, 484–406 BC.
[6] Hazelwood, R. R., Dietz, P. E., & Warren, J. (1992). The criminal sexual sadist. *FBI Law Enforcement Bulletin, 61,* 12–20.

be problematic, because the offender will begin to lose respect for the detective and might begin to manipulate the detective and try to take control over the interrogation.

Anger excitation offenders or sexual sadists are generally more intelligent and engage in fantasy more than any other offender type, so their crimes are often extremely well planned out, including their response to police if ever brought in for questioning. They actually believe they are intellectually superior to the police, and regardless of the evidence you may have against them, will very likely waive their rights and speak about the incident. They have an exaggerated self-image, and may believe they will obtain more information from the police than they will provide to them. Because they are so egotistical and self-centered, they love being the center of attention, so we need to be prepared for a very lengthy interview. They will have a plan of how they will respond to the police and any evidence against them. If caught in a minor discrepancy they will try to ignore it or claim police misunderstanding of their previous statement. However, their well-thought-out plan is actually their weakness, because they are very rigid and tend to stay with their plan or story even when it seems to be failing. Therefore, the key to these offenders is to disrupt or knock holes in their plan/story. If we can do this, they are likely to make major mistakes because, while they are good at making plans, they are not very adept at improvising or thinking on their feet.

These offenders will favorably respond to compliments about how important they are, but are likely to respond very negatively to any criticism; even the smallest slight may cause them to veer away from the main topic. The detective should act as if he is actually learning from the offender or that the offender is teaching him something; this increases these offenders' natural tendency to talk, because they see themselves as being in a superior position. The goal is to keep them talking to give them an opportunity to vent or express themselves; this may take an extended time investment, so we need to be prepared. However, these offenders can and will talk themselves into jail, and detectives need to be prepared to listen, because this love of hearing themselves talk, being the center of attention, and their belief they are smarter than the detective is their downfall. Open-ended questions are their favorite because it allows them to continue talking, many times about anything but the incident. The detective must be strong enough, however, to maintain control and keep the interview focused on the incident instead of wandering to other subjects.

Using a bluff or false evidence with anger excitation offenders should only be attempted in limited circumstances and masked with as much undeniable truth as possible. They are more intelligent, their offenses are typically more planned out, and they tend to be better prepared than any other offender. Therefore, they generally have taken steps to limit or eliminate leaving behind forensic evidence at the scene. They are typically in absolute control at the scene and with the victim and they know what they have done to avoid leaving evidence behind. They are also liable to have taken the time to self-educate themselves in police tactics and procedures such as crime scene investigation and forensic science. This information is likely used during their planning of the incident and in efforts to clean up the scene and avoid arrest. So, bluffs are very difficult to run on these offenders and therefore should be carefully constructed and woven with enough truth to be plausible; if they realize you are bluffing and you have no real evidence linking them to the crime, they are likely to spend the rest of the interview just giving you a hard time.

Caution

This is not an offender with whom to "wing it." Do not start an interview without being prepared with all of the case facts and knowing exactly what information you are trying to get from the interview. These offenders will be sizing up the detective throughout the interview and looking for any weak points, and if they find them, they will try to take control of the interview and manipulate the detective into safer areas. However, if the offender is ever caught in the act or we do have undisputable evidence of their guilt, a more direct approach can be used with much greater success.

Opportunistic

Opportunistic offenders are somewhat different than other sex offenders, primarily because by definition, opportunistic offenders are not typically sex offenders. They usually commit their sexual assaults during the commission of other crimes, and many times the rape itself is not planned. It is often the case that the opportunity presented itself and the offender committed an additional crime. Therefore, it may be difficult to talk about the sexual assault without talking about the other offenses, and not possible to talk about the other offenses without eventually talking about the sexual assault. Because of their criminal diversity, it is also very likely that these offenders have more extensive police experience than many other "regular sex offenders," and are probably much more acquainted with the legal process, including previous incarceration. This also means they may understand very well how rapists are treated in the prison system by other prisoners. Thus, for this offender type, greater success is likely to be found by first concentrating on the dominant crime prior to initiating questions on the sexual assault. We want to make sure we have all of the facts and the real motive behind the original crimes before we move onto aspects of the sexual assault.

Typically, these offenders will go out of their way to avoid being labeled as a sex offender, and will respond to efforts to *minimize* their acts or participation in the sexual assault, such as emphasizing that the sexual offense was out of the ordinary for them and their other crimes. Therefore, the offender is not "really" being considered as a "regular sex offender," but rather as a criminal who got carried away, made a mistake, committed a one-time incident never to be repeated, or was simply in a situation where the offender (as a man) was unable to stop his "lust." These offenders would be accepting of any efforts to minimize this aspect of their crime.

Partners or Gang Rapists

Gangs

As mentioned earlier, the main goal for the interview of multiple offenders is to identify the *group leader* and the *reluctant participant* and then the remaining suspects and their exact criminal participation in the assault. We want to interview the reluctant participant first, primarily because this is the person who did not want to be there or knew what was happening was wrong. And because the reluctant participant recognizes that what happened was wrong, this is the person who is most likely to provide information as to what exactly happened and who else was involved. This does not mean this interview is going to be easy, because the reluctant participant is part of a criminal gang or group of close friends and may feel some loyalty and be afraid of being labeled a "snitch." These issues need to be overcome before aspects of the crime can be discussed. Detectives may have to use a combination of sympathy and empathy toward the victim along with *rationalization* as to why it is important to identify and arrest the other offenders and *minimize* their own possible participation in the event.

Once information is obtained from the reluctant participant, we can begin interviews with other participants based on those who were least culpable or participated in the least amount. The same tactic to *minimize* their participation and *project* blame onto the leader for their current legal situation works to great advantage to get the other members to begin to provide information. The last member would be the identified leader. By this time, it is likely several others would have already provided information against the leader, and a better picture of what happened during the incident would be known. If the other members of the group have already made admissions or confessions as to what happened, a much more direct approach can be used on the leader, including some direct accusations of his lead role in the affair. It is better to approach him as if we already have the information of what happened and have a very strong case against him. It is essential to give leaders the impression that the only way they can save themselves is to provide their side of the story and perhaps mitigate their participation.

Partners

Like other instances where criminals work together, the general idea is to attempt to pit one offender against the other and hope they will provide evidence against each other. In non-sex-related crimes, the strategy for partners is first to determine the nature of the working relationship between the partners. For example, determine if it is a case of two equal partners or if it is a case of a leader–follower type situation. If this is a case of equal partners, then the approach of trying to convince one partner to provide information against the other is often successful. In these situations, one team of detectives might interview one suspect while another team interviews the other, and the teams then convince each partner the other is providing information against him. This is generally very successful.

In instances where there is a leader–follower type situation, then typically efforts are made to interview the weaker follower first with the intent to turn him against the leader, who is probably more involved and more culpable than the weaker follower. Partner sex offenders are somewhat different because sex offenders do not often operate on an equal basis; between the partners there is always a leader and a follower. Basically, the personality of the leader will not allow someone else to be on his level and thereby exercise any *control* over his actions or fantasy. Although he may allow the follower to accompany him because the follower is needed or provides some assistance, there is definitely a leader and follower role. Although the same approach of interviewing both partners at the same time is a good tactic, it is important to remember that many times it is the leader of the two that may come forth and provide information against the follower; while the follower thinks he is protecting his partner by not talking or by denying the partner's participation in the incident.

▶ Offender Statements

One of our main goals of the offender interview/interrogation is to obtain the offender's version of events. A statement against self-interest or a confession is very powerful evidence and has long been established as one of the best pieces of evidence against a suspect. A confession statement should include the complete offender's version of events before, during, and after the event. Specifically, we want to know where the offender was before the incident, how he came into contact with the victim, what happened during the event, and what happened after the event. What we are looking for is not just a statement agreeing with our facts, but rather those specific events or portions of the statement that we can then go out and validate as being truthful.

This is a very critical point that is lost on many detectives, particularly those who are so dependent on a confession to resolve their case; that is, the suspect's confession is not the end of the investigation; rather, it is the start of even more investigative effort to substantiate every part of it.

Sketches

At some point after the offender begins to make admissions or has confessed to the crime, the detective should take the time to have the offender prepare a sketch or a graphic representation of the scene or events surrounding the incident. This means the offender is given a piece of paper and asked to prepare a sketch of the scene as they remember it. For instance, in cases where the offender had entered the victim's residence and assaulted the victim in her bedroom, the suspect is asked to sketch the bedroom of the victim and show in the sketch the location of the bed, other items of furniture inside the bedroom, and where the victim was located on the bed. This is another form of a confession or admission from the offender, produced by his own hand, and is going to be used not only to corroborate the victim's statement and crime scene examination, but also to help validate the overall voluntariness of the confession, admission, or interrogation process. Especially important is a sketch where the offender may diagram the entire scene as he remembers it and then indicate by placing an "X" over his entry point, and then place a dotted line on the sketch to indicate his route of travel from entrance point through the scene to the victim, and then his route out of the scene as he escaped. It is not unusual to note while the offender completes the sketch that he did things at the scene that were unknown to the police at the time of the crime scene examination. An example is the offender who describes a method of entry that was unknown to the police such as an unlocked window or that the door was unlocked, or he spent time walking through the house prior to accosting the victim, or after the rape he went looking for items to steal or had spent time cleaning himself off in the bathroom. One offender noted he had eaten some leftovers from the refrigerator prior to leaving. This fact was unknown by the police at the time of the scene examination but was later confirmed by the victim. It is not unusual after the interrogation and sketch for the detectives to return to the scene to attempt to collect other potential evidence. This type of information is invaluable because it is something that only the offender or someone who was actually at the scene would know about.

There are times when more details are provided by the offender from a sketch than from the confession or admission. A well-prepared sketch can be as valuable as any written admission or confession.

False Confessions

A tremendous amount of psychological pressure is generated through the interrogation process so the detective's tactics have to be carefully balanced with his attempts to gain admissions or a confession in order to avoid obtaining *false confessions* from persons who may be susceptible to that psychological pressure. There is a very real possibility of obtaining false confessions, and many persons throughout the last several years have been freed from prison based on DNA evidence that essentially proved they did not in fact commit the crime. However, what is very important is the number of these persons who had also confessed to a crime they had not committed. Therefore, our concern is not just obtaining a confession or admission from offenders, but also to substantiate, confirm, and validate their admissions or confession. It is imperative for all detectives to ensure the truthfulness of any suspect's confession, so every element of the confession must be checked and verified to have occurred as indicated by the offender. **Case Study 9-3** highlights this situation.

Case Study 9-3

During the course of an extensive interrogation, the suspect, with the help of the police detectives, began making admissions based on themes offered by the police. Eventually, the suspect began to confess and he made a statement. A short time later however, the police returned to the suspect because his statement did not conform to the scene or events, and the suspect again made a statement clarifying certain points. A short while later, the police returned a third time because the second statement also did not conform to the information they had, so the suspect made a third statement, this time covering all the points the police asked. Based primarily on the suspect's confession, he was convicted of murder. During his appeal, it was shown that the confession was more the product of the police than a statement from the suspect. One important note was that the murder weapon was a .38 caliber pistol that the police could never show the suspect ever possessed before the incident. They also could not explain what happened after the murder, even though the suspect was never out of the sight of a number of witnesses. At least five witnesses had also observed another man in the area who fled the scene right after the victim was shot. The police had ignored all of this other information and had concentrated solely on the suspect, determined to get a confession or admission from him.

This case study is an example of an overreliance of the confession by many detectives who may typically depend on a confession in order to solve their case. The result in this case was the wrongful conviction of the suspect.

One technique that has always worked to eliminate the possibility of a false confession is to obtain some piece of information from the offender that is unknown by the police but can be verified or substantiated. In the case study, this might have been where the suspect actually obtained the weapon and what happened to it after the murder. Since the police were never able to put the gun into his hand and the weapon was never recovered, this was critical information that was not asked for or satisfactorily answered. If an offender cannot provide independent information that only the suspect would know about the event, then it is very possible you do not have the right suspect. It is our job as detectives to both punish the offender and to exonerate the innocent.

▶ Conclusions

As with the victim interviews, interviewing sex offenders can be a very lengthy and stressful process, and it takes discipline and practice to remain nonaccusatory and seemingly unaffected when dealing with an offender engaged in some of the most deviant crimes known to man. Because of the powerful nature of confessions as evidence in court, the interrogation process and the various techniques used are going to be a focus of defense attorneys who will be looking for any perceived coercion or unethical conduct by the police.

▶References

Carney, T. P. (2004). *Practical investigation of sex crimes: A strategic and operational approach.* Boca Raton, FL: CRC Press.

Kebbell, M., Alison, L., Huren, E., & Mazerolle, P. (2010). How do sex offenders think the police should interview to elicit confessions from sex offenders? *Psychology, Crime, and Law, 16*(7), 567–584.

Napier, M. R. (2010). *Behavior, truth, and deception: Applying profiling and analysis to the interview process.* Boca Raton, FL: CRC Press.

Zulawski, D. E., & Wicklander, D. E., (2002). *Practical aspects of interview and interrogation* (2nd ed.). Boca Raton, FL: CRC Press.

CHAPTER TEN

The Crime Scene and Evidence[1]

The investigation of a sexual assault, like other violent crimes, begins with the initial notification to the police, which has great investigative value that is frequently not recognized by detectives. There are some important investigative questions that detectives should be concerned with answering; these initial questions should include but are not necessarily limited to:

- Who made the call?
- If the report was not made by the victim, then who was the caller? What is the caller's relationship to the victim?
- From where was the call made?
- When was the call made?
- What exactly was reported?
- Did the caller identify an offender?
- How was the report made—in person or by phone?
- Is there a recording of the call to 911?

One of the first automatic steps in all violent crime preliminary investigations should include obtaining a recording of the telephone notification received by the department or its 911 call centers for later review by the detectives. With the recording available, there is no doubt as to what exactly was reported to the police and often it is possible to hear such things as the tone of voice and excitability of the caller, and other background noises or voices that may prove to be important in later stages of the investigation. If there are background voices on the recording, then they are likely to be important witnesses that will need to be interviewed as well. The importance of the recording is being able to compare what was initially reported

---

[1] Much of the material in this chapter has been taken from Adcock, J. M., & Chancellor, A. S. (2013). *Death investigation*. Burlington, MA: Jones & Bartlett Learning. Used by permission.

on the phone to what was reported to the first responding police officer, and then what was later reported to the detectives during the victim interview. We are looking for consistency from the initial report all the way through the victim's interview. Consistency, as repeated many times in this text, should be seen as another example or form of corroboration of the victim. Additionally, if there are any inconsistencies between any of the reports, they need to be addressed and explained during the course of the investigation rather than in court.

Many times the initial report of the incident is not always made to the police, but instead to a friend, a relative, or directly to a medical facility when the victim is seeking medical treatment. This may seem to be *counterintuitive behavior* because we generally expect that if someone is a victim of a crime, the first persons to be notified would be the police. However, first reporting the incident to someone other than the police happens frequently enough that one should not to draw any inferences when it occurs. It need only be addressed and simply explained by the victim.

▶ First Responders

First responders are typically the first uniformed patrol officers to arrive at the scene. Their initial actions at the scene and how they react to the victim will often set the tone for the subsequent investigation. The first responder has three basic responsibilities: 1) Attend to the victim, 2) secure and protect the scene, and 3) gather the basic information about the assault and call for assistance.

Attend to the Victim

If the victim is not already at a hospital setting, then the first task is to quickly assess the physical wellbeing of the victim to determine his or her immediate medical needs and if emergency treatment of the victim is necessary. Once immediate medical needs are addressed, then the officer can start making other assessments such as any special needs based on language, cultural, mental, or physical impairment. If the victim is younger than 18 years of age, then the efforts will have to be made to contact his or her parents. Some jurisdictions have victim advocates available as part of a multidisciplinary approach to sexual assaults, and these advocates are trained to help the victim through the initial investigative process and may respond either to the scene or to the hospital. In jurisdictions without advocates, the initial responding officer should take the time and inform the victim of the general procedures of the preliminary investigation. This would include the need to conduct a crime scene examination to look for physical and forensic evidence, the need for the victim to have a medical examination, and the need for a detailed statement by the detectives. It is also important to explain the importance of not bathing, cleaning up, changing clothing, or even using the restroom until after the medical examination to prevent the loss of potential evidence.

We have been taught as a society to contact the police when we need help, so it is not unusual for the victim to form a bond with the first responder, particularly in especially violent incidents, because the first responder is like the cavalry who has responded to and rescued the victim. Many times a positive, professional, and compassionate response by the first officer will go a long way toward the victim's willingness to cooperate with the subsequent investigation and their final recovery. Remember, one of the chief concerns of many victims is the fear that he or she would not be believed if he or she made a report, so the first responder must remain supportive and nonjudgmental while receiving the report. A calm and empathetic demeanor will go a long way to reassure the victim. Other small gestures like offering to contact a family member or friend to meet the victim at the hospital, arranging for a someone to watch her children while she is examined and interviewed, or informing her that while at the hospital the detectives will need to take the clothing she is wearing for evidence and suggesting that a friend or family member bring a change of clothing with them so the victim can change at the hospital will go a long way in taking care of the victim.

Secure and Protect the Scene

This includes determining exactly where the offense took place, defining that scene, and quickly checking for any other persons remaining at the scene and for any fragile evidence. For instance, in some crimes that take place inside the victim's residence, the scene would include not just the location where the sexual assault took place, for example in the bedroom, but would also include the point of entry and exit, and any other location that the offender may have taken the victim to or may have gone himself, such as the bathroom or other rooms when looking for something to steal. If the victim is already aware that something is missing or knows the offender stole something from her residence, this is also very important to note. In situations where the incident may have taken place in a hotel or motel or some other building, the scene may have to be expanded to cover whatever escape route the offender may have used, such as the stairwell or elevator. Identifying the specific locations and protecting them for later examination are important first steps. Remember, it is always easier to collapse a scene when such a large area is not needed, but it may become difficult to expand a scene to take in additional area once the public or the media arrive on the scene. If the incident is not being reported at the scene, then the officer will need to determine the location of the incident and who is in control of that location. For instance, is the scene located at the victim's residence or the offender's residence, or some other location? The officer should pass this information on to his or her supervisors who can determine if another officer should be dispatched to the scene to secure it, pending the arrival of crime scene technicians or detectives.

Establish the Elements of the Crime and Call for Assistance

This is a limited inquiry to gather the basic facts of who, what, when, where, and how of the criminal act. If the incident is being reported at a medical facility or somewhere other than a private setting, then the officer needs to conduct the initial interview with the victim out of the public eye or somewhere she cannot be overheard or observed by others. This is an embarrassing ordeal for the victim and we want to ensure we do not add to the trauma by allowing others to hear any of the details of the incident. At this stage it is not necessary to get into great detail concerning the whole incident, but rather to determine the basic criminal offenses that were committed. This would include both physical and sexual assaults, if the offender broke into the house, or if he may have also stolen something from the victim or the scene. Other basic facts that need to be covered are the identification of the offender, if known, or at least a physical description or clothing description of the offender. Ask the victim to describe any vehicles that may have been seen or any vehicle that was involved in the incident in as much detail as possible. Also, ascertain if the victim has told anyone else about the incident besides the police; this is going to be a very important part of the follow-up investigation, so identifying these other potential witnesses is critical.

One very important fact to determine is *when* the offense took place. If it occurred contemporaneously with the call to police, then detectives or crime scene technicians may need to respond to process the scene and make arrangements for the victim's medical examination as soon as possible. However, if the initial complaint to police was delayed then any scene examination and the victim's own medical examination may become more problematic and the need for either is decided on a case-by-case basis by detectives assigned to the case. Generally, 72 hours is a standard timeframe in which the physical examination of the victim is still considered viable to collect evidence. Even if there is no forensic evidence, there still may be evidence of physical trauma that can be observed and documented during a physical examination. However, there have been cases where forensic evidence has been collected up to 96 hours after the event; therefore, this is a decision best made case by case by detectives and medical personnel based on the individual circumstances.

As mentioned previously, delayed reporting is quite common based on the shock of the incident and the victim's perceived shame, guilt, or humiliation. Although the delay may pose problems with the crime scene examination and subsequent investigation, this should not be a concern to the initial responding officer. Instead, the officer needs to remain sensitive to the victim and not give any impression the complaint is without merit or that he or she not being believed. It is difficult to outline all of the possible scenarios that influence the duties of the first responder. The key to these and other situations is to remain flexible and adjust to the particular situation and circumstances. Examples of other possible duties are described in the following sections.

Arrest Suspect if Still at the Scene

It is relatively uncommon for the offender to be present at the scene upon the arrival of the patrol officer. One possible exception includes incidents of marital rape, that is where a spouse has reported a sexual assault by her spouse who is also living at the same residence and who may still be at the residence when the victim makes her complaint. Other examples include the interruption of an assault in progress—literally catching the perpetrator in the act. For these types of incidents where a suspect or offender is taken into custody at the scene, or can be easily identified through eyewitnesses, the thrust of the preliminary investigation may be somewhat different. Our concern in this situation is twofold. First, to get the suspect out of the area and back to the station where he can be quickly interviewed, because his interrogation is going to be the major focus of the preliminary investigation. Our second concern is to get the suspect to a medical facility to collect the necessary biological samples (blood and DNA), obtain a physical examination, and collect any other potential forensic or trace evidence from her body or her clothing.

Identify and Separate Witnesses

If any witnesses are present at the scene—whether they are eyewitnesses to the event or may have interacted with the victim before or after the incident—they should be identified and separated. If it is not possible to separate them, then at least ask them not to discuss the event to keep them from comparing what each may have seen. It is important that witnesses only provide what they personally observed and not be influenced by others. Every effort should be made to identify anyone who came into contact or interacted with the victim before and/or after the incident as he or she may be an important witness who might provide potential corroborating evidence to the victim's statement.

Look Beyond the Scene

As an agency policy for incidents that take place within a residence, one patrol should respond to the scene and additional patrols should respond to the general area to look beyond the scene. These additional patrols should be looking for any vehicles driving away, anyone riding a bicycle, or even anyone walking in the area. Anyone observed in the area should be stopped and a field interview with the person should be conducted. This is especially important because some offenders may travel to the victim's residence by vehicle, bicycle, or even by walking and will make their escape in the same manner. In cases where the offender may have attempted a sexual assault, but for various reasons the assault was interrupted or not completed, it is not out of the question for some offenders to escape and then proceed over to another victim they had previously identified. So, while the police are responding to victim number one, the offender is actually on the way to assault victim number two. Anyone seen in the area as the patrol is en route to the initial report should be noted and, if possible, field interviewed for later contact by detectives. If no one is noted, then efforts should be made to note the vehicle descriptions and license plates of any vehicles located within the surrounding area. This effort to locate anyone in the area is particularly important when the event takes place in the early morning hours when normal traffic is limited. For those incidents that take place during the daytime with normal traffic, this may not be practical or possible.

Avoid Cross-Contamination

The interview and subsequent medical examination of the victim and offender are the responsibility of the detectives, but a major concern for the first responder is to avoid any potential cross-contamination of evidence. Steps taken to avoid cross-contamination include removing the suspect and when appropriate, the victim, from the scene as soon as practical. If the suspect or victim were found at another location, we generally would not want either of them brought back to the scene until they have been examined or the scene is processed to avoid any possible cross-contamination. These efforts to avoid cross-contamination may include transporting either the offender or victim in a police vehicle to the hospital or to the police station. Of course, they should never be transported together, but even when transported separately, they should never be transported using the same vehicle. At the hospital, the same examination room should not be used to examine the victim and offender. Until they have both been examined at the hospital and their clothing has been received as evidence, they should not even be interviewed using the same interview room at the police station. The rationale for this extra effort is to ensure any potential trace evidence such as hairs and fibers found on either the victim or offender cannot be argued by the defense to have been deposited on the other person's clothing through inadvertent or accidental means such as riding in the same car or even being interviewed in the same room prior to the evidence collection.

This is where the concept of *Locard's law* or the *theory of transference* becomes so important. Locard's law is the basis of modern crime scene examination and states a simple premise that whenever someone enters a scene, he brings something with him from the outside environment, such as any hairs or fibers and other items of trace evidence he may have on his clothing. A good example would be pet hair, lint, or dust from your residence or workplace that is routinely and unknowingly deposited on your outer clothing as you go through your normal life. As one enters another location or the crime scene, those same hairs, fibers, lint, and dust will naturally fall off into that other room or crime scene. Whenever you leave that other room or crime scene, you will also take something with you in the form of other hairs, fibers, or other items of trace evidence already inside the scene and now unknowingly attached to your clothing. Further, when two persons are in close personal contact with each other, such as during a violent assault, these same hairs and fibers are often exchanged between the two.

Case Study 10-1

A young girl was lured by a child molester to get into his truck to help him search for a lost puppy. The child did so but instead was driven to another location where the man removed her bathing suit, threw it onto the floorboards of his vehicle, and then began to fondle her. Afterward she was allowed to get dressed and he dropped her off a short distance from her house. The police were called to the victim's house and after her interview the bathing suit was collected as evidence. A short time later, a suspect was identified and his truck processed for evidence. Later laboratory analysis of the bathing suit discovered a number of carpet fibers that matched the carpet samples taken during the vehicle examination. In his police interview, the offender had denied touching the child or that she was ever in his truck. During his trial he could offer no explanation as to how the carpet fibers ended up on the child's bathing suit and instead tried to insinuate it was a result of cross-contamination caused by the police. However, the police were able to show that the child was actually interviewed at her house and the bathing suit was recovered and packaged immediately. The offender was interviewed and his truck examined approximately 10 days later, so there was no possibility of any accidental contamination. The man was later convicted of child molestation.

Case Study 10-1 highlights the importance of cross-contamination issues and should not be taken lightly. Remember, the defense attorney is not likely to challenge the forensic analysis of the evidence as much as the manner in which it was collected. Many times decisions to transport the victim or the offender are made very quickly without considering these potential problems. This is also one of the reasons we attempt to limit the number of persons entering and leaving the crime scene. Theoretically, everyone entering or leaving has a chance to introduce foreign hairs or fibers into the scene or remove something from the scene as they leave. Limiting the number of persons into the scene limits the chance of such contamination.

Brief Responding Detectives

One of the other chief responsibilities of the first responder is to record all of his actions and the times they occur, from when he was dispatched through his arrival at the scene and his actions, all the way up to the arrival of the detectives or crime scene personnel. Of special concern are the overall reactions of the victim, a brief explanation as to what happened, and any spontaneous statements or comments that may have been made by the victim or any witness, or anything else the first responders may have observed that could benefit the investigation. This information should be presented to the responding detective or be placed into his written report.

Upon arrival at the scene detectives now must evaluate the scene, and depending on the agency, will either begin to process the scene themselves or will call on their crime scene technicians to do so. The detectives also have some very important duties as well, including making arrangements for any significant witnesses to be interviewed and for necessary statements to be taken. They should also attempt to conduct canvass witness interviews to try to locate additional witnesses from around the scene.

▶The Canvass Interview

One of the most important investigative steps in the preliminary investigation is the canvass interview. Canvass interviews are conducted in and around the scene, including places of business or employment, for key actors in the case. The purpose is to gather information from those who may not have seen the incident itself, but we think may have heard something or seen something before or after the incident, or may know something about the crime, the victim, or offender. Some may be or become hostile, reluctant, or uncooperative witnesses; therefore, the right approach could make the difference between obtaining information and walking away with nothing. Another aspect of the canvass interview that cannot be overemphasized is the organization of the process. It is crucial that every effort is made to contact as many people in the surrounding area as possible. In instances where there is no answer to the door of a residence, a follow-up procedure needs to be in place that will insure contact is made with each and every one of these absentees.

Research by Wellford and Cronin[2] reported one of the key features of successful police departments in solving homicides is the ability of the department to conduct thorough, timely, and accurate canvass interviews. Although the cited study was designed around homicide investigations, the concept is essentially the same with sexual assault and other violent crimes. The canvass interview is essentially a fishing expedition looking for witnesses, and although it is often manpower intensive and time consuming, it is a vital step in a successful case resolution. One suggestion when conducting a canvass interview in a residential neighborhood is to look around for a sofa or easy chair, swing, or rocking chair sitting on a front porch as this generally means there was someone (usually elderly) who sat there all day long and probably saw something. This person who probably spends his or her time watching the happenings of the street and neighbors is generally an

---

[2] Wellford, C., & Cronin, J. (2000). Clearing-up homicide clearance rates. *National Institute of Justice Journal*. NCJ 181728.

excellent source of information. Spend some time with that person to find out what goes on in the neighborhood or other information about the victim or suspect. Many times the elderly are a wealth of knowledge about their area and the people who live there. This information not only reflects what happened that was unusual but also that which could be considered normal, such as the neighbor's boyfriend coming by, the people who walk the street every day at the same time, delivery people, and so on. The importance of canvass interviews cannot be overemphasized. Unfortunately, this is often a weak point in preliminary investigations because inexperienced detectives do not understand the value of an all-out effort to locate other potential witnesses. This is one of the first areas the case detective or supervisor should review and make certain that a good effort is made to gain additional evidence or identify other witnesses.

The remainder of a preliminary investigation of sexual assaults is traditionally conducted simultaneously in three parallel tracks consisting of *the victim, the suspect,* and *the crime scene.* In a perfect world this would mean three separate detectives responding to work the investigation one concentrating on each track. Unfortunately, we do not live in a perfect world and quite frequently detectives are called upon to conduct all three tracks as best they can.

▶ The Crime Scene

Many times the only thing separating a criminal from being held responsible for his actions is a good crime scene examination and subsequent follow-up investigation. The crime scene examination is as important to sexual assaults as it is for homicides and other serious crimes. For all crimes, the crime scene is perhaps the only instance in which both the victim and the offender, for whatever period of time, were together at one location. Therefore, it is the most logical place to find physical evidence linking all three—victim, offender, and location—together.

Legal Considerations

Generally, there are very few legal problems conducting a crime scene examination when the incident takes place within the victim's residence her vehicle, or in an open area with no right to privacy. The victim only needs to give consent to perform the examination, or in the case of those incidents that take place in open areas, there is no warrant requirement. However, in other incidents that may take place in the offender's residence or vehicle, or in other places that are under the control of another, then a search warrant is required. This is based on three Supreme Court decisions. This concept was initially decided in *Mincey v. Arizona,*[3] and has been reiterated and refined in

---

[3] *Mincey v. Arizona,* 437 U.S. 385 (1978).

Thompson v. Louisiana[4] and *Flippo v. West Virginia*,[5] Although these three cases dealt specifically with homicide investigations, it is clear from these Supreme Court decisions that there is no *crime scene exception* to the search warrant requirement. Where this might become an issue are cases of marital or domestic rape where the offender may cohabitate with the victim and therefore may have the same right to privacy as the victim over the scene. In these incidents, obtaining a search warrant is the better answer before conducting the examination and may eliminate any defense arguments to suppress the potential evidence because it was obtained without the suspect's consent.

It is important to note these decisions do not mean the police cannot enter a scene to protect life, arrest suspects if they are still present, remove others to protect the scene, and do a general walkthrough to make sure there are no safety issues or that there are no other persons remaining at the scene and then to secure the location. These limited actions would be considered appropriate under emergency or exigent circumstances. However, once the scene has been secured and there is no other danger of evidence being damaged or destroyed, then the police must apply for a warrant before processing the scene. Obtaining a warrant or consent for the examination is normally the responsibility of the responding detective, not the crime scene technician.

Crime Scene Examination

Crime scene examination for sexual assaults is not always pursued in the same vigorous manner as for other violent crimes. Many times this is based on a false perception that the vast majority of evidence is going to be found on the victim or suspect and thus likely recovered during the medical examination. So, there is sometimes a hesitancy to look at the scene as anything more than a "check the block" exercise or something that must be done because of agency protocol instead of a real effort to locate and collect physical evidence. This is a false belief and the crime scene should be examined in the same manner and purpose we do every other violent crime scene. The detailed, step-by-step technical aspects of crime scene examination, documentation, and proper evidence collection cannot be fully covered here. This particular subject has become so technical that dozens of textbooks are devoted to nothing but scene examinations and various aspects of forensic science. Instead, this chapter provides an overview of some of proper scene examination techniques and important general concepts that can be applied to nearly every crime scene regardless of the crime.

One key to conducting any crime scene examination is to have an understanding of what has supposedly occurred. This concept is especially important in conducting these particular scenes, because throughout the examination, in addition to documenting the scene and collecting evidence,

---

[4] *Thompson v. Louisiana*, 469 U.S. 17 (1984).
[5] *Flippo v. West Virginia*, 528 U.S. 11 (1999).

we are also looking for consistency; that is, evidence that the scene or physical evidence matches what the victim is alleging took place. Consistency found at the scene is another form of corroboration for the victim and can be as valuable as other items of physical evidence. Therefore, if the victim says the offender forced entry into her house, then obviously we are looking for some signs of forced entry. If the victim says she was attacked in her bed, then we are going to focus attention on the bed. Everything that we find within the residence that matches the victim's story is a *consistency*. Things found at the scene that do not match or that directly contradict the victim's initial statement need to be reported back to the detective as soon as possible so they can be addressed; hopefully, these conflicts can be clarified during the victim's initial interview if possible. If they are not addressed during the initial interview then they will need to be addressed later with the victim.

Process the Scene the Same Way Every Time

There is a long-standing argument between police professionals on aspects of the crime scene examination of sexual assaults and whether or not it is necessary to conduct the scene examination. This conflict usually comes into play based on a prior or current relationship between the victim and suspect, such as when the victim and the offender may have engaged in consensual sex at the same location in the past or in cases of marital rape which may take place in the marital bed where generally both husband and wife sleep. In both instances it is logical to assume that there may be DNA evidence or other trace evidence such as body or pubic hairs from the offender left behind prior to this particular incident during a previous consensual act. The value of such evidence may be problematic since forensic evidence cannot determine if they were deposited during a consensual act or during a forced act, or when exactly they were deposited. However, it is important that a scene be processed in the same way every time based upon the general concept that: "*It is better to have the evidence and not need it, than to need the evidence and not have it.*"

For instance, in the case of marital rape, when a husband rapes his wife and it takes place in the marital bed, it is assumed consensual marital sex has also taken place there. The question is always: Is there any value to the crime scene examination? Maybe not, but what if the husband and wife were estranged, had no consensual relations for a period of time prior to the incident, or no longer shared the marital bed? Now such forensic evidence may help establish evidence of the incident. Unfortunately, we do not always have this information in the preliminary stages of the investigation while the scene is being processed so we do not know how any item of evidence is going to fit into the subsequent investigation. Therefore, the scene should be processed in the same manner every time; if the evidence is later determined not to have any value then it can be disposed of or returned.

There is another reason to process the scene in the same manner every time. This is due to the heightened public awareness of crime scene processing techniques and forensic science from popular TV shows on this subject, such as *CSI: Crime Scene Investigation, Cold Case, Forensic Files*, and many other modern police dramas. Based on these shows, juries now expect to see much of what they have seen on TV presented to them in court. This is known as the "*CSI* effect," and it has created problems across the United States in a significant number of prosecutions when the jury was basically disappointed in the manner in which the scene was processed. These issues have led to the acquittal of criminals despite some good physical evidence linking them to the scene. Most defense attorneys are aware of this phenomenon as well and will take advantage of any half measures taken by the police in this area. Their goal is to imply their client was identified based on an incomplete or unprofessional police investigation.

The Crime Scene Examination Is an Opera, Not a Slam Dance

A crime scene is not just about taking pictures and throwing fingerprint powder around. Like an opera, the crime scene examination should be processed step-by-step, based on an established and organized plan. Consider the opera—it is performed within a set program of music, singing, and stage movements. It is well organized and scripted, and if the same opera were to be preformed the following evening, it would have the same music, singing, stage movements, and timing. The crime scene examination generally takes place along a similar basic program of events, with minor exceptions due to the particular dynamics of each scene. For example, before any examination of the scene takes place, it should be videotaped, photographed, and sketched before anything is touched or moved. Only after the scene is documented does the search for evidence begin. The practice of following a set program and order of events is seen in our search for forensic or latent evidence. There is generally a particular order in which we search for and collect forensic and latent[6] evidence. Typically, we search for trace and biological evidence before we begin to search for latent prints and before introducing any chemicals or other potentially damaging examinations to the scene. The idea is to collect all those possible items of evidence that are readily observable and collectable before introducing any foreign substances to the scene.

A Crime Scene Examination is a Marathon, Not a Sprint

There is, within reason, no time limit to processing a scene. Therefore, there is no need to pressure or hurry the crime scene technicians to complete their task and no reason to neglect specialized examinations or analysis if warranted. Sometimes this is a particularly difficult concept to teach and enforce because we, as Americans, tend to be rather impatient and therefore seek instantaneous answers and results. Even worse, many of us believe crime scene examination is like what we see on television—important evidence should be readily observable and found immediately. The reality is

---

[6] Latent evidence refers to something hidden or not visible to the naked eye. A fingerprint is a good example that might be visible only after application of fingerprint powder.

that crime scene examination may take several hours to several days, and in some cases even longer. It all depends on the scene and the amount of evidence that is contained in the scene, so the marathon versus sprint analogy essentially reminds us we are under no time constraints and should never hurry through the processing of a scene. We do need to balance this concept of taking our time with the fact that the scene may be at the victim's residence and therefore we want to be able to make it available to her as soon as practical.

Burned Bridges

This concept deals with movement of things inside a crime scene, and it essentially expresses an understanding that once an object is picked up or moved it can never be placed back exactly where it was when it was first found. Thus, by picking up an item of evidence or moving the body, we have "burned the bridge" of the scene integrity. The item in question can be placed close to where it was, but never *exactly* where it was. No object or item of evidence should ever be touched or picked up until it has been thoroughly documented through photography and measurements for the crime scene sketch; it should only picked up when you are ready to collect it as evidence. In other words, the one and only time an item of evidence should be picked up or moved is when it is collected as evidence. Once the item has been documented and picked up, then it should be properly packaged and removed from the scene and any chance of contamination.

Behavioral Evidence

The scene examination should not just be about picking up physical and forensic evidence; instead, we should also be looking at the scene for what else we can learn about the offender, because these types of events provide a great deal of offender behavioral evidence. This concept is best described in **Box 10-1**.

BOX 10-1 Behavioral Evidence at the Crime Scene

The crime scene is the one place offenders tell us all about themselves, such as their age, intelligence level, maturity, criminal sophistication, criminal experience level, and their goal or motivation for the crime. Unfortunately, we are not always listening to what they have told us about themselves.

One of the best examples of displayed offender behavior is a case in which an offender has committed a residential burglary in order to gain access to the victim. In addition to other physical evidence, we would be looking for how the offender was able to commit the crime, such as how he gained entrance to the residence and victim. We are basically looking to identify the *modus operandi* (MO), which is basically translated as the *mode of operation* or *how* the offender was able to commit the crime. This also includes what method, tools, or approach to the victim were used. Based on the totality of events as described by the victim and observed at the scene, we are looking to answer some very important questions including those listed in **Box 10-2**.

BOX 10-2 Questions About the Offender's MO

- How prepared was the offender to commit the offense?
- Did he bring his own tools, weapons, or other items with him or did he use whatever he happened to find at the scene?
- Did he take these things away with him or did he leave them in place?
- What precautions did he take to prevent his discovery or aid in his escape?
- Did he make an effort to avoid being identified such as wearing a mask or gloves, or placing something over the victim's eyes or head to keep her from seeing?
- Was physical and forensic evidence found or not?
- Was the offender able to control the victim or was there difficulty in controlling the victim?
- What was the criminal sophistication or experience level of the offender?
- Were there other crimes committed such as theft or robbery? If so, what was the dominant crime?
- What stands out as being odd or unusual?
- What stands out as actions by the offender that were unnecessary to committing the crime or to facilitating his escape?

Answering these types of questions can tell us a lot about the offender. The level of organization and preparedness of the offender can be an indication of his intelligence and maturity level. This is seen in efforts to hide his appearance and may also indicate a higher degree of criminal experience. The ability to control a victim is often seen as an example of self-confidence or criminal sophistication. Answering these questions may also identify his MO, which we may use to link the offender to similar cases. However, we must remember that an MO is basically learned behavior, and therefore we should expect an MO to change or evolve as the offender gains additional experience from committing other crimes. For instance, with a serial offender, we should expect a change in MO about every 6 weeks or so as he gains experience or develops new techniques.

Examining offender behavior at the crime scene may also tell us a lot about his personality characteristics, much in the same manner as we learned from the behavior-orientated interview technique we used with the victim. This is important because there is a big difference between an offender who plans the crime, brings necessary tools and weapons he will need with him, makes an effort to prevent discovery of his identity, and attempts to leave no physical or forensic evidence behind compared to an offender who appears to act on impulse, was not prepared to commit the crime and must use items from the scene to assist him, makes no effort to hide his identity, or does not appear to be concerned with leaving behind physical or forensic evidence. These recognized crime scene behaviors when combined with other information from the victim interview, will help paint a fairly accurate picture of the type of offender involved in the incident. In addition to the MO aspect of the crime, or the "how" the offender was able to commit the crime and escape, we are interested in offender behavior that is known as the *signature aspect*.[7] The signature aspect refers to offender actions and behavior that go beyond what is necessary to commit the crime and may provide the "why" of the crime. The signature tends to be more individualistic behavior and is more reflective of the offender's own unique personality, goals, and motivation. Although a signature may evolve somewhat over time, the basic theme tends to stay the same. Therefore, we always need to look for the signature aspect to link cases together, because it is likely to remain the same whereas the MO may change whenever the offender is confronted with a new set of circumstances. **Box 10-3** outlines the differences between MO and signature in a particular scenario.

BOX 10-3 Differences Between MO and Signature

The offender surprised the victim by suddenly placing his hand over her mouth to prevent her from calling out and then placed a knife against her throat to seek her compliance. He further threatened to harm her sleeping child if she resisted, but promised not to harm her if she did what she was told. Once the victim was compliant and offered no further resistance, the offender instructed her to undress and then put on a red nightgown and pair of red high heels he had brought with him. Once she had complied with his demands he put on a condom and initiated his sexual assault but made demands for her to repeat certain phrases as he engaged in vaginal sex with the victim. After ejaculating he placed the condom into a paper bag he had brought and then retrieved the clothing and shoes and placed them back into the bag he had brought with him to carry the items. He then instructed the victim not to move for 20 minutes. The offender then departed. Crime scene investigation noted the point of entry was an opened window in another room and the offender had departed through the front door.

In this scenario the offender's entrance and exit from the residence and his approach to the victim would all be considered as part of his MO, since his actions all dealt with *how* he was able to enter and escape, gain and maintain control over the victim, and obtain compliance to his demands. The use of a condom was also evidence that he tried to avoid leaving any evidence behind. However, aspects of the sexual assault such as making the victim dress in red nightgown, wear high heels, and making her repeat certain phrases to him are aspects of his *signature*, because they had nothing to do with committing the crime, avoiding leaving evidence, or making his escape. Making the victim change clothing or put on certain objects or to repeat certain phrases during the sexual assault are things that are much less likely to occur with

---

[7] Douglas, J. E. & Munn, C. (1992, February). Violent crime scene analysis: Modus operandi, signature, and staging. *FBI Law Enforcement Bulletin*.

other offenders. Instead, these are examples of the uniqueness of the *signature* and why we want to concentrate on the signature, when available, to link different instances together.[8]

For crime scene examinations there must be a concerted effort to completely document and examine the scene for physical and forensic evidence, but there is also a need to fully examine and document the various aspects of the MO and possible signature aspects noted at the scene.

Scene Documentation

As with other crime scenes, efforts should be made to fully document the scene through photography, which should document the area we normally would for any other type scene. It is important to note the scene should be first photographed in its entirety before anything is added to the scene such as evidence tents. **Figures 10-1** and **10-2** demonstrate this point. Figure 10-1 shows the scene and potential evidence on the floor as it was initially found. Figure 10-2 is the same scene once evidence tents have been placed on those items of evidence identified by the crime scene technician. Then, close up photographs of each item as identified or marked by evidence tent should be taken as documented in **Figure 10-3**.

FIGURE 10-1 Initial photograph at the crime scene before any processing takes place. This is also known as an overall scene photograph.

[8] Hazelwood, R. R., & Burgess, A. W. (2008). *Practical aspects of rape investigation: A multidisciplinary approach* (4th ed.). Boca Raton, FL: CRC Press.

FIGURE 10-2 Important items of evidence are marked with evidence tents. This is also known as an evidence establishment photograph.

FIGURE 10-3 A close up photo of the evidence. A close up photo may be necessary for smaller items to fully depict the item as it was found.

This is an important aspect of general crime scene investigation that is frequently overlooked or skipped. Instead, the first action upon entering the scene is often to immediately begin placing evidence tents on the visible evidence and then stop to photograph the scene, but not always taking individual photographs of each particular item of evidence. As a general rule, if you have used an evidence tent to mark or identify a particular piece of evidence, you should take an individual close-up photograph of that item, with another close-up photograph that includes a measuring device. Special photographs may also be taken to focus attention on specific areas of the scene and specific pieces of evidence. For instance, in **Figures 10-4** and **10-5**, the victim, a 12-year-old female, reported that her male relative would come into her room and stand next to her bed and masturbate while she slept. She reportedly observed him on several occasions but was too frightened to say anything. The scene was initially photographed as depicted in Figure 10-4 and then searched using an alternate light source. Suspected semen stains were found in the carpet and were marked using the yellow markers and then re-photographed to depict the location of those stains. In this case, evidence tents were too big to be used and were confusing as to the location of each stain, so the yellow markers were used instead.

FIGURE 10-4 Photo of scene as it was initially found.

FIGURE 10-5 Plastic markers are used to identify suspected semen stains on the carpet.

Scene documentation also includes a written report reflecting the technician's observations of the scene and should include those facts that may not be discernable in photographs, such as the time of day, odors, indoor or outdoor temperatures, or other weather conditions.

Search for Evidence

Like other crimes of violence, searching for trace evidence is a large part of the crime scene examination. Even when offenders make a concerted effort to avoid leaving trace evidence at the scene such as wearing gloves, using a condom, or making the victim clean up afterward, this does not mean they are always successful. Hairs and fibers may be transferred, and bodily fluids such as saliva or blood may be deposited at the scene. Even in instances when a condom was used, semen may come out of the condom as it is removed and be deposited onto the victim or other object; we call this *spillage*, and this may occur despite the best efforts of the offender not to leave evidence behind.

The first step to locating trace evidence is to attempt to visually locate evidence by simply taking your time and looking over the area with the naked eye. It is surprising how much can be seen without any assistance if one takes the time to look closely and carefully. Items that are observed should be photographed, added to the crime scene sketch, and then collected as they are found. It is important when dealing with hairs and fiber-type evidence that they are collected as soon as they are found to ensure they are not lost if a sudden breeze or other air movement causes them to be disturbed and accidentally moved onto the ground and lost.

The visual search then progresses by employing a simple light source such as a flashlight and using oblique lighting techniques. Oblique lighting is simply directing a light source nearly parallel across the surface of an object. This helps to create a contrast and exposes much minute detail that is unobservable when the light is focused straight down. A good example is footwear impressions that are very difficult to observe when a light is shone directly onto the floor, but are relatively easy to observe when the light is shone at an oblique angle. It is the same with hairs, fibers, and most biological stains, which are often easy enough to observe using a regular flashlight.

Alternate light sources are also very effective in locating fibers and biological stains, which may not be visible with the naked eye or other normal light sources. Ultraviolet (UV) light is especially suited to locating semen at the scene, because it will fluoresce. Photographs of the stain can be taken without a flash or the need for any other special filters or equipment.

Additional photographs can be taken when suspected biological stains are found. In **Figures 10-6** and **10-7** are close ups of a towel from the motel room that was initially identified in Figures 10-1, 10-2, and 10-3. The yellow markers on each photo are used to point to potential stains that were observed on the item as it was being collected. Based on this observation, the towel was spread out and an alternate light source was then used to view the suspected stains. **Figures 10-8** and **10-9** show the stains using an alternate light source set at 450 nm and using an orange filter over the camera lens. The stains are consistent with the offender using them to clean himself off after he had assaulted the victim. Notice the photos also captured the evidence tents so there is no doubt as to which item was being photographed.

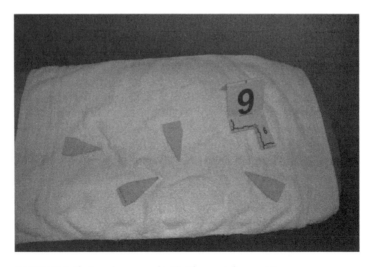

FIGURE 10-6 Plastic markers are used to identify suspected semen stains.

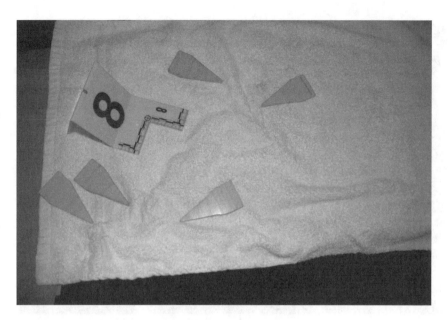

FIGURE 10-7 Plastic markers are used to identify suspected semen stains.

FIGURE 10-8 The towel is viewed using an alternate light source and special filter over the camera lens. The stains are readily seen when using this technique.

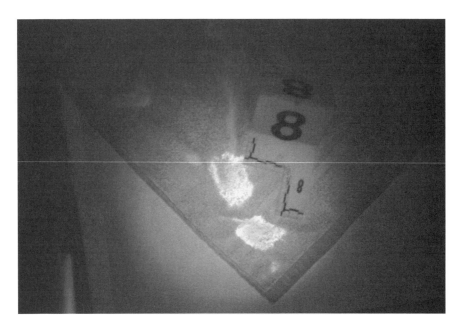

FIGURE 10-9 The towel is viewed using an alternate light source and special filter over the camera lens. The stains are readily seen when using this technique.

Collection of Evidence

In the past, evidence technicians were trained to simply collect certain items such as bed sheets, pillowcases, blankets, or other bedding items and submit them to the crime lab for the examination and collection of any trace or biological evidence. However, currently most crime labs do not accept such large items because of the amount of storage space they require. Instead, technicians are now expected to conduct some of the initial examination of these larger items at the scene and collect those readily visible or identifiable items of evidence and submit them for examination. This does not mean that larger items such as bedding are no longer collected if deemed important, but the crime laboratories are simply overwhelmed with the amount of evidence submitted and are not always able to accept such large items for examination. Laboratories prefer to do many examinations in stages by following what is known as the *best evidence* concept; that is, the laboratory will prioritize the evidence submitted in each case and examine items in what they believe will give the best evidence for the least amount of time and cost. For instance, the sexual assault kit from the victim is believed to provide the *best evidence* that can link the suspect to the victim, generally through DNA analysis. If the DNA is unsuccessful, then the remainder of the kit is examined for fingernail scrapings for possible DNA. If those efforts are unsuccessful, they will then proceed with the personal clothing of the victim and suspect; first their underwear, then their outerwear, and then any hair and fiber evidence. If examination of the clothing is also unsuccessful, only then are they likely to accept or even look at the bedding for any additional forensic evidence.

However, if at the scene the technician has found what they believe to be biological stains as depicted in Figures 10-8 and 10-9, the lab is likely to first go to those exhibits and complete their analysis. In the case with the towels (Figure 10-8 and 10-9), they were actually small enough items to be submitted directly to the laboratory for examination. In other instances, it is necessary to collect the stain off the medium where it is found. There are two basic methods to collect a stain from a medium. The first is to remove the entire stain by cutting it out of whatever it is on and packaging the whole stain. This works best if the stain is on some type of fabric or medium that is easily removed. The more accepted method is to collect the stain using a cotton swab dampened by a few drops of distilled water. The wet swab is placed onto the stain and in a circular motion the stain is swabbed, and the potential biological matter is then transferred to the cotton swab, which is air dried and then submitted as evidence. The cotton swab is the most widely used and most accepted method of collecting biological stains, including blood. Cotton swabs and/or other biological stains should be air dried and then placed into a paper container, and never placed into a plastic bag or container. One important thing to remember when collecting biological samples is to avoid potential contamination of the samples. We avoid contamination by making sure each biological sample is collected using a clean pair of gloves. If a cutting instrument is used to cut out a stain it should only be used once and then discarded, and the collector should wear a mask or a face guard and avoid breathing, coughing, or sneezing during the collection process. It is not unheard of to find the crime scene technician or the detective's DNA when evidence is processed at the lab. This of course calls the entire collection effort into question and gives something for the defense to counter any potential damaging forensic evidence with.

Biological evidence and DNA analysis are perhaps the best forensic tools we have to positively link the victim, suspect, and scene together. But, there has been a tendency in recent years to concentrate so much attention on this one aspect of crime scene examination that some valuable evidence may not be collected or is intentionally ignored. In teaching crime scene courses, it is not an infrequent comment by detectives or even crime scene technicians that once they find a suspected semen stain at the sexual assault crime scene or are informed a semen stain has been found on the victim's clothing or during her medical examination, they tend to bypass or ignore the other evidence such as hairs and fibers. The general thinking was, since DNA is a more positive means to link a suspect to the scene or victim, then there was no need to continue searching or collecting other evidence and thus they could reduce their time spent at the scene. This has created an overreliance on DNA analysis to solve crime. If the laboratory analysis comes back with a good DNA profile then detectives may be successful in linking the suspect to the scene or to the victim. However, it is also just as likely for the lab to report they were unable to produce a suspect profile or were unable to produce a complete profile based on contamination or other factors we may not be aware of at the time the stain was collected. Even worse, the stain we believed was the suspect's might later be determined to be that of a previously unknown consensual partner deposited some time before the incident. In such cases, attention would then be given to other types of trace evidence such as hairs and fibers, provided they were collected during the examination. But, we could be at a loss to link a suspect to the scene if the other trace evidence was not collected as well. As mentioned earlier, this is another example of why we should be processing the scene in the same way every time, even when we believe we have found semen or another biological stain. DNA is a fantastic forensic tool and its use and development is continuing, but it is not the end all to forensics or crime scene examination.

Collection of Standards

When dealing with hairs and fibers, it is important not just to collect any hairs or fibers that may be present at the scene, but also to make sure we collect standards from the remainder of the environment. Using a house as an example of a crime scene, we would want to collect fiber standards from all carpets in the house. If there are domestic animals in the house, then a standard of each of their hair or fur is needed as well. These standards are necessary in anticipation of searching the suspect's clothing, vehicle, or residence for any possible transference of fibers from the scene to the offender. In cases that take place inside a family home or inside a family car, it may be necessary to obtain hair and DNA samples from other family members who occupy the house or are routinely inside the vehicle. These may be needed to compare and eliminate any hairs found at the scene. It may also prove important to identify and compare any hair that may be found on the suspect's clothing, vehicle, or residence.

It is also necessary to obtain standards from the victim and suspect, and generally these samples are collected during their medical examination and are contained within the rape kit. Other standards, particularly DNA samples, may be needed from others in certain circumstances such as someone who has previous consensual sexual relations in the same bed. In those instances, it may be necessary to collect standards from anyone who may have had consensual sex with the victim as well.

For hairs and fibers recovered from a suspect or victim, the value is twofold. First, how common is that particular fiber? The more common the fiber the less important it will be because the chance of coming into contact with it is greatly increased. Obviously, the more uncommon the fiber the greater evidential value it holds because the chance of accidentally picking up that fiber may be reduced. The same thing with hairs; if they can be linked back through forensic examination to the victim or suspect, then it is going to be much more valuable evidence than hair that cannot be further linked to another person. Secondly, it is very important to note where exactly the hairs or fibers were recovered. It is very easy to transfer hairs and fibers onto outer clothing. It can happen even during innocent contact with another person, walking through a particular area, or while riding in a vehicle. It is somewhat more problematic to find foreign hairs and fibers in a person's underclothing because generally the outer clothing would have to be removed or the under-clothing exposed in order for hairs and fibers to be deposited there. It is far more significant if the hairs and fibers were found in a person's underclothing than on a person's outer clothing.

Search Beyond the Scene

After the crime scene technicians have documented the scene, completed their forensic examination, and have collected all of the visible physical and forensic evidence, it is recommended that an additional, more conventional search of the scene be conducted. This is sometimes known as a *search beyond the scene* and is designed to find additional physical or forensic evidence in the loca-tions away from the actual scene. For example, there are many instances when police have found the suspect's fingerprints on an item in the refrigerator or on a glass or other household items or on a countertop where the offender may have gotten something to drink, something to eat, or otherwise moved some household object. For incidents where the offender has forced entry into the victim's house, it is also very important to look outside the residence, particu-larly around windows or doorways where the offender may have watched the victim from outside. At different scenes, fingerprints on window ledges or windowpanes and door handles have been recovered. Because some offenders use an opened door or window to gain entrance, it is wise to look for prints even at closed windows or locked doors to see if the offender may have first tried that particular location before finding another way into the residence. Footwear impressions as well as cigarette butts have been found on the ground or in flowerbeds underneath a window. Even an offender's semen has been found on the exterior wall underneath a window where he had masturbated outside while watching the victim on previous occasions. These spots outside the victim's residence are often the second best location to obtain additional physical or forensic evidence and should not be overlooked.

Completion of Crime Scene Examination

At the completion of the crime scene examination and after the scene is released, if the scene was examined pursuant to a search warrant, it is now necessary for the detective to file a search warrant return in the same manner as other search warrants, advising the court of the items seized during the execution of the warrant. It is also important for the detective to coordi-nate with the crime scene technicians to have a clear understanding of all of the items of evidence that have been collected as well as a clear understanding of the potential forensic examination of that evidence at the crime lab. Evidence collected during the examination should be submitted expeditiously to the lab, as typically there is a long waiting list of cases pending examination, so it is beneficial to get the evidence into the queue as quickly as possible.

▶ The Victim Examination

For sexual assaults, the victim is also a very important source of evidence, because her body and clothing frequently contain physical and forensic evidence that are vital for a successful prosecution. However, we must make certain that the concept of the victim being a "crime scene" does not mean we forget that we are dealing with a human being who has been subjected to a severe traumatic experience. Although we want to recover the evidence from the victim, we do not want to cause any further emotional problems by our attitude or how we treat them. Therefore, it is important that we also take note of several other important issues that may play a part in how the victim perceives the process. One of the larger issues in the modern United States is the very different cultural issues that now confront us from the wide variety of immigrants present in the country. In earlier U.S. history, most immigrants were primarily European and their cultures were relatively similar to U.S. culture, so there were not many great cultural conflicts in terms of criminal investigation. However, with the influx of other immigrants from Asia, the Middle East, and the sub-Indian continent there has been a cultural shift in some areas of the United States. It is imperative that we understand that there may be some important religious or cultural conflicts for some victims, such as a general reluctance to discuss such personal matters with a male or increased modesty levels that may make victims with these backgrounds hesitant to undergo the medical examination. In these situations it may take some talking to the victim and sometimes her family to convince them of the importance of the examination and collection of evidence. Many times the medical personnel may be better suited to providing this explanation. In many instances, language barriers may hamper the ability to adequately convey these issues to the victim or her family; in these instances it is probably going to be necessary to contact a translator. Most large hospitals that serve diverse populations may already have identified translators who are available to assist.

For most hospitals it has become standard procedure to afford victims some greater sense of privacy when they arrive for examination, and the victim is often placed into a separate examination room and not forced to wait outside in the regular waiting room with other patients. This has not always been the case, but more and more this is the accepted practice. If a victim's advocate did not respond to the scene, then this is often when the *victim's advocate* or *rape crisis worker* will most likely respond and first make contact with the victim.

Victim's Advocate or Rape Crisis Worker

As stated earlier, victim's advocates should be seen as a "positive" for the detective in his investigation, and it is well to establish and then maintain a good working relationship with them. These workers are there specifically to attend to the needs of the victim and provide her with some degree of comfort and understanding. This allows the detective and police personnel to remain focused on their job and duties. The victim's advocate should pick up on the same theme as the initial responding police officer; that is, offering an explanation of the process and what is about to happen at the medical examination and the importance of collecting the evidence. Then, they will explain about the expected police interviews and then provide information on possible follow-up treatment. When a good professional relationship has been established between the victim's advocate and the detectives, we will see results in our subsequent victim interviews. It starts as the victim's advocate begins to explain the investigative process and the need for the victim to speak to detectives. Words of encouragement for the victim, reassurance to her of the professionalism and competence of the police detectives who will interview her, and the necessity for the victim not to hold back any details of the event will make a huge difference. The victim's advocate instills in the victim a sense of trust and confidence in the police even before she has a chance to meet them, and helps make establishing rapport with the victim easier for the detectives. Again, this takes time, training, and mutual trust of the two agencies to be able to work together in this manner. But, when this relationship is present, the resulting interviews are generally more productive and the victim will likely become a much better witness in court. With the advent of the Sexual Assault Nurse Examiner (SANE) program, much of the victim advocate's earlier responsibilities to monitor the forensic examination have diminished, but that does not mean they are not needed during the examination. When the victim's advocate is present, she can lend the emotional support necessary to help the victim and allow the SANE to remain neutral and objective in his or her evaluation and also allows the SANE to concentrate on the forensic examination rather than also be aware of the victim's emotional state.

It is unfortunate that many detectives do not take the time and energy to reach out, get to know, and even train with the victim's advocate. Even worse is when they turn their backs on victim's advocates or fail to appreciate the impact they can have on the victim's recovery and the case itself.

▶ SANE Program

One of the best developments in sexual assault investigations has been the SANE program, which is designed to better address the needs of the sexual assault victim in the emergency room and during the medical examination. Since its inception in the mid to late 1970s, the program has become an integral part of the multidisciplinary approach to conducting sexual assault investigations that incorporate the various aspects of the medical profession, social services, the police, the crime lab, and the prosecutor's office. This multidisciplinary approach is often referred to as the Sexual Assault Response Team or SART, which is a community response from various agencies to conducting sexual assault investigations with emphasis on addressing the needs of the victim after the incident.

The SANE[9] practitioners are essentially registered nurses with specialized forensic training in conducting sexual assault medical examinations and properly documenting and collecting forensic evidence. They can be the detective's best friends in the medical field or at the hospital emergency room. So, developing and maintaining a professional relationship with the SANE nurses is one of the more important things a detective can do if he wants to be successful in his investigations. The SANE program is a major fix of the earlier nightmares of how we used to conduct sexual assault investigations. Prior to the SANE program, the most difficult and frustrating aspect of the entire investigation was often trying to get the on-call ER doctor to perform a sexual assault examination of the victim when she was brought to the hospital. One would think that the victim in these circumstances would be a priority for examination based on her complaint and what happened to her. Unfortunately, this was not always the case. Years ago, many doctors were absolutely intent on avoiding anything that could land them in court as a witness, so it was not unusual for victims to have to wait 3 or 4 hours, or sometimes even longer in the waiting room before someone finally saw them. The long wait in the public waiting room and obvious unsympathetic and disinterested attitude of many doctors only added to the victim's trauma. With the advent of the SANE program however, these nightmares are almost nonexistent. The SANE nurses are specially trained and are willing to conduct the necessary examinations. Another major plus is that they know they will be expected to testify in court. Perhaps the best advantage of the SANE program is the ability for detectives to speak with the nurse after the examination and get a fairly good understanding of the allegation as reported by the victim and the preliminary results of her examination. For prosecutors the SANE program is equally beneficial, because unlike so many in the medical profession, the SANE nurses are specifically trained on the proper methods to collect, package, and store forensic evidence. They understand aspects of chain of custody and cross-contamination, so these issues seldom come up at trial. SANE nurses are willing to go to court and render an expert opinion about the results of their examinations.

The SANE nurse is actually responsible for accomplishing much more than just performing a physical examination and/or collecting evidence

---

[9] The term SAFE (sexual assault forensic examiner) is also used at some locations to identify the person who is conducting the sexual assault examination of the victim. The two terms are essentially interchangeable.

from the victim. **Box 10-4** illustrates some of theis other key tasks, duties, and responsibilities.

BOX 10-4 The Role of SANE Nurses

During the course of their examinations, SANE nurses are expected to:

- Obtain information about the victim's current and past health issues and how they relate to the crime.
- Determine from the victim the basics of the sexual assault.
- Assess psychological functions and state of mind to determine if the victim can orientate herself to what is happening at the present time, including where she is, who she is, the day of the week, and the approximate time.
- Determine if there are any indications of suicide or self-harm present.
- Collect urine and blood samples (especially in cases of suspected drug- or alcohol-facilitated sexual assaults).
- Treat the victim for most minor injuries such as cuts and abrasions.
- Refer the victim to a medical facility for more serious treatment or follow-up treatments.
- Provide the victim with prophylactic medications for the prevention of sexually transmitted diseases (STDs).
- Provide the victim referrals for follow-up medical or psychological care and treatment.

Much like the arguments between professions over conducting a crime scene examination, there are similar arguments about the actual need for a medical examination when the victim reported that the offender used a condom or that she suffered no real injury. Following the same logic with the crime scene examination, we never really know what the results of the examination are going to be, so we always should follow protocol and have the examination completed within the standard 72-hour time period. On more than one occasion during the medical examination, a condom was actually found inside the victim when it slipped off the offender's penis and he was unable to retrieve it. Further, on more than one occasion, the offender has attempted to use a condom but the condom broke while being used. Thus, semen was found inside the vagina of the victim despite the efforts of the offender to prevent it. However, had the detective determined that since a condom was used there would be no viable evidence to obtain, it would have been lost. Also, even when a condom is used, there is still important evidence that can be collected from the victim. Each company produces its own formula for lubrication and/or spermicide that may be added to the condom. Vaginal swabs may be able to collect these substances and subsequent laboratory examination may be able to identify the specific brand name of the condom used by the offender. If an offender is ever found and he has that brand name of condom in his possession, it can be strong circumstantial evidence linking him to the victim or scene.

The medical examination of the victim, regardless of whether it is performed by a medical doctor or SANE nurse, follows a standard protocol of talking with the victim about what happened and completing a general intake form to record and document the victim's recollection of the events of the assault. Shortly thereafter, the victim's clothing is collected, making sure each item of clothing is individually wrapped (to prevent cross-contamination). The process is helped by the use of standard rape evidence collection kits that are used for every victim. Generally the rape kit is one the police and supporting crime laboratory have agreed to be the standard for that particular state or jurisdiction. It contains envelopes for collecting hair standards, including head, pubic, and if present, limb hair. It also contains a series of swabs used to collect possible samples from the mouth, vagina, and anus, depending on what the victim has reported. In addition to collection of samples, the victim is examined for possible trauma to the genitalia. If trauma is present, then it is addressed, and if possible, photographed for use as evidence. However, it is important to remember that not all forced sex acts cause injuries. For example, a woman who routinely engages in consensual sexual intercourse may not show signs of trauma even after being sexually assaulted unless the incident was exceptionally brutal or some foreign object was used during the assault. In a great many occasions the medical report may only be able to state there were signs of recent sexual activity, but no signs of trauma were present. Again, this does not indicate the sex act was actually *consensual,* only that no trauma was inflicted during the incident.

The medical examination of the victim is specifically designed to find and collect various items of trace evidence that might have transferred from the suspect onto the victim. This includes hairs and fibers, as well as possible DNA evidence from semen or from other biological fluids, such as saliva obtained from bite marks or from the victim's breasts if the suspect attempted to lick or suckle them. It is also possible to collect saliva from the outer vaginal area if the suspect attempted to perform oral sex on the victim during the assault. Even if no DNA profile can be developed from the swab, it may be possible to identify the presence of amylase, an enzyme found in human saliva, which may be seen as corroborating the victim's complaint as to what happened during the assault.

▶ Associative Injuries

There are a great number of injuries that are not what we would normally consider to be "sex related," meaning trauma to the genitalia or injuries caused during the actual sexual assaults. These non-sex-related injuries are referred to as *associative injuries.* Examples of associative injuries include trauma to the head and face caused by slapping, punches, or other blunt-force trauma; various self-defense injuries such as cuts, contusions, or lacerations to the hands, forearms, or legs; and broken fingernails, pulled hair, and bite marks are also a frequent finding. In more severe cases, there may be evidence of ligature marks on the ankles, wrists, or throat if the victim was bound or choked during the assault. Documenting the presence or absence of these injuries can be as important as the collection of any forensic evidence, and they can serve as another example of victim corroboration.

An example of associative injuries is demonstrated in the following scenario of a victim who reported jogging along a walking path in a small park. Suddenly, she was tackled from behind by an unknown assailant. She landed hard on her front side and was forced onto her back. The assailant then forcefully removed her jogging shorts, underwear, running shirt, and bra, leaving her naked on the ground. He then mounted her and vaginally raped her. Based on her report, there are certain injuries we would expect to find during her physical examination such as abrasions to her hands, elbows, forearms, shoulders, or knees as she fell forward and then hit the ground. If the offender tackled her and had his arms wrapped around her, she may have been prevented from reaching out with her hands to brace the fall, and may have hit her head on the ground instead, but there should be some contusion on her body reflecting where she came into contact with the ground. We would also expect to see signs of fabric abrasions as the clothing was forcefully removed, and additional abrasions on the victim's backside and buttocks from coming into contact with the ground with her bare skin, or even fingernail scratches as her pants were forced down by the offender. Other similar examples of associative injuries are on victims who reportedly were dragged or were on their knees and elbows while being assaulted from behind on a rug. The physical examiner would be looking for the presence or absence of abrasions or rug burns on the knees, elbows, back, or buttocks. When such injuries are found, they are in effect corroborating evidence to the victim's report. When under the previous scenario they are completely absent, this is an inconsistency, because it is not what we would expect to find under the circumstances of the victim's report. This is not necessarily evidence of a false report, but it is something that needs to be addressed at some time during the examination.

All injuries noted during the physical examination including genital and associative injuries need to be recorded in the SANE written report and should be photographed. From the detective's perspective, it is important to remember that in some instances when the victim is examined within a few hours after the incident the injuries may be documented and described as being red or swollen, because the contusion may not be present at the time of the initial examination. Therefore, it may be advisable to re-interview and if possible re-photograph the injuries 24 hours after the initial physical examination in order to capture these contusions that will likely be more visible. The victim's clothing should also be examined to look for the same "associative injuries" consisting of the rips, tears, grass stains, dirt, other ground debris, and impacted dirt or mud spots on the knees, hips, elbows, or shoulders. The same may be true of the victim's underwear, because if her outerwear were removed, then her underwear may have come into contact with the ground and may have the same stains or dirt and ground debris. Again, if the rips and stains are found they should be looked at as a consistency with the victim's statement, and if they are not found, then efforts should be made to determine why they are missing.

▶ Male Victims

There is no standardized procedure for the medical treatment of male victims, but the examination has the same basic goals of documenting any associative injuries and explanation of the sexual assault. The male genitalia is examined for any signs of trauma, including bites and lacerations, and in some cases the penis swabbed for possible saliva and offender DNA. If rectal penetration occurred, then the examination would be looking for any signs of trauma and rectal fissures or tears as well as any rectal bleeding and discharge. Pubic hair and head hair combings should also be taken as well as known standards and fingernail scrapings. Even if the report is delayed in some cases, a medical examination may be beneficial particularly if the assault involved anal sodomy or insertion of a foreign object and the victim reported an injury resulting from that assault. The victim's clothing should be collected as evidence in the same manner as with a female victim and forensically examined for the same signs of violence and traces of semen or other biological fluids and other stains.

At the conclusion of the physical examination, the SANE nurse will seal the various samples and standards that were obtained from the victim and place them back into the rape kit and then seal it with the evidence seals that come with the kit. The completed rape kit is then released to the police. If possible, detectives should be present to talk with the SANE nurse and get a brief summary of her findings. Especially important are findings of any trauma, whether they are related to the sexual assault and centered on the genitalia or there are any associative injuries. Additionally, detectives should determine if there were any comments or spontaneous statements made by the victim that may have investigative value.

Generally, detectives are almost always interested in asking one question: "What do you think?" What they are looking for is the SANE nurse's perspective on the victim and particular aspects of the sexual assault. Detectives should be looking for an initial assessment of the victim's report, and whether from the SANE perspective the examination provided any consistency with the victim's allegations of what happened. In the case of inconsistency, determine if the SANE nurse can provide any explanation. Again, this does not infer we are looking for any evidence of a false report, but rather if there are any issues that need to be explained or covered during the victim's initial interview. This exchange between the SANE nurse and the detective is an integral part of the investigation because it provides yet another piece to the total investigation. Many times it provides the detective with additional investigative steps or helps to confirm some theories that may have developed as the case has progressed on other fronts, such as from the crime scene or the offender examination or interviews.

▶ Suspect Examination

If a suspect is identified or taken into custody contemporaneously with the event or within the same 72-hour period, he should also be examined by a

SANE nurse. For this examination, it is necessary for the suspect to either give his written consent for the examination or to obtain a search warrant to have him examined and for various biological standards such as hair, blood, and other DNA samples to be collected as well as having his clothing seized. As with the victim, the suspect is examined to collect any potential transfer of hairs and fibers as well as swabbing of the genital areas for possible DNA transfer–type evidence. If the victim reports that she was digitally penetrated, then the suspect's fingers and hands may also be swabbed to attempt to obtain any vaginal secretions or victim DNA that may have been transferred to the suspect during the assault. The suspect is also examined for any injuries such as scratches or abrasions that may have been caused by any possible defense efforts of the victim. On more than one occasion, the victim reportedly put up a vigorous defense by scratching and even biting the offender in an effort to resist the assault. Not only would we be interested in locating these scratches but also would compare possible DNA from underneath the fingernails of the victim and the presence of scratches on the suspect. In the case of bite marks on the suspect, we are looking to collect possible victim DNA on the bite mark as well as a dental comparison with the victim if possible. In the same manner as with the victim, it is possible to also have associated injuries on suspects, both on their bodies and on their clothing. The suspect's clothing is also collected as evidence in the same manner as the victim's clothing.

It is very important to note any comments or spontaneous statements that may be made by the offender during the examination, such as explanations of injuries if offered or other general denial statements such as, "I never touched her," or other similar statements. Because this is a suspect of a violent crime, it is advisable to have a police officer present in the room for protection of the SANE personnel, to prevent possible destruction of evidence, and to prevent the escape of the suspect from the treatment facility.

▶ Conclusion

As with other violent crime scenes, every effort needs to be expended on locating and collecting whatever physical and forensic evidence we can identify at the scene or during the medical examinations that can possibly link the suspect and victim together. Finding such evidence is not always possible; we might not be able to find such as items as the traditional trace evidence we expect to find during the medical examination, such as hair, transferred from the suspect to the victim or victim onto the suspect. Although this transfer does in fact take place, studies have shown that such hair transfers actually take place less than 20% of the time.[10] To continue with this theme, it is not unusual for some offenders to fail to ejaculate, or they may go through

[10] Exline, D. L., Smith, F. P., & Drexler, S. G. (1998). Frequency of pubic hair transfer during sexual intercourse. *Journal of Forensic Science, 43*(3) 505–508.

extraordinary efforts to destroy or eliminate any trace or forensic evidence prior to their departure. As an example, one serial offender actually made his victims shower, douche, and even made a few victims shave their entire pubic area following the assault. This same offender also stripped the bedding and placed it into the victim's washing machine, and in one case put bedding into the bathtub and filled it with water and bleach. All of these efforts were to avoid leaving behind any physical or forensic evidence that could link him to the scene. This was very effective in most instances, but there were still a few cases where the offender was not so lucky, and some evidence was found despite his best efforts. What was more effective for locating this particular offender was that his signature and behavioral aspects were used to link him positively to other victims. So, in many cases we may be left with associated injuries or other behavioral aspects that may link the offender to multiple offenses or can be used to show consistencies between the victim and those other identified factors.

Therefore, to be successful in resolving these cases, detectives should assume at the onset of the investigation that no physical or forensic evidence will be found that can positively link the suspect, victim, or scene together. Using this concept should prevent an overreliance on DNA or other forensic analysis and require the detective to depend instead on the basics of criminal investigation. If the subsequent analysis provides no forensic evidence, the case was already continuing based on this possibility, so confirmation of what we already planned on may not prove to be such a detriment to the investigation. If forensic evidence comes back with positive results, it is an unexpected prize and the case is only made stronger.

CHAPTER ELEVEN

Investigation

▶ Latent Investigation

After the preliminary investigation—including the crime scene, victim's medical examination, and victim interview—has been completed, things typically begin to slow down as the investigation enters into the latent or middle stages. Hopefully by this stage detectives have established an understanding of what happened and a direction in which the remainder of the investigation should go. During the initial stages of the investigation, a multitude of things is going on as the detectives respond to the potential twists and turns of events. There are relatively few cases in which the prosecutor is ready to proceed with an indictment and prosecution upon completion of the preliminary investigation; there are cases when this does happen, but they are very few and very far between. The best examples are those cases where the suspect was apprehended while committing the criminal act and subsequently confessed to the crime. Such cases are fairly straightforward and tend to have an abundance of evidence and witnesses. Although the offender's statements will have to be followed up on and confirmed and the physical and forensic examinations will still need to be completed, in general these are not difficult cases to complete. Even in relatively simple cases, however, there is almost always some additional investigative activity needed to complete the case.

Regardless of the status of the case, the detective needs to take time to sit down, read, and understand the entire investigative file and all of the various reports completed or accumulated thus far. This is a basic step in all criminal investigations, but so many detectives do not take the time to complete it, or do not understand its importance. One of the main reasons to read and review the file is to make sure the detective has received all of the written reports from all of the detectives or uniformed officers participating in the preliminary investigation. The more personnel involved in the preliminary investigation, the greater the chance of someone not completing reports as required. This is especially true whenever the investigation involves multiple agencies. Because police officers are notorious for not completing written reports, it is incumbent on the case detective to make sure they are completed and added to the investigation.

Another very important rationale for this seemingly common-sense task is quite simple: to get organized and stay focused. Whereas during the preliminary investigation, the detective may be subjected to several twists and turns as often conflicting information is funneled in to them, the latent investigation is marked by more planning and prioritizing of the remainder of the investigation—basically determining what remains to be done and sometimes in what order those tasks need to be accomplished.

Sitting down and actually reading the investigative file and all of the documents contained therein allows the detective to know for certain exactly what facts, evidence, and circumstances have been validated or verified and what facts still remain to be confirmed. The use of an investigative plan has proven to be helpful in the latent stages of an investigation.

Investigative Plan

An investigative plan can be simply defined as a "to do list." It consists of any questions raised but not answered during the preliminary investigation or new questions that arise throughout the investigation. It is a list of the many investigative leads or tasks that need to be completed to answer those questions. An investigative plan is a very important investigative tool and acts as a basic road map or reminder of things that need to be accomplished. An investigative plan is not an investigative report; rather, it is a set of investigative notes. It can be formalized by an agency on a preprinted form or can be completed on a piece of scrap paper. It should be a "living document" designed to be added to, updated, or edited as the case progresses.

Because it is an informal document, it can be adjusted to the individual detective's own preference and be either handwritten or typed. We can use a simple bulleted, phrase, or comment format or provide a detailed description of what needs to be accomplished. Essentially, the detective should be able to go to the investigative plan to quickly determine the tasks that need to be accomplished, rather than go back through the entire file or to try and recall from memory what is still remaining to be done. The investigative plan is especially helpful when dealing with multiple cases at the same time. **Box 11-1** presents an example of a basic investigative plan; it uses short statements to list the leads that need to be accomplished to keep the investigation on track and notes those leads already accomplished.

As the leads are accomplished they are checked or crossed off. As new leads are developed, they are simply added. Using technology (e.g., maintaining the list with a smart phone or computer) makes it easy to go through at regular intervals to edit the plan by taking out those leads that have been

BOX 11-1 Sample Investigative Plan

1. Interview/statement John Smith, bartender
2. Interview SANE Nurse Nancy Smith
3. Obtain copy of 911 recording
4. Criminal background check of:
   - Bob Jones (done 9/2/11)
   - Phil Johnson
5. Obtain DNA samples from Phil Johnson and Bob Jones for lab
6. Obtain ambulance run reports/interview attendants (George Sears, Ralph Smits)
7. Interview Sally Smith (done 9/4/11)
8. Interview waitress Sherry Johansson (done 9/3/11)
9. P. Johnson says he was at sister's house—check alibi
10. B. Jones says he was at Tip Top Tavern—check alibi
11. Interview Mrs. Barbra Woodard (911 call came from her house)

completed, removing those leads that are determined unnecessary, and adding those leads which are identified as "to be accomplished." The investigative plan is likely to be edited and changed several times throughout the investigation as leads are followed up on and new information that needs to be verified is added. The updating of the investigation plan is a continuing process throughout the investigation and will help keep the investigation on the right path.

As the case progresses, it is strongly suggested that the detective sit down at least once a month to review whatever progress has been made or what new information has developed, and again edit and update the investigative plan. Studies have shown that in many of the famous serial murder investigations, the name of the offender appeared within the police investigative records—generally within the first 30 days of the investigation—but for one reason or another the information was never pursued or the offender was not properly eliminated as a suspect. When reviewing a cold case, one of the first steps is to review those initial police reports to see if each person who came to the attention of the police was properly vetted and eliminated as a suspect. One last important reason for completing an investigative plan is that if the case is ever transferred from one detective to another, it provides the new detective with a chance to review what direction the previous detective was pursuing.

The latent stage of sex crime investigations typically turns from the crime scene and victim to focus almost exclusively on the suspect. If a suspect has been identified or is already known, then this stage is generally used to confirm and validate alibis and other statements by witnesses or those provided by the suspect. If a suspect has not yet been identified, then the investigation is going to turn to efforts to identify him.

▶ Known Offenders—Date or Acquaintance Rape

Many citizens still think of rape as a stranger coming out of a dark alley or breaking into a house and violently forcing sex on a woman. This same group would probably believe that the police will eventually identify and arrest him; the prosecutor would then bring the case to court with the offender being sent to prison as the end result. As previously discussed within this text, this is seldom the case. In the vast majority of cases, the victim and offender are known to each other and there is not always a great deal of violence or physical trauma. Many incidents are committed within the context of some type of interpersonal relationship such as acquaintances, dating, or even within a marriage. These cases are marked more by insistence and coercion of the victim rather than physical violence, so unless either the victim or the offender is a public figure, it is quite likely no one will ever know about the incident because it will not be reported in newspapers or on television. Because of the confusing nature of these incidents, there is a very good chance there will be no arrest and prosecution. A previously established relationship and lack of physical violence make these offenses very difficult to investigate and prosecute. With these types of cases, we generally see a delay in reporting the incident to the police or a lack of reporting at all.

In these cases, several of the traditional investigative hurdles are addressed and answered and our position from an investigative perspective is quite strong. First, the identification of the suspect is basically solved because he is known or can be identified by the victim. The second issue is that the offender generally admits to being with the victim during the time frame of the incident, and generally to having sexual intercourse with the victim. Although undoubtedly he will claim the intercourse was consensual, at least we can establish it occurred, which is one of the elements of proof needed to establish a criminal offense.

Because consent is going to be the most expected defense, most of our effort should be expended to either validate consent or establish the victim's non-consent to the act. There are some basic investigative steps we can take toward this goal. The first step is to try to establish the exact relationship between the victim and the offender. For instance:

- Do they simply know each other, or do they socialize together?
- Do they know each other from work or school?
- Do they just live within the same apartment complex or dorm?
- Do they have a superior–subordinate relationship (e.g., student–teacher, worker–supervisor)?
- Are they currently or were they ever in some type of dating situation?
- Was there any prior consensual sexual relationship between them?

One of the biggest questions we want to answer on this point is: Does the offender offer a different idea or understanding of the relationship than the victim? It is not uncommon in these situations for the offender to claim a much greater relationship than the victim reports, and such conflicts need to be clarified. This is where canvass interviews of friends and associates of both the offender and victim can reveal important information—particularly when we can establish that a relationship described by the offender as a boyfriend–girlfriend or a dating situation is not necessarily accurate. Combining this type of fact with a good victimology can help to establish whether or not the victim is likely to engage in consensual intercourse with a casual acquaintance.

If the defendant claims that there was a relationship or that he was dating the victim, then we want to tie him to the specific details of their relationship. Examples of such background questions include:

- How long have they been in the relationship?
- When did they meet?
- Do they know each other's families?
- Does he have any photos of him and the victim together?
- What future plans were made, if any?
- Do any of his friends known about the victim? Who? When? What?

The second basic step is to carefully identify each and every specific action of the victim to communicate her nonconsent to the offender. This basic step should have been covered during the victim's interview when we were trying to identify any unequivocal "nos" communicated to the offender through her resistance and whether they were expressed passively, verbally, or physically. In addition to the victim's expressions of nonconsent, we also need to focus on any special situations such as medical conditions or physical problems of the victim that might ordinarily preclude sex or her interest in sex. Again, what we are trying to show is any lack of consent, or in some cases, inability to have sex. Examples include if the victim was menstruating at the time of the incident, was experiencing a yeast infection, was under treatment for an STD, or was suffering from another condition such as a cold or the flu, a migraine headache, or particularly if she was vomiting or experiencing diarrhea. These conditions might not be considered to be conducive to consensual sex and may further establish the victim's nonconsent.

The third basic step is to look at the offender. We are concerned with his actions leading up to the actual assault and if there were any particular efforts to set up the scene, and manipulate or otherwise isolate the victim. We also want to understand what the offender did verbally or physically to overcome the victim's expression of nonconsent or resistance. As stated earlier, the majority of these incidents do not always involve physical force; instead the offender may have used coercion, or didn't take "no" for an answer. This aspect should have been covered during the victim interview. These three basic steps are used in combination to get an understanding of the whole event.

At this stage of the investigation we have initially looked at the crime scene and then conducted a victimology assessment to study and understand the victim. Our next step is to turn our focus to the offender where there are some commonalities as well as subtle differences between the stranger and acquaintance offender.

Background of the Offender

One key step regarding any offender is to conduct a detailed background investigation or check of the offender. What we are trying to determine is if this is an isolated event or if there are other occasions when similar events took place. This background investigation includes a criminal history check to determine if he has ever been accused or implicated in any crime in the past, but particularly for any crime related to sexual assaults. If the offender has committed any criminal offenses, then it would be beneficial to get copies of all related police reports involving the offender.

For instance, a suspect was implicated in a sexual assault involving a residential burglary at night. A criminal history check only revealed a few arrests for petty theft and one for trespassing. Both seemed to be unrelated to a sex crime until the reports were obtained and revealed that the thefts in question involved stealing female underwear from a clothesline and from an apartment complex laundromat. The suspect was arrested for trespassing after entering a house through an unlocked back door and was observed leaving by neighbors. The owners checked their house, but because nothing was missing they declined to press charges.

Based upon the initial criminal history checks it did not seem like the previous arrests had anything to do with the current sexual assault case under investigation. However, the arrest reports indicated the crimes were in fact related, because the theft of female underwear and entering houses without committing a crime are two of the "nuisance crimes" that many sexual offenders typically start out committing. The reports showed a progression from a beginning or fantasy stage to an actual sexual assault. They were also used with great success in the interview of the suspect, who ultimately confessed to several rapes and confirmed he had committed several other thefts of underwear that he used for masturbation purposes.

In many cases it might be beneficial to review even those police reports where the offender was a reported victim. On more than one occasion, reviewing reports where the offender reported being a victim of a crime has led to a much better understanding of the offender as **Case Study 11-1** demonstrates.

Although the suspect in this case study made these reports as a victim, it helped in the presentation of his murder investigation for the prosecutor to

Case Study 11-1

A background investigation of a murder suspect revealed a series of reports made over the course of the preceding few years of thefts and burglaries at the suspect's house, vehicle, and place of employment. In each incident the suspect was supposedly the victim of the crime, but interestingly, his statements to different police departments were very similar to each other. Furthermore, the suspect presented the same type of evidence to the different departments to validate his claim. It appeared as if the same thing was happening to him time after time regardless of where he was living. When all of the reports were compared together it was fairly obvious that the offender was making false reports in order to make false insurance claims or to cover up thefts of property he himself was committing. The importance of this information helped paint a picture of a suspect who was able to lie repeatedly and convincingly to the police and keep the lies going for a period of time. It was apparent from his previous successes of making false reports that he thought he was much smarter than the police, and thus believed he could get away with murder.

---

show how the suspect was experienced in staging a scene and making a false police report. This information was also invaluable in the suspect interview.

Our main interest in conducting a criminal background check is to see if there are any reports involving the suspect in the past to determine if there are any similarities between previous incidents and the one currently under investigation. It is not uncommon for the suspect to have been arrested several times for sexual assault but for one reason or another he was never prosecuted. This is especially common in cases of acquaintance rape. Either the victim decided to drop the charges or the case was based solely on a "he said, she said" type situation, and the prosecutor declined to prosecute. Suspects who have gone through one police investigation without having been prosecuted are generally hesitant to put themselves in a position to have to go through it again. Therefore, any prior reports of a similar situation should be looked at very carefully as a pattern of suspect behavior.

In addition to a criminal background check, we also want to do a general personal background check on the offender. We attempt to identify close friends, associates, and co-workers who routinely interact with the offender on a personal, social, or professional level. As many victims and offenders tend to know each other, it is possible that many of the associates and friends of the offender may also know the victim. In these circumstances, in addition to the general background information about the offender, it is beneficial to determine the extent of the relationship between the two. Of particular importance would be any comments made by either the offender or the victim concerning the incident in question or about each other.

We are also looking to identify the suspect's current or past girlfriends, ex-wives, consensual sex partners, or anyone else that may have a close personal relationship with the offender. These people are likely to know the most personal information, history, or prior behavior of the offender. They are very rich sources of information on the suspect, and as noted previously, no one wakes up one day and decides to rape someone. Instead offenders are developed over the course of many years and many similar events may take place leading up to the crime.

Former girlfriends or associates may turn up other instances where the offender displayed this same type of behavior. This may include aspects of fantasy, paraphilia, sexual dysfunction, and what was needed to arouse the offender or to overcome a dysfunction. Remember that acquaintance rapes make up more unreported rapes than stranger rapes, so it is possible that former girlfriends or dates may disclose that similar events took place with them, but they declined for one reason or another to report them; therefore, a simple criminal history check of the offender does not always reveal this information. Thus, face-to-face interviews of former wives, girlfriends, or other dates may be necessary.

One thing to remember is that these same consensual partners may also have been sexually, physically, and emotionally abused or subjected to other types of coercion by the offender during long periods of their relationship. Some wives may have also actively or passively participated in some of the assaults themselves and therefore may be reluctant to talk to the police. As noted earlier in the text, sexual offenders like to have power and control over everyone in their lives and there are frequent instances of domestic abuse, infidelity, and other selfish acts. This is particularly apparent when we are dealing with the wives of sexual sadists who may have spent years under extreme emotional distress while they were being groomed into sexual slaves. The possible psychological and emotional trauma of these victims cannot be overstated and has to be considered when attempting to speak to them.

Unfortunately, many detectives do not like this aspect of the investigation because they are essentially expanding the investigation and potentially searching for additional victims. Instead, most detectives want to concentrate on the incident in question and do not want to look at anything that may have occurred before or after the incident to see if there is any other evidence. This is an example of *investigating in a vacuum*, where the investigator is concerned only with what happened during this singular event, does not try to see if there is any evidence of prior incidents, and does not look at what may have happened afterward. The result of this is generally a very weak case that—unless there is something unique to the particular case—is generally not going to be prosecuted. This allows the offender to reoffend and may help him to increase his confidence in committing additional crimes as he gains experience.

What some detectives fail to realize is when other *victims* are identified, this takes away the concept of miscommunication between the offender and the victim. Instead, these other victims may begin to establish the offender's modus operandi (MO). It is also not uncommon for former girlfriends who have been interviewed to decide to come forward and make a complaint. This may create additional work for the detective, but it also helps in the potential prosecution of the offender. As an example, in the military, our experience has shown that if an offender has assaulted a victim within his own barracks, there is a very good chance he assaulted or attempted to assault other females. A canvass interview is always conducted with each female within his unit— and in some cases, they are extended to include all females who were ever assigned to the unit at the same time as the offender. This almost always reveals other victims who were either assaulted in the same manner as the current victim, or who the suspect attempted to assault but never reported the incident, or who did not report the assault as a sexual assault but as some type of harassment.

One other thing we are especially looking for in the offender's background or in other cases is whether or not there is any evidence of *predatory conduct* by the offender. Predatory conduct refers to actions of the offender to manipulate or isolate victims in such a way that they feel they are unable to effectively resist. Such efforts might include inviting a victim to a particular residence to attend a party, yet when the victim shows up no one else is there, or offering to give the victim a ride home and then stopping in an isolated area and demanding sex and threatening to force the victim out of the vehicle if she does not comply. A variant of this tactic can be seen in **Case Study 11-2**.

Case Study 11-2

An offender brought his Jet Ski to a lake where he would make contact with females and spend some time talking to them. After a while he would offer to take them on a ride across the lake. He then allowed them to get onto the back of the Jet Ski and he would take off across the large lake to several small islands where he would stop because he claimed he needed to relieve himself. The females also disembarked onto the island and he would suddenly demand sex or he would simply drive the Jet Ski away, leaving them on the island, usually dressed only in a swimsuit. The beach where they started from was quite a distance away, making swimming back a near impossibility. Several times the victims had been single parents who had left their children at the beach since they thought they would only be gone for a few minutes. The victims were never physically assaulted nor otherwise threatened but felt forced to succumb to his demand or be stranded. Afterward he would bring his victims back to the beach and then race off to another location where he would load the Jet Ski into his truck and leave the lake. The offender's activity only became known to the police while they were investigating a related incident; several of the victims had made a report to the local sheriff's department, but the investigations were not aggressively pursued. All of the victims felt they had made an obvious mistake and did not feel the police had actually believed them. Sadly, although several reports were made, there was never any follow-up action by the responding department. There were probably several victims who never reported their victimization.

This case study shows an example of predatory conduct. Using the con approach, the offender selected females he thought he could intimidate or threaten with being left alone on an island far away from their children who would be left unattended if they did not return. The offender, when questioned, readily admitted to having sex with the women, but maintained each incident was consensual. However, when each victim was questioned and came back with the same basic story of the offender's actions although they did not know each other, the offender's predatory behavior and his MO became quite clear.

Similar predatory conduct has occurred in the military, particularly at the basic training units where new soldiers are initially inducted into the service. At this point in their careers, trainees are 100% under the control and influence of their drill sergeant, who is responsible for their initial training. The drill sergeant can make any soldier's initial training easier by granting certain special privileges or miserable by holding them to proper standards, solely at his discretion. Like all predators, some of these drill sergeants can pick out likely targets who may be susceptible to a quid pro quo offer of special privileges such as use of cell phones, easy duty, or guarantee of a passing score on a physical training test in exchange for sex. There are others who simply take advantage of their positions over a trainee and make no effort to try to groom them or offer them anything; instead, they maneuver the trainee to a location where they are isolated and simply make sexual advances. Victims taken by surprise might not say no or actively resist the sergeant; it is not unusual for the trainee to be told not to say anything about their victimization because no one will believe them over a drill sergeant. Again, in these cases, if one victim comes forward, generally there are other victims who have not come forward who are identified during canvass interviews.

There is a very important investigative concept in sexual assault investigations that essentially explains that when these cases are not aggressively investigated, they are seldom prosecuted: *Whenever we allow these investigations to generate into a "he said, she said" incident, with no other evidence available, a tie will always go to the offender.* This concept simply reflects the general hesitancy of a jury to convict anyone based solely on the word of the victim. Whether this is morally right or wrong does not matter; it is a fact we have to live with. Therefore, we need to make certain we use everything at our disposal to obtain some other evidence that will corroborate the victim's allegation.

Common Characteristics, Circumstances, and Issues in Acquaintance Situations

With acquaintance-type situations there are some common characteristics, circumstances, or issues that appear time and time again during the investigations. The following sections describe some of the more common factors and the efforts we may have to take to overcome these issues.

Age of Victim and Offender

Often in these cases we are dealing with victims and offenders who are both in the 16–29 year age group. This particular age group is generally considered to be at high risk for victimization because of their age, maturity level, life experiences, and because they are most likely to engage in other high-risk behaviors, such as alcohol or drug usage. This age group is also typically actively engaged in dating or romantic situations, sometimes for the first time. Frequently, they have left home and are residing in another location for the first time and may not have a family support structure nearby. Many are entering the workforce and beginning to live independent lives, and some may for the first time be living together with peers of the opposite sex within the same building, such as an apartment complex, barracks within the military service, or in college dorms. They also tend to spend more time socializing with their peers who are also probably in the same situation.

There is little we can do as detectives to overcome the age of the victim; it is one of the facts of these incidents that we have to deal with. Our only recourse in these situations is to conduct a detailed victimology, as covered earlier in the text, to show the basic personal characteristics of the victim and to establish victim corroboration. However, what may be more important is the age of the offender. If the victim and offender are the same age or within 1 or 2 years of each other, there is not too much difference. But, 4 to 5 years' age difference is very important because of the difference in life experience and maturity level between them. Examples of where age difference would be significant are the comparisons between a high school freshman and a high school senior, a college freshman and a college senior, or a college student and a high school student. In these circumstances, we can see how a victim may be manipulated or controlled by an older, more mature offender. We also see this same type of incident play out with older offenders who target young teenagers over the Internet, showering them with attention, which makes them feel good about capturing the interest of an older and more mature man. In reality these offenders are simply using the lack of maturity, life inexperience, and general naiveté of their victims to overcome any reluctance or resistance to sex. This is one of the reasons we have established legal ages of consent for sexual intercourse.

Males and Females Have Different Expectations

Evan Mark Katz,[1] advertised as a woman's dating coach on the Internet, summed up the different expectations between men and women regarding sex in his article, "Men Look for Sex and Find Love. Women Look for Love and Find Sex." This is a problem within our society and culture and we see it repeated many times in our investigations when men and women have different ideas about sex and the issues of consent or force. Typically, men are taught or learn to be more aggressive, and sex is often seen as an opportunity to "score" and "conquer," to add a notch to the bedpost, or show their manliness to their other male friends. It is the hedonistic pleasure of sex and male prowess rather than the possible ramifications of the act that concerns them.

Women tend to be more passive and coy. The sex act, although also seen as pleasurable, is culturally used as a way to attract and keep a potential partner. Because women will bear the ultimate potential ramification of the sex act—pregnancy—women tend to be more cautious and selective in their sexual partners. Also, in our society, where a man may be respected, envied, or seen as "manly" for having multiple sex partners, females with multiple sex partners are often looked down upon as being promiscuous and having low moral standards. Simply put, males will typically have sex as circumstances present themselves and if they are able; women will typically have sex when the circumstances and partner are right for them.

Unfortunately, our society and therefore our juries overwhelmingly tend to place much of the blame on the victim for sex crimes and view the victim's conduct before, during, and after the incident very critically. Basically, the incident is viewed from the perspective of: Could the incident have been prevented if the victim stayed home or did not put herself at risk? Right or wrong, this thought process influences prosecutors and police in how these crimes are viewed. Robin Warshaw[2] identifies an interesting term that captures this concept very succinctly: *justifiable rape*, wherein the victim's pre-crime behavior is seen as a trigger to a male's response. Whereas this is not a legal term or concept, it does explain how the incident may be viewed by the offender, police, prosecutor, or the jury as a noncrime. She identifies such pre-crime conduct as:

- The woman invites the male out on a date
- The man pays for the date
- She dresses suggestively
- They go to his place rather than to a movie
- She voluntarily drinks alcohol
- She voluntarily consumes illicit drugs

---

[1] Katz, E. M. (2003–2012). Men look for sex and find love. Women look for love and find sex. Retrieved June 10, 2012, from http://www.evanmarckatz.com/blog/men-look-for-sex-and-find-love-women-look-for-love-and-find-sex/

[2] Warshaw, R. (1988). *I never called it rape*. New York, NY: Harper and Row; pp. 42–43.

Many times men see these actions as indications of the victim's interest in sexual relations. If the victim then says no or offers resistance to their advances, the response is seen as teasing, leading them on, or just an attempt at playing hard to get rather than an outright refusal. Studies have shown that many men consider more aggressive behavior as being justified under these circumstances. These different expectations of males and females play no part and should not be used as an excuse for any criminal act, but they are likely to be a major portion of the investigation and potential defense in court as we learn how the victim and offender each saw the particular circumstances. Therefore, a detailed victim interview as mentioned earlier is especially important to counter any perceived justification of the offender; it should focus instead on the victim's actions to make her nonconsent known to the offender.

Use of Alcohol by Victim and Offender

The use of alcohol by the offender and/or the victim is one of the most common denominators in many of these cases; it is present in about 50% of sexual assaults. Alcohol usage has increased, particularly among females who join their male peers in binge drinking—that is, intentionally drinking to the point of intoxication. Alcohol and drugs alter one's ability to make sound judgments and assess risk, cloud thinking and logical reasoning, and may lead to increased aggression. Alcohol also prevents effective communication, and more importantly, lowers inhibitions of both the victim and the offender. Under the influence, we do things we would not ordinarily do if we were not under the influence. One example of this is the *Girls Gone Wild* video series, in which young college coeds are approached while "partying" and drinking alcohol and are encouraged to "flash" or show their breasts or even undress while being videotaped or photographed. Some may even go further and perform sexual acts on camera. It is doubtful that most would do such things if they were sober, and certainly many have regretted their decision once they sobered up. Perhaps the best description of lowering of inhibitions is: It releases the brakes of our conscience, allowing us to do what we know we should not and otherwise would not do. When we combine the age and maturity levels of the victim and offender, add in a dating situation with different expectations of sex between males and females, and then mix in alcohol or drugs, we end up with a dangerous cocktail. The story of what occurs within such a situation is often very difficult to unravel.

Some offenders will intentionally take advantage of victims through the use of drugs or alcohol. Examples of these incidents are covered in greater detail later in this text, so they are not further addressed here.

Mixed Signals

Another common theme in many of these cases is the presence of confusing or mixed signals that may be sent out by the victim or misunderstood by the offender. A woman might go to a man's residence when dressed provocatively and drink alcohol and engage in consensual "petting" or foreplay, but might not have any intention or desire to have sexual intercourse with the man. However, from a man's perspective, these activities may lead him to believe the woman is *interested and willing* to engage in sex. There is no doubt that legally, a firm and positive "no" from the victim is all that is needed to establish nonconsent. Unfortunately, a victim might say "no" verbally, but then respond "yes" from the man's point of view with other nonverbal or physical means. Consider, for example, a victim who reports that she invited her date to her apartment to watch a movie. They began consensually kissing and petting on the sofa, but when the offender made additional advances she told him, "no" and "stop," several times. But, he continued his advances and eventually raped the victim. The offender, when interviewed, reported that the victim did say, "no" and "stop," but then unbuttoned her own shirt to expose her breasts and began touching his genitalia as part of a mutual foreplay activity. The offender claimed she seemed to be responding positively to his advances so he continued. It becomes difficult not just for the offender but also for the police to determine at which point seduction and consensual acts turn into criminal behavior. Add in alcohol that clouds the judgment of both victim and offender and it becomes even more confusing.

It is also clear that under similar circumstances the victim has delivered a firm "no," but many offenders simply do not take no for an answer or ignore the request and continue with their advances. This is the reason why we spend so much time during the victim interview to cover in detail what she did to express her nonconsent or offer resistance to the sexual act.

Previous Consensual Contact Between Victim and Offender

Perhaps the greatest problem with acquaintance rape cases exists when the victim and offender have a history of consensual sexual relations with each other. The question in these circumstances is always going to be whether there was a clear expectation from the offender, based on previous consensual sexual relations, that such sexual advances would be welcomed or consented to by the victim. While it is always important to document the efforts made by the victim to show her nonconsent, it is going to be especially important in these situations. The longer a consensual sexual relationship existed, the more likely the offender may be to believe any advances would be welcomed. This will likely be his defense or explanation when confronted with the victim's complaint.

These issues should be covered during the victim interview, and they are likely to be an important aspect of her statement. We want to determine if their consensual sexual relationship is continuing or had previously ended. If the relationship had ended, then it might be important to document that this in no way confers that previous consensual sex with the offender makes the victim liable for continued sex with the offender. This issue is fairly clear with the police if the victim has given a clear "no" to the offender.

Especially difficult are relationships that were long term, involved cohabitation, or were in a marital context. These cases may require additional work to establish the exact circumstances surrounding the event.

Marital Rape

Historically, the crime of rape was defined as sexual intercourse with a female who is not a man's wife, without her consent. It is only since 1993 in the United States that the concept of rape within a marital context was even illegal; prior to this, a husband could be prosecuted for some type of physical assault against this wife, but could not be charged with rape. Marital rape does in fact take place, often within the context of other domestic assaults, and may occur without any physical force or with just what is needed to overcome resistance. However, depending on the offender, marital rapes may involve physical force and violence in the same manner as some stranger-on-stranger incidents. Women who are raped in these situations may have been raped multiple times before they decide to report their victimization or to take steps to get out of the marriage. They are also more likely to have experienced forced oral and anal assaults than other acquaintance-type situations. Drug and alcohol abuse by husbands are also a great influence and danger.

One difficulty in these cases lies in convincing the victim to press charges against her husband. As in other domestic abuse situations, the wife may initially make a complaint but eventually decline to follow through with the prosecution. Some wives may hesitate to report these problems to the police out of fear of retribution by their spouse, embarrassment, fear of reaction by their family and friends, or out of a need to protect their children. Some victims, based on ethnic or cultural backgrounds, may still see sex as an obligation or a duty of a wife to perform for her husband and may not see the husband's actions as criminal, and thus would be reluctant to press charges.

Many times the victimization of a wife may not come to the attention of the police until she is located and interviewed by the police after the husband was arrested as a suspect in a different sexual assault. It is only then that the police identify the wife as a victim as well. This is very likely, particularly when dealing with anger excitation offenders or sexual sadists, who make an effort through grooming and coercion to turn their wives into sexual slaves. In these circumstances, the wife is likely to have experienced severe mental, physical, and sexual abuse, including sexual torture, over a period of time. This is another reason why we always want to interview wives and ex-wives, because it is not uncommon to find another victim of the offender.

There are other fairly common examples of marital rape that include incidents where the wife and husband are experiencing marital problems and may not be sleeping together in the same bed or even in the same house. A common theme is that the husband comes over to the wife's house for a visit and makes sexual advances, thinking the wife will be receptive. She is not receptive and the advances become nonconsensual. A second related theme is the husband and wife who may live in the same house, but no longer share the marital bed or engage in normal consensual sexual intercourse and the wife wakes up to the husband attempting to engage in sexual relations with her. These cases are somewhat easier to work if there has been a clear "break" of the marital relationship, such as an announcement by either party that he or she intends to seek a divorce or if a divorce action has already been initiated, or if the victim has made it very clear she is not interested in sex with her spouse.

Another concept is the *expectation of consent*—within a marriage one partner assumes or expects the other partner will consent to any sexual advances. Expectation of consent is not a legal term but rather a "cultural understanding" that is generally accepted between married partners that when one seeks out sex, it would naturally be within the marriage. Unfortunately, the police are often confronted with situations in which one partner attempts to have sex with the other while he or she is asleep or during a dispute and the partner who was asleep decides to make a criminal complaint against the other. There is seldom a report of any physical assault, threats, or any other coercive action by the offending partner and technically the actions may meet the elements of proof for an offense because the partner did not actually give consent. However, if the actions were not forced or the initiator stopped once he or she was told to stop, did those actions actually cross the line to a criminal offense? Unless some type of nonconsent has been clearly communicated to the other partner beforehand, this is going to be a difficult investigation and will certainly never be prosecuted. Sadly, these cases often place the police into a position of marriage counselor or referee rather than an investigative agency and causes the police to expend a great deal of resources to get to the basic facts.

It is critical to take each complaint seriously because we never know which incident we are likely to be confronted with when we start our investigation. Therefore, each complaint and victim must be carefully evaluated and not simply discounted or ignored because the victim and offender are married.

Superior–Subordinate Relationship

There is a school of thought that says any superior–subordinate sexual relationship should be looked at as coercive in nature. This comes from the concept of a subordinate who must depend on the superior to keep his or her job or get a promotion. Many times we see these situations as quid pro quo, or this for that ("If you do something for me, then I will do something for you."). Perhaps the best example of a quid pro quo situation is the infamous "casting couch" where Hollywood movie moguls or producers would offer starlets a chance to get into the movies providing they had sex with them. In the business world it is the same concept: Sleep with the boss and you get promoted, or a bigger project to supervise, or a raise. We see this also in the military where a sergeant or officer will use his influence to provide something for the victim he has targeted in exchange for sex. The military has severe penalties for officers or noncommissioned officers who engage or even attempt to engage lower ranking soldiers in any sexual acts, because in the military superiors also decide who will go out on dangerous missions, who will be assigned less pleasant duty stations, or who may have undesirable duty. Thus, there are many opportunities to coerce to the victim in order to gain his or her compliance. A quid pro quo situation should always be looked at as coercive because the victim's actions are not based on consent, but what she may have to do to protect herself.

There is also a good chance that those who have not complied or could not be coerced may suffer at the hands of the superior through a poor evaluation or loss of a job or position. Often these incidents result in civil torts against the business or the superior. Any previous lawsuits would be valuable evidence of prior conduct by the offender. Although these incidents seldom involve force, there is generally some subtle coercion or other pressure applied to the victim to seek her compliance, and there are generally multiple victims. A good canvass interview of the business or other subordinates who have worked for the suspect will often provide other potential victims or other information that may be useful.

Offender's Sense of Entitlement (Athletes, Movie Stars, Rock Stars)

One of the key factors we see in acquaintance-type situations comes from the offender's sense of entitlement; that is, that somehow he feels he is entitled to sex from the victim. An example of this sense of entitlement is a man who has spent a lot of money on a date and believes he is entitled to sex as a return on his investment. We also see this same concept of entitlement played out with college or professional athletes, movie stars, and rock stars. Because of their perceived value on the court, field, stage, or movie screen, they are often shielded from arrest or punishment by coaches, universities, professional teams, record labels, or movie studios. What is created is a special class of persons who believe they are no longer held to the same standard as everyone else. Regardless of what they do, someone is there to take care of them and thus they begin to develop the concept that they can do whatever they want to do. They begin to think they are entitled to sex simply because they want it. The fact that they are often surrounded by groupies or fans who make themselves readily available for sex plays into this thinking.

The problem is, not all fans are groupies. Some may only want the chance to be up close to the celebrity or are impressed with any personal attention shown to them. Unfortunately, the offender has probably gotten away with so much for such a long time that the concept of "no" may be foreign to him. Again, we see examples of this when the victim claims she verbally and physically resisted, but the offender would not take no for an answer. We also see signs of entitlement in how the suspects interact with and treat others, their own selfishness, and a general "I'm above it all" attitude displayed during their interviews. These observations tell a lot about their egos and personality characteristics, which were likely to have been expressed during the incident as well.

Regardless of the circumstances of the assault, there are a few investigative tactics that have proved to be very successful in obtaining corroboration of the victim's complaint. One of the best investigative techniques in an acquaintance-type situation is a pretext phone call made by the victim to the offender.

Pretext Phone Calls

A pretext phone call is a call made under the direction of the police by the victim to the suspect, with the intent to engage the suspect in conversation about the incident and hopefully obtain admissions or other incriminating statements. These conversations are typically overheard, meaning the police are also listening in on or recording the call. This tactic can be especially useful when the offender and victim know each other and no violence or physical force was involved in the incident. **Box 11-2** presents an example of a pretext phone call made by a victim who reported she was sexually assaulted after passing out from drinking alcohol at a party. She reported waking up in bed naked at the offender's residence with pelvic pain and thought she had sex the previous night, but did not remember anything.

BOX 11-2 Example of a Pretext Phone Call

Sally: I was calling about last night.

John: I was going to call you, too.

Sally: Yeah, things sort of went a bit too far for me. I guess I had a little too much to drink. I mean, like I woke up naked at your house. How did I get there and what happened?

John: Yeah, well there was no way you could drive home after the party, so I just took you home with me. You know, and well, so I put you to bed.

Sally: Did you undress me?

John: Yeah, well you sort of, you helped too.

Sally: I did?

John: Yeah, well you were a little out of it. Maybe you just don't remember.

Sally: Not really. Did we have sex?

John: You don't remember?

Sally: No, I don't remember anything.

John: Well, yeah a couple of times actually. Don't you remember?

Sally: No. I told you I don't remember anything. I guess I must have passed out.

John: Well no, not completely passed out, you were sort of in and out of it.

Sally: Well, did you at least use protection?

John: Oh yeah, no worries there.

Sally: Because I don't want to get pregnant. I'm not on the pill or anything.

John: Oh, you won't. I was careful.

Sally: Why did you have sex with me when I passed out?

John: I'm sorry; I guess I got a little too excited.

Sally: I think you took advantage of me when I passed out. You never even gave me a chance to say yes or no.

John: I know. I'm sorry. It won't happen again.

Note the pretext phone call above was not accusatory or confrontational and was more of a question-and-answer type of conversation. This approach is generally better for obtaining incriminating statements from the offender rather than a direct approach that may cause the offender to become defensive or unresponsive. The idea behind the phone call is not to allow the victim to vent but rather to engage the offender in conversation. In this example, the offender did not make major confessions of assaulting the victim but did make a number of very important admissions. Specifically, he admitted to bringing the victim to his house, that she was intoxicated, that he undressed her, and that he put her into his bed. He admitted to having sex with her, indicating he probably used a condom although he did not specifically say it. The real value of a pretext phone call is in the subsequent suspect interview, where such admissions are very helpful in overcoming the offender's likely resistance to admitting his guilt.

Along the same lines, some victims may be able to personally confront the offender and engage him in conversation while wearing a wire or while equipped with a digital recorder to record their conversation. This is almost always a better approach because the conversations tend to be longer and the offender tends to explain what happened in greater detail, but it does require a special victim who is first able to make such a personal confrontation, and second will not get carried away and get violent or angry herself.

Although we prefer a recorded verbal conversation, if the victim is hesitant over additional personal communication with the offender, there are other options available such as text messages over cell phones, instant messaging (IM) over computers, or through emails, which may achieve the same purpose of obtaining admissions from the offender. In some cases with certain offenders these nonpersonal confrontations may even be better because they might be more likely to write extensively on the subject and provide more details or explanations in written form. However, there are a couple of disadvantages of using this medium.

First, it is far easier for the offender to simply ignore a text or IM, or delete an email from the victim without answering. It is harder to hang up on someone when they call. Also, sending a text or email allows the offender a chance to think about his reply and formulate a well-reasoned response rather than having to think on his feet as with a telephone call. With text messages or emails there is always going to be an issue of whether we can prove the response came from the offender or if someone else who had access to his cell phone or email account responded. Lastly, once communication has taken place using these mediums, there is always a chance that the offender will continue to communicate with the victim and the victim will respond to the offender without police knowledge. As we have made records of their conversations completed in our presence for our case, it is just as easy for the offender to begin to document any additional conversations with the victim initiated or conducted without our knowledge. Therefore, all of these factors need to be taken into consideration before such a pretext call or contact is made.

The pretext phone call is best completed during the initial victim interview or shortly thereafter, but before the suspect interview because the offender may be hesitant to talk with the victim after he is aware that she has made a criminal complaint against him. If during the suspect interview he invoked his rights and declined to be interviewed or make a statement, a pretext phone call is no longer an option.

Effects on the Victim

Victims may suffer a great deal of emotional trauma from offenses involving acquaintances, usually even more than those involving strangers. For stranger offenses, the circumstances are often beyond their control—they were engaged in normal life activities, and were attacked. For acquaintance-type offenses, victims will have to deal with issues of self-confidence, wondering if they somehow allowed themselves to get into a dangerous situation; issues of misplaced trust, because they gave their trust to someone who took advantage of them; and various feelings of guilt that they were not able to control a situation. After all, our society and culture have placed the responsibility for the results of sexual intercourse on women. It is one thing to anticipate an assault by a stranger and to prepare for it; it is more difficult to comprehend that a trusted friend or relative may also be a threat. It may be difficult for the victim to recognize or see what happened to her as rape, especially if no physical force was used. These are some of the reasons why these offenses are not always reported to the police.

▶ Unknown or Stranger Offenders

Unknown offenders commit what are known as *stranger-on-stranger* offenses, wherein at least the victim does not know the offender. This is the type of crime with which the public tends to associate the offense of rape and on which most police training is focused. There are a few advantages for the police in these cases that we need to take advantage of as we investigate. First, stranger rapes are generally more likely to be reported in a timely fashion or contemporaneously with the event. Second, there is generally more offender behavior to be evaluated, along with more available physical and forensic evidence. Lastly, the investigation typically will focus less on consent and more on identifying the offender.

Identification of an offender is obviously going to be a major part of the investigative effort, and there are a couple of different ways to do so. The more traditional way is through the use of photographs of previously identified or arrested suspects. This is still depicted on TV or in movies where the victim sits and goes through books of photographs of formerly arrested persons, or the police have taken the description of the offender and gone through their arrest photographs themselves and come up with likely suspects which are then shown to the victim for a possible identification. Along the same lines are suspects who may be identified through a subsequent police investigation and a photo or physical lineup is prepared. Whether we conduct a photo lineup or a physical lineup, this is a critical step and we want to make certain it is conducted in a manner that will not be able to be challenged. For instance, if we are looking for a blond, white male who is clean shaven, we do not want to put in photographs of dark-haired white males with beards or mustaches, nor do we want to include Black, Asian, or Hispanic people in this lineup. We do not want to be seen as ensuring the victim pointed out the right suspect, because our choice was the only one in the photo array or physical lineup that matched her description. In a physical lineup, the victim is typically placed into a room or a place inside a room where she is out of the sight of the offender. An advantage of a physical lineup is the possibility of the victim being allowed to hear them speak and even repeat certain phrases or sentences used by the offender during the assault. Many times the identification is based first on a photo array and then followed up with a physical lineup containing the suspect.

In some cases the victim may report seeing the unknown suspect at a party or social setting prior to her assault. In this case, locating any personal photographs of those attending the party from personal cameras, cell phones, or some type of surveillance camera is also an acceptable tactic. If the victim is able to identify a suspect through any of these techniques, whatever was used, such as the photo array shown to the victim, other personal photographs, or photographs to document participants of the physical lineup, will all become important evidence in future criminal proceedings. It is worth the extra effort by the detectives to take away any argument for unfairness; therefore, the other photos or stand-ins must be as close as possible in appearance, height, weight, and physical stature to the victim's initial description and should not contain police personnel or anyone else that the victim may know or be able to immediately rule out as the offender. Regardless of the method, the lineup procedure is likely to be challenged by the defense; therefore, the photos that were used and in what order they were shown to the victim need to be thoroughly documented. In a physical lineup, the participants should be photographed in the order they were standing. Again, this is to show that the lineups were not overly suggestive or prejudicial to the suspect.

The use of photos or physical lineups is a traditional method used to identify or eliminate potential suspects that is still used today, and many times it is the only technique available. However, in many instances we can also rely on forensic evidence gathered from the crime scene to enable us to identify an unknown offender.

▶ Forensic Evidence

Combined DNA Index System

The use of DNA technology to help solve crimes has become a fundamental tool for modern-day law enforcement. But, in order for it to be used, we first have to collect a sample from the crime scene, such as semen, saliva, or blood, and then we have to be able to compare it to a suspect's DNA. When a potential suspect has already been identified, it is simply a case of sending both the crime scene sample and the suspect's known standard to the laboratory and then comparing the results. It becomes relatively easy in these cases because either the suspect will be placed into the donor pool or match the sample collected from the scene, or he will be eliminated as a donor to the DNA sample. If we do not have a potential suspect already identified, we can expand our efforts through use of the Combined DNA Index System (CODIS). CODIS is essentially a national centralized DNA database, established and funded by the FBI. It allows allows police laboratories throughout the country to share DNA data collected from their crime scenes with evidence from any other crime scene and then compare this data with any previously identified offenders. Entering the DNA information into the database is the function of the supporting crime lab and does not directly involve the police department.

CODIS consists of three separate indexes for comparison of biological evidence. The first is the forensic index, which contains the DNA profiles extracted from evidence collected at crime scenes. The second is the convicted offender index, which contains the DNA profiles of identified individuals, generally taken upon their conviction for certain criminal offenses. Each state has different "qualifying offenses" that require a DNA sample to be collected and placed into the database. The third index is maintained for unidentified bodies that have been found. The concept is designed to assist police who may come up with a tentative identification of an unknown body and then collect DNA samples of the parents or siblings of the deceased to compare to the unknown remains.

The benefit of CODIS is that once any data obtained from a crime scene are entered into the database, they remain there until they are removed by the responsible crime laboratory. Police in multiple jurisdictions are now able to compare information across the country and share leads with other jurisdictions for every new case that is reported. A weekly comparison search is conducted for all of the new offender profiles and from any new crime scenes. Once entered into the database, at a minimum a forensic profile it will be checked 52 times a year for possible matches. Any resulting matches from other crime scenes or identified offenders are provided to the local or state laboratory that originally submitted the DNA profile and eventually to the police agency that submitted the original crime scene evidence.

IAFIS

Much like the CODIS database, the Integrated Automated Fingerprint Identification System (IAFIS), is essentially a national fingerprint and criminal history database maintained and supervised by the FBI. It is designed to enable police crime laboratories across the country to conduct an automated fingerprint search of crime scene latent prints and compare them to the various fingerprint cards taken from arrested suspects. The system can be accessed 24 hours a day, 365 days a year. The IAFIS provides not only fingerprints, but also corresponding criminal histories, mug shots, scars, tattoos, physical characteristics, and aliases.

The benefit to the IAFIS is like that of the CODIS: once data obtained from a crime scene are entered into the database, they remain there until they are removed by the responsible crime laboratory. Police in multiple jurisdictions are now able to compare information across the country and share leads with other jurisdictions. After every suspect is arrested, his or her fingerprints are obtained and entered into the IAFIS system to be compared to any latent print recovered from a crime scene.

Violent Criminal Apprehension Program (ViCAP)

If we are still unsuccessful at identifying a potential suspect from forensic and physical evidence, then we need to expand our search. One method is to determine if this particular investigation is similar to any other recently reported cases, either based on the MO, signature, or some type of forensic evidence. This effort is known as linking cases together and our intent is to determine if the same offender may have been involved in any other case that we are investigating or that any other department is also investigating. This includes a check of our own local records and those of neighboring cities or communities and should also include any similar cases from around the same state or across the country. In addition to possibly identifying a suspect, we also need to know if we are dealing with a first-time offender or with a possible serial offender. Whereas we can easily check the surrounding police departments and our state agencies, it is not so easy to pick up the phone and call all departments in all 50 states. The Violent Criminal Apprehension Program (ViCAP) can be used to make inquires across the country.

ViCAP was created in 1985 and was designed to collect, analyze, and correlate information on violent crime including homicides, sexual assaults, missing persons, or unidentified human remains. ViCAP is a nationwide database where certain crime scene criteria and offender characteristics from individual cases are added to the database for comparison with other cases. If any similarities are found, investigators can contact the agency with the other case, and they can compare details to see if there is an actual match between them. The ViCAP database is essentially a series of questions designed to capture aspects of the victimology as well as specific crime scene and forensic evidence, and a series of questions designed to identify specific offender behavior. The offender behavior helps identify the MO and possible signature for that offender. ViCAP is a very good investigative tool and has been instrumental in solving many cases, including cold cases and serial offender cases that took place across the country.

Since 2008 the ViCAP database was finally made available for all law enforcement agencies through a secure URL. This allows for real-time access by any authorized agency to the database, where a search for similar cases can be conducted 24 hours a day, 7 days a week. Although this is a good investigative tool, it is unfortunately greatly underutilized. To increase the usage, many states have set up their own ViCAP programs, generally monitored or supervised by the state police agency. There is a weakness in that participation is strictly voluntary, meaning there is no legal requirement for an agency to add any case to the database. The strength of the database is limited by the amount of information contained within the database, so detectives are encouraged to enter information on both solved and unsolved stranger rapes into the database.

Another very important tool we have at our disposal to provide some investigative leads is the Criminal Investigative Analysis (CIA), which is the new term for what is still commonly known as an offender profile.

Criminal Investigative Analysis

The *criminal investigative analysis* or CIA is not a psychological profile of the offender, although it does focus on identified offender behavior and identified personality characteristics. The CIA is more of a look at the entire event including the crime scene, forensic evidence, and victimology assessment, as well as the various offender behaviors. It includes how the crime was committed and the interaction between the offender and victim. This allows for a better understanding of offender's motivation, criminal sophistication, and possible prior relationship with victim. Behavioral evidence at crime scenes may also provide some insights into the personality characteristics of the offender. It is not designed to provide a by-name suspect identification, for that is an impossibility. Rather, it can help to focus attention onto a particular suspect or what type of person would have acted in that manner, helping to narrow the possible offender pool. **Box 11-3** lists some of the basic information that can be gained from a CIA.

BOX 11-3 CIA Basic Information

A CIA can provide basic information on the offender such as:

Sex and race
Approximate age
Maturity level
Possible criminal history and sophistication
Level of planning or preparation
Possible employment history
Possible military service
Social adjustment

BOX 11-3 (continued)

Sexual adjustment or abnormalities including dysfunctions

Alcohol or drug usage

Educational level

Interpersonal skills

Anger control issues

Manner of dress and personal appearance

Pre-crime and post-crime behaviors

Victim selection process

Historically, the CIA was pioneered by the FBI during the late 1970s with the original Behavior Science Unit with such famous practitioners as Howard Teeter, John Douglas, Robert Ressler, Robert Hazelwood, and Ken Lanning. Their combined research taught law enforcement a new way to look at violent crimes through the offender's displayed behavior. Their research established two main ideas surrounding this concept: behavior reflects personality, and behavior can be discerned from the crime scene.

Behavior Reflects Personality

Generally speaking, offenders' behavior while committing crimes will be reflected in their personality characteristics in normal life. If the offender was able to exert control over the victim, seemed well prepared to commit the crime, and took precautions to avoid identification, he is likely to express the same personality traits in his non-criminal life. Such an offender would likely be more intelligent, orderly, and compulsive than an offender who appeared to be more spontaneous, had difficulty in controlling the victim, and did not pay attention to leaving forensic evidence behind. The second offender we would generally see as being less intelligent with less self-confidence. This is one of the reasons why so much time is spent learning about the offender during the victim interview and why such effort is expended throughout the crime scene examination to identify the various offender behaviors.

Behavior Can Be Discerned from the Crime Scene

As stated previously in this text, the crime scene is the one place where offenders tell us all about themselves. The behavior described by the victim and other crime scene factors allow us to identify the offender type that is likely involved in the crime. If we can identify the offender type, then we might also identify potential pre- and post-crime behaviors and the likelihood that the offender was involved in previous offenses or will commit another offense. It may also provide interview techniques, a sense of the likelihood of the offender still having evidence linking him to the crime, and, sometimes more important, a sense of the likelihood of increased violence by the offender.

The initial goal of the CIA at this stage of the investigation is to assist in narrowing the search for the offender. For instance, if we recognize that the offender in question is an anger excitation or sexual sadist type, we can generally eliminate possible suspects who are of the power reassurance type. The CIA may also be able to provide us with possible investigative leads or strategies to find the offender. **Case Studies 11-3 and 11-4** provide examples of using this strategy to locate an unknown offender by formulating an investigative plan and strategy based on the offender typology. They bring up another important concept of CIA: *The best predictor of future behavior is past behavior.*

Case Study 11-3

Police in a small rural town were having difficulties identifying an offender who broke into the residence of an elderly female and raped her. Nothing similar had happened in this town for a number of years, and the police were stymied about what to do. No new residents had moved into the area recently and no strangers were observed by the close-knit neighborhood. Based on the general facts of the crime and the interaction with the victim, the offender was identified as a power reassurance type. Based on this finding, it was likely that the offender would live in or around the small town or would feel comfortable within that neighborhood. One strategy for identifying the offender that was offered to the department was for the patrol officers to actively contact and conduct a field interview of any males who were seen walking or riding their bikes alone through the area at night from about 10:00 PM until dawn. Within a few days, the police contacted a young male who was out walking through the area at night. They had initially discounted him because he lived some 50 miles away and was only visiting his grandmother who lived in the same neighborhood. Under urging, the police did a more detailed background check on the young man and quickly discovered he was actually raised by his grandmother and had lived in the same neighborhood area for a number of years prior to his moving to another town. So, rather than being a stranger, this young man was very familiar with the area and had lived just one street away from the victim. After obtaining additional evidence, the police were able to arrest the young man prosecute him for the assault.

Case Study 11-4

Multiple police jurisdictions were investigating a series of rapes and attempted rapes in which the offender would gain access to a house and confront the victim who was normally in bed. Several crimes were linked through DNA, and several others through other factors, but so far the police were unable to identify the offender. The offender was identified as a power reassurance type, and a similar strategy to the one used in Case Study 11-3 was suggested, along with an additional suggestion to pay attention to any suspect who may have been interrupted while trying to enter a house. Such suspects may have been classified as only burglars and therefore discounted as potential rapists. The suggestion was to go back and re-contact any offender who had been identified during this time and obtain a DNA sample. Within a few days, a suspect was arrested for an attempted burglary of an apartment. The task force re-contacted the suspect, who denied any involvement in the rapes and voluntarily gave a DNA sample. Weeks later, the sample was positively linked to the DNA previously collected during several crime scene investigations. The offender was later arrested and made a full confession to all of the known rapes and several other attempted rapes and burglaries.

Note that in both cases, the suggested strategy did not identify a specific person, but based on previously established behaviors of this offender type, gave the police a starting point to begin to identify the offender. For individual offenders we can look at their MO and their possible crime scene signature to be able to predict how they are likely to respond in the future.

In using a CIA to link cases together, we want to look at the MO to determine how the offender was able to carry out his attacks and escape detection, as well as the signature aspects that are unique to a particular offender. The MO, as stated earlier, is based on experience or *learned behavior* and is therefore much more likely to change over time as the offender becomes more experienced. For serial offenders, we can expect an MO to change every 6 weeks or so. Many times a change is the result of public awareness. For instance, if the MO of the offender was to gain entrance to a victim's residence through an unlocked rear door, once the public becomes aware of the series of attacks, people become more security conscious and begin to lock their doors and windows. This means that the offender must adjust his MO in order to continue his attacks. One offender in Arkansas was using a blue light in his vehicle to pull over women along the highway at night. Once they stopped, he would kidnap them at gunpoint and take them to another location and rape them. There were several similar instances, but once the public became aware of the ploy, women were refusing to stop along the highway, even for highway patrol officers in marked vehicles. The offender then changed his tactics and began to assault females at their residences. Initially, the police assumed these assaults were committed by a different offender based on the MO, but when the behavior of the offender during the sexual assault was compared to the previous assaults, it was clear it was the same offender who was forced to change his MO but retained his signature.

A more reliable method for case linkage is an *offender or crime scene signature*, because even when the offender's MO changes, the signature or the motivation of the offense does not. Although there may be subtle changes to his signature as the offender gains more experience and refines his fantasies, the general theme behind his signature is going to remain the same and will remain fairly unique to that offender.

A CIA can be a very effective tool, but it is not by itself going to solve a case. It may only assist providing additional information about the offender and suggest additional investigative leads. It may also provide possible interview suggestions, be used to support a search warrant, or indicate the likelihood of increased violence of the offender in future cases. However, there are instances when a CIA can actually be very counterproductive to an investigation; **Case Study 11-5** is a good example of this.

Case Study 11-5

During a review of an unsolved and well-publicized serial murder investigation, the police department received four unsolicited offers to conduct "profiles" of the crime and offender. The department, under public pressure for six unsolved homicides and with little physical or forensic evidence available, jumped at each offer. The department cooperated in each instance, hoping for any possible insight into the crime and the offender. Unfortunately, none of the so-called experts had the education, training, police experience, or qualifications to conduct such analysis. The results were four totally different interpretations of the crime and the offender. This caused the investigation to suddenly divert and go off into a different direction each time a new "profile" was received. If viewed separately, it was as if each "expert" was describing completely different investigations. One analysis was so inadequate that it was clearly almost a word-for-word copy of the professional text from which its findings were based. Another so-called expert completely misinterpreted one of the autopsy reports, causing the department to change its theory of that particular crime. The result of these efforts was a lot of frustration, wasted time, and wasted resources by the department with no progress toward the outcome. After coordinating with a true expert on behavioral analysis, all four reports were totally debunked and set aside.

Always exercise caution when seeking a professional to conduct a CIA on a particular case. The FBI or other professionally trained law enforcement officers are almost always a good starting point, and a request for a CIA can be made through ViCAP. Some non-law enforcement professionals are also highly qualified, but there are a lot of charlatans who believe a formal college education, with no actual practical experience, qualifies them to render such an opinion. A good analogy is that a graduate of medical school does not immediately open a practice and start seeing patients; instead, he continues his classroom instruction with supervised practical experience for several more years. Case Study 11-5 is an example of what happens when so-called experts volunteer their services only to create more problems than they may have solved.

Once an offender is identified by whatever means, the investigation is far from over. As in the case with the acquaintance offender or someone who is already known at the time of the victim's initial report, our attention now focuses on the offender to link him further to the scene or in some cases to eliminate him from being involved. This generally will involve validating the results of the offender interview such as any possible alibis.

▶ Alibis

An alibi is evidence or an explanation offered by the suspect to show he or she was not at the scene at the time the offense was committed. It should never be accepted at face value. Once an alibi is accepted we have basically eliminated that suspect from involvement, because he had no opportunity to commit the offense. Thus, it is extremely important that we exercise caution in this area and check out each and every alibi thoroughly. If a suspect claims he was at a particular place or with a particular person at a particular time, we must refute or validate that alibi. As a general rule, three independent means should be used to validate the alibi before the suspect can be cleared, but there are some important considerations to remember in this process:

1. An alibi provided by a relative is considered only half as reliable as that of other persons. This is based on the fact that relatives often provide alibis for their family members whether they are true or not. Therefore, using the rule of thumb requiring three independent sources to validate an alibi: If the wife or husband of the suspect provides an alibi for the suspect, this does not count as one source, but only half of one source. An additional two and a half sources are needed to completely eliminate the suspect. In many cold cases that have been reopened, the new suspect turns out to be one that had been eliminated too quickly and without proper validation very early on in the case.
2. The alibi must cover the same time period as the event itself or an other critical aspect of the crime. Regardless of an alibi for before or after the event, it is the suspect's whereabouts during the event that is important.
3. A credible and documented alibi may only mean the particular suspect was not present at the time of the criminal offense.

There are some instances when it is very difficult to validate the whereabouts of a suspect. For instance, those who live alone and claim they stayed home all night and had no contact with anyone else are very problematic. Canvass interviews of neighbors, checking Internet usage and telephone records, and in some cases conducting a polygraph are means to validate these alibis. In cases where we cannot validate the alibi, we may have to use other measures to eliminate the suspect, such as forensic evidence or motive and means. Unless another suspect is eventually positively identified, this person should remain on a possible suspect or person of interest list.

Another investigative effort which may be helpful is the use of a timeline wherein we can establish the offender and victim's activity before, during, and after the incident. This is used to not only link possible cases together, but to help establish or refute the offender's alibi or version of events.

▶ Timelines

A timeline is a separate written report designed to put all of the events relating to the crime into proper chronological order in one document. Although it can be used for any crime, its value in sex crime investigations becomes very evident when confronted with a complicated series of events, multiple offenders, or serial offenders. Timelines as an important investigative tool are based on an old adage: *Nothing happens in a vacuum. There is always a before, a during, and an after for every event.*

This is true for every event, but especially so when investigating crime. So many times detectives want to focus on the event itself, more specifically the crime scene and witness statements or suspect admissions, and they do not always take into consideration important circumstantial evidence that may have led up to the crime or may have transpired after the crime. Whereas the crime scene records the *during* aspect, the timeline is designed to concentrate on the *before* and *after* of the criminal act.

There is no particular format or style for constructing a timeline, and several commercially available computer programs are designed to create timelines and various link analyses. These special computer programs can produce high-quality and very professional-looking products, which are very useful, especially in court. But, they are also costly to purchase and maintain and may take additional training in order to fully use. However, a workable and useful timeline can be created using a regular word-processing program or any one of the spreadsheet programs readily available on most computers.

Which program is used depends on what is available for the individual detectives or their agency and how proficient they are with the use of different programs. We have found that using a simple spreadsheet program produces one of the easiest timelines to use and understand. One value of using a spreadsheet program is that no additional training is needed and multiple detectives or administrative support personnel can be used to update the document as new information is obtained if it is placed on a common server or computer. The purpose of a timeline is to place all of the various pieces of the investigation into one document in chronological order. Often the timeline is the only place in the entire case file where all of the facts and circumstances from all documents and statements can be found. More importantly, it also is the one place where all of the various events can be seen in context with other facts and circumstances.

The value of placing these seemingly unrelated events into some chronological order is the ability to paint a picture of premeditation, establish or destroy an alibi, and to possibly link others to the crime as co-conspirators. In the case of a serial offender, these events could link common cases together with other aspects of the offender's life. **Table 11-1** is a basic example of the simple timeline for a possible serial offender. Even in this small and limited timeline, it is possible to recognize a pattern to the offender's activity. It may also identify other potential investigative leads or identify a weakness in the investigation or identify an area where additional evidence is needed to establish a particular fact.

TABLE 11-1 Sample Timeline for a Potential Serial Rapist

Date	Time	Event	Source
3/24/2010		Henry rents apartment on Castle Drive	Rental contract
3/30/2010		Henry and wife move into apartment	Witness
3/30/2010	2:30	ATM receipt from Arthur Street ATM $40	Bank records
4/4/2010	1:45	ATM receipt from Arthur Street ATM $40	Bank records
4/10/2010	14:25	Henry's daughter born	Birth certificate
4/12/2010		Wife returns home from hospital	
4/15/2010	2:00	Brenda Tuttle raped in Newton Apartments, Arthur Street	Police report
4/15/2010	8:00	Henry calls in sick to work	Timecard
4/16/2010	8:00	Henry reports to work	Timecard
4/19/2010	3:00	Debit card used at 7-Eleven on Arthur Street	Bank records
4/25/2010		Henry receives collection notice for vehicle	Subpoena
4/27/2010	14:00	Daughter medical appointment	Dr. records
4/27/2010	21:00	Domestic disturbance at Henry's house	Police report
4/28/2010	2:30	Kathy Winchell raped in Garden Apartments, Arthur Street	Police report
4/28/2010	4:00	ATM receipt from Arthur Street ATM $40	Bank records
4/28/2010		Henry scheduled day off	
5/5/2010		Apartment rent is late	Lease info
5/7/2010	9:00	Wife travels to mother's house for visit	Wife statement
5/7/2010	23:54	Debit card used at 7-Eleven on Arthur Street	Bank records
5/8/2010	2:45	Connie Sullivan raped in Newton Apartments, Arthur Street	Police report

Collateral Materials

In addition to the general offender background information mentioned previously, wives, girlfriends, and other witnesses may also be able to provide access to another very important facet of the offender, which Hazelwood and Burgess[3] call *collateral material*.

Collateral materials are the personal property that may be collected and maintained by certain offenders and may include a wide variety of items such as personal writings, books, newspaper clippings, files, or magazines. Frequently, the offender may have a special place within the residence he shares with his wife and children that only he has access to. This may include the basement or attic, an office, or even something smaller such as a trunk, suitcase, or filing cabinet. In many cases the collateral material is no longer found as books, handwritten notes, or pictures, but instead has been purchased or maintained digitally with a personal computer or other digital storage devices. This eliminates the need for a special hiding place and allows the offender to collect much more of this type of material.

Collateral material is found in four categories known as *erotica, educational, introspective,* and *intelligence.*

Erotica

Erotica are materials that serve a sexual purpose for the offender. What material this may consist of depends upon the individual offender and any paraphilias or sexual fantasies he may have developed. It may include inanimate objects such as underwear, shoes, inflatable dolls, or mannequins. It could also include any number of books and magazines, photographs, and even personal drawings or writings. It is not unusual for male offenders to have a collection of softcore magazines such as *Penthouse, Playboy, Hustler,* or other similar magazines. The evaluation as to the importance of this material includes whether it is secreted away from everyone else in the family, there is a serious financial investment in buying the items, the material is never thrown away or otherwise disposed of, and it relates to the offense under investigation.

Educational

Educational collateral materials are items such as professional articles or textbooks that may provide the offender with direct knowledge or information concerning crime scene investigation, forensics, DNA analysis, legal matters, profiling, or psychology. Such material would be used to educate the offender on police tactics and capabilities that could be used to help him commit crimes and escape detection by the police.

---

[3] Hazelwood, R., & Burgess, A. W. (2008). *Practical aspects of rape investigation: A multidisciplinary approach* (4th ed.). Boca Raton, FL: CRC Press.

Introspective

These materials provide the offender with information about his particular sexual or personality disorders, behaviors, or interests. These are collected in order to rationalize his deviant sexuality. Perhaps the best examples are pedophiles who may collect material on pedophilia to show that they are not necessarily deviant, but just not politically correct, and that their system has just not been accepted by the rest of society yet. Examples would also include articles on offender research, causation, and self-help books or audiotapes by subject matter experts on their particular interests.

Intelligence

Intelligence collateral materials are collected and maintained for use in future crimes. These may include index cards, notebooks, or file folders containing names and addresses, photographs, or even surveillance notes on future or past victims.

The importance of collateral material is that it can provide some *direct evidence* that links an offender to a crime and victim, such as personal property taken from the scene or the victim. It may also include photographs and/or audio or video recordings of the offender's assaults. Some material may also only provide *indirect* or *circumstantial* evidence that can link the offender to the scene or victim; examples include writing or pornography that is related to the same theme displayed in the crime. What may be shocking in some cases is the sheer amount of material that some offenders may have in their possession—sometimes carefully packaged, stored, or even formally categorized for easy retrieval when needed.

It is important to note that this material may have such great value to the offender that even when he is being investigated, he may still elect not to dispose of any of this material, regardless of how incriminating it may be. The value of collateral material comes into play during the suspect interview, when at the appropriate time the detective informs the suspect that it has been found and recovered. This may have the equivalent effect of the seizure of someone's life work, so the fact that his most coveted property was handled or is in the custody of another could be devastating to the offender.

▶ Linking Cases Together

One of our goals in this stage of the investigation is to look for other victims and establish if we are possibly dealing with a serial offender. A serial offender is someone who has committed multiple offenses. Forensic evidence is the best and most sure method to link suspects to multiple cases, and it is difficult for a suspect to offer a defense when his DNA or fingerprints are found at multiple scenes with multiple victims. Unfortunately, this is not always the situation, so we have to then look at other ways to link offenders to other cases. There is a myriad of things we can use through the course of the investigation to link cases together.

The matrix shown in **Table 11-2** is a good example of the many factors we can use to link cases together in a serial offender investigation. It was created to reflect the review of several adjacent police agencies experiencing a series of rapes of women, primarily in their apartments or houses, and at least one was attacked outside her house. As the word of the various assaults got out through police channels, all of the police agencies came together to exchange information. Communication is the key to these investigations, and getting every adjacent police agency involved was a good move. During a series of meetings, each department shared its particular case facts and evidence with the other departments. One suggestion at these meetings was to take all of preliminary investigations and construct the matrix to see if they could come up with a proactive investigative plan. The matrix was designed to identify the basic MO of the offender, which included the timeframe of the incident, where it occurred, the method of entry, and the approach of the offender. It also focused on the sexual aspects of the incident and offender sexual behavior; that is, what the sexual interest of the offender was and what sex acts were demanded and performed. Lastly, this particular case focused on the verbal behavior of the offender, because he provided abundant personal information about himself to several victims.

One of the advantages of the matrix is that it provides a basic understanding of the offender and how he commits the crime, including anything he may do that is unusual or unique. This understanding helps the police to review any previous unsolved cases to see if there were other cases within the area they had not yet linked to the offender, and more importantly, to be able to quickly recognize the offender for any newer cases that may be reported during this timeframe.

Table 11-2 shows nine cases that were evaluated to see if they could be linked to one offender. During this type of review a number of factors are considered, including the time of the event, method of entry, and the offender's approach to the victim. This type of information reflects the general MO of the offender and how he was able to commit the crime and escape. Additional facts came from aspects the offender's verbal, sexual, and physical behavior. For instance, this particular offender engaged in some revealing verbal exchanges with his victims after the assaults that included detailed information about his family background, with mention on several occasions that he had a young daughter. The physical behavior was also important because he seldom used physical violence, as most victims were either unable to actively resist or complied with demands out of fear. However, note that in Cases 4, 5, and 7, he reportedly choked the victim from behind. This was determined to be an effort to gain control, overcome resistance, and ensure compliance of his victim; once they complied, the physical assault stopped. This offender was noted to routinely engage in multiple sexual assaults including vaginal, anal, and oral sex and demanded different sexual positions.

TABLE 11-2 Matrix Linking Cases Together

Event	Case 1	Case 2	Case 3	Case 4	Case 5	Case 6	Case 7	Case 8	Case 9
Time 2200–0600		x	x	x	x	x	x	x	x
Victim's residence		x	x	x	x	x	x	x	x
No forced entry		x	x	x	x	x	unk	x	x
Victim sleeping		x	x		x	x	x		x
Choked from behind				x	x		x		x
Express concern for victim	x	x	x	x				x	x
Victim moved within house		x	x	x		x		x	x
Negotiates with victim			x		x			x	x
Multiple sex acts		x	x					x	x
Vaginal sex	x	x	x	x	x	x	x	x	x
Sex in sitting position		x	x						
Anal sex		x	x					x	x
Oral sex		x	x			x			x
Ejaculates in vagina	x	x	x		unk		unk		x
Ejaculates in mouth		x	x					unk	x
Displays weapon	x			x					x
Washes victim off		x				x		x	x
Offender smokes		x	x	x		x			x
Extended time with victim		x	x			x		x	x
Provides personal info		x		x		x		x	x
Mentions daughter		x		x		x			x
DNA	x	x	x						x

Note that there appears to be a wide variance in the offender's sexual demands across many cases, and with the physical behavior on others. This often causes much disagreement among the police about whether they are dealing with the same offender. However, when examining the physical and the sexual behavior displayed by the offender, the differences are related to the victims rather than the offender. In cases where the victim showed an active effort to resist or escape, more physical force was applied and the resulting sexual behavior was also limited. In cases where the victim offered no resistance and was compliant with the offender's demands, we see more sexual behavior in the form of multiple assaults. In these cases we also see more verbal behavior by the offender as he spent more time with these victims, including holding long conversations and smoking cigarettes with them. In several cases with compliant victims, he moved them from place to place within the residence, such as from the bedroom to the living room and once from the bedroom to an outside deck where the victim was sexually assaulted. With a more compliant victim, we also see attempts to destroy some physical evidence by making them wash in the shower after the assault. The unique aspect of this particular offender was reflected in the amount of time spent with the victim after the assaults, the verbal behavior and personal information he provided about himself, and the multiple sex acts and positions demanded.

When using a matrix, it is important to remember that there are seldom two cases in any series that will link completely together. This is because each offense will involve different circumstances based on the individual victims, the location of the assaults, the increasing experience of the offender, and any number of things that may present themselves to the offender. For instance, in two of the cases the offender entered the residence in the early morning hours, but the victim was not actually in bed. In Case 4, the victim was using the bathroom and was surprised by the offender standing in the hallway as she exited the bathroom; in Case 8, the victim was surprised as she was watching TV in her living room. Cases 2, 3, and 9 are matched to the offender through DNA analysis, but absent the forensics, the cases are all very similar and could be linked together through the offender behavior. However, Case 1 is almost completely different from the others. The offense took place outside the normal timeframe, the victim was accosted outside her apartment and not inside, and the assault was rather quick, with little interaction or verbal exchange between the victim and offender. If not for the DNA match to the same offender, it is likely this case would not be considered to be part of this series. This is an example of a very important concept when dealing with serial offenders: Generally speaking, the first cases in the series are atypical or different from those in the later part of the series. This is because during the first cases the offender may lack the experience or the self-confidence in his abilities.

Based on a review of all nine cases noted in the matrix, a firm link can be established in at least seven of these cases through the offender's behavior or through forensic evidence. Only in Cases 5 and 7 is the offender not positively linked into the series. This does not mean they were committed by another offender, but rather that there may not be sufficient evidence or information provided at the time of review to firmly establish that link. In these cases, more effort should be expended to gain additional information, perhaps through a re-interview of the victim.

The matrix was created by using a simple spreadsheet program which allows for easy editing as new information is developed throughout the cases. Note that in some places the information is noted as unknown because it was not collected or asked about during the initial police investigation, or in several cases, the victim declined to submit to a medical examination.

NCIC Offline Checks

Another effective tool, especially when dealing with a potential serial offender, is a National Crime Information Center (NCIC) "offline check." This is a special request made through the NCIC to query their database to determine when and where the offender or his vehicle came into contact with police and when his name or vehicle information was checked through the NCIC. As most people know, it is routine for police officers who stop a vehicle for a possible traffic violation to ask for an NCIC check to determine if the vehicle was reported stolen. Further, if the driver of a vehicle or a person is stopped for suspicious behavior or whenever someone is arrested, there is an additional NCIC check for his criminal history to determine if he is being sought by police elsewhere or if he has any current arrest warrants on file. Each one of these contacts through NCIC is recorded in the NCIC database, which can be retrieved during the offline check. This provides the time, date, and agency that requested the information and the reason the individual was checked. If the individual was driving a vehicle, that vehicle information is also provided. For background purposes, it positively places the offender at a specific place at a specific time, which is then recorded on the timeline for later comparison to other events, but also provides the detective another place to go for information. Specifically, a police department can determine why the offender was checked out, or what he was doing at the time.

What is especially helpful is being able to identify the type and description of any vehicles a suspect may have been driving during previous contact with police. If, for instance, the offender is driving a pickup truck at the time of the investigation, but previous encounters with police can identify, via the NCIC check, previously owned vehicles that may be unknown at the time of the investigation. An offline check also provides information from Immigration and Customs Enforcement (ICE) about whether the suspect ever departed the country and was processed through one of the U.S. points of entry upon returning to the United States. Information on a particular offender is readily available on the NCIC server for the preceding 6-month period. However, information beyond 6 months in the past up to 10 years can be obtained if specifically requested through NCIC. Although an NCIC online check may not be beneficial for every case, if we are working on a serial offender, it can be a very effective tool to use to document his current movement and other activities.

▶ Conclusion

There are many instances when, regardless of our efforts, we are unable to identify a suspect; or, if we have identified a probable suspect, there is not enough evidence available for a successful prosecution. In these cases, whatever efforts were expended were not necessarily wasted. If these suspects are sexual offenders, is it very unlikely they will stop. Many times escaping an arrest and prosecution may embolden them to reoffend. However, many states as well as the U.S. Military have eliminated the statute of limitations on the offense of rape, which means that even if we are unsuccessful in identifying a suspect immediately, if a suspect is ever identified, prosecution will still be possible provided we took the time to conduct a professional investigation. Additionally, we should also make certain we have done all we possibly can to link this offender to any other crimes, such as ensuring DNA and fingerprint evidence is submitted by the crime laboratories to CODIS and IAFIS. This is automatic for some crime labs, but it never hurts to make sure this was accomplished prior to closing a case. Lastly, we also want to add the case into the ViCAP database. This may not only assist another police department with a current or future investigation, but may lead to additional evidence that could lead to the solving of this case as well.

▶ References

Ainsworth, P. B. (2001). *Offender profiling and crime analysis*. Portland, OR: Willan Publishing.

Benedict, J. R. (1998). *Athletes and acquaintance rape*, Thousand Oaks, CA: Sage Publications.

Holmes, R. M., & Holmes, S. T. (2002). *Profiling violent crimes: An investigative tool* (3rd ed.). Thousand Oaks, CA: Sage Publications.

Palermo, G. B., & Kocsis, R. N. (2005). *Offender profiling: An introduction to the sociopathological analysis of violent crime*. Springfield, IL: Thomas Publishing.

Warshaw, R. (1988). *I never called it rape*. New York, NY: Harper and Row.

CHAPTER TWELVE

Drug- and Alcohol-Facilitated Sexual Assaults

Drug-facilitated sexual assaults (DFSA) and alcohol-facilitated sexual assaults (AFSA) are incidents in which the victims are too intoxicated or have been rendered unconscious at the time of the assault and are thus unable to give knowing and voluntary consent to sexual intercourse. Although we see more and more of these incidents in recent years, drugs and other intoxicating substances, particularly alcohol, have been used for hundreds of years as a means to lower the inhibitions of victims and thus take advantage of them. The poet Ogden Nash succinctly sums up the concept: "Candy is dandy, but liquor is quicker."[1] This translates to a widespread belief that getting a woman drunk increases a man's chances of having sex with her. The problem arises when the woman drinks to the point where she can no longer give consent and it becomes a criminal act. Alcohol in combination with other drugs has become an expedient way to render a victim unconscious and thus unable to give consent. This is not a new concept either. An example is the Mickey Finn, which is a combination of chloral hydrate and alcohol, which causes the victim to fall relatively quickly into a deep sleep. The original concept of Mickey Finn was to help facilitate the robbery of victims by rendering them unconscious so that when they awoke, they were unaware of what happened to them.

Drug- and alcohol-facilitated sexual assaults are also a little different than most of the incidents described in other chapters of this text. They can be committed by strangers or acquaintances, and happen quite frequently during dating situations. Often the victims unwittingly participate in their own victimization through their voluntary use of illicit drugs or through voluntary intoxication through alcohol. These cases present some of the most challenging investigations that detectives have to deal with on a routine basis. Unfortunately, there is often a delay in reporting. One reason victims delay is worry over their own criminal misconduct through voluntary use of illegal

---

[1] Ogden Nash (1902–1971), "Reflections on Ice-Breaking" Published in Hard Lines. Simon and Schuster, 1931.

substances and for fear of incriminating friends who may have been present at the social gathering that precipitated the incident. When this happens the victim might have to decide to admit to committing a criminal offense, and she might also have to also identify others who were present and also used the illicit substances. Another frequent problem is that victims are uncertain of exactly what happened to them. Because of the drugs or alcohol, there are gaps in their memory and ability to recall what happened. They wake up confused and uncertain of where they are at or how they got there. They have no memory of being sexually assaulted, but believe something may have happened to them because they have the feeling of having had sex from genital soreness, their sanitary napkin or tampon was missing, or they woke up dressed but their clothing was improperly placed on their body. This presents investigators with a great number of difficulties as they seek to unravel exactly what happened.

Whereas these cases are difficult and often frustrating, they are not impossible to solve; but they do take patience, special attention, and understanding from both the police and prosecutors. The offenders in these types of cases are also very different from the other offenders discussed earlier in the text. In these cases there is seldom any force or coercion of the victim because the drugs or alcohol have already rendered the victim into such a condition that force is not needed. Instances of drug- or alcohol-facilitated rape are also somewhat less likely to be reported to the authorities than incidents of forcible rape. Many times victims hesitate to report because they do not want others to know about the rape, they may fear retaliation by the offender, they have no idea who actually raped them, and/or they have a very real perception that with no exact memory of the event, there will be no evidence to validate their claim. When victims choose not to report their assault or police do not take such instances seriously, offenders are allowed to continue to find new victims. Any detective should take these cases seriously, whether or not they have teenage daughters, nieces, or other family or friends attending high school, college, or in military service.

This chapter has been divided into separate sections on alcohol-facilitated sexual assaults and drug-facilitated sexual assaults because, although they are closely related, there are some very important differences in the offenders involved and the other circumstances surrounding the incidents.

▶ Alcohol-Facilitated Sexual Assaults (AFSAs)

Alcohol is a particular problem in sexual assault investigations, and as noted throughout the text, it plays some part in well over 50% of all incidents that are reported. This includes consumption by either the victim or offender, or in many cases both. Alcohol has been a favorite drug of choice of offenders for hundreds of years for lowering inhibitions or overcoming any potential victim resistance. Its popularity comes from several reasons, including: Alcohol is a legal substance, it is socially acceptable, and therefore it may be openly purchased and consumed by adults. The real reason it is used to such an extent is that it works. Alcohol in moderation is present in some fashion or form in many social situations and it is associated with recreation, having fun, interacting with others, and for many, with sex. Alcohol has oft been described as "liquid courage," and the lowering of inhibitions seems to facilitate flirting, sexual attraction to another, or possibly lead to developing a personal relationship. This plays into an important teaching point used when we talk about sex: "*If men thought eating asphalt would help them have sex, we would be driving on dirt roads in a matter of months.*" Essentially, whenever any product or thing is said to increase the chance of having sex when it is consumed or used, it will become very popular. Because of alcohol's effects and the mere *possibility* of having sexual intercourse, alcohol has taken on an almost mythical importance in social settings, particularly for youth. We frequently see this with younger and sometimes underage victims who are not interested in any of the social aspects of alcohol, but rather in its intoxicating effects.

The main intoxicating effects of alcohol are the lowering of inhibitions, motor skills, and cognitive abilities of the consumer. As a person becomes more intoxicated, there is a decreasing ability to process information and make sound and logical judgments and a decrease in motor control, speech, reaction time, and impulse control. This makes it harder for people to stop once they have begun to engage in a particular behavior. If the consumption continues, it will ultimately result in a loss of consciousness, or "passing out," as it is more commonly known. In extreme cases there is a very real possibility of death from alcohol poisoning.

Alcohol also contributes to sexual victimization, not just because of its effects on the cognitive abilities, but also on risk perception.[2] For instance, if a woman was sober, and a man gave her a very strong drink, she would likely recognize its strength as soon as she tasted it. It is likely she would further dilute the drink before consuming it and her "internal safety mechanism" may lead her to think the man was deliberately trying to get her drunk. This would make her cautious about his intentions and she would take steps to avoid him and refuse any other drinks from him. However, after having a couple of "normal" drinks, the same woman might become somewhat intoxicated and it would become more difficult for her to notice the drink was stronger. Victims may also make unwise decisions such as accepting a ride or accompanying someone they do not know to his apartment, or allowing someone they do not know to stay at their house. Alcohol impairs the capacity to take in and analyze information, make complex decisions, and recognize potential dangers; thus, it lowers that internal safety mechanism. Instead, intoxicated people focus on

---

[2] Norris, J. (2008). *The relationship between alcohol consumption and sexual victimization.* Harrisburg, PA: National Online Resource Center on Violence Against Women Applied Research Forum. Retrieved June 11, 2012, from http://www.vawnet.org/Assoc_Files_VAWnet/AR_AlcVictimization.pdf

whatever information is most available, but do not always catch some of the less obvious information.

Predatory offenders use two general strategies or approaches (both can be used with alcohol and/or drugs). The first is known as the *proactive approach*, which is the intentional effort to get victims drunk or give them an incapacitating drug without their knowledge. In these situations the victim is then maneuvered to another location to be sexually assaulted. The second approach is known as *opportunistic*, which is simply to take advantage of someone who is already too intoxicated to give knowing consent.

The most common rape-risk situation for adult and college-aged women is the opportunistic type of situation where they are sexually assaulted after they have become voluntarily intoxicated. A jury's negative perceptions of a victim's behavior and credibility can be a significant barrier to successful prosecution, because society tends to have difficulty distinguishing between drunken sex and rape. The question becomes: Was the incident actually rape, or is it a case of next day regret, or "buyer's remorse"?[3]

Victims

As discussed earlier, the credibility of the victim and establishing corroborating evidence are essential elements in all sexual assault investigations. It is even more important in these cases because the introduction of alcohol into the situation can cause many people on the jury to remember something they may have done while under the influence of alcohol that they regretted. For alcohol- and drug-facilitated rapes, we can break this down into four components identified by Scalzo as:[4]

1. Actual credibility
2. Ability to perceive at the time of the incident
3. Ability to remember what happened
4. Existence of corroborative evidence

Actual Credibility

Credibility is essentially the truthfulness of the victim and can be based on a combination of her background (victimology) and corroborating evidence, such as other witness testimony or forensic evidence. The problem in these situations is that a victim who was voluntarily intoxicated at the time of her rape may feel shame or self-blame and may be reluctant to reveal

---

[3] Scalzo, T. (2007). *Prosecuting alcohol facilitated sexual assaults*. Alexandria, VA: National District Attorney's Association, American Prosecutors Research Institute.
[4] Scalzo, T. (2007). *Prosecuting alcohol facilitated sexual assaults*. Alexandria, VA: National District Attorney's Association, American Prosecutors Research Institute.

embarrassing details or try to limit her own participatory conduct. In many cases this becomes very problematic because her reaction could cause the police to believe she is withholding certain facts or is simply being untruthful. Credibility in all rape cases is important, but especially in these incidents where the whole case is going to come down on issues of consent. The victim must be able to state unequivocally that she indicated her nonconsent to the act while masked in an alcohol fog and be believed by the jury.

One of the factors that will come into play is whether there is a motive for the victim to lie about the incident. The defense will call into question the victim's conduct and imply that the complaint was the result of drunken sex and next day regrets. Because this is certainly going to be one of the key defense points, we can blunt some of these issues through establishing victim credibility during the victimology assessment. Examples would also include: The victim's complaint was timely and she came forward as soon as possible to make the complaint; she told someone immediately following the incident about what happened; and she has a consistent statement about what happened. We also want to consider if there was some other reason why she would not be interested in consensual sex such as: At the time, she was menstruating and she was wearing a tampon or sanitary napkin, or she was previously injured, and at the time even consensual sex was painful to her. Lastly, did she have other underlying medical issues such as a yeast or fungal infection, an STD, or some other uncomfortable condition that made even consensual sex uncomfortable to her?

Ability to Perceive

Relating to victims' credibility is their ability to perceive or grasp what was happening to them at the time of the incident. It is clear that the ability to perceive or understand what is happening is going to be influenced as the level of intoxication increases. If the victim loses consciousness, then she has no ability to understand what is going on and therefore cannot give knowing consent to the act, and the issue may prove to be moot. In instances where the victim is intoxicated but is still conscious, we have to look at some other factors such as: Is the victim able to relate in any detail what exactly happened? How much alcohol did she consume? Who else was present at the scene, and where was everyone prior to the assault? Using other witnesses, we may have to determine other factors relating to the victim and her activity such: her ability to perform simple tasks such as walking, mixing a drink, lighting a cigarette, using the restroom, or standing without support. Was her speech slurred, was she speaking too loudly, or was she able to fully participate in a conversation and understand what was being said? Was she responsive or in a nonresponsive state? Did she understand what was happening around her? Could she use her cell phone, send or receive emails, or text message? Could she use her credit card, debit card, or use an ATM, or was she able to pay for a purchase? Lastly, what was her physical condition, such as her clothing, makeup, or hair? Was she crying, vomiting, or spilling drinks? All of these simple tasks become difficult or are impacted as the victim consumes more alcohol and the effects are generally apparent if other witnesses are asked.

Ability to Remember

The victim's ability to remember what happened is also a good source of credibility, and the more details the victim is able to recall that can be verified will benefit establishing the victim's credibility. However, alcohol does diminish the ability to remember, and the more alcohol that is consumed, the greater the memory impairments. Large quantities of alcohol consumed rapidly may result in the victim experiencing either a fragmentary or an en bloc blackout.[5]

Fragmentary blackouts "occur when people may recall portions of the episode after the incident when cues for events are provided. Fragmentary blackouts involve a more transient, perhaps forgetful memory loss for which aspects of experience are recalled via provision of pertinent cues" (p. 15).[6]

En bloc blackouts have "definitive starting points, contain amnesia for all events within a discrete period, end with a sense of lost time, and require a high blood alcohol concentration." The *en bloc* blackout is not a "process of forgetting, but rather one of not remembering" (p. 15).[7]

If victims are unable to remember every detail of the assault, then we must concentrate on those aspects they can remember, starting with what was going on before the incident and what may have happened after the assault or as they regained consciousness. Concentrate on the offender's behavior and identifying other witnesses who may be able to provide other information or perspectives on the assault. Going over the event in short sequences may help to trigger or cue a memory. Examples include: After he brought you the drink, then what happened? After you were dancing then what happened? After he started kissing you then what happened? Breaking down the event into these smaller sequential events is very helpful in allowing the victim to slowly recall what may have happened.

Existence of Corroborative Evidence

As oft repeated in the text, corroborative evidence is not a legal requirement but it is vital if we want to first get the prosecutor's interest to take the case to court and then to present it to a jury in order to get a conviction. Regardless of the circumstances of the sexual assault, corroborative evidence may

---

[5] Scalzo, T. (2007). *Prosecuting alcohol facilitated sexual assaults.* Alexandria, VA: National District Attorney's Association, American Prosecutors Research Institute.

[6] Scalzo, T. (2007). *Prosecuting alcohol facilitated sexual assaults.* Alexandria, VA: National District Attorney's Association, American Prosecutors Research Institute.

[7] Scalzo, T. (2007). *Prosecuting alcohol facilitated sexual assaults.* Alexandria, VA: National District Attorney's Association, American Prosecutors Research Institute.

compensate for lack of the victim's memory. Finding an offender's DNA inside the victim can establish sexual intercourse even when the victim says she cannot remember that it happened. Such forensic evidence would be great to have, but corroboration need not be so conclusive; it just must give the jury some context in which to evaluate the victim's credibility. However, information obtained from witnesses can show that the victim was too intoxicated to perceive the act or give knowing consent for the sex act; for example: the victim was unable to walk unassisted, lit up the wrong end of a cigarette, vomited or urinated on herself, could not undress herself, was unable to understand simple commands, or was so drunk she was helped to bed to go to sleep. Because of the condition of the victim, we may have to depend on others to gain this type of information and thus we can come up with some effective corroborating evidence. There is almost always some way to corroborate the victim's statement; if we look hard enough, it is generally there. Unfortunately, many times the detectives just do not want to spend the time to do it.

Case Study 12-1 is a typical example of an alcohol-facilitated sexual assault. The offender is known to the victim as a co-worker, but they have never had any type of sexual or romantic relationship. The offender went to the victim's house to "talk," and after drinking some alcohol the offender made sexual advances toward the victim.

Case Study 12-1

We were both off that day, and James, a guy I know from work, came over to my house for lunch. It wasn't a planned visit; he just showed up and knocked on my door. I think he was looking for someone to talk to about his wife, because I know they were having problems. He came in and we talked for a while—just small talk about work and things. Then he asked for a drink so I gave him a small glass and set a bottle of gin on the table and got a thing of orange juice out of the refrigerator. James said he didn't like small glasses so I went and gave him a regular water glass and he poured a drink. I then poured myself a drink and sat back down. I don't drink hard liquor that much so mine was pretty weak. We talked for a while longer and then I made us some sandwiches for lunch, and then we ate them. We kept talking; he was telling me about wife and family and some of their personal issues. I only had two weak drinks and was actually starting on my third when I decided it didn't taste very good and actually poured most of it down the sink while he was using the restroom. When he came out, I went to the bathroom. I started to feel a little sick and was sitting on the toilet trying to take deep breaths to avoid throwing up. I must have been in the bathroom for a while still sitting on the toilet when James just walked into the bathroom and took my hand and tried to make me stand up. I was telling him to stop and tried to take my hand away from him but he kept pulling me up, trying to make me stand up. I finally was brought to my feet, but my panties and shorts were still around my ankles and I was off balance and, well, we both fell into the bathtub and I hit my head and I think he hit his too but not too hard. I was telling him to stop and I was getting mad because my head hurt. He then stood up and grabbed me by both arms and pulled me up out of the bathtub and then tried to kiss me. I moved my face away and said for him to stop, but he reached up and pulled my chin and turned my face toward his and kissed me on the lips. I broke away and said to stop. He began walking backwards and pulling me forward, out of the bathroom and into the small bedroom. He then turned us both around and began pushing me backwards onto the bed. I was telling him to stop and I didn't want to do this, but it was like he didn't hear. He got onto the bed beside me and began touching me under my shirt and then rubbed my vaginal area with his hand. He kept trying to kiss me, but I was getting scared and actually started to get sick. I managed to push him back and then turned to my right side and got sick. I was throwing up on a pillow near my head. I know I threw up like three times, and tried to wipe my face with my hand. I was starting to feel really dizzy and then realized he had moved down to the foot of the bed and had got in between my legs and was performing oral sex on me. I was telling him to stop and I rolled over to my side because I thought I was going to get sick again. He then sat on the edge of the bed and began touching me again like, rubbing on my butt, and then he then put his finger in my butt. I called out to stop because it was hurting and he did. I tried to throw up again but was just sort of gagging. He then pushed me over to my stomach and then tried to enter my vagina with his penis from behind. But I don't think he was hard enough to actually penetrate. I said to stop but thought maybe he will just do it and get it over and then leave me alone. I was getting sick again from smelling the vomit on the bed and I pushed the pillow away from my face. He continued for a while and then just stopped and I'm not sure if he ever actually penetrated because he wasn't very hard. He turned me over onto my back again and then got into the bed and like straddling me, he moved up and then leaned forward where his penis was like in my face, and started telling me to suck him and make him cum. I was starting to feel sick again and turned my head to the side. He kept telling me to suck him and once he took his penis and rubbed it across my lips but I closed my eyes and kept my head turned. I guess he was getting frustrated because he got off of me and started getting dressed again. I rolled onto my side again and started to throw up again. He must have left because when I finally rolled over after a while I realized he was gone. I got up and pulled my panties and shorts up and went to the bathroom and splashed water on my face. Just a few minutes later two other friends came over and I told them what happened and they called the police for me.

The suspect, James, was later interviewed and corroborated nearly every event as stated by the victim, including falling over into the bathtub, but maintained it was absolutely a consensual event and even indicated that the victim was the aggressor.

One only need to apply the four components of credibility as previously described to this case study to see how a complaint like this should be approached. The victim's credibility was established by a prompt report and consistent statements to the police. The offender was a married coworker and there had never been any dating or even flirting between them at work or in any previous social contacts. The victim had a good reputation as an occasional social drinker and was often the designated driver when she and her friends went out. The victim was able to perceive what was going on that she was getting tipsy and actually threw her third drink away instead of finishing it. She was also able to relate what happened and could put events into sequential order as she gave her statement. She reportedly was in the bathroom feeling sick when James entered and made her stand up, with her shorts and underwear around her ankles. This is a very important aspect because there is no chance of a misunderstanding, no missed signal, no flirting, or mention of any conversation indicating she was interested in sex. Instead, she was unexpectedly disturbed in what most of us would agree is the most private setting and most private circumstance in our normal lives. She was feeling the effects of the alcohol to the point she and James lost their balance and fell into the bathtub and struck their heads. James then, despite her verbal and physical resistance, brought her into the bedroom where she was assaulted on the bed. Shortly thereafter she said she got sick and threw up. She was able to describe the sex acts, even to the point of not being sure he had penetrated her because he was not erect enough to do so.

Perhaps the best evidence is the various corroborating evidence, including her friends who provided descriptions of the victim as being extremely distraught but able to tell them what happened and who was involved. The police viewed the scene and noted the shower curtain was damaged and there was vomitus in the bedroom and also some on the victim's shirt. During his interview, the offender confirmed nearly everything the victim alleged but steadfastly maintained they were both drunk, and that it was actually the victim who was the initiator of the event and that the actual sexual acts were consensual. In this case, his confirmation of the sex act coupled with the victim's credibility, corroborating evidence, and some basic common sense that says it is unlikely that a person who has just gotten sick to their stomach is going to be ready and eager for consensual sex, and who really wants to have sex with someone who is throwing up?

One of the more important aspects of this case was after a detailed victimology and review of all case facts, the police department found no reason for a false report or for the victim to lie about what happened. The defense attorney would try to focus attention solely on the behaviors of the victim; however, we need to also take a look at the offender's behavior before, during, and after the incident and focus on the elements of proof to be successful. James was later convicted of attempted rape.

The Offender

Our major task in the investigation of these incidents is to determine if the offender is a predator or if the offender was just as drunk as the victim and did not intentionally rape anyone. This is often difficult because predators want to be seen as "regular guys doing what regular guys do," and that they were presented with an opportunity for consensual sex and merely made a mistake. But, with some effort, we can look at the offender's pre-crime behavior to determine whether there was predatory behavior. The more predatory behavior we can identify, the better able we are to show his criminal intent. An immense challenge in AFSA cases occurs when the offender was drunk as well, because offenders will attempt to use alcohol as an excuse for their actions and any rape. All investigations should include the offender's level of intoxication. Predators will often go to extra lengths to get their victim intoxicated yet will not drink as much because they will have to be able to manipulate the victim and maintain control over the situation. Based on witness interview, we can try to determine how drunk the offender was. What was his capacity to do things such as walk, talk, or drive? Did there appear to be any planning or manipulation on his part, such as ensuring the victim always had a drink or mixing the drinks himself, encouraging the victim to take shots of hard liquor, or taking some other actions to increase the amount of alcohol consumed by the victim? Did the offender maneuver the victim to a place where she was alone or take her away from friends or others to a place where she could then be assaulted? These are some predatory behaviors that we are looking for to show this was more of an intentional plan rather than just an opportunity that came along. The more sober and in control of his faculties the suspect was, the easier it is to show his behavior was predatory, especially if the victim was extremely intoxicated. The more predatory the defendant's behavior, the easier it is going to be to show that the actions are consistent with nonconsent. **Case Study 12-2** is an example of offender predatory conduct.

Case Study 12-2

Virginia and Raymond were co-workers who knew each other from work, but each had a different set of friends and had never dated or socialized with each other outside the work place. Several of the younger employees, including Virginia and Richard, got together after an office party at a local hotel and began drinking very heavily. Many of them had rented rooms at the hotel and intended to stay the night instead of trying to go home after drinking. Virginia became intoxicated and was slurring her speech, stumbling, and hesitant while walking, and had even mistakenly gone into to the men's restroom instead of the women's restroom. As the evening wore on, the employees gradually retired to their own rooms until only Virginia and Raymond remained. Virginia stated that she was also ready to go to her room and as she started to leave, Raymond came up to her, put his arm around her, and slowly walked her outside to the rear of the building. She was able to walk with Raymond's assistance but did not know where they were going. Raymond walked a short distance outside and into a small alley between buildings. He then stopped and tried to kiss Virginia, who later stated she told him no and did not kiss him back. Raymond then sat down on the concrete and pulled on her hand until she also sat down on the ground. Once she sat down Raymond pushed her back onto the concrete and began removing her pants. Virginia stated she was totally taken by surprise because there had been no conversation, no flirting, and no real interaction with Raymond prior to being led outside. She protested and said, "no" and "stop" and tried to get up, but Raymond lay on top of her and then vaginally raped her. Virginia said she was totally unprepared and did not know what to do but was afraid to do anything. After a short period of time, Raymond stood up and helped Virginia get to her feet and pull her pants up. He walked her back to the hotel lobby, where he then walked away.

Case Study 12-2 is an example of predatory conduct wherein the offender simply waited until the victim was totally incapacitated and no other witnesses were around to offer help to the victim. Witnesses confirm that Virginia was drinking heavily but was not flirting or giving the impression she was interested in sex. During his interview Raymond maintained that the act was completely consensual and even claimed Virginia was the aggressor. The verification of Virginia's intoxication, the location of the act in a public street when each had a hotel room available, and the fact that no witness observed any interaction between the two prior to the incident or while they were drinking were used to demonstrate the predatory conduct of Raymond.

Initially, both the police and prosecutor believed that Virginia's complaint was not a sexual assault but rather an example of drunken sex that Virginia regretted. This belief was held despite Raymond's failed polygraph examination on the issue of Virginia's incapacitation and the fact that he continued his advances despite Virginia telling him "no." It was only after the whole event was examined from the predatory behavior perspective that they were convinced that a criminal act was actually committed.

Many times offenders in these situations will talk about the incident to the police because they want their actions to be seen as opportunistic or a mistake or misunderstanding, as opposed to predatory. Therefore, they may willingly tell their side of the story. In these cases, we are interested in the offender's version of events, including his explanation of what happened before, during, and after the event. As discussed earlier, one of the things we are looking for is an admission that sexual intercourse or some other sexual act between the victim and offender did take place. The interviewer also needs to cover other very important areas such as such as:[8]

- Did he see the victim drinking?
- How much did the victim drink?
- What kind of drinks?
- Who gave her the alcohol?
- How many drinks did the victim consume?
- How many drinks did the suspect consume?
- Who purchased the alcohol?
- Did he think the victim was drunk? If not, what did the victim do to indicate she was not drunk?
- Was the victim awake during the entire sexual act?
- Did the victim fall asleep during the sexual act?
- Why would victim think she was raped?
- In what positions did they engage in sex? (Is this possible based on the victim's level of intoxication as reported by others?)
- Where did sexual intercourse take place? (Consistent with a consensual act?)
- Was there any prior interaction with the victim?
- How long has he known the victim and under what circumstances?
- How did the event end?
- What did the victim and offender do afterward?
- Has anyone else ever accused him of rape or other misconduct before?

These incidents are difficult but not impossible to investigate, and, like other acquaintance rape situations, it may seem like a case of "he said, she said," but with a little effort some corroborating evidence is generally available if an effort is made to find it. Prosecuting these cases also presents problems, and these are addressed in more detail later in this text.

▶ Drug-Facilitated Sexual Assaults (DFSAs)

DFSA incidents tend to follow a similar pattern to those involving alcohol, wherein the victim ether has voluntarily consumed an illicit or recreational drug for its intoxicating effects, or was surreptitiously given a drug that caused the victim to lose consciousness. In either case, the victim is sexually assaulted once she is under the influence of the drugs or incapacitated. With

---

[8] Scalzo, T. (2007). *Prosecuting alcohol facilitated sexual assaults*. Alexandria, VA: National District Attorney's Association, American Prosecutors Research Institute.

alcohol-facilitated incidents we might be confronted with underage drinking by the victim, but with drugs we must also deal with the possibility that the victim may have voluntarily consumed an illegal substance, such as a recreational drug, prior to the assault, thus complicating the investigation. This causes many victims to delay reporting the incident because of their own criminal conduct. DFSAs are different in several other ways; first, the victim is almost always unconscious at the time of the assault. She is rendered unconscious by the use of drugs and then removed by an offender to a place where she is sexually assaulted. Secondly, opportunistic incidents do occur, such as a victim who is found incapacitated from the effects of a drug she has voluntarily consumed and is then sexually assaulted, but the majority of DFSAs are well-planned events where the offender selects either a victim he knows or a complete stranger and assaults her. In these incidents, the offender is prepared with his own particular drug of choice, which he will typically add to the beverage of his selected victim and then wait for the drugs to take effect. These drugs run the gamut from legitimately produced prescription drugs such as Rohypnol, commonly referred to as the date rape drug, or other commercially produced sedative hypnotics, to the various illicit drugs such as GHB or even heroin. The choice of drug is generally limited by the offender's preference and his access or ability to obtain them. These incidents are sometimes called *anonymous rape,* because there is often no direct interaction between the victim and offender until the victim is already drugged. Examples include victims who report being at a night club and dancing, then feeling dizzy or nauseous and then waking up in a strange place, naked or clothing out of place, with no memory of how they got there or what had happened to them. Lastly, the offenders who use this technique are far different from any other offender type we have thus far discussed and identified.

These offenders are often very intelligent with higher education levels; some may even have earned graduate or post-graduate degrees. They tend to have highly developed social skills and therefore have an ability to socially interact with people. Perhaps the biggest difference is that many of these offenders are older, well-established professionals, from a higher social economic level, and are well known and respected in the local community. DFSA offenders also do not always demonstrate some of the other characteristics of other offender rapist types. **Boxes 12-1** and **12-2** outline some basic similarities and differences between the two types of offenders.

BOX 12-1 How DSFA Offenders Are Similar to Other Offenders

DSFA offenders are known to be:
- Liars
- Manipulators
- Impatient

(continues)

BOX 12-1 (continued)

- Egotistical and selfish
- Display poor empathy toward others
- Sexually selfish and hedonistic
- Narcissistic
- Operate with sense of entitlement

BOX 12-2 How DSFA Offenders Are Different from Other Offenders

DFSA offenders do not always:

- Have a criminal history
- Show criminal versatility
- Exhibit poor behavior controls
- Show irresponsibility
- Live parasitic lifestyles
- Experience short-term marital relationships
- Abuse alcohol or drugs
- Have abusive relationships

The major goal and motivation of these offenders is sex in the same manner as it is for acquaintance rapists. However, these offenders want no interaction with the victim at all and are looking for a 100% nonresistant victim, much in the same manner as necrophiles. They are not driven by anger, fantasy, or an inability to control themselves. In fact, of all of the offenders, this type is generally the least impulsive. They clearly understand what they are doing is wrong but are able to justify their actions because, like other offenders operating with a sense of entitlement, it gives them what they want and that is all that is important to them.

It is not unusual for some offenders to work in pairs to facilitate the drugging of their victims. This is seen primarily in younger offenders who may frequent nightclubs and take turns finding victims. Typically, females go to nightclubs in groups. One of the partners will distract the others in the group while the second offender picks out his target and then slips a drug into the target's drink. Once the drug begins to take effect and her friends are distracted, the victim is escorted out of the nightclub to a location where she is sexually assaulted. The next time they go out the partners may switch places or responsibility to distract others in the group and allow the other partner to sexually assault the victim. The partners may or may not both participate in the sexual assault. It is also not uncommon for males to become victims of DFSA in the same manner as females. These incidents may take place in "straight bars" or "gay bars."

A difficulty in these cases is that the victims who report these incidents are usually uncertain whether they were sexually assaulted because they have no memory of what happened to them. They report having been at a nightclub with friends enjoying themselves, and the next thing they knew they were waking up naked in strange place with no memory of how they got there, who brought them there, or what happened to them. Many victims are only able to describe an unexplained genital or anal soreness, that their clothing has been rearranged or is missing, that there is unexplained presence of semen on their clothing or body, or that their tampon or sanitary napkin is missing. It was not uncommon when these incidents first started to be reported in the 1980s for the police to simply dismiss such complaints outright, believing it was a case of voluntary intoxication where the victim got drunk, had sex with someone, passed out, and now was concerned about what people would think about her.

It is important to note there are some major differences between what we would consider typical sexual assaults and DFSA incidents. Some of these differences are listed in **Boxes 12-3** and **12-4**.

BOX 12-3 Typical Sexual Assaults

Coercive or forced rapes are marked by:
- Power, anger, and control
- Physical "blitz" assaults possible
- Victim's resistance possible
- Victim is aware of what is happening
- Physical assaults to overcome victim resistance are possible
- Sexual torture, sadism, mutilation, and murder are possible
- Sexual satisfaction from "control," infliction of pain, humiliation
- Threats made to victim if they report crime
- Efforts made to conceal offender's identity (mask, gloves, or clothing)
- Assault may or may not be a planned event
- Offender may be prepared with "rape kit"
- Offender is unable to claim that "nothing happened"

BOX 12-4 DFSA Sexual Assaults

DSFS incidents are marked by:
- Lack of force or physical assaults
- No fear or resistance by victim
- Sexual gratification comes through intercourse and control over victim
- May involve victim in illegal acts (drugs)
- Victim is completely unaware of what happened to her
- Sexual torture is unlikely
- Almost always a 100% a planned event

(continues)

BOX 12-4 (continued)

- Rape kit, but different contents
- Efforts to hide his actions, but some injuries make it difficult to conceal the act
- What stands out as actions by the offender that were unnecessary to committing the crime or to facilitating his escape?

The major difference between these offenders and incidents is the lack of force or coercion; in DFSA cases the victim is incapacitated, so there is no chance for the victim to resist and force is simply unnecessary. Victims are seldom forced to consume or take drugs as they have voluntarily taken them for their intoxicating effects or were surreptitiously given them by the offender. As there is no need for physical force to be applied, the victim typically shows no signs of force, such as ripped clothing. Sadistic torture is also unlikely because there is no satisfaction to inflict pain or suffering on a victim who cannot appreciate what is happening to them. The majority of injuries that occur are caused during sexual intercourse because the victim is unconscious and therefore unprepared, so vaginal tears are a frequent finding during subsequent medical examinations.

LeBeau and Mozayani[9] have identified four general components to the DFSA modus operandi (MO) as *means, opportunity, plan,* and *setting,* which form the acronym MOPS:

- *Means.* Means generally refers to the offender's access to drugs and a general understanding of how they are used and what effects they may have on the victim's alertness or memory.

- *Opportunity.* This is the ability to carry out the attack on the victim without any chance of discovery or interference. For offenders who use their own residence, it might be a time when their family is away and thus they will not be disturbed.

- *Plan.* A plan is not just about how to carry out the act, but rather how the offender is going to avoid arrest and prosecution. This may include what he will use to dissuade his victims from making a complaint, such as denying any sexual assault ever took place, telling them that sex was consensual even or that they were the sexual aggressor, or convincing them no one will believe what happened because of the offender's or victim's reputation. One tactic often used is to provide them with illicit drugs prior to the assault, such as cocaine, marijuana, or other drugs they would voluntarily consume while "partying." This presents a problem for victims, because if they make a complaint of sexual assault they will also have to admit they were abusing illegal substances, thus making reports unlikely.

---

[9] LeBeau, M. A., & Mozayani, A. (2001). *Drug-facilitated sexual assault: A forensic handbook.* San Diego, CA: Academic Press.

- *Setting.* Setting is the location where the assault takes place. This could be a hotel, motel, or the offender's residence. The main consideration is to have a location where he is in total and absolute control and thus unlikely to be disturbed for a number of hours.

As the MOPS model indicates, these offenses are not opportunistic but planned events; this is because the offender must be ready with the setting where he intends to assault the victim before he provides the drugs to them. Once the victim has been given the drugs and they begin to take effect, the offender is essentially committed and must then react to complete the assault. It is highly unlikely that he would provide drugs to a victim and then try to seek out such a setting while the victim loses consciousness. For the most part, these are rather passive offenders, so they tend to strike only when everything falls into place. In circumstances where the victim does not cooperate, does not drink alcoholic beverages, or otherwise cannot be induced into taking the drugs, the victim may escape and avoid an assault.

In instances where the victim is in a nightclub or other similar social setting and is provided the drugs, the offender may attempt to be seen as a friend, boyfriend, or rescuer of the victim who by all appearances is clearly intoxicated. The offender then slowly makes their way outside to "get some fresh air" or to "take her home," and then takes the victim to the setting he has already established and commits the assault. It is not unusual for these offenders to be exceptionally well prepared at the setting and photograph or videotape the entire assault, which will be used to relive the excitement of the assault, aide in masturbation, or to improve his actions. These offenders tend to rely on their plan even if events or circumstances change because they typically have poor improvisational skills. LeBeau and Mozayani[10] noted that most DFSA offenders will have underdeveloped intimate and personal relations and may never have had a normal intimate relationship. Therefore, "sex with something (rather than someone) impersonal, compliant, and ephemeral" may be all they are "emotionally capable of." Although these offenders may know they are committing an offense, their sense of entitlement will justify their actions, they will seldom feel any remorse for their actions, and they will likely deny that they committed the act. If they admit to sex with the victim at all, they will argue the act was totally consensual. It is important to note from an investigative perspective that there is no requirement to prove the offender provided drugs to the victim; rather, it is only necessary to prove that the victim was incapacitated and could not give consent at the time the sexual act was performed.

DFSA Investigative Techniques

From a police perspective, DFSA cases are very difficult because there is almost always a time delay between the event and report to the police, and

---

[10] LeBeau, M. A., & Mozayani, A. (2001). *Drug-facilitated sexual assault: A forensic handbook.* San Diego, CA: Academic Press.

the victim is generally unable to provide any specific details about what happened during the sexual assault. These cases are also very difficult because of other issues of potential illegal acts by the victim through her voluntary ingestion of illegal substances, and potential witnesses may also be involved in illegal drug usage prior to the assault, making them hesitant to admit their own criminal conduct as well. For these type of cases we must adjust our investigative techniques away from concentrating on offender behavior, identifying offender typology, issues of consent, or victim resistance that were so important with coercive offenders. In these cases the focus is on events leading up to the assault and events that took place after the assault.

Some important information that victims should be able to provide during their interview includes:

- What are their normal drinking habits?
- How much did they have to drink that night?
- What physical effects were different than normally experienced?
- Did they ingest any prescription or over-the-counter medication?
- Were they prescribed any medications? If so, what?
- How much control did they have over their drinks?
- Who provided the drinks?
- Did someone give them a "special" drink?
- Did they take any shots of alcohol?

These questions are not designed to be accusatory; rather, they are used to determine what is normal for the victim and what was different the night of the incident. This is a very important aspect of the interview because typically the offender will place drugs into the victim's alcoholic beverage and the effects will initially mimic alcohol intoxication. We are looking to answer questions such as: How was this particular incident different from other times when the victim was consuming alcoholic beverages? Who may have placed the drugs into their drink? When and how were the drugs given to the victim?

One final question that is very important and may cause some difficulties with victims is whether or not they had voluntarily consumed any illegal substances prior to the assault. Regardless of whether or not they consumed illegal substances, there is no justification for the sexual assault. It is also important to ask if they are missing any personal property. Personal property could be anything from valuables such as money or jewelry to personal items stolen from their purse or an item of clothing. Again, it is important to ask victims what led them to believe they were sexually assaulted. As described earlier, the victim will report being uncertain, but that when they awoke they experienced unexplained genital soreness or vaginal discharge, found semen on their clothing or body, or their clothing was improperly placed on them or missing.

Unfortunately, victims are generally incapacitated or unconscious during the sexual assault and are often unable to describe exactly what happened to them. However, there are instances where some victims experience what are known as "flashbulb memories,"[11] which are described as short periods of consciousness where they may briefly wake up but might not understand exactly what is happening to them. This is not a complete consciousness, but rather a brief 30–60-second span of time where they become aware of something happening to them, but they are unable to move, react, or even speak and then fall back into unconsciousness. One example is a victim that reported waking up, realizing she was naked in a room where people were walking over her, but she did not know where she was and could not otherwise move and then lost consciousness again. Other victims report waking up and realizing someone is on top of them having sex, but they are unable to call out or move from under them, and then they pass out again. In one aspect of these cases we are fortunate because issues of consent and resistance are far easier to establish, since a heavily intoxicated or unconscious victim is considered to be unable to give voluntary consent and any issue of resistance is also not applicable. The issue is then whether the victim was sufficiently intoxicated or unconscious and therefore unable to give knowing consent.

When dealing with the *before* aspect of the incident, it is important to get as many details from the victim as possible concerning the last place she remembers being, the people she was with, and what she was doing. The goal is to identify persons who saw the victim before she became intoxicated or drugged and may be able to confirm how much or how little she was drinking or who may have bought or served any drinks. If the location was at a bar or nightclub or other location that served alcohol, it is also important to identify waitresses or bartenders who can help establish how much the victim drank, what type of liquor she consumed, and if anyone offered to buy her drinks. Then, similar to alcohol-facilitated incidents, try to get an impression from everyone who had contact with the victim prior to the incident of how intoxicated the victim appeared, and whether or not it was typical for her to be so intoxicated. What is especially important is to identify anyone who may have come to the rescue of the victim or escorted the victim out of the establishment or away from others. Many times these canvass-type interviews are the only way to identify potential suspects.

Once ingested, the typical date rape drugs such as GHB or Rohypnol do not take effect instantaneously; if a victim consumes a drug-laced drink, she will not suddenly fall to the floor and pass out. Instead, as with all drugs, there is a delay while the drug is ingested and enters the bloodstream. The time from ingestion to when the drug begins to take effect is known as the

---

[11] LeBeau, M. A., & Mozayani, A. (2001). *Drug-facilitated sexual assault: A forensic handbook.* San Diego: Academic Press.

onset of action, and each drug has its own particular onset of actions. Alcohol causes a synergetic effect when combined with drugs, wherein they are enhanced by each other and often result in a quicker onset of action. For instance, if a drug takes 15–20 minutes before one begins to feel the effects, when taken in combination with alcohol, the onset of action could drop to 5–10 minutes. Offenders often put drugs into alcoholic beverages to take advantage of these drug interactions.

When interviewing victims, we can discover signs from their description of their drinks and the after effects that they had ingested drugs. If the victim noted any aftertaste from her drink, it may have been laced with drugs. For instance, GHB (gamma-hydroxybutyric acid, a common date-rape drug) has a very salty aftertaste. Frequently, pills that are crushed and placed into a drink may not have completely dissolved in the liquid before being consumed, and victims may describe their drinks as containing grit that they felt on their tongue as they drank. Lastly, we are concerned with the general effects of the drugs as described by the victim. These symptoms are important because they may help identify the drug that was used. **Box 12-5** is a collection of some of the most common symptoms (the list is not all-inclusive, but fairly representative of what we find in these cases).

BOX 12-5 Common Effects of Drugs

Confusion	Dizziness
Drowsiness	Psychomotor impairment
Impaired judgment	Reduced inhibitions
Slurred speech	Impaired judgment
Heaviness in limbs	Numbness
Feeling flushed/warm	Feeling very drunk after only one or two drinks

---

Finally, we want to look at the *after* of the event and are concerned with a couple of important factors. First, when did the victim regain consciousness? This is a relative term, however, because the victim may regain consciousness but not be able to think clearly as an after-effect of the drug. Some drugs may take 24 hours or longer to get completely out of the system and for the victim to return to normal function. This is often referred to as the *duration of effects,* or how long the drugs affect the body. For instance, cocaine has a very rapid onset of action of just a few minutes, but the duration of effects may be limited to 20–30 minutes. Other drugs, particularly the stronger depressants, may have duration of effects of 8 or more hours. The combination of onset of action, duration of effects, and the symptoms experienced can be used to try to determine the type of drug that was taken by the victim.

Second, where did the victim regain consciousness? Were there any witnesses who came into contact with the victim? The location is important because it may prove to be the scene where the assault took place, which will need to be processed as any other crime scene, or it may be another location that can provide links to the offender. Of great importance is locating those persons who first came into contact with the victim after the event and gaining their impressions of the victim, including her alertness and ability to think logically, speak, and move. Some of the "hangover" or lingering effects of the drugs contribute greatly to the delay in reporting, because the victim may still be too confused to realize what happened. Other contributing factors to the delay in reporting are the victim's feelings of guilt or self-blame because of her voluntary ingestion of alcohol or drugs and lack of memory of exactly what happened.

Fitzgerald and Riley[12] describe another victim dynamic of DFSA incidents:

> The ability to sense danger is critical to a person's ability to implement self-protection strategies. When faced with the threat of being raped most people employ one or more protective measures such as verbally negotiating with the assailant, cognitively assessing their options, screaming, stalling, attempting to escape and/or physically resisting. If these efforts fail to prevent the rape victim may "fight back" in other ways. They may use their sensory and cognitive abilities to memorize details about the assailant's physical characteristics, the location of the crime, and other factors that can be used to aid authorities in apprehending and prosecuting the offender.

The coercively or forcibly raped victims at least know what happened to them and had some chance to mentally prepare for what was happening or at least recognized threats to their own safety. This mental awareness is not available to the DFSA victim and the experience has been aptly described as "mind rape,"[13] where even the consciousness or awareness of the victim has been robbed or violated.

▶ DFSA and AFSA Victim and Crime Scene Examination

For cases involving drug- or alcohol-facilitated assaults, there are some special considerations for the crime scene and for the victim's medical examination.

---

[12] Fitzgerald, N., & Riley, K. J. (2000). Drug-facilitated rape: Looking for the missing pieces. *National Institute of Justice Journal*. Originally published by the National Institute of Justice Journal, U.S. Department of Justice. Retrieved June 12, 2012, from https://www.ncjrs.gov/pdffiles1/jr000243c.pdf

[13] Fitzgerald, N., & Riley, K. J. (2000). Drug-facilitated rape: Looking for the missing pieces. *National Institute of Justice Journal*. Originally published by the National Institute of Justice Journal, U.S. Department of Justice. Retrieved June 12, 2012, from https://www.ncjrs.gov/pdffiles1/jr000243c.pdf

Victim's Examination

Like other victims, it is strongly encouraged that the DFSA victim undergo a medical examination up to *96 hours* after the event. Note that this timeframe is beyond the normal accepted time limit of 72 hours for the standard victim medical examinations. Although there may be limited chances of obtaining any biological evidence during the examination, there is still a very good chance of obtaining possible *toxicological* evidence, because of the length of time some drugs stay within the body. Therefore, it is strongly recommended the victim undergo the examination to collect the necessary biological samples. The best sample for toxicological examination is urine, and detectives should be aware of the importance of collecting a sample from the victim if she happens to appear at their office prior to any medical examination. So, if during her interview the victim asks to use the restroom and she cannot "hold it," the police can provide a small plastic medical specimen cup to the victim to use to collect her own urine sample. There is no medical or legal necessity for the collection to be made by medical personnel as long as the specimen cup was not previously used or contaminated. Explain to the victim the importance of collecting as much of the sample as possible (up to 100 mL). The specimen cup then needs to be sealed and properly identified, and can be submitted directly to the crime lab for analysis in most jurisdictions. It is important that the sample be obtained as soon as possible, as every time the victim urinates, she is eliminating the drugs from her system. The police should not try to induce the need to urinate through encouraging the victim to drink large amounts of coffee, water, or other beverages because this results in a diluted urine sample.

Whether the sample is collected during the medical examination or by the police, when submitting it to the crime lab, it is important to advise the toxicologist that the case involves a possible DFSA, and therefore we are requesting a full spectrum analysis of the sample. This is important because routine toxicology examinations do not specifically look for these drugs, so they have to be specifically requested. The full spectrum analysis will identify all of the drugs that may be in the sample. This presents a double-edged sword to the police, because on one hand it will identify any of the so-called "date rape drugs," but it will also identify any illicit drugs the victim may have voluntarily ingested such as marijuana or cocaine. Therefore, prior to submission of the sample to the lab most states require a special permission or authorization form from the victim to conduct the examination. It is important to note that one of the tactics of some offenders is to supply the victim with some illicit substance to consume before she is incapacitated and sexually assaulted. Providing so-called recreational drugs to the victim could be a way to render the victim incapacitated, similar to providing alcohol to get the victim drunk or as a way to get her involved in participatory criminal conduct. For either reason, the intent is to scare the victim into not reporting the sexual assault, because she will also have to admit to using drugs prior to the assault. The laboratory will have specific questions about the samples and those answers should be provided along with the samples. These questions listed in **Box 12-6** should be covered or clarified during the victim interview.[14]

BOX 12-6 Victim Interview Questions Relating to Lab Specimens

- How much time elapsed (approximately) between the alleged drugging and the collection of specimens?
- Did the victim consume alcohol? How much?
- Was the victim also taking prescription or over-the-counter medications?
- Did the victim consume recreational drugs (e.g., marijuana, cocaine, Ecstasy)?
- Did the victim urinate prior to the collection of a urine sample? If so, how many times?
- What general symptoms did the victim describe?

The medical examination is also important because if any injuries are inflicted during these incidents they are generally the result of internal trauma, which is likely to be found only during the medical examination. It is also important to note the presence of any associated injuries.

Scene Examinations and Offender Residences

Like other similar crimes, DFSA cases may involve multiple scenes, including the original location from which the victim was removed, vehicles used to transport the victim, the location where the assault took place, and where the victim was eventually found or regained consciousness. When any of these locations can be determined, a crime scene examination should be conducted in the same manner as other crime scenes, including the search for all of the traditional forensic evidence such as fibers, hair, and other biological evidence. However, a search should also include a detailed look for any type of alcohol, prescription medications, and any other controlled substances. Additionally, all prescription medications found at the scene should be photographed, identified in a written report, and collected as possible evidence. As with other cases involving controlled substances, it is not unusual for suspects to place controlled or illegal substances into prescription vials of other drugs such as antibiotics, vitamins, or other legal medications. Particular interest should also be paid to prescribed medications involving some type of depressants such as sedative–hypnotics (sleeping pills), muscle relaxers, or any other anti-anxiety medication that, when used in combination with alcohol, could disable the victim.

---

[14] LeBeau, M. A., & Mozayani, A. (2001). *Drug-facilitated sexual assault: A forensic handbook*. San Diego, CA: Academic Press.

A wide range of drugs has been used to facilitate these incidents. It is very important to remember that not all offenders use illegal substances; many may simply use whatever drugs are already available to them through a legal prescription. **Box 12-7** lists some common legal and illegal drugs that have been identified in DFSA cases (generally used in combination with alcohol).

BOX 12-7 Common Legal and Illegal Drugs Used in DFSA

Alprazolam (Xanax)	Chlordiazepoxide (Librium)	Lorazepam (Ativan)
Triazolam (Halcion)	Diazepam (Valium)	Prazepam (Centrax)
Flurazepam (Dalmane)	Clonazepam (Klonopin)	Oxazepam (Serax)
Flunitrazepam (Rohypnol)	Temazepam (Restoril)	Carisoprodol (Soma)
Chloral hydrate	Marijuana	Meprobamate (Equanil)
Opiates	Scopolamine	Cocaine
Diphenhydramine	Ketamine	
Gamma-hydroxybutyric acid (GHB)		
Methylenedioxymethamphetamine (MDMA) (Ecstasy)		

At a fresh scene, also consider collecting any drinking glasses that may still be present. Latent prints found on the outside and forensic analysis of any residue in the glass is possible and can be very important evidence. If there is any remaining liquid inside a glass it should also be collected in a plastic medical specimen cup or clean glass jar. If any vomitus is found at the scene or on the victim's clothing, it should also be collected in a plastic specimen cup as this will be a good source for toxicological evidence. The stomach contents will likely have a greater concentration of any drugs, because they had not yet been absorbed into the bloodstream. Locating and documenting vomitus is also important as it may help establish the nonconsensual nature of the offense.

If the incident took place inside an offender's residence or if we are going to conduct an examination of his residence with a search warrant, the examination should be expanded in an effort to locate many different types of evidence. This takes a great deal of preparation and consideration. Because we are often dealing with controlled substances, it is a good idea to conduct the scene examination in conjunction with narcotics officers who can help identify substances that we may not be as familiar with. For instance, some drugs such as GHB are frequently overlooked because they are clear liquids that could easily be disguised in sport drink bottles or other such containers. Narcotics officers are generally better trained and have more experienced looking for such substances. Because some drugs may be produced clandestinely, the scene examination should also include searching for the basic ingredients for making them, any drug-related literature or recipes, Internet correspondence or searches for such recipes, and vials or bottles used for packaging.

A search of an offender's residence should also include efforts to locate items such as sexual devices or toys, lubricants, condoms, and any camera or recording equipment. The items are not as important as the evidence we might be able to gain from them. For example, sexual toys should be collected in an effort to obtain the victim's DNA. Lubricants or condoms may seem unimportant, but there are occasions when traces of a lubricant may be found in the victim's underwear or recovered during the medical examination. Although it may not be possible for the laboratory to identify the specific bottle where a stain in the victim's underwear came from, they may be able to establish that it came from that particular manufacturer, which could at least provide circumstantial evidence linking the offender to the victim. The same is true of condoms that are recovered because the lubricant or spermicide placed on the individual condom is unique to that brand and may be linked to samples obtained from the victim during the medical examination.

The "treasure trove," however, is any recording equipment that is discovered. One of the markers of this particular offender type is how commonly they video record their assaults, essentially making their own pornographic movies, starring themselves and the victim. Finding such equipment, especially if it is already set up in a particular place within the residence, is very powerful evidence. In the past such recordings were generally stored on VHS tapes. With the advent of digital imaging, such recordings are now often stored on a computer or burned onto DVDs; therefore, it may be important to also obtain the offender's computer, cameras, and other media storage devices for later forensic examination.

Lastly, we want to look for any personal items from the victim, which, as previously described, are often kept as *trophies* or *souvenirs.* These items become so important to offenders that it is very unlikely they will dispose of them, even if they think the police are coming to their house; instead they may try to secret these items away. If such materials are found, they may not necessarily be the personal effects of the particular victim in the case that we are working on, but instead the personal property of other victims who may not have reported the crime to the police, or who reported their victimization to another department. Any such items should be carefully documented, and whenever possible, we should try to locate their owners. It is not unusual for victims to be identified through personal items or upon reviewing video recordings that were recovered from the offender. Many victims have reported they had no idea something had happened to them or that they had ever been assaulted.

▶ Offender Interviews

DFSA offenders present a challenge to interview and interrogate. As previously described, they are often older and well educated, socially adaptable, and well respected within the community. These offenders may seem cooperative but irritated that they could be suspected of such a crime and indicate that they simply want to clear their name. Although they are intelligent and have the ability to engage an attorney, it is surprising how many offenders waive their rights and go through a police interview. This is an example of their ego, narcissistic personality, and their belief that they are smart enough to convince the police of their innocence. They rely on their social standing and reputation within the community and the fact that in their mind they have already *damaged* the only witnesses to their criminal acts. *Damage* does not refer to any actual physical trauma, but the victim's uncertainty as to what happened; this damage commonly causes victims not to make a complaint. They have also damaged any testimony of the victim by providing them alcohol, other illicit substances, or through the drugs that were given to the victim. By rendering the victim unconscious, they have hindered the victim's ability to describe what happened to her and thus damaged her credibility or believability. Based on the fact that the victim is already damaged and the victim's credibility is challenged when compared to the offender's social standing, the offender is likely to be very confident during the interview. Bluffing with false evidence is not generally successful with these offenders, because it is likely they have planned the event very well and ensured they did not leave behind any physical or forensic evidence.

One advantage we have during these incidents is the fact that most offenders opt to use the consent defense, and therefore will admit to having *consensual* sex with the victim. The importance of this statement is that they have admitted to penetration of the victim, which is one of the major elements of proof to substantiate a rape offense. Although the offender may maintain the act was consensual, if through other evidence we can establish that the victim was incapacitated at the time of intercourse, we can confirm a rape took place. When the consent defense is used, it is important to determine the circumstances surrounding the event, whether the victim was able to give knowing consent, what was said or done by the victim to indicate her consent to sex, and if the victim was awake and an active participant during the sexual act. How the encounter ended is also important to cover, especially if the victim has reported waking up in a strange place or with no memory of what happened. Questions should also cover their goodbye, exchange of numbers, comments to each other about the previous day/night's activity, and plans to get together again. Usually, reports of conversations with the victim starkly contrast with the victim's statement of being totally incapacitated.

The DFSA offender will typically not display any remorse or empathic feelings toward the victim and will likely continue to deny any criminal intent or involvement to the absolute end. Although you are likely to obtain admissions to sexual intercourse, it is highly unlikely to obtain a full confession, unless he realizes confessing will ultimately be in his favor. One particular weakness for these offenders is how rigid they are once they have a plan in place; although they have a great ability to make plans and carry them out, they generally have very poor improvisational skills. Thus, they are often unable to think on their feet or adapt to changing situations and information. Therefore, if the offender can ever be "knocked off his game" or presented with unexpected facts such as a video made during the incident, the identification of his drug source, or other evidence he is unaware of, it could cause him to make substantive errors during the interview.

▶ Conclusion

These cases are difficult but not impossible to work and prosecute, but they do take extra effort to successfully resolve. Scalzo[15] has identified one other very important concept when investigating and prosecuting AFSA and DFSA cases, which she describes as *victim likeability*—that is, how the victim is seen and accepted by the jury. Although this is not a legal concept or a requirement, the fact is jurors tend to believe people they like and disbelieve people they do not like. So, they may decide a victim who engaged in risky behavior may not be as worthy of protection as a victim who did not engage in risky behavior or was clearly taken advantage of during the incident. Thus, the very things that might make a victim particularly vulnerable for assault in the first place, such as being intoxicated or using drugs, are also likely to make the victim seem less credible in a jury's eyes. Victims who are seen as putting themselves in jeopardy may be viewed unsympathetically or with skepticism since they "assumed the risk of rape" by becoming intoxicated to the point of being unable to protect themselves. Therefore, it is imperative as part of our investigation that we make an effort to make the victim "likeable," by highlighting the predatory nature of the offender, or the defense mechanisms the victim put into place that were overcome by the offender. Examples include going out in the company of other friends as mutual protection and a history of not drinking alcohol to the point of intoxication or otherwise engaging in similar high-risk behaviors. In these cases, a good victimology assessment can be helpful in making the victim likeable and thus believable to the jury.

---

[15] Scalzo, T. (2007). *Prosecuting alcohol facilitated sexual assaults*. Alexandria, VA: National District Attorney's Association, American Prosecutors Research Institute.

▶Further Reading

Fitzgerald, N., & Riley, K. J. (2000). Drug-facilitated rape: Looking for the missing pieces. *National Institute of Justice Journal*. Retrieved from https://www.ncjrs.gov/pdffiles1/jr000243c.pdf

Kilpatrick, D. G., Resnick, H. S., Conoscenti, L. M., & McCauley, J. M. (2007). *Drug-facilitated, incapacitated, and forcible rape: A national study*. Rockville, MD: U.S. Department of Justice.

LeBeau, M. A., et al. (1999). Recommendations for toxicological investigation of drug-facilitated sexual assaults. *Forensic Science Communications, 44*(1), 227–230.

Olsezewski, D. (2008). *Sexual assaults facilitated by drugs or alcohol*. Lisbon, Portugal: European Monitoring Centre for Drugs and Drug Addiction.

Scalzo, T. (2007). *Prosecuting alcohol facilitated sexual assaults*. Alexandria, VA: National District Attorney's Association, American Prosecutors Research Institute.

CHAPTER THIRTEEN

False Rape Allegations

Why is it that rape victims must be able to show that they did not contribute to their own victimization?[1] Why does "proof of the guilt of the offender" depend upon the "proof of the innocence of the victim"?[2] As we have documented earlier, not only will we have to find corroborating evidence to validate the allegations of the victim, but all the victim's actions before, during, and after the assault will certainly be questioned and subject to scrutiny and cross-examination by a defense attorney.

Text after text on the subject of rape and its effects on females is often full of vignettes of harsh and insensitive treatment of victims by the police, medical professionals, and later by the courts. This is a sad indictment of our treatment of victims. It is also one possible explanation for why many experts believe that incidents of rape are greatly underreported by women. However, such callous treatment of the victim does not occur in a vacuum: There is little doubt the criminal justice system places a heavy burden on rape victims. However, police find themselves being placed in a very difficult position. They have the duty and obligation to initiate an investigation based on the victim's complaint, yet many times their efforts turn out to be a complete waste of time and effort. This is often the result of victim's failure to tell the complete truth about what happened or a decision to intentionally make a false complaint. As stated earlier, there is a hot debate over the exact number of false rapes, but there are relatively few, if any, experienced detectives who have not been intentionally misled by a false complaint. As addressed previously in the text, every false complaint costs time and money, puts a drain on limited manpower resources, and takes police away from helping real victims. For those falsely accused there is also a high price to pay for false complaints, including ruined

---

[1] Hiberman, E. (1976). *The rape victim.* New York, NY: Basic Books; p. 13.
[2] MacKellar, J., & Menachem, A. (1975). *Rape: The trap and the bait.* New York, NY: Crown Publishers; p. 79.

personal and family reputations, the financial cost of defending themselves in court, and for some, even the cost of their freedom.

From the police perspective, we genuinely want to believe the victim and find the person who assaulted or abused her. False reports create a frustrating experience that only serves to validate some of the rape myths and cause indifference on the part of many detectives to rape victims—especially if they present without any visible injuries or begin to display any *counterintuitive behaviors*. The concept of false rape reports is not new and there are many historical and modern examples that have also led to some of the harsh treatment of victims over the years.

▶Historical Examples of False Complaints

Perhaps the oldest documented false complaint is found in the *Old Testament* (Genesis 39:7–20): The wife of Pharaoh's Captain Potiphar repeatedly tried to seduce Joseph while her husband was away. Joseph refused and ran away. Enraged after failing, she told her husband that Joseph had attacked and nearly raped her. Her false complaint resulted in the sentence of Joseph into an Egyptian prison where he remained for several years.

More recently, there have been many other examples across the United States of false rape complaints. We previously discussed the case studies of Kathleen Webb and Tawana Brawley, who both falsely reported being raped. Webb's false report led to the wrongful conviction and incarceration of Gary Dotson. Brawley's false report served to fuel the fires of racial discord when she reported being raped by white police officers.

Another example is the infamous 2006 Duke University lacrosse player case in Durham, North Carolina. Crystal Gail Mangum, an African American woman who worked as a stripper, dancer, and escort, falsely accused three white members of the Duke University men's lacrosse team of raping her during a team party. The complaint immediately hit the media and like the Brawley case, was portrayed as a racial incident, and it resulted in three white students being accused and suspended from college. All three were then vilified by local and national media. Many people, including the local prosecutor, Mike Nifong, openly inferred that the alleged assault was a racial hate crime and then used the case as a vehicle for his pending reelection. Nifong was reelected but was eventually forced to withdraw from the case in January 2007 after the North Carolina State Bar filed ethics charges against him. On April 11, 2007, over a year after the arrest of the three accused, the North Carolina state attorney general, who had assumed the investigation and prosecution of the case, dropped all charges and declared the three players innocent and victims of prosecutorial misconduct. The attorney general's decision was based on several inconsistencies in Mangum's accounts of the evening and unimpeachable evidence for alibis provided by two of the accused students. In June 2007, Nifong was disbarred, becoming the first prosecutor in North Carolina ever to lose his law license based on his actions during a case. Mangum was never prosecuted for making a false complaint.

These are just a few examples of the more well-known and publicized false complaints, but there are many other examples, several of which are described later in this chapter. The problem with false reports is that they add to the general suspicions of victims by the police, increase the demand on the victim for corroboration and evidence, make prosecutors leery of taking some cases to court, and make it more difficult for juries to convict offenders. The concerns about false rape complaints seem to justify the insistence and search for corroborating evidence and the placing of victims in the position of being "suspects" themselves, to avoid prosecuting and punishing an innocent man.

▶ Statistical Data: How Many False Complaints Are There?

As mentioned earlier, even the mention of "unfounded" or false complaint statistics strikes a sour note among feminist and other experts who are very quick to point out that rape is the only category of crime in which data reflecting *unfounded statistics* are even mentioned. Susan Estrich and Susan Brownmiller[3], among other feminist writers, continually challenge the accuracy of these unfounded statistics. Brownmiller argues that because rape was always defined by men rather than women, men were able to use and benefit from rape as a means of perpetuating male dominance by keeping all women in a state of fear. So the concept of police unfounding rape complaints was seen as just another means for the police (men) to exercise control over women. Brownmiller also reported as fact that the unfounded or false rape rate was actually only about 2% of the total number of those reported. This figure has been referenced repeatedly in the last 30 years by feminists and others in professional articles and texts refuting the alleged high number of unfounded and false complaints. Subsequent research, however, noted that this figure was not based on any actual study or analysis of the issue but came from a speech delivered by Lawrence H. Cooke, New York Appellate Division Justice, to the Association of the Bar of the City of New York. Justice Cook's cited reference was the Commander of the New York's City Rape Analysis squad. This particular data from the '*commander*' was never published or subjected to any type of a peer review, so its basis and validity was never determined.[4]

Estrich challenges the unfounded statistics mainly because of the manner in which the police are allowed decide on their own which cases have merit and require additional investigation, and which do not have merit and are subsequently unfounded. Because this decision normally rests only with police, Estrich contends it is proof positive that police are unfairly and unduly

---

[3] Brownmiller, S. (1975). *Against our will: Men, women, and rape.* New York, NY: Ballantine Books.

[4] Edward Greer. *The truth behind legal dominance feminism's two percent false rape claim figure,* 33 Loy. L.A. L. Rev. 947 (2000). Available at: http://digitalcommons.lmu.edu/llr/vol33/iss3/3

skeptical of rape victims.[5] The implication is quite clear: Estrich believes the high number of unfounded cases is the result of sexual bias or prejudice against women by male-dominated police, rather than a result of actual false complaints made by women.[6]

As discussed earlier in the text, because of the criticism directed against the police, many departments have simply stopped using the term *unfounded*—even in cases where the victim has clearly lied and filed a false police report, the case will be closed without such a determination to avoid any further critique. This serves to skew statistical evaluation because not all departments are using the same definitions or criteria, and some are not using the term at all. The real problem is that there is no official mechanism for collecting and reporting such statistics accurately. While some detectives or even entire police departments may exhibit some sexual bias and prejudice, it cannot be used to explain the fact that some victims, for many different reasons, do make false rape complaints. For the detective it is almost counterproductive to be concerned or to worry about such statistics in the first place, because the reality is that even if 90% of the reported rapes were completely false, that means that 10% are true and we still have to do what we can for those real victims. Therefore, such a collection of statistics is more a philosophical and theoretical project and should have no bearing on the conduct of an investigation.

This is not to say that false reports are unimportant, because they do cause a lot of problems for law enforcement, legal, and medical personnel responsible for investigating these incidents. Perhaps the most significant impact of false rape allegations is on the legitimate victims. Having suffered pain, fear, shock, and humiliation, they must now face the possibility of disease, pregnancy, and a damaged sense of personal wellbeing, compounded by having to prove they are not lying.

Many detectives look at the concept of false reports through the lens of being frustrated, being lied to, and having their time wasted. In reality this is not true, because detectives are paid to investigate reported crimes and this is what they are doing. If they determine a crime was not committed or the victim has lied about the offense in question, then they in fact have done their job. So, instead of looking at victims with suspicions or doubt, they should be looking at each reported crime as a chance to improve their understanding of the dynamics of the event, help them better read and understand people, become better interviewers, and learn to approach investigations with logic and not emotion.

---

[5] Estrich, S. (1987). *Real rape.* Cambridge, MA: Harvard University Press; pp. 15–16.

[6] One confusing area described by Estrich is the use of the term *unfounded*. There is no clear standard for the use of the term, and it is used interchangeably by many agencies to reflect anything from insufficient evidence to prosecute to making a false complaint. Many agencies unfound cases if they determine the incident did not take place as reported by the victim or the victim no longer wishes to pursue the investigation. Other agencies insist they will unfound a rape complaint only if the victim admits she lied about the incident.

To fully understand this concept of false rape complaints, we have to look at some of the reasons they are made.

▶The Dynamics and Range of False Rape Complaints[7,8]

There are thousands of reasons behind making a false rape complaint and they are spread across a wide spectrum or continuum. At one end, the victims may have simply misinterpreted their willing involvement in a sex act and may be seeking some immediate escape, forgiveness, or absolution from their perceived wrongdoing by shifting the blame onto someone else. On the other end of the continuum are victims who set out to intentionally manipulate the criminal justice and healthcare systems to solve some acute personal or psychological crisis in their lives. Some have even intentionally set out to punish another person as revenge for some other act against them.

The following case studies provide examples of what is considered as the lower range of the continuum of false complaints.

Case Study 13-1

Sondra, a soldier, was found in the room of another soldier during a surprise inspection. This violated unit policy in force at the time because she was in the male barracks which were off limits to females. Sondra and the other soldier were ordered to get dressed and report to the unit commander, but while being led away, Sondra collapsed and had to be helped to walk downstairs. She later claimed to her chain of command that she had been held against her will and repeatedly raped by the other soldier for several hours the previous night. Sondra later admitted during her interview with police that she was lying, and only made the allegation because she did not want "to get into trouble" because she was in the other soldier's room. Sondra admitted to having consensual intercourse with the other soldier.

Case Study 13-2

Carol reported she had just broken up with her boyfriend and was walking through a park toward her vehicle, when she was stopped in the middle of a

---

[7] McDowell, C. P., & Hibler, N. (1983). False allegations of rape in the military community [unpublished paper]. Washington, D.C.: U.S. Air Force Office of Special Investigations.

[8] Hazelwood, R. R., & Burgess, A. W. (2008). Practical aspects of rape investigation: A multidisciplinary approach (1st ed.). Boca Raton, FL: CRC Press.

grassy area by a black male who called her by her name. She stopped to talk with him and the male told her he had been watching her for several months and he knew her routine, and even knew a lot of personal information about her. Carol stated that she got scared when he made statements such as, "I want to control you, to possess you, and I love you." Carol stated that she tried to walk away, but suddenly the man grabbed her from behind, forced her to the ground, and then he tried to rape her. Carol said the man tried to force her to have oral sex with him and when she refused he struck her several times across the face and pulled her hair. Eventually, he obtained an erection and he vaginally raped her. When he was finished he stood up and ran away from the area in an unknown direction. Carol said she was dazed and got dressed and then drove to her place of work and reported to her boss she needed time off because of the attack. Carol then said she went home, bathed, douched, and threw away the clothing she was wearing. She did not report the incident to the police until 3 days later. Several days later during a subsequent interview Carol admitted she had lied in her earlier statement and made up the report because she was upset about breaking up with her boyfriend. Carol was under psychiatric care and reported she was confused when her boyfriend broke off the relationship with her, and she thought she might somehow gain him back and make him feel guilty through a report to the police that she had been assaulted.

Case Study 13-3

Sharon was very upset when she called her husband, who was working a double shift at work. She reported that the previous evening she had been at her next-door neighbors' house and accepted their invitation to spend the night because her husband was working all night. After all their children were in bed, they began drinking wine and watching pornographic movies. Sharon then reported the male neighbor became sexually aggressive towards her and although she said "no," he overcame her resistance while assisted by the wife, who helped hold her down and forcefully removed her clothing. Sharon told her husband she did not want to make a complaint to the police, but he called the authorities anyway. Sharon later admitted she had consensual sex with both of the neighbors and felt guilty about cheating on her husband, so she made up the false complaint. Although she never wanted to make a police report, her husband insisted on calling the police.

There is also a misconception that only women make false complaints dealing with sexual assaults, and as the following case shows this is not the case.

Case Study 13-4

A mid-20s black male reported to the local hospital emergency room that the previous evening he had been jogging along the roadway in the early evening when three white males drove past him in an unknown type of car and then turned around and approached him. He was still running when he was unexpectedly grabbed from behind, thrown to the ground, and his sweatpants were forcefully pulled down. He then stated he must have "blacked out" for a long time and when he came to he was lying in the snow, his pants were still around his ankles, and his anus hurt. Upon examination by medical personnel, they noted a minor tear on the anus. The victim was able to accurately describe the outdoor area where he was assaulted and was able to take the detective to the scene. An examination of the scene, however, revealed an open area covered with several inches of snow with no signs of disturbance. The victim claimed to have blacked out and lain in the snow for an extended period of time before he was able to get up. The night in question was later determined to be the coldest night in recorded history for that particular area, yet the victim experienced no cold-weather injuries. When confronted with these inconsistencies, the victim suddenly requested the incident be dropped and refused to cooperate with the police any further. An interview of medical personnel revealed the "victim" had only asked for a blood test for venereal disease and to be checked for AIDS. He had only mentioned the assault after an inquiry was made as to the necessity of the tests. The victim had asked the medical personnel not to call the police but under their protocol it was a requirement.

Case Study 13-5 is another example of a false complaint made at the lower end of the continuum. It was not made with any intention to actually get anyone into trouble but to gain attention.

Case Study 13-5

A 19-year-old female reported being at the local bowling alley around 10:00 PM with a few friends when she said needed to go to the restroom. When she came out, she noted her friends were not inside the bowling alley, so she thought they might have gone outside to smoke. She then exited the bowling alley herself and walked outside to look around but did not see them. A man was outside smoking, leaning against the wall, and she asked him if her friends had gone outside. The man directed her around to the side of the bowling alley and she walked around the corner to go find her friends. She reported that she was then suddenly attacked from behind and thrown violently to the ground. It was the man who was smoking cigarettes outside the bowling alley. He was able to quickly gain control over her and then forced her pants down and vaginally raped her. She reported trying to struggle and called out several times for someone to help but she was not heard. After the man was finished, he stood up and then fled the area. She got up and went back into the bowling alley where she found her friends again. She said she was in so much shock she never thought about reporting the incident to the police or to her friends, so she sat down and stayed with her friends for a while longer, and then everyone went back home and she went to her apartment. After "sleeping on it" she made her report the following morning. The victim was only able to provide a limited amount of information on the suspect, and many aspects of her story changed as she retold it. A check of the security camera inside verified that she was at the bowling alley with a group of friends and had gone to the restroom as reported. However, she was then seen to return directly back to her friends who had also never left the bowling alley. The camera verified the victim had never left the interior of the bowling alley as she claimed and when confronted with this inconsistency and the video tape, the victim admitted she had made up the story because she was upset that a friend she had consensual sex with the day before was ignoring her. This was her way to get him to pay attention to her. She also admitted she was concerned that others would think her "loose" or promiscuous because she had casual sex with the other boy.

In each of these cases, each person tried to use his or her status as a "victim" to solve some crisis or provide an immediate escape from some situation or problem in his or her life, including avoiding punishment, attempts at sympathy and to gain attention, or as a way to request medical treatment. Similar examples include being caught in the act and worries about reputation and being perceived as sexually "loose" or promiscuous after consensual sexual relations with a stranger or casual acquaintance. Others include efforts to cover up or explain a sexually transmitted disease or an unwanted pregnancy to either a mate or parents. In juveniles, common themes of false reports are an effort to explain to their parents evidence of recent sexual activity, violations of curfew, or their voluntary consumption of alcohol or drugs.

In each of the incidents described in these case studies, the victims had some sort of "hidden agenda," or something they wanted or expected in return for their complaint. These particular complaints all seemed to be a "spur of the moment" thought or decision—what we term *ad hoc* or *after the fact*—meaning, the false report was something they felt at the time may rescue them from their situation, or provide some immediate comfort to their bruised ego and self-esteem. In these cases there was no real preparation, nor were their complaints well thought out, and there was no effort to come up with any corroborating evidence to substantiate their allegations. Due to the obvious lack of preparation coupled with the recognition of the victims' hidden agendas, these cases were all fairly rapidly determined to be false complaints. Out of all of the victims who make a false report, victims in the lower continuum are the most sympathetic, because there is generally no malicious intent or effort to get someone else in trouble. These tend to be spontaneous or impulsive ideas to get them out of some situation, and then they are unable to stop or control the process once it gets started.

At the other end of the spectrum are cases that often involve a great deal of detailed prior planning; we call these *premeditated*. These tend to have well-thought out plans that often include a fair amount of corroborating evidence provided by the "victims" to add credibility to their claims. There are several general motivations behind these types of complaints such as: *providing an alibi, seeking sympathy, revenge,* or *other malicious intent.* The following case studies are examples of premeditated false complaints.

Case Study 13-6

The victim, a female college student in her early 20s who was married but currently separated from her husband, reported she had been sexually assaulted in her vehicle in an isolated area by an unidentified male hitchhiker she had picked up to give a ride. She reported being physically assaulted and then tied up with fishing line, with her hands tied over her head to the hand straps located in the interior of her vehicle. After she was tied up, she was then was cut with a broken bottle on the chest and thighs near her genital area. (Although she described her injuries as cuts, they were actually shallow scratches that did not bleed.) During her interview, she could only provide a scant description of what happened and of the suspect, who she said ran away after tying her up and cutting her. However, she never indicated there had been any attempt at sexually assaulting or raping her.

During a subsequent victimology assessment, it was discovered she had previously reported a sexual assault when she was in high school in which the suspect, whom she could not accurately describe, assaulted her and had cut her forearms with a broken bottle and then ran away. The previous incident was remarkably similar to her current report, including being physically assaulted with no attempt to rape her. It was also learned from family and friends that picking up a hitchhiker was totally out of character for the victim. A broken bottle and fishing line were found inside the victim's vehicle that the victim admitted were hers and were already inside the car when she picked the man up. It was also learned that this victim was the female weightlifting champion for her weight classification in the local area, and was in fantastic physical condition, but reported being "overpowered" and unable to resist the suspect. This victim never admitted to making a false complaint, although her fingerprints were the only ones found on the broken bottle shards. In all subsequent interviews, she was always accompanied by her husband, who after reconciling their differences, insisted on remaining in the interview room while she was interviewed. The victim eventually asked to drop the complaint. Her report was also viewed as an attempt to get attention and sympathy.

Other victims make a false rape complaint for totally malicious reasons, and these are the more serious of false complaints. An example of a malicious complaint that includes making a report against a particular person as revenge for some particular wrong or problem with the victim is found in the case file below.

Case Study 13-7

Helen, a college student in her mid-twenties, reported that she had been sexually assaulted and raped repeatedly over the course of several months by her boyfriend. She had been afraid to come forward to the police but finally had worked up the nerve to report her victimization. During her interview she provided great detail concerning each incident, the scene, and other subtle details that made her complaint very believable and easily corroborated. Her boyfriend was interviewed and actually corroborated a great deal of the victim's statement concerning the times, dates, and locations of each sex act, but of course maintained that each incident was consensual. The boyfriend was firm in his denial of using any force or coercion towards the victim and voluntarily took a polygraph examination to test the veracity of his denial. To the surprise of the police, the boyfriend passed the examination without any difficulty. That fact combined with other background information collected on the boyfriend led the police to question the veracity of the allegation. The police examined the victimology of the victim and discovered she was also a criminal justice major and was very familiar with police procedures and basic criminal investigations.

Shortly after the polygraph examination, Helen hysterically called the police late in the evening alleging an assault by her boyfriend. She claimed that she had walked out of her house to get something from her car and as she was walking back her 'boyfriend' suddenly came up grabbed her from behind and held her in a threatening way, demanding she drop the charges against him. He then produced a knife, which he put under her sweatshirt and used to cut her across her chest to show he was serious. The victim did have several scratches across her upper chest and mid abdomen, which were documented during a medical examination. Helen was extremely distraught and wanted to drop the investigation because she was afraid of her boyfriend and thought if she dropped the charges he would just leave her alone.

Her original complaint of rape began to unravel when the police responded to this new complaint and located the boyfriend. They quickly discovered he had an airtight alibi for his presence the entire day including the time frame of the alleged assault. He and four friends were nearly fifty miles away and their car had broken down on the highway. They were forced to call a tow truck to come and get them off the highway and another friend had to drive out to pick them up and bring them home.

When the victim was confronted with this inconsistency, she finally admitted that she had fabricated her original complaint and also admitted to scratching herself on her chest and abdomen using a bottle opener because she thought it would provide more evidence to validate her complaint. Helen admitted that the boyfriend had never forced or coerced her into having sex with him, but she was upset because he had been too rough with her. The 'roughness' of the sex act was actually the result of his sexual inexperience rather than any force or criminal coercion. Helen explained he was now starting to pressure her to get married, although she did not feel ready. She made the complaint because she wanted to both punish him for being so rough with her and cause him to break up with her and leave her alone. She insisted she never thought the complaint would ever be prosecuted because it was a case of 'he said, she said,' so there was no chance of him being convicted.

The problem with this particular case was that the victim was very believable. Knowledge gained from her law enforcement classes regarding police procedure and the typical behavior of rape or domestic assault victims enabled her to play the part very well. Even after the boyfriend passed the polygraph, there were several detectives that still believed the victim was telling the truth because of the amount of corroborating evidence.

As noted in the Case Study 13-7, these types of complaints are especially bad because they could lead to an innocent person being accused of a crime and quite possibly being sent to prison. Even if the accused are later acquitted or charges are dropped, they are going to have to deal with a certain percentage of the public who will still believe they were involved and may have simply gotten away with the crime. Another example is victims who set about using their status as a victim for purely selfish reasons because they think they can turn their victimization into a monetary gain. An example of this is provided in **Case Study 13-8**.

Case Study 13-8

A woman reported that as she was visiting a major theme park she had been accosted and raped as she was attempting to use the restroom. The victim's clothing had been torn and she had obviously been struck in the face numerous times as her lip was cut and her face was swollen. During the hospital examination the sexual assault nurse examiner (SANE) reported signs of recent sexual activity and recovery of semen in her vagina. Surveillance cameras showed the victim walking into one of the smaller public restrooms and then walking out several minutes later. Police were still uncertain because the manner in which the victim reported the crime did not seem to be consistent with other victims. Several days later, however, a man came forward to the police claiming the victim's rape complaint was a false report and the victim was intending to sue the theme park, alleging they failed to protect her from assault. The man reported that earlier on the day of the incident the woman in question had come by his house rather unexpectedly and initiated consensual sex with him. She then went to the theme park with her brother. Later the victim was re-interviewed, and, after being confronted with the man's statement and other inconsistencies, admitted that the rape complaint was in fact a scheme to provide evidence of a rape to the police because she and her brother intended to file a multimillion-dollar lawsuit against the theme park. It was her brother who was waiting in the women's bathroom and had actually struck her in the face and tore her clothing. The consensual sex earlier that day was to be able to have semen in her vaginal tract when she was examined at the hospital.

As shown in these case studies, as the false complaints proceed along the spectrum from unplanned to planned, the reports tend to increase in intensity and detail. At each step along the way, the amount of violence reportedly used against the victim increases and the event often becomes increasingly complicated and involved. In the preceding cases, the victims made an effort in their reports, some more elaborate and involved than others, to provide evidence to the police that they thought would substantiate their claims. The premeditated, well-thought out false complaints create serious problems for the police because the false victims can be quite convincing. Unlike some of the other false victims, they are often able to provide details of the event, they can provide physical evidence substantiating their complaint, and due to their agenda or reason for making the complaint, they are seldom willing to drop the complaint and can be very vocal in demanding action from the police. Most victims are very well rehearsed in their story, have staged the scene to resemble a sexual assault or a break-in, and many times will self-inflict wounds.

Self-inflicted wounds add to the realism of the report by providing "evidence" to the police and medical personnel that they are truly victims of some personal outrage. These injuries can be quite convincing when presented to the layman, because it is not "normal" for persons to intentionally inflict injuries and pain upon themselves, especially just to make a false complaint. These "victims" are initially believed because they do not present themselves as being insane or even mentally unstable during their treatment. But to the experienced detective, most of the injuries are inconsistent with injuries that we would expect to see during a real sexual assault. Common injuries presented by false victims are sharp, forced injuries, which are generally very shallow incised wounds. Interestingly, the injuries seldom involve the more sensitive areas of the body such as the breasts, nipples, clitoris, or anus, and seldom involve the face. Instead, what we tend to see are long, linear cuts across the abdomen, top of the legs, arms, or on the back—all within the range of motion of the victim, meaning the victim was able to inflict the wounds herself. To understand what might motivate someone to injure him or herself, one must first understand what it means to be a victim and what he or she could possibly get out of being victimized.

▶ Being a Victim[9]

To be a victim of any crime can be a traumatic experience, and the more "personal" or threatening the crime, the more it can affect the individual's sense of safety and security, and in turn, the more damaging it can be to one's sense of wellbeing. Rape is one of the ultimate "crimes against persons" because not only is the victim's sense of privacy invaded but also her personal safety is violated. The victim of a rape therefore requires understanding, attention, and the willingness of others to lend support and assistance to aid in her recovery. Because of these needs, police and the criminal justice system, together with healthcare professionals, have designated responses to provide that immediate care and attention to the rape victim. The intent is to treat the victim immediately, with follow-up treatment to help return the victim to normalcy as quickly as possible. This immediate understanding, no-questions-asked support, and care are also what attract the false victim to make a report. MacDonald[9] refers to false victims as "pseudo victims" who seek out and demand the same service and attention to help them through their own individual problems by carefully manipulating the criminal justice and healthcare systems. They want and expect to receive the same attention, sympathy, understanding, and concern that they believe the genuine rape victim receives. This not only includes compassion and attention from healthcare officials and police, but more importantly, from their own families.

False rape victims, especially those that tend to plan out their reports, are often seeking the attention they believe is lacking from their families. This desire for attention is usually in the form of concern, sympathy, and support and more often than not, their false rape complaint was not the first time they tried to gain attention from family or loved ones: They have probably tried lesser efforts to get that attention in the past. Therefore, false rape complaints are especially likely when some real or perceived need for which the pseudo victims lack adequate coping responses arises; this need prompts them to manipulate others into helping them out of the situation. This manipulation is similar to a special category of mental disorder commonly referred to as Münchausen syndrome.

Emir Asher first coined the term *Münchausen syndrome* in 1951 to describe patients involved in self-mutilation in order to support false claims of injuries or disease. Asher took the name from the central figure in a book about Baron

---

[9] McDowell, C. P., & Hibler, N. (1983). *False allegations of rape in the military community* [unpublished paper]. Washington, D.C.: U.S. Air Force Office of Special Investigations.

Karl Friedrich Hieronymus Freiherr von Münchausen, a retired soldier known for his tall tales and fabulous adventures that often took the form of "serious narration of palpable absurdities."[10] Münchausen syndrome is well known in medical fields and ranks along other well-established phenomenon in medical literature, such as malingering, hysterical conversion reactions, self-mutilation, and factitious disorders.[11] One essential feature is the intentional production of physical symptoms to support claims of illness or injury. This can include complaints of pain when it is not present to the extreme of accepting an injection of medicine or a drug such as penicillin that they know they are allergic to, and then suffering through the expected reaction. These patients appear to be compulsively driven to make complaints, and then use their complaints to manipulate doctors and hospitals into giving them attention. With a false rape complaint, the victim is basically trying to manipulate the criminal justice system (police) and the healthcare officials to achieve her goals. *Münchausen syndrome by proxy* is frequently found in child abuse cases where mothers intentionally inflict injury or induce illness on their own children as an excuse to bring them to the hospital for treatment. In these cases the injury and illness of the child are used to manipulate medical personnel into giving attention to the mother, who in a sense becomes a "victim" herself, needing comfort, consoling, and consideration because of the injury or illness of her child.

The degree to which pseudo victims defend their victimization can be in direct proportion to their need to be seen as a victim. Some victims, regardless of the evidence presented to them, are unlikely to ever admit to a fabrication of their complaint. If confronted, they are likely to become enraged at the suggestion and storm out of the interview, questioning detectives' competence and threatening some type of legal or tort action against them.

The vast majority of false rape complaints, however, are found at the lower end of the continuum where the circumstances surrounding the complaint, the lack of corroborating evidence, and often the lack of conviction by the victim leads to a fairly rapid determination of a false complaint. False rape complaints at the higher end of the continuum can be rather problematic, because although less frequent, they tend to require a great deal more attention and investigative effort due to the complainant's preparation of physical and forensic evidence and a staged scene to corroborate the complaint.

---

[10] McDowell, C. P. (1983). *False allegations of rape in the military community* [unpublished paper]. Washington, D.C.: U.S. Air Force Office of Special Investigations.

[11] American Psychiatric Association. (2000). *Diagnostic and statistical manual of mental disorders (DSM-IV-R)*, Washington, D.C.: Author; "Factitious means not real, genuine, or natural. Factitious disorders are therefore characterized by physical or psychological symptoms that are intentionally produced or feigned. The sense of intention is subjective, and can only be inferred by an outside observer."

▶Recognizing False Complaints

There are certain common factors that tend to be present in nearly all false rape complaints that we have termed as *red flags*[12]—things that when we see or recognize them, cause us to pay closer attention. It is important to note that there is no single element or *red flag* that we can point to that shows for certain an incident is false. Instead, we look at a number of things and then using the totality of circumstances, approach to look at the entire event. Generally, when each factor or red flag is considered alone or in a vacuum without any other evidence or information, it may not mean anything, but when placed into combination with other factors or other red flags, can validate the determination of a false complaint.

The following sections identify some areas where red flags are likely to appear. It is important to note that these areas of the investigation are not special or anything extra, but rather a normal part of the investigation. These steps will be taken anyway, but we are now focusing on the victim's response or behavior.

Enthusiasm of the Victim[13]

This refers to the victim's level of interest in making the initial report to police, so one of the first things we want to look at is the manner in which the incident was reported to the police. Delays in reporting the incident, although also common in actual rapes, are nearly always present in false complaints. Again, with good reason this does not present a problem per se but is one of the factors to watch out for. Probably more important is the fact that many false complaints are not initially reported directly to the police but rather to friends, spouses, or associates during a personal conversation, or to medical personnel while seeking treatment for suspected pregnancy or venereal disease. In fact, many times it is the friends or family members who insist that the victim make a report; it is usually evident that family or "friends" seem to be more concerned with reporting the assault than the victim. As a result, many false victims we see were "convinced," or nearly "coerced," into reporting the incident by spouses, family, or friends rather than coming forward on their own.

Along with the initial report, we also look at the general nature of the report and what the victim claims happened and her reaction to the incident. We understand the concept of *counterintuitive behaviors* and how the victim may respond in unusual manners, but some victims might go way beyond what we could possibly call counterintuitive behavior, as demonstrated by the **Case Study 13-9.**

---

[12] The term "red flags" was first coined by John Douglas and Corinne Munn in their article *Violent Crime Scene Analysis: Modus Operandi, Signature and Staging, FBI Law Enforcement Bulletin,* February, 1992.

[13] McDowell, C. P., & Hibler, N. (1983). *False allegations of rape in the military community* [unpublished paper]. Washington, D.C.: U.S. Air Force Office of Special Investigations.

Case Study 13-9

Donna was admitted to the hospital following an attempted suicide after claiming she had injected ammonia into her veins and had sliced her wrists. While in the hospital, she told her attending doctor she had attempted suicide because she was gang raped nearly 1 month before by four unknown black males behind a building near where she lived. She claimed she was dragged into the woods by the men, where she was vaginally, anally, and orally assaulted by all four suspects. She reported being so upset that she wanted to commit suicide because she could not deal with what happened to her.

Upon admission to the hospital, she had unexplained scratches on her back and stomach, and recent trauma to her vagina and anus that she claimed occurred during the assault 1 month prior. The hospital reported the incident to the police, but because of the fragile mental condition of the victim, the attending doctor refused to allow the police to talk to her. The doctor felt she was so upset over the attack, she might attempt suicide again if forced to talk about the incident. Instead of letting the victim talk to the police, the doctor inserted himself into the case to act as an intermediary—asking the victim questions posed by the police and then returning to tell the police her answers. This was most unfavorable to the police, but the doctor used his position to stand in their way of contacting the victim in person. Based on third-hand information, a crime scene search was eventually conducted in the area identified by the victim through the doctor, but the scene was inconsistent with the information she was providing through her doctor.

During her victimology assessment, the police learned Donna had willingly talked to her friends about the incident on several occasions since her hospitalization, but had provided different versions of the incident to her friends and boyfriend. Her parents were interviewed several weeks later, and the police learned she had told her parents that only two men were involved in her assault, and both had been immediately caught, arrested, confessed, and were already sent to prison. Therefore, she would not need to testify in court and once released the case would be over. In reality, since Donna had never talked to police about this incident, there was no way to investigate her complaint; therefore, there was no chance to identify, arrest, and convict any suspects, or even verify her story. She was later released from the hospital without notifying the police and then immediately left the area without having ever officially talked to the police about the incident. The doctor in question was later brought before the state licensing board by the police department where he had to defend his actions. Although he retained his medical license, he was sternly rebuked for his actions.

Case Study 13-9 highlights how manipulative some victims can be when telling their story to the untrained layperson. In this case, the doctor was absolutely convinced that she had been assaulted and believed he was doing the right thing in protecting her from the police and any further trauma. He could not explain why the victim who reported being raped a month before had recent trauma to the vagina and anus. Even worse, he had never asked the victim about it during all of his treatment, because he had never realized the inconsistency in her report.[14] What he actually succeeded in doing was preventing the police from conducting a criminal investigation.

The victim (Donna) in this case study was contacted by police a short time later for an interview concerning her allegation. When contacted by the police, the victim was surprised and shocked that the police had tracked her down and were still interested in investigating her complaint. Donna steadfastly refused to be interviewed or make any statement about her "rape" and asked to be left alone, and slammed the door in the face of police detectives.

Part of the problem with false victims is that they were never actually assaulted, so they have to make up emotions and think about how they should be responding to the incident. Because they are not real victims, they must decide on what to do from what they have seen on TV or in the movies, what they have read in books, or what someone else has experienced. Victims, as a rule, are generally not that familiar with the investigative process, so when they report that they could not identify their attacker during their initial interview, or could only provided a limited amount of information about what happened, they generally assume that the police will not have anything to investigate and will close the case. As noted in Case Study 13-9, many false victims are surprised if they are re-contacted by the police for follow-up interviews and learn that the investigation has continued.

Generally, once false victims have reported the attack and have begun to receive the desired attention, their interest in the case and willingness to cooperate with the police wanes. After all, many never intended to get anyone in trouble and never expected the police to do more than take a report. Besides, they have been rescued from whatever situation was causing them problems and as far as they are concerned the event is over. What we frequently see in these situations where the victim is re-interviewed are dramatic changes in details of the event from what was originally reported to what they are now reporting; or, they claim during a re-interview they cannot remember the exact details of the event.

Medical Treatment

Another common factor is victims' general indifference to the incident and to their alleged injuries. It is also not uncommon for victims to balk when requested to undergo a medical examination in order to collect physical evidence and look for other evidence of injury. Although this also might occur with a real victim for various reasons, the reluctance to undergo medical

---

[14] Police believe that the scratches and other injuries were self inflicted immediately before her hospitalization as a way to validate her complaint.

treatment might also be followed by a change in the facts of the assault, which would negate the necessity for conducting the examination. **Case Study 13-10** is a good example of how the details change when victims realize they may have to undergo a physical examination.

Case Study 13-10

Deborah, a 28-year-old wife, initially reported being assaulted and vaginally raped by an unknown male in her vehicle while in the parking lot of a night-club. Once taken to the hospital for examination and treatment, she was briefed on the extent of the medical examination and then suddenly changed her allegation completely, stating she had only been touched through her clothing and was not actually raped, as she initially reported. Based on this new statement, no medical examination was necessary and she was returned to the police station where Deborah gave her statement of what happened. However, as she was being interviewed, the details of the incident began to change and eventually she confessed she had been seeing her boyfriend inside the club when other friends of her husband had come in and saw them together. The rape complaint was her way to distract her husband's attention from the fact that she was having an affair with another man.

Victim Reports Pre-assault Incidents

It is also important to listen carefully when victims report activities that may have occurred prior to the assault, such as receiving threatening messages, either by phone or by written notes, or they report the feeling of being under some type of surveillance by unknown persons leading up to the assault. The implication is they are being targeted and threatened by an unknown offender. **Case Study 13-11** is a good example of such claims by the victim.

Case Study 13-11

A married 47-year-old female reported on multiple occasions to the local police that she was receiving threats against her life from unknown persons. These threats came in the form of phone calls and notes that were left on her vehicle, and finally someone actually spray-painted a threat on her garage door. This caused the police to respond to the victim, and they set up several surveillance cameras focused on the residence. They informed the victim that they could cover the entire house with the exception of one corner of the house, which based on the layout was considered as an unlikely point of entry. Several days later in the early morning hours, the victim reported to the police via a 911 call that two males had entered her residence and had physically and sexually assaulted her inside the house. The police responded to the scene and checked the surveillance cameras, but they had not recorded any activity surrounding the house. They looked at the house and found the point of entry to be the very location they were unable to cover by the surveillance camera. The entry was made by removing the window screen, opening the window, and apparently crawling through. Inside the house the police noted some minor disturbances, such as a houseplant that appeared to be turned over but was not broken and the dirt was not scattered on the floor. The chairs of the dining room table were tipped back or laid on the floor but were not otherwise disturbed. In the bedroom was a wadded up strip of duct tape that the woman reported was used to wrap her wrists together and a wire coat hanger she claimed had been inserted inside her vagina as part of her torture and sexual assault. The victim claimed to have put up a fight but was overcome by two offenders who were larger than she was. As the offenders left the scene they stole some jewelry from her dresser, but during the crime scene search the jewelry was recovered inside a baseball cap that was supposedly dropped by the offenders as they left.

The victim was examined at the hospital but there were no internal injuries and no signs of a sexual assault. The coat hanger however, was later found to have vaginal secretions from the victim on it and the duct tape did have some hair and skin cells from the victim on it. After additional questioning the victim finally admitted to making the false report and staging the scene to resemble a break in and struggle. She further admitted to putting the duct tape around her wrists and then removing it and wadding it up. She had also had carefully inserted the coat hanger into her vagina to add realism to her claim. She was trying to make her husband pay attention to her.

When a victim reports receiving prior threats, it is important to note that typically she is the only one in her family or residence who ever received the threats. No one else in the house ever receives the threatening phone calls, and any notes the victim reports receiving are almost always thrown away so the police are usually left with the word of the victim that they were received. There have been occasions when the victim has produced a note that was constructed of pieces of text clipped from different sources such as magazines and newspapers then pasted on a piece of paper to form written text. Research has never identified a single case where such a letter has ever been found to be genuine.

Does the Report Solve a Problem for the Victim?

MacDonald identifies one of the basic reasons for a false rape complaint is to receive assistance or solve a problem for the victim. This problem can be anything from alcohol, drug abuse, or financial problems to getting attention from a spouse or boyfriend. Many times this is the hidden agenda behind the complaint. So one question that should be answered is: Will the complaint solve some immediate problem for the victim? Several cases studies already presented demonstrate this concept—if the victim was not successful, then she was attempting to solve a problem by making the report. This is an example of why a victimology assessment and the victim's background are so important. Many times we are able to see how a false rape complaint may in fact help the victim solve some immediate problem in her life. Remember, these incidents are not always so well thought out, and by the time these "victims" are at this stage of dealing with problems, they are often desperate for help or some relief.

Previous Rape Complaints Made by the Victim

A history of previous complaints of rape or sexual assaults by the victim demands a closer examination of the facts and circumstances. A comparison of the current complaint to previous reports normally yields obvious similarities. The similarities may include the same description of the suspect, similar weapon used or displayed, and the same method of attack. An example is found is **Case Study 13-12**.

Case Study 13-12

Linda called the police from her house and reported she had been raped while in the parking lot of the local post office. Linda said she stopped at night to buy some stamps from the vending machine, and when she returned to her car she was accosted by a man hiding in the rear seat of her vehicle. He threatened her with a knife, lifted up her dress, removed her underwear, and raped her in the front seat of her vehicle. Linda reported that after he was done, he ran away. She drove home and called her husband who was working out of state.

When asked to go for a medical examination, Linda refused and claimed that in the time since she called her husband, she had already bathed, douched, and thrown away her underwear and dress, although she could not remember where she had disposed of the articles. It was also noted that Linda was a heavy-set woman and her car was a smaller compact. She had no associative injuries or bruises, and physically it did not seem possible for the event to have happened in the front seat of her car as she claimed. When Linda was confronted with these facts she became extremely upset, swore at the detective, and refused to cooperate any further. She then stood up and walked out of the interview room and continued to insult the police until she was outside the police station. It was later learned Linda had filed a similar report in an adjoining city the preceding week. In that incident she reported being raped by a man hiding in her vehicle behind a department store. The physical description of both suspects and her description of both assaults were nearly identical. Linda's main concern expressed to police during both incidents was that hopefully her husband who was working out of state would now return home.

It is not unusual for victims who have been successful in making a false complaint in the past to try the same tactic again. This reinforces the need for a good background check of the victim's history and victimology assessment.

▶Victim's Description of the Events[15]

During their interview, most rape victims can recall the basic events of the assault in reasonable detail. This includes the description of the sex acts that occurred, the order in which they were performed, and statements or instructions given to them by their attacker. True victims usually provide additional details of the event—sometimes important details, sometimes unimportant or trivial details. Examples of specific details true victims can provide include the rapist having body odor or bad breath or the offender's apology after the assault. Conspicuously absent from false complaints are descriptions of problems relating to sexual dysfunction on the part of the offenders. In reality, a high percentage of rapists experience varying degrees of sexual dysfunction during the attack, including not only failure to achieve an erection, but premature or retarded ejaculation.

In contrast, false victims providing their statement about what happened typically respond in one or two general ways; with a general lack of concern or interest in the entire process, or telling the story with great relish and enthusiasm. In the first instance the victim's story is generally lacking any real detail of the assault, often accompanied with the explanation of some type of self-handicapping behavior such as keeping her eyes closed or being rendered unconscious by alcohol, drugged by some unknown substance, overpowered by multiple offenders, or for some unexplained reason she just "blacked out."

Sometimes noted during the interview is the victim's almost total lack of interest in the entire process; this is not a case of "zoning out" as if she is dealing with stress, but rather as if the whole process was boring to her or was taking too much time. Similarly, such conduct may be marked by the victim actually falling asleep during the interview or medical examination. **Case Study 13-13** is a good example of the victim's lack of interest and actually falling asleep during the interview process.

Case Study 13-13

Louann, a 17-year-old, claimed she had been raped in a college dorm after being "lured" into the building by three unknown male students who claimed her boyfriend, a fellow student, wanted to talk to her. She claimed she was taken to one of the rooms where they began taking her

---

[15] McDowell, C. P., & Hibler, N. (1983). *False allegations of rape in the military community* [unpublished paper]. Washington, D.C.: U.S. Air Force Office of Special Investigations.

clothes off, held her down on the bed, and then raped her. After the assault she was allowed to get dressed, and she called for a ride to pick her up and take her home.

A few hours later she told a friend what happened, and the friend convinced her to report the rape and actually drove her to the police station to make a report. Louann initially refused to go to the hospital for an examination and only consented when told of its importance to the police investigation. During her initial police interview afterward, Louann was very unresponsive, even disinterested in the process and kept falling asleep. Eventually she said she was tired and asked to discontinue for a while and go home, agreeing to come back the following day to complete her statement. Louann never came back, and when she was contacted to arrange for an interview appointment, stated she felt the police were not really interested in investigating the crime and that she knew nothing would happen. She refused to cooperate any further and wanted to drop her complaint. Other witnesses developed during the preliminary investigation claimed Louann had called them on the phone after she got home and was very angry over what had happened. She admitted to having consensual intercourse with two students, but when the third student came into the room and also wanted to have sex she got mad, because the two students started laughing at her and she thought she was just being used, and decided to leave. As part of the victimology, it was learned this was the second rape report filed by Louann, and she had declined to complete the previous report as well.

Falling asleep during the interview is very unusual unless the incident took place in the early morning hours, the victim had been consuming alcohol, or it was a result of a drug-facilitated incident. In those incidents it is very likely for the victim to be exhausted, and as discussed earlier, a detailed interview can be delayed. But absent a medical condition or those other particular facts, it is highly unusual for a victim to fall asleep during the interview process. Falling asleep is an avoidance behavior because when the victim is asleep, she does not have to answer questions and can be anywhere she wants to be in her own mind.

It is equally unusual for the victim to provide information about her victimization in a matter-of-fact, emotionless manner—as if she had rehearsed it prior to coming to the police, or so haltingly it seems as if the victim is making up the story as she is talking. False victims generally seem well prepared in certain areas and are able to provide very detailed information concerning that aspect of the incident. However, when questioned in an area they did not anticipate, they become very vague and begin to answer questions in more general terms with few specific facts or details, or try and steer the interview to safer areas. Additionally, as the story is repeated, two distinct differences are noted. Either the story remains the same, without the addition of any further details, or the details of what happened or the basic facts change dramatically as it is retold. As mentioned earlier, this is not what we would expect as we interview the victim, because as a story is told and retold we expect to be gaining more information and more details as the victim begins to recall what happened.

The second general response we may see is the victim relating the incident with relish or enthusiasm, such as supplying a great deal of unsolicited graphic details of what happened. In this situation it becomes evident the victim is trying to "shock" the investigator through what might be termed as *overkill* or *exaggeration*. Because a false victim was not subjected to the incident she is describing, she lacks the genuine feel of a real victim who was traumatized. She is usually just describing some event that she is making up, has read about, or has seen on TV.

Another frequent occurrence during false victims' interviews are unexpected gaps in their stories. These gaps are quite noticeable if the detective is paying attention to the victim, because they are in often in sharp contrast to an otherwise detailed account of the incident. Such examples include detailed descriptions of all the events leading to the sexual assault and afterward, but when talking about what happened during the assault, there is a sudden vagueness when it comes time to describe the sexual assault, such as:

- "I don't know how, but he took my pants off."
- "Suddenly, my dress was off and he was having sex with me."
- "We were kissing and the next thing I knew I was naked."
- "I told him no several times and afterwards he just got up and left."
- "We came back to my apartment and the next thing I knew we were in bed."
- "Then my leggings fell down and he was raping me."

Although some gaps can be expected with real rape victims due to the embarrassing nature of the incident, most real victims will be able to explain what happened and fill in the missing details. This is why we go back over the statement a number of times. This is in contrast to most false victims, who seem to have problems going back to fill in such missing details as simple as, "How did he get your pants off?" The importance of this becomes apparent, for example, when an overweight female says, "We were kissing and suddenly my leggings were on the floor." This is a huge gap in the story, because how do such tight pants suddenly fall to the ground or end up on the floor? There is something missing, like how they were completely removed. But again, since she did not actually experience this part, she might not catch the importance of her statement. Responses of "I don't know," "I don't remember," or "He just did it," are almost standard responses when questioned further or asked to clarify. Generally, false victims cannot supply such details because they did not anticipate these questions and do not know how to respond.

Description of Sex Acts

As noted throughout the text, the sex acts involved in an actual assault are often demeaning and humiliating. They run the gamut of oral, vaginal, and anal sex, and the order in which they were performed is predetermined only by the attacker. Cunnilingus, vaginal, or anal intercourse followed by fellatio is not uncommon. In real victims, while embarrassed and degraded because of the acts they were forced to perform, they usually can describe such acts. In false victims, only those sex acts they are familiar with are traditionally reported, and acts that they perceive as "dirty" or "undignified" are frequently not included in their report of the assault. One reason may be the false victim's reluctance to debase herself any further than necessary; thus, few will want to acknowledge more than vaginal intercourse, unless other acts are within their experience or repertoire. Reports of anal sodomy and fellatio are greatly underreported in false rape complaints, and many remain ambiguous about whether intercourse occurred or only admit to enough penetration necessary for the offense of rape to have occurred.

Identity of the Suspect

Contrary to popular myths, in the majority of rapes committed, the victim and subject are of the same race and are known to each other, either through work or normal social situations or by some prior personal relationship. In false complaints, there is a higher probability that the suspect will be an unknown, a friend of a friend, or a slight acquaintance whose name they cannot remember, and many will report being raped by someone of another race. The most predominant stereotype is the unknown black male suspect attacking the white victim. This allows the false victim to also play upon the perceived prejudices of police and society with regard to interracial rape. This also allows the victim to shift the blame to an "unknown assailant" and relieves her of the responsibility of falsely accusing a real person of a crime. With an unknown offender who will never be identified, there is no chance of the case ever being solved and the victim is able to remain a victim.

Self-Handicapping Behaviors

We also want to pay attention to what are known as *self-handicapping behaviors*, in which the victim reports being unable to assist the police in identifying the offender or offering any real information because of what happened to her. The key statement that seems to be present in many false rape complaints is, "*I blacked out.*" Blacking out or losing consciousness basically excuses anything that may have happened to the victim and completely eliminates the possibility that she can describe what happened to her or who was involved. There are many reasons why a person might lose consciousness without the use of drugs or alcohol, but they generally involve some type of trauma to the head or fainting. Fainting is a temporary loss of consciousness primarily due to an inadequate supply of oxygen to the brain. Fainting is a mild form of shock and may be caused by many things, including the sight of blood, exhaustion, weakness, heat, or strong emotions such as fear. But, even when consciousness is lost, it is not for an extended length of time as depicted on the television or in the movies.

Other examples of self-handicapping behaviors include multiple offenders, being blindfolded, or the incident happening in a dark alley or at night, meaning "she could not see the offender." Remember: Multiple offenders, the event occurring at night, or being unable to see the offender are not in themselves particularly important facts; they only become important when other red flags are also present.

Force and Injuries to the Victim

The next consideration is the amount of force used or described during the assault. One thing the majority of real rape victims report is the sense of being totally overwhelmed by fear, and that they submited to the assault because they did not want to be injured or killed. As noted earlier with the various approaches used by rapists, many victims are really unable to escape or defend themselves. So, any physical resistance by most real victims is quite limited; the actual force level used by the rapist might consist more of threats of violence and physical intimidation than actual physical force. In contrast, false victims often report exaggerated attempts at self-defense; frequently, they claim they were in a serious physical, even life-or-death struggle, and may have resisted by kicking, scratching, or punching their attacker. But, because the attacker was simply too big for them, or there was too many of them, their resistance was eventually overcome. As previously discussed, victims who respond in such a physical manner are likely to produce an extremely violent response from the offender, which is likely to produce some serious injuries on the victim. Yet, the false victim is more than likely untouched or does not describe any violent response to her actions.

False victims may also present injuries as corroborating evidence of the assault. Although they claim to have been injured by the rapist, their injuries are not the typical or expected injuries resulting from rape and sexual assault. There are two main characteristics to these injuries that may distinguish them from real complaints: the wounds or injuries themselves, and the concern shown by the victim for her injuries.

The false victim may present a wide range of possible injuries and wounds, but most do not appear to be particularly serious, life threatening, or have sexual overtones. Injuries may include scratches, abrasions, cuts, and bruises, and may be found throughout the body. However, lips, face, eyes, and the genital areas are almost universally void of any serious, disfiguring injuries (see **Figure 13-1** and **Figure 13-2**). Although there may be injuries surrounding the breasts and genital areas, normally no injuries are found on the sensitive areas such as nipples, areola, anus, labia majora, or the clitoris.

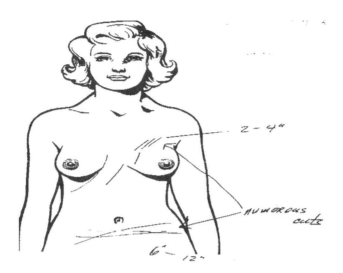

FIGURE 13-1 An example of a SANE medical report where the injuries to the victim are sketched on a diagram. Note that the injuries are inconsistent with a sexual assault.

If present, injuries will normally be located within the reach and the range of motion of the hands and arms of the victim. Again, false victims' intent with self-inflicted injuries is to provide the corroborative evidence and gain the sympathy they believe they need, not to cause themselves any great pain or permanently disfigure themselves.

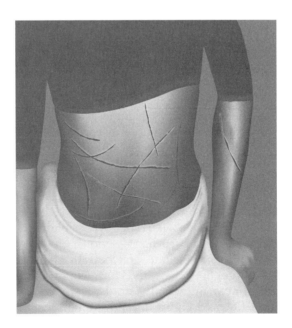

FIGURE 13-2 An artist's depiction of the long lateral incised wounds on the back of a victim from a reported sexual assault. Note that all of the injuries are within the range of the victim and do not involve any sensitive areas.

Because false victims have not actually experienced an attack, they are forced to create what they think may happen during an assault, but they have no idea of the amount or intensity of the violence which may result if the rapist becomes physically abusive. To them an injury is an injury. In reality, injuries sustained in actual assaults will reflect a lot of emotion such as hatred, contempt, and, above all, anger. It is very likely that injuries to real victims are severe and specifically targeted on their genital areas. Insertion of foreign objects into the vaginal tract and removal of the victim's nipples would be more consistent with the injuries expected during sexual assaults. This dichotomy of injuries being present, but not consistent with injuries caused during extreme violence or rages, will be evident and recognizable by most detectives.

This leads to the second characteristic, when the false victim has a tendency to accept her injuries with a certain nonchalance and unconcern described as the "martyr effect." Perhaps of equal importance to the location and existence of reported injuries is the lack of *associative injuries*. For example, when a victim reports being raped on the ground, we would expect to see rips, tears, or stains on her clothing. Likewise, if there are no abrasions found on her back, buttocks, knees, elbows, shoulders, or other high points on her body, this is a red flag. Victims who report being raped in automobiles yet show no signs of fabric burns or bruises from door knobs, gear shift levers, or steering wheels, which are known to occur even during consensual intercourse in automobiles, should be questioned further. Conversely, if they have damage to clothing but no physical injuries, then it is also suspect as noted in **Case Study 13-14.**

Case Study 13-14

Julia, a 14-year-old white female, reported being kidnapped on her way home by a large, older, unknown black male who forced her off a pathway and dragged her into the woods and then across a small creek where he stopped in a small clearing and ripped her shirt off and pulled down her pants. The victim reportedly fell to the ground and "blacked out." She woke up as she was being dragged fully clothed through the grass and mud and was eventually pushed into a small creek, and the offender then ran away. She then ran to her boyfriend's house and called her parents. Julia was examined at the hospital and found to be sexually active, but no signs of recent sexual activity were noted. She had no scratches, abrasions, stains, or bruises, although her clothing was torn, grass stained, and wet. Under questioning, Julia later admitted she had gone to another boy's house, where she had remained past her curfew. They concocted a story about her being raped to cover her coming home too late, and Julia also admitted to tearing the top buttons off her shirt, and being dragged through the grass and creek by the other boy to appear as if she had been dragged away by the man to match her story.

▶ Crime Scene Examination

Crime scene examinations are also an important investigative step with any investigation, but specifically we are looking for signs of a staged crime scene— that is, where physical evidence has been added or removed and the scene altered with the specific intent to misdirect a police investigation. Elaborate methods have been used to stage crime scenes, including messages written in blood, warning notes or letters left by the suspect for the victim, and evidence of forced entry. One common finding is unnecessary, inconsistent, and excessive damage to the residence/crime scene or the victim's personal property. Generally speaking, when a sex offender has forced entry into the house and commits a rape, it is consistent and even expected for them to steal property from the house. Disturbances are likely as they search for cash or other valuables, but it is generally inconsistent for them to then go through the house causing damage to the walls or to damage personal property or effects. **Case Study 13-15** is an example of a victim's statement that was inconsistent with the crime scene.

Case Study 13-15

Connie, a 30-year-old wife, reported that an unknown black male broke into her residence in the early morning hours, held a knife to her throat, and vaginally raped her. Connie related that she had accidentally left the garage door open, and thought the entrance into the house was made through the door leading from the garage. She had also for some unclear reason allowed her 7-year-old daughter to sleep in her master bedroom, while she slept in her daughter's room. Connie was never able to adequately explain why she and her daughter had exchanged rooms on that particularly night, and insisted several times it was the only time she had ever left the garage door open, and the first time her daughter slept in her room. The crime scene examination revealed no signs of forced entry into the house, nothing stolen or disrupted, and no signs of semen or hairs and fibers on the daughter's bed, although Connie was certain he had climaxed during the rape. There were no witnesses to the break-in, and her daughter did not hear or see anything. As part of the crime scene examination, the master bed was examined and semen stains and several different colored pubic hairs were discovered. Connie's husband was working out of state at the time and had been gone for several months already at the time of her report. After additional interviews, Connie admitted to having several affairs while her husband was gone, including having sex with her boyfriend in the master bedroom. Connie refused to admit she had lied about being raped, and became very uncooperative and declined to cooperate any further with the investigation. It was later determined that Connie had previously made another similar complaint at a former residence in another city and state, and when the police challenged her report, she also refused to cooperate any further. Connie's main concern was that her husband was scheduled to return home within a week.

▶ Confronting the Victim

Confronting the victim of any crime with suspicions of making a false complaint should never be undertaken lightly and should not be based on a gut feeling or a few minor inconsistencies or inconsequential facts. There should be some substantial measure of proof or irreconcilable differences between the victim's statement, other witness statements, crime scene examination, medical examination, and any evidence collected during the preliminary investigation before the victim is ever confronted. If the police are mistaken, then they are likely to increase the amount of trauma suffered by the victim and whatever rapport was developed between the detective and the victim will undoubtedly suffer irreparable harm. Stressing that additional interviews are necessary to clarify the inconsistencies found in her prior statement(s) is a useful tactic. Efforts should be made not to place the complainant into a psychologically stressful situation.

One suggestion is to insert an additional investigator into the interview process, even to the point of allowing him to take over. The victim should be asked about any inconsistent evidence and be given a chance to explain or reconcile it. The detective must remain supportive because one of the main goals of the false rape complaint is to regain self-esteem, and any direct challenges to the victim's credibility may result in increased self-defensiveness. The goal must remain to allow the complainant a chance to change her statement or provide additional information.

The reaction of the victim in these situations varies. At the low end of the spectrum, there is often an embarrassed, tearful confession mixed with relief that her lie is over. The amount of energy needed to keep the allegation going is often too much for most people to bear. Some victims even provide a detailed description of their efforts to establish the incident and the reasons why it was thought to be necessary to make the false report. Those at the upper end of the spectrum, however, may have already convinced themselves of their status as a victim, and no amount of confrontation or evidence is likely to change their mind. This type of victim has internalized all of the distortions and it has become a part of reality. Predictably, they will act outraged and may even storm out of the office, threatening to make a complaint with some higher authority or go to the media.

▶ Conclusions

A good preliminary investigation will identify problem areas in the majority of these types of cases, and the behavior-orientated interview technique is perhaps the best tool we have to sort these situations out. It is extremely difficult, if not impossible, for a false victim to come up with sufficient details and keep them straight during their initial interviews or to keep a story going for an extended time period. But we also have to remember that red flags are good to note and recognize, and they may cause us to take a closer look at those areas. We need to look at them not just because they may be signs of a false complaint, but because if we have noticed this is a problem area, it is likely the defense will also notice such a problem area. Therefore, we need to get it clarified and explained before we go to court, and if we do not, we are likely to see the defense bring the issue up again in court.

The subject of false rape complaints is very complicated. The scope of the problem is vehemently denied by feminists, who attempt to explain away statistics as inaccurate and/or as examples of sexual bias. For police, the subject often results in multiple personal anecdotal examples of some of their wasted efforts. Each side has an equal share of horror stories concerning the entire issue of rape and sexual assault. False rape complaints must be recognized as a problem for police and criminal justice professionals, legitimate victims, society, and even the false victim. The police, more than anything, want to "catch the bad guy." But, they are concerned with wasted effort and expenditure of limited manpower and assets investigating reported incidents that did not actually happen. For real victims, it is even worse, because they must pay the price of the false reports harming their credibility and taking resources from their investigations.

False rape victims will continue to surface time and time again, whenever they are stressed, need assistance, feel threatened or ignored, or any of the other countless reasons or hidden agendas for filing false complaints. It is for this reason that false rape complaints will undoubtedly continue to be a major problem. The only response to this challenge is education and training of police officers and healthcare officials to recognize and identify likely false complaints at their earliest stages. Once identified, the "victims" can be directed toward agencies other than the criminal justice system to tend to their problems.

▶ Further Reading

American Psychiatric Association. (2000). *Diagnostic and statistical manual of mental disorders, fourth edition, text revision (DSM-IV-R)*. Washington, DC: Author.

Estrich, E. (1987). *Real rape*. Cambridge, MA: Harvard University Press.

Hiberman, E. (1976). *The rape victim*. New York, NY: Basic Books.

MacDonald, J. M. (1974). *Rape: Offenders and their victims*. Springfield, IL: Charles C. Thomas Publishers.

MacKellar, J., & Menachem, A. (1975). *Rape: The trap and the bait*. New York, NY: Crown Publishers.

McDowell, C. P. (1983). *False allegations of rape in the military community* [unpublished paper]. Washington, DC: U.S. Air Force Office of Special Investigations.

McFadden, R. D., Blumenthal, R., Farber, M. A., Shipp, E. R., Strum, C. & Wolff, C. (1990). *Outrage: The story behind the Tawana Brawley hoax*. New York, NY: Bantam Press.

Warshaw, R. (1988). *I never called it rape*. New York, NY: Harper & Row.

CHAPTER FOURTEEN

Working with Prosecutors[1]

As with other subjects covered in this text, there are hundreds of specialized texts and writings on the subject of trial, court procedures, and courtroom tactics. This chapter emphasizes the importance of working with the prosecutor to ensure we are operating within the law, to point out what the prosecutor is looking for when he decides to take a case to court, and to describe some of the difficulties in prosecuting sex crime offenses. Not working with or not listening to the prosecutor is one of the more common mistakes that leads to unresolved and unprosecuted cases. This close working relationship is especially important when dealing with these particular offenses because of the many difficulties that will have to be overcome to get a conviction. This is truly where a partnership is needed, and when it works there is success, and when it does not it will affect how your cases are brought to court.

▶ The Prosecutor

The prosecutor is more commonly known in most jurisdictions as the district attorney. They are elected officials responsible for a specific geographic jurisdiction as determined by state law and may be limited to a single county or in some states may encompass a multi-county district or judicial circuit. There is generally one district attorney (DA) who supervises several other deputy district attorneys who are assigned to assist in the prosecution of various criminal cases. More and more jurisdictions are also establishing a special prosecution section to deal with special victims of crimes such as child and domestic abuse and/or sex-related crimes. This is an example of the multi-disciplinary approach to the investigation and prosecution of rape and other sex crimes. This specialized prosecution allows for the prosecutor to develop some experience and expertise in these often complicated crimes.

---

[1] Much of this chapter has been adapted from: Adcock, J. M., & Chancellor, A. S. (2013). *Death investigation*. Burlington, MA: Jones & Bartlett Leaning.

The district attorney and his office are chiefly responsible for coordinating the government and community's response to crime, from the initial screening when the prosecutor decides whether or not to charge a case, through all court proceedings, sentencing, and in some cases in the appellate process. The district attorney's general duties and responsibilities include, but are not necessarily limited to:

- Providing guidance to police agencies on criminal procedures and the law during the course of the investigation.
- Assessing investigative reports provided by the police within his jurisdiction and determining whether there is sufficient evidence to file a criminal complaint
- Determining if the criminal complaint warrants presentation in criminal court or would be more appropriately handled through pretrial diversion or other remedy.
- Representing the community in the prosecution of offenders in criminal or civil courts.
- Directing the county grand jury.
- Protecting and properly applying victims' rights legislation.

Because of the many complexities in these cases, the prosecutor and the detective should be working hand-in-hand to achieve their common goal: Identifying offenders so that they may be brought to justice and punished, and thereby preventing them from victimizing or harming others again. Remember, cases are not over for the police once an arrest has been made, and prosecutors should not find out about a case only after an arrest. This teamwork is not just about being prepared for court, but should be worked on or established on daily basis. The advantage is to be able to quickly receive legal advice as necessary concerning search warrants, rights advisement, assistance in obtaining investigative subpoenas, preparation of arrest warrants, and input and recommendations on investigative leads as the preliminary investigation is developed.

This aspect cannot be overemphasized, because unlike the police who have a narrower role in the investigation—basically to find out what happened and identify evidence that establishes those facts—the prosecutor must look at the end product and what evidence he has or what additional evidence he is going to need in order to present evidence in the trial. For instance, finding a key piece of evidence at the scene is very good for the police and may help to establish some key fact needed to identify the offender. The prosecutor, however, now has to determine how exactly that piece of evidence is going to be introduced into court, which may require additional witnesses or additional facts that are unrelated to the general police investigation of determining what happened. Therefore, the prosecutor often requests additional investigative leads from the police to help firm up the evidence base during the preliminary investigation when there are likely more detectives involved in the case.

Asking the assistant DA to respond to the scene or to the station during victim interviews or suspect interrogations is a good way for the prosecutor to develop an interest and assume ownership of the case. The term *ownership*, as mentioned earlier in the text, reflects the notion of personal interest, investment, or involvement in the case. By owning the case, we generally are expressing our determination and commitment to see it through to the end, which is particularly important for these sometimes long-term cases. It is advantageous for both the detective and the DA to assume ownership. A good working relationship between the detectives and the DA is based on a general *trust* between the two agencies; the value of this trust is immeasurable, not just for the serious cases, but for all offenses and violations. This general trust developed between the agencies will sometimes result in the prosecutor being more willing to prosecute an "iffy" or otherwise difficult case.

Whereas our job as detectives is traditionally to deliver a well-documented and thoroughly investigated case, there are also other tasks prosecutors frequently ask of detectives to assist in during the preparation for court, such as conducting background checks on potential defense witnesses. An important concept relating to all criminal investigations that is especially relevant in sex-related offenses is that *the investigation is not over until the offender has been convicted*. On more than one occasion, detectives have conducted investigative leads and interviewed newly identified witnesses even during a trial because of new information or allegations that came out unexpectedly during testimony. It is not uncommon for the defense to be quite silent about their possible defense or to introduce surprise pieces of information during court that often shift the focus of the trial from the offender and his actions to the actions and behavior of the victim.

Theoretically, if we have conducted a thorough investigation, these instances are going to be few and far between, but they still happen. Remember, it is up to the prosecution to present evidence of guilt; the defense however, does not have to present any evidence of their innocence. The same with information, the prosecution has to ensure the evidence they provide to the jury has been validated for its truthfulness and reliability. Theoretically, defense is under the same obligation to present truthful evidence in court, but many times the defense may simply present an alternate theory of events or of the crime without really having to present any evidence. The purpose of this tactic is to confuse the jury, and it almost always results in extra work during court to tie up any loose ends.

Additionally, because the U.S. jury pool is so inundated with television programs revolving around police, crime scene examinations, and forensic evidence, there is often an unrealistic expectation that they are going to see the same fantastic results during the trial in which they are jury members. These high expectations and their influence over the jury are known as the *CSI effect*, and it is a real problem, especially when presenting a case with no or limited forensic evidence. This often causes the prosecutor to hesitate to take cases without such evidence to court or forces him to change his tactics or court presentation.

Detectives are especially helpful in these types of cases to help explain the lack of forensic evidence or to reemphasize other evidence that is available. Many times crime scene technicians are called to testify not just to introduce physical or forensic evidence found during the scene examination, but rather to educate the jury as to their efforts to find that evidence and what a lack of evidence actually means. As most detectives know, *the absence of evidence is not evidence of absence,* meaning we can say that if we found a fingerprint, the offender or whomever left the print was perhaps at the scene, but we cannot say that if there were no prints found, the offender was not present at the scene. Actually, we can only say that the offender may not have left any prints or left prints that we did not find. So, our courtroom testimony sometimes amounts to something like a college lecture to educate the jury on the reality of scene examinations and to counter some of these very unrealistic TV programs and perhaps to lower jury expectations. As detectives, our understanding of these key principles may provide the prosecutor with a better understanding of how to combat the lack of forensic or physical evidence by using such educational testimony or through the use of expert witnesses.

In many jurisdictions, the DA's office also has its own set of trained investigators to assist local police in completing serious investigations as well as helping to prepare cases for prosecution. These are commonly referred to as *district attorney investigators.*

District Attorney Investigators

These investigators operate under the direct auspices and legal authority of the district attorney and are often granted full peace officer powers under state law. Essentially this means DA investigators have full powers of arrest and warrant as other police officers within the state. Whereas they are not responsible for conducting routine police investigations, they are instead used in a wide variety of instances. DA investigators are often made a part of the critical incident response team that is called upon when an incident involving the use of "lethal force" by a peace officer occurs within the county. Generally, their duties are focused on providing much of the follow-up investigation on cases submitted to the DA by local law enforcement agencies and other county departments. Some of these cases include such serious felony cases as homicides, sexual assaults, robberies, gang cases, narcotics, insurance fraud, career criminal prosecutions, arson, child abduction investigations, and other major cases. District attorney investigators also assist other law enforcement agencies upon request where assistance, additional manpower, or special expertise may be desired. Many of their duties include locating witnesses, serving subpoenas, witness preparation for court, preparation of courtroom exhibits, and properly accounting for and securing evidence obtained from the police.

In some jurisdictions the DA investigators by statute also assume *original* jurisdiction over some criminal offenses and therefore may be the primary investigative agency in a wide variety of cases. These include abuse of judicial process (perjury, witness intimidation, falsification of evidence, conspiracy to obstruct justice), welfare fraud, nonsufficient checks, parental child abductions, election code violations, crimes committed by public officials, corporation code violations, environmental health violations, and so on.

▶ Decision to Prosecute

Prosecution of the suspect is not always an automatic result at the end of the investigation or even after an arrest has been made. Before prosecutors will take a case to court, they want to be absolutely certain they have the necessary information and evidence to win the case—not just to justify any expenditures and the cost of the trial, but also because of some other very important considerations that might not seem relevant, but do play an important part. These considerations include double jeopardy; that is, if the offender is acquitted at trial, he can never be tried again for that same offense. Basically, the prosecution gets one shot at taking a suspect to trial for a particular crime. So, if they take a chance on an uncertain case and the offender is found not guilty or acquitted by the jury, then they are prevented from ever pursuing the offender again for that offense. There is another very important issue to remember as we discuss prosecutorial decisions, which is that the district attorney is an elected official, and losing cases generally results in decreased political support. Thus, many difficult cases are not brought forth, to the frustration of the police and to victims.

The major question for most detectives is: What exactly is the prosecutor looking for, or what does the detective have to show in order to get a case to court? **Table 14-1** is a good example of what prosecutors are looking for in order to make a charging decision. The table shows the responses of prosecutors from 150 different locations across the United States who were asked to rank various factors or elements of the crime that influenced their decision to file charges or go forward with their prosecution.

Looking at Table 14-1, it is interesting to note that two of the top 10 deciding factors included the application of physical force and injuries to the victim. As stated earlier in the text, both the prosecutor and police feel more confident in moving forward with cases in which physical force was applied to the victim as there is little doubt in that *something* happened. The second highest criteria is also interesting because it deals with proof of penetration; as stated earlier, this is important because it is a main part of the elements of proof for a rape and what the prosecutor is going to have to show in order to establish that a criminal offense actually took place. This also highlights

TABLE 14-1 Rank Order of Important Factors in Filing Rape or Lesser Charge

Rank in filing decision	Factors	Percent choosing this factor
1	Use of physical force _ _ _ _ _ _ _ _ _	82.0%
2	Proof of penetration . _ _ _ _ _ _ _ _ _	78.0%
3	Promptness of reporting _ _ _ _ _ _ _	71.3%
4	Extent of suspect I.D. _ _ _ _ _ _ _ _ _	67.3%
5	Injury to victim _ _ _ _ _ _ _ _ _ _ _ _	63.3%
6	Circumstances of initial contact _ _ _	61.3%
7	Relationship of victim and accused _	60.7%
8	Use of weapon _ _ _ _ _ _ _ _ _ _ _ _	58.0%
9	Resistance offered by victim _ _ _ _ _	54.0%
10	Witnesses _ _ _ _ _ _ _ _ _ _ _ _ _ _	36.0%
11	Suspect's previous record _ _ _ _ _ _	31.3%
12	Age of victim or suspect _ _ _ _ _ _ _	24.7%
13	Alcohol or drug involvement _ _ _ _ _	12.7%
14	Victim's previous arrest record _ _ _	10.7%
15	Sexual acts other than intercourse . _ _ _ _ _ _ _ _ _ _ _	9.3%
16	Location of offense _ _ _ _ _ _ _ _ _ _	4.0%
17	Accomplices _ _ _ _ _ _ _ _ _ _ _ _ _	3.4%
18	Race of victim and suspect _ _ _ _ _	0.7%
19	Occuption of suspect _ _ _ _ _ _ _ _ _	0.7%

From: Forcible Rape, A National Survey of the Response by Prosecutors, Prosecutors Volume 1, The National Institute of Law Enforcement and Criminal Justice, Law Enforcement Assistance Administration, Department of Justice, March 1977. Originally published by the National Institute of Justice, U.S. Department of Justice.

the importance of the suspect interview and obtaining an admission from the suspect that he had intercourse with the victim. Even when he claims the intercourse was consensual, he is admitting to penetration and this is one fewer element that has to be established in some other manner. Other top-10 criteria include the promptness of reporting, the strength of the suspect identification (ID), circumstances surrounding the initial contact between suspect and victim, their pre-offense relationship, if a weapon was used, and victim resistance. We have discussed all of these factors throughout the text and now we can see why they are important to have covered and properly documented in our investigation; these are the very things a prosecutor is going to look at when you present your case for prosecution. Therefore, it will behoove the detective to make sure these elements are covered during the investigation itself, as well as highlighted during the presentation to the prosecutor.

Continuing with this concept, it is also important to note which of these same criteria were viewed by prosecutors as being important when it came to obtaining a conviction. **Table 14-2** compare these criteria to what the prosecutors considered during their charging decisions, and what they believed was important when they obtained a conviction. It is interesting to note that the same criteria prosecutors were looking for in order to take a case to court were the same things that they believed led to convictions, only in slightly different order of importance.

For detectives it is clear that to get a case into court and then obtain a conviction, they need to concentrate on these criteria. One important note is

TABLE 14-2 Most Important Factors Involved in Obtaining a Conviction of Forcible Rape

Rank in obtaining conviction	Rank in decision to file charges	Factors	Percent choosing this factor
1	1	Use of physical force _ _ _ _ _	83%
2	5	Injury to victim _ _ _ _ _ _ _ _ _	76%
3	3	Promptness of reporting _ _ _	70%
4	2	Proof of penetration _ _ _ _ _ _	68%
5	9	Resistance offered by victim _ _ _ _ _ _ _ _ _ _ _ _	66%
6	8	Use of weapon _ _ _ _ _ _ _ _ _	64%
7	4	Extent of suspect I.D. _ _ _ _ _	64%
8	7	Relationship between victim and suspect _ _ _ _ _	55%
9	6	Circumstances of initial contact _ _ _ _ _ _ _ _ _ _ _	54%
10	10	Witnesses _ _ _ _ _ _ _ _ _ _	52%
11	11	Suspect's previous record _ _ _ _ _ _ _ _ _ _ _ _	26%
12	12	Age of victim or suspect _ _ _ _ _ _ _ _ _ _ _	24%
13	15	Sexual acts other than intercourse _ _ _ _ _ _ _ _ _	22%
14	13	Alcohol or drug involvement _ _ _ _ _ _ _ _	9%
15	17	Accomplices _ _ _ _ _ _ _ _ _	7%
16	18	Race of victim and suspect _ _ _ _ _ _ _ _ _ _ _	6%
17	14	Victim's previous arrest history _ _ _ _ _ _ _ _ _ _	6%
18	16	Location of offense _ _ _ _ _ _	5%
19	19	Occupation of suspect _ _ _ _	1%

From: Forcible Rape, A National Survey of the Response by Prosecutors, Prosecutors Volume 1, The National Institute of Law Enforcement and Criminal Justice, Law Enforcement Assistance Administration, Department of Justice, March 1977. Originally published by the National Institute of Justice, U.S. Department of Justice.

that forensic evidence and strength of suspect ID were of lower importance in convictions than use of force, victim injuries, and victim resistance. Clearly, convictions can still be obtained without a great deal of forensic or physical evidence. This particular survey was completed years before the prevalence of DNA evidence use and yet convictions were still possible. Now that we have reliable methods to use DNA and other forensic evidence, cases should be even easier to get to court and get convictions. Unfortunately, we have erroneously come to believe a case without DNA or other forensic evidence is not prosecutable.

Other factors that are likely to generate prosecutorial interest are almost any serious crime involving juveniles, young children, or babies as victims, or whenever juveniles or young children are accused of committing a serious crime, because of the media and public interest. Additionally, almost any incident involving the sexual torture of the victim or incidents where injury was inflicted in a particularly brutal manner will capture media attention and thus become more known by the public, thus providing additional pressure to take such cases to court. The typical case of the stranger who runs out of the forest to attack a jogger captures more media interest then a victim who reports being assaulted by her date in her apartment. It is likely the *date* or *acquaintance rape* would likely never even make the local newspapers unless it involves someone of importance, because almost any incident involving a well-known local person or perhaps a well-known celebrity is going to garner additional publicity and media attention. This translates to added pressure on the prosecutor to take the case.

Regardless of the potential media pressure, caseload, how difficult the case may be, or experience level of the individual prosecuting attorney, no district attorney who must stand for reelection wants to take a chance of losing a major case and suffer voter or media criticism or loss of confidence in his abilities. Therefore, DAs are always going to be wary of taking any dubious cases to court, despite the public outcry. So, if we want them to take our case, we want to be able to convince prosecutors they have a winnable case. One effective way to provide the prosecutor with the case facts in an easy-to-understand format outlining the basics of the case is to prepare a *prosecution summary*. This may be an informal or formal report outlining the general case facts, the evidence, forensic findings if available, and the identity of potential witnesses with brief descriptions of their expected testimony. Essentially, we are reducing the entire investigation—which when presented as a case file or final investigative report may run into the hundreds of pages of written investigative reports, witness statements, or other documents collected during the course of the investigation—into very a easily understandable synopsis that should be used in combination with a face-to-face briefing about the entire investigation.

Box 14-1 is an example of what an uncomplicated prosecution summary might look like.

The form used and substance of the report can be altered to fit individual cases or agencies and is not necessarily limited to sex crimes, but can be

BOX 14-1 Sample Prosecution Summary

Prosecution Summary

Police Department/Agency

City, State

Case number_____   Investigating officer_____

Offenses: Violation of _____[State law citation]_____ ; [list all applicable offenses, e.g., rape, aggravated sexual battery, burglary, kidnapping]

Subject: Jones, Johnny A.; Male; [other identifying data deemed appropriate]

Victim: Patterson, Sarah J.; Female; [other identifying data deemed appropriate]

Synopsis of event: At approximately 02:20 on May 3, 2009, at 3445 Montgomery Road, Apartment C, [city, state], Johnny Jones, during the hours of darkness, unlawfully entered the residence of Patterson through a closed but unlocked window and accosted Patterson while she slept in bed. While holding a knife to her throat and threatening to harm her children if she resisted, Jones then raped and anally sodomized her. He then fled the area but was linked to the scene from fingerprints found on the window and through DNA from semen recovered during Patterson's medical examination. Patterson also positively identified Jones in photo and physical lineups.

Evidence:

1. Fingerprints found on window exterior match Jones'

2. Semen/DNA recovered during Patterson's medical examination

3. Photographs of genital injuries of Patterson, obtained during medical examination

4. Knife found on Jones's person at the time of his arrest

5. Testimony of Patterson and her identification of Jones during photo and physical lineups

6. Surveillance photo at convenience store near crime scene depicting Jones, taken shortly after incident; Jones wearing same sweatshirt as described by Patterson

7. Statement of Jones he was 50 miles away at the time

8. Cell phone records reflecting Jones called while in the area of the crime scene

9. Photo array of photo lineup and photos of physical line up when Jones was identified by Patterson

Forensic evidence/analysis:

1. Jones's latent prints on window exterior

2. Jones's DNA sample and semen sample found during medical examination of Patterson

Witness and expected testimony:

1. **Patterson:** Will testify she was sleeping in her house when she was accosted, raped, and anally sodomized by Jones; her identification of Jones in photo and physical lineups

2. **Officer Majors:** First responding office will testify about his first contact with Patterson and her emotional state; securing the crime scene pending arrival of crime scene techs

3. **Felix McWilliams:** Will testify he works at Night and Day convenience store and was working when Jones

(continues)

BOX 14-1 (continued)

came in and bought a pack of cigarettes shortly after the incident was reported; will authenticate the surveillance photograph taken by surveillance cameras

4. **Officer Murphy:** Crime scene technician will testify about crime scene processing and collection of latent print outside the living room window

5. **Victoria De Jesus:** SANE nurse will testify to the medical examination of Patterson, the collection of evidence, and photographs of injuries; offer expert opinion as to emotional state of Patterson and her collection of evidence

6. **Kimberly Richards:** Victim's advocate will testify to her observations and interactions with the victim

7. **Detective Evans:** City detective, will testify to the arrest and interview of Johnny Jones and Johnny Jones's alibi of fishing at the lake 50 miles away from scene; also to the examination of Johnny Jones's cell phone records, placing him around the scene at the time of the incident; will testify to collection of DNA sample from Johnny Jones

8. **Eric Potter:** Latent print examiner state crime lab, will testify to his results of the IAFIS search for the latent print and his later identification/verification of Jones as the donor of the print recovered from the scene

9. **Luther Edwards:** DNA analyst at the state crime lab, will testify to his analysis of the semen recovered from Patterson and comparison with Jones DNA sample

10. **Detective R. Patrick:** Will testify to his arrest and interview of Jones and will introduce his confession statement and video-recorded interview

---

adopted for use in any case. It can also be used as a good investigative tool when initiated at the start of the investigation, with the evidence and witness information entered into the form as they are developed. This also shows the detective where the investigation might be weak and where he needs to look for additional evidence in order to strengthen his case.

▶ Multiple Victims and Jurisdictions

One of the key issues to establish by the prosecutor is the jurisdiction to bring the case to trial. This can become somewhat problematic when the offense and case they are currently working on are in one jurisdiction and other similar offenses occur in other jurisdictions. This can be especially difficult when the offender has crossed state lines, and then there are two separate jurisdictions and laws to deal with. Most of these decisions will be based on state law and court precedence, but are an additional factor to be considered and perhaps overcome. Even when offenses are committed within the same legal jurisdiction, there is now the problem of how to prosecute. Again, for detectives, sex-related cases are somewhat difficult to investigate, but even more so for prosecutors. Depending on individual state laws, many times they are unable to combine cases together into one trial and instead must prosecute each offense separately.

This adds to the overall cost of prosecution and typically forces the prosecutors to make some difficult decisions, such as limiting prosecution to the strongest case to achieve a conviction of the offender and then either declining to prosecute other cases or accepting some type of plea bargain by the offender.

▶ Plea Bargaining

Plea bargaining or "making deals" is sometimes a necessary evil in the U.S. justice system; it is basically an agreement with the offender to plead guilty, but for a lesser crime or for a reduced punishment. We see this used in one of two general ways.

The first instance is when a reduced charge or a reduced sentence is used as leverage to induce a co-conspirator to testify against his other co-conspirators. Generally, this is offered to the person who first comes forward with an offer to assist or it is offered to the person with the least culpability or involvement in the crime. As an incentive for his testimony, one of the offenders may be offered a much lower range of punishment, and in some cases, may escape any punishment at all through an offer of immunity. Immunity, as noted earlier in the text, is essentially an agreement that the person would not be punished for any illegal act he may have committed, providing that he testifies truthfully against others. Although we do not like to reward criminals with reduced punishment or even escaping punishment, many times it is simply the price we have to pay to punish those offenders who are more culpable.

The second instance where we see plea bargains used is when the prosecutor, for one of many different reasons, may accept a guilty plea by an offender in exchange for reducing his charges, say from a very serious felony such as rape or attempted rape, to some relatively minor offense such as assault and battery. This unfortunately means the offender is not convicted of a sex-related offense and therefore may not have to register as a sex offender. It is difficult to say how these negotiations go because there are so many different dynamics at play with each individual case. These types of plea bargain decisions are made by the prosecutors and are not always the result of prosecutors trying to ease their case load or their unwillingness to take on a difficult case; many times they are forced into these positions because of the overall cost of the prosecutions, the various difficulties with evidence, or sadly because the police investigation simply lacks the necessary evidence to prove the more serious offense.

Very few prosecutors are making decisions about plea bargains in a vacuum, meaning they are aware of the publicity and how it might play out, they are aware of the evidence they have or they lack, the feelings of the detectives involved in the case, and perhaps most importantly they are very aware of the feelings of the victims and their families. Therefore, such decisions are seldom made without prior consultation and agreement of the victim's family, and hopefully with the concurrence of the detectives. Many victims consent to the agreements because they allow the offender to be convicted and punished but avoid the possibility of the victim having to testify in court and having to relive the experience and go through the embarrassment. This, however, does not always sit well with victims who want the opportunity to face their attacker and testify against them.

When we teach the concept of plea bargaining in various police courses, we are very familiar with the frustration and misunderstanding of detectives of the necessity for the prosecutors to make these difficult decisions. Although we understand their frustration, we generally remind them of the importance of developing every piece of information, locating every witness, validating every statement or alibi, and presenting the case in a manner that gives the prosecutor enough *ammunition* to achieve success.

It should also be noted that many states have laws restricting the district attorney's discretion to plea bargain certain crimes or capital offenses.

▶ Stages of a Criminal Prosecution

There are certain steps or phases for every prosecution in which the police and the district attorney will play a very important role, beginning with an arrest of the suspect and generally ending after the trial by acquittal or conviction. Each of these stages is discussed in the following pages.

Arrest

Criminal prosecution can be said to begin when a suspect is arrested and taken into custody because it is at this stage that the government (represented by the police) has taken the first step toward bringing the offender to justice. The arrest may be made in the following scenarios:

1. If the officer observes the offender committing a crime in his presence, the offender may be taken into immediate custody.
2. Based on probable cause to believe that a crime has been committed by that person. The best example of this circumstance would be responding to the scene and the suspect is present and admits to the crime or is immediately identified by the victim or other eye witnesses. The offender may be taken immediately into custody at this point.
3. Based on an arrest warrant. The arrest warrant is issued based on probable cause as outlined by the detective and authorized by the judge or magistrate. An example is when the offender has been identified sometime during the investigation but not necessarily at the scene. This is a formal process and requires the formal written authorization of a judge or magistrate in the form of an arrest warrant in order to take the offender into custody.

The entire process of the arrest, taking the offender formally into custody, and the subsequent administrative processing at the police station is known as the *booking* procedure. Booking actually refers to an old procedure where each arrestee was taken to the supervisor at the police station and their name and other information relevant to the offense were recorded in a ledger book. The general booking procedure today includes taking the suspect's fingerprints, photographs, and in some states a DNA sample is also taken. When the police complete the booking process, suspects for the more serious cases such as homicide and rape are generally held in temporary detention inside the city or county jail pending their initial appearance in court. During this initial hearing, issues regarding retention in jail or release prior to trial are settled.

Bail

In most minor or routine cases, it is often possible for offenders to gain a rather quick release from detention through a bail system wherein suspects can put up some type of cash or property guarantee in exchange for their release until their initial court appearance. Release on bail is essentially the suspect's promise to appear at all future court proceedings with the understanding that if they fail to show up, the court could forfeit the bail. In some relatively minor offenses, suspects may be released on their "own recognizance," which is really no more that their promise to show up for their court proceedings. Bail for more serious cases like homicide and rape are often more involved and sometimes impossible to achieve because of state law that may prevent bail from being offered, or because the bail is so high—sometimes in the hundreds of thousands of dollars that—it becomes impossible for the suspect to post. Each state has its own rules and regulations relating to bail.

Arraignment

The suspect's first court appearance following arrest is known as the *arraignment*. Typically, an arraignment takes place at the earliest opportunity, but generally within 24 to 48 hours. It is not unusual for many large cities to have night court, and thus first arraignments may be conducted at night. The arraignment is designed to ensure suspects are brought to a judge soon after their arrest, ensuring they are not held incommunicado and they are advised exactly what charges are being placed against them in the complaint filed by the prosecutor. It is the responsibility of the judge to try to establish the identity of the accused and that he understands the English language and understands the process taking place. The judge will also attempt to determine if the suspect has legal representation and may assign a public defender to aid in his defense. The first issues of bail are discussed and the judge makes an initial ruling.

Lastly, the judge attempts an initial pleading to the crime where the defendant chooses to plead "guilty," "not guilty," or "no contest" to the charges.

Generally, at this stage the defendant pleads not guilty and additional hearings for bail or preliminary hearings are then set as the legal process is initiated.

Preliminary Hearing or Grand Jury Proceedings

The next step in the process is the bringing of criminal charges against the offender. Charges are brought in one of two ways. The first is a preliminary hearing in front of a judge or magistrate where the prosecution presents a portion of their case to establish there is sufficient evidence to continue with the prosecution. This is a mini trial, and although the defense attorney may ask questions of the various witnesses, he is generally limited in presenting his defense. This is a good time for the defense attorney to understand what evidence the government has in its possession.

The second way to bring charges is through presentation of the case to a grand jury. The grand jury is a panel of citizens selected from the local community or judicial district to determine whether it is appropriate for the government to proceed with a criminal prosecution. The grand jury is meant to protect suspects from inappropriate prosecution by the government. The grand jury members are drawn from the general population and may serve not by the case but for a certain period of time. During their empanelment they may hear numerous cases or conduct their own investigation into certain matters as guided by the district attorney. If the grand jury members feel there is sufficient evidence to prosecute, they issue what is known in some jurisdictions as a "true bill" or an indictment.

In the federal system, cases must be brought by grand jury indictment, but states are free to use either process. If the judge during the preliminary hearing or the grand jury is not satisfied that there is sufficient evidence or probable cause to bring the case to court, then the charges against the offender are generally dropped at that point. However, because the offender was never in jeopardy, meaning he was never in danger of losing his freedom during either process, it is possible to re-arrest or seek an indictment of the offender at a later time if additional evidence or information is developed.

Pretrial Motions

Prior to the trial court proceedings, there are often other court hearings that take place. These court hearings are known as pretrial motions and are based on issues or questions that need to be settled before court and may be brought forth by either the prosecution or defense. Essentially, each side is offered a chance to present evidence or arguments defending their position before the judge. The judge then makes a ruling over the issue outside of the normal court and without the jury being present; the main idea is to decide these issues so as not to interfere with the normal flow of the court presentation once the trial has begun. There are many possible pretrial motions, but generally they revolve around obtaining necessary information about the criminal complaint from the police and prosecutor, the defendant's mental competency to stand trial, or around issues of the admission of certain items of evidence or witness testimony.

Discovery

Discovery is one of the standard pretrial motions and is essentially where the government (prosecutor) must provide to the defense all of the evidence they have collected against the accused. This includes both physical and testimonial evidence accumulated during the investigation that might be introduced as evidence in court. This also includes all of the police investigative reports; lists of property and/or physical evidence seized; crime scene reports, sketches, and photographs; any results of forensic testing/examination that have been requested or completed; and the list of witnesses the prosecution potentially plans to call in their case.

This ensures the government is not going to use any "secret evidence" and further gives the accused a fair chance to plan his defense against the allegations and to challenge the admissibility of evidence. These types of hearings are routine; they are now more of a formality rather than any type of adversarial procedure, as with other hearings and the criminal trial itself.

Competency or Insanity Hearings

A competency or sanity hearing is an attempt by the defense or the prosecution to show that the accused's mental condition at the time of the act will or will not prohibit prosecution for his particular crime. Generally, the issue revolves around the defendant's ability or capacity to understand or appreciate the nature and illegality of his actions at the time the crime was committed, and his current ability to participate or assist in his own defense. In these cases, the defense will often present expert witnesses to testify as to the incompetence or inability of the accused to understand or appreciate the nature of the crime, either based on a temporary situation or because of long-standing mental problems. It is important to remember that every state has particular laws and procedures for determining the competency of the accused to stand trial. But in almost every case, if the result of the hearing determines the accused was insane or mentally incompetent at the time the crime was committed or is incapable to assist in his own defense, it is likely he may not be held responsible for his actions. It is important to note that because of the depravity and deviance of the acts of some offenders, particularly some sexual sadists, it is a natural assumption by laymen that they must be insane or mentally deficient to be capable of perpetrating such acts against another person. However, this is seldom the case. Typically, sexual sadists clearly understand that what they are doing is against the law, and they simply do not care. Their actions are based on their desires and wishes and how their actions affect others likely never enters their mind; their main concern now, however, is to escape punishment so they are free to reoffend.

Again, it is difficult to outline specifics on this particular issue because each state has its own laws and views this concept quite differently.

Suppression Hearings

A suppression hearing is an attempt by one side to prohibit or suppress the introduction of evidence or testimony into the proceedings. These hearings are often based on some alleged constitutional violation of rights. These include but are not necessarily limited to:

- 4th Amendment problems which generally revolve around the alleged improper seizure of evidence
- 5th Amendment problems revolving around the alleged improper or lack of rights advisement, and the conduct of the interview or interrogation of the offender
- 6th Amendment problems generally revolving around the right to legal counsel
- 8th Amendment problems generally revolving around alleged cruel and unusual punishments or excessive bail
- 14th Amendment problems generally revolving around allegations of equal protection claims

Other common examples include efforts to suppress victim identification based on an improper photo or physical lineup and suppression of an offender's statement or introduction of some physical or forensic evidence.

Each of these hearings is essentially a mini-trial wherein the side seeking to suppress some part of the evidence at the criminal trial presents evidence in support of their claims, and the other side has a chance to present counter evidence and arguments in support of their position. The judge then makes a decision based on the case facts and established precedence as to what evidence is going to be admissible and what evidence is going to be inadmissible or suppressed. Evidence suppressed or judged to be inadmissible cannot be used in court by either side.

Motions in Limine

This is a hearing used to exclude or *limit* the testimony anticipated by one side or the other. The motion essentially seeks to avoid irrelevant, inadmissible, or prejudicial evidence at any point in the trial. If the judge agrees that the expected testimony may be irrelevant or prejudicial to the case, he may limit a particular witness's testimony. We see this many times when we have statements, admissions, or confessions from co-conspirators that might implicate the defendant, and in many cases motions are made to limit testimony surrounding the victim's background such as his chaste character or sexual history. Many states have already made this subject off limits except in limited circumstances.

Other motions in limine particular to sex crime prosecutions involve limited questions to the victim regarding her previous sexual history. At one time this was a common tactic by the defense and it was used to show the victim was not of chaste character, implying that she may be promiscuous and therefore likely to have consented to the act or her complaint should not be believed. Changes to the law have fairly well eliminated this aspect from ever coming out in trial unless there is an overwhelming reason behind it.

There are other occasions when the defense will attempt to insert frivolous motions that are designed to embarrass, harass, or intimidate the victim,[2] such as requests for psychological examinations, counseling records, private medical records, and employment records, or any number of similar requests designed not necessarily to obtain exculpatory evidence, but rather to influence the victim to drop the charges for risk of divulging other personal information. Many times this works against the defendant because it angers the victim even more and makes many more determined to go forward. This is why the prosecutor should actively resist any such motions—even if the judge rules in favor of the defense, the victim will see that the prosecutor did his part and may not feel like she was abandoned.

Admissibility of Forensic Evidence or Expert Testimony

Other pre-trial motions frequently revolve around the admissibility of expert opinion testimony or attempts to suppress the admission of certain scientific or forensic examinations and techniques. These are commonly known as *Daubert hearings.*

Daubert Hearing

A Daubert hearing is used as a basis to introduce new scientific evidence or forensic techniques, and expert opinions resulting therein. The name is based on the Supreme Court decision rendered in *Daubert v. Merrell Dow Pharmaceuticals* (509 U.S. 579 [1993]), which substantially changed the standards of how scientific evidence and expert witness testimony are evaluated as admissible in court.

Prior to the Daubert decision and two subsequent but related decisions, *General Electric Co. v. Joiner* (522 U.S. 136 [1997]) and *Kumho Tire Co. v. Carmichael* (526 U.S. 137 [1999]), all federal and most state courts followed the "Frye standard" or the "general acceptance test" when seeking to admit scientific evidence. The Frye standard was based on another earlier

---

[2] Hazelwood, R. R., & Burgess, A. W, (2008). *Practical aspects of rape investigation: A multidisciplinary approach* (4th ed.). Boca Raton, FL: CRC Press.

Supreme Court decision in *Frye v. United States*, 293 F. 1013 (D.C. Cir. 1923). In the Frye decision, the court determined that an expert opinion on a specific scientific technique was admissible when there was a *general acceptance* by the relevant scientific community of the technique's reliability.

In Daubert, the Supreme Court ruled their earlier Frye decision was now superseded by changes in the Federal Rules of Evidence (1975), specifically Rule 702, which governs expert testimony. Rule 702 states:

> If scientific, technical, or other specialized knowledge will assist the trier of fact to understand the evidence or determine a fact in issue, a witness qualified as an expert by knowledge, skill, experience, training, or education, may testify thereto in the form of an opinion or otherwise.

The court determined such a rigid standard initially established by Frye, requiring a *general acceptance* by the scientific community, would be at odds with the new, more liberal thrust and general approach of relaxing the traditional barriers to "opinion testimony" as outlined in Rule 702. This new rule establishes a standard requiring a valid scientific connection to the specific inquiry as a precondition to its admissibility.

Rule 702 essentially has two requirements. First, the evidence must be reliable, and supported by accepted scientific methods and procedures. Second, the evidence must be relevant, and sufficiently tied to the specific facts of the case that it will help the jury in resolving a factual dispute. The judge in the trial court is charged with the role of "gatekeeper" to determine if the expert witness and his or her evidence will assist the jury to understand or determine the true facts of a case.

Daubert now allows the judge to evaluate the methodology underlying the expected expert testimony and whether it is scientifically valid and applicable to the facts at issue. This evaluation is based on four basic criteria:

1. Whether the theory or technique can be and has been tested;
2. Whether the theory or technique has been subjected to peer review and publication;
3. A determination of the reliability based on the known or potential *rate of error* of the technique or procedure; and
4. What the general acceptance of the theory in the relevant scientific community is.

For instance, when DNA analysis and bloodstain pattern interpretation were first introduced, they almost always required a hearing prior to the trial for the judge to be satisfied that the analyses were reliable enough to be used in court. Because these techniques have become so widely accepted across the country, there are seldom any instances where either of these forensic techniques or procedures are challenged. With the additional development of new scientific and forensic techniques or the use of nonstandard-type expert witnesses, these Daubert hearings are quite common. Although it is primarily the prosecutor's job to get the evidence into court, it is also one of the detective's responsibilities to assist in locating potential expert witnesses and be familiar with developing forensic techniques that may be invaluable to the investigation and to eventual court proceedings.

Trial

Trial is where the accused are finally brought to court to face the charges against them, and the evidence collected about their acts are finally presented to the jury. Like an "opera," criminal trial procedures follow along a set path and distinct phases. **Box 14-2** lists the various stages of a criminal trial.

BOX 14-2 Stages of a Criminal Trial

Jury selection
Opening statements
Prosecution case in chief
Defense case in chief
Prosecution rebuttal
Closing prosecution arguments
Closing defense arguments
Prosecution rebuttal statements
Charging the jury
Jury decision
Sentencing

Note that the prosecution is allowed to present rebuttal evidence after the defense case and is allowed a second chance to rebut the defense's closing arguments. This is because the defendant is assumed to be innocent at the time of trial, and it is up to the prosecution to present evidence of guilt. Therefore, the prosecution is allowed to rebut any evidence presented by the defense. In the U.S. judicial system, the defendant has a constitutional right to a trial by jury, or if he chooses, he may elect to be tried by a judge alone. Per this belief system, the accused is presumed to be innocent of the charges, and it is the government or the prosecutor that bears the total burden of proof in a criminal trial. Although defendants have the right to present evidence and witnesses on their behalf, it is not necessary to do so. There have been many times when defendants have chosen not to put on any defense of their own because they did not feel the government had established their guilt. The prosecutor must prove to the jury the defendant committed the crime, not beyond all doubt, but beyond a reasonable doubt. A jury or judge makes the final determination of guilt or innocence after listening to opening and closing statements, examination and cross-examination of witnesses, and jury instructions. If the jury fails to reach a unanimous verdict, the judge may declare a mistrial, and the case will either be dismissed or a new jury will be chosen. If a judge or jury finds the defendant guilty, the court will sentence the defendant.

▶Prosecution Problems with Sexual Assault Cases

Sex crime cases are among the most complicated of all prosecutions because of the sometimes horrific nature of the crimes, the amount of potential medical and forensic evidence, and because of all the issues of victim credibility and corroboration. But, in nearly every case, the prosecutor must deal with the even bigger problems of jury bias and the rape myths from which much of the bias originates. Remember, in sex crime prosecutions there are always *two* persons on trial: the defendant *and* the victim, with the jury often looking at individual's accountability and responsibility in order to assess the believability of each. We can also expect that female jury members might judge the victim based on their own concept of what *they would or wouldn't do*, and that male jury members could very well be thinking, "There but for the grace of God go I."

The prosecutor will need to confront the bias and educate the jury about accepting that rape and other sexual assault crimes almost always place the onus on the victim to prove she is telling the truth, rather than looking at the misconduct or criminal acts of the offender. He will need to remind them how we as a society look at other violent crimes, such as being robbed at gunpoint; in such cases, we would not automatically look at the victim as if we expect her to be lying about the incident. At the same time, the jury cannot hold the victim to some higher standard of conduct than anyone else and emphasize that it was the defendant's actions that led to the criminal act. Most of these issues should be addressed during their *voir dire*[3] and jury selection to make sure the jury is going to be willing to take these matters into consideration as they hear the evidence.

As the case progresses, there are other areas and evidence which should probably be covered and brought out during the prosecution's case in chief through the victim, witnesses, suspect statements, or expert testimony to counteract the various rape myths and potential jury bias. These special areas may include but are not limited to the topics that follow.

---

[3] *Voir dire* is a French phrase meaning "to tell the truth," and describes the procedure for *selecting* or *empaneling* the jury on a particular case. During voir dire, each side is able to ask questions of the jury members to identify anyone who may be prejudiced for or against the accused. Those potential jury members who are found to be to be unable to be fair to either side can be eliminated from the jury pool by the judge. During this process each side also gets a limited number of challenges they may use to eliminate anyone they feel may be unsympathetic to their side.

Relationship Between Victim and Defendant

If the defendant is a stranger and there was no relationship between the two, this issue is not as great because issues of consent are not as likely. In cases where the defendant and victim both know each other, then it becomes important to establish the exact relationship and perhaps to educate the jury that the vast majority of reported rapes involve people that know each other. The greatest difficulty is in cases where the victim and suspect had a previous sexual relationship with each other; in these cases, *when* and *if* the relationship was ended may become a central issue.

Delay in Reporting

It is important to note that there is a delay in reporting in many rape and sexual assaults and that such a delay does not always mean there is a problem with the complaint of the victim. In fact, the delay may be the result of shock, denial, or fear of repercussions from the defendant if she reported, or other such similar reasons. As noted in the prosecutor survey, a delay in reporting is not necessarily that important if a logical explanation can be provided.

Lack of Witnesses

As covered throughout the text, there are very few instances where the sexual act is observed by anyone else. Generally speaking, there are only two persons present when the crime occurs, so this lack of witnesses to the event can be countered with other witnesses who observed the victim and/or defendant before or after the incident and can talk about their demeanor or if either told them about what happened.

Lack of Injury to the Victim

There is a school of thought and there are rape myths out there that say if the victim did not resist or is not injured, then there is no evidence of a forced act. As we know, the vast majority of victims do not actually offer resistance and use of force and injuries to victims are almost the exception rather than the rule.

The Problem Victim

Problem victims are the typical high-risk victims such as prostitutes, hitchhikers, and alcohol and drug abusers. They are very difficult cases to present and are perhaps the best examples of where *victim likability*, as discussed earlier, comes into play. It is difficult to get some members of the jury to actually like the victim, but not impossible; for instance, if the victim is a prostitute, it is also likely the defendant knew the victim was a prostitute, and therefore he was likely engaging in having sex with a prostitutes. If the victim was drinking and using drugs, it is also likely the defendant was doing the same. Therefore, the defendant can also be shown to have serious character flaws, which may negate some of the negative feelings toward the victim. It is also interesting to note that when referring back to prosecutors' criteria for convictions discussed earlier, the victim's past criminal record was rated as number 17 of 19, so it is likely it would play a part, but maybe not as much as we might expect.

Alcohol and Drugs

Any involvement with alcohol and drugs is a potential problem, but it is important to remember that alcohol is involved in nearly 50% of all sexual assault cases, so it is an issue in a large number of cases. Of great concern for this situation is whether the victim voluntarily consumed alcohol or drugs, or the offender slipped them to the victim surreptitiously. Is there any evidence of predatory conduct on the defendants part? Such predatory behavior may help balance out any participatory conduct on the victim's part, such as voluntary intoxication. The prosecutors' criteria for conviction relating to drugs and alcohol was rated as number 14 out of 19. Again, it might be important in some cases, but may not be as big a problem as we might think.

Alcohol-facilitated sexual assault (AFSA) cases are difficult because jurors tend to look at the circumstances as crimes of opportunity or as mistakes in fact rather than as planned assaults or the result of predatory conduct. It is not uncommon for them to look at the case, and because of the combination of age, maturity, and alcohol for both defendant and victim, they may forgive the defendant or decide not to hold him accountable. The detectives during the investigation and the prosecutor during the trial need to focus on the activity and behavior of the defendant, and highlight that the defendant's actions were intentionally, deliberately, and specifically intended to take advantage of the incapacitated victim who was not able to give consent.

Good Guy Defense

This can be a double-edged sword for the defense if they are blaming the victim and putting on a "good guy" defense; basically, that the conduct alleged by the government and the victim is totally out-of-character for the defendant. We see this many times when the defense concentrates on the conduct of the victim, and tries to show that the defendant's alleged conduct during the incident conflicts with his otherwise law-abiding life. This can be a good tactic, particularly when the defendant appears to be a good-looking, well-mannered, and well-educated person who does not seem to match the same person as described by the victim. The double-edged sword is best explained in the adage, "Those who live by the good guy defense die by the good guy defense," and it only works when the offender is truly a *good guy*. However, opening up a good guy defense also allows the prosecution to bring in witnesses such as girlfriends and ex-wives to present evidence that they are not such good guys and very capable of committing the crime in question. Locating and interviewing other victims are also very important—even if they cannot be used as direct evidence in the case in point, it may be possible to have them as possible rebuttal witnesses if the defendant attempts to use the good guy defense. The mere fact they have been located and are available to call as witnesses may cause the defense to seek other strategies.

Consent Defense

For consent defenses, there is no question if sexual intercourse between defendant and victim took place, because it is generally admitted by the defendant. The real question is whether or not the victim gave knowing consent. As stated earlier, in cases involving alcohol- or drug-facilitated sexual assaults in which the victim was determined to be unconscious, there is no issue of consent as knowing consent cannot be given by an unconscious person. For other issues, a victim's statement that identifies the number of times they resisted the advances of the defendant is vital. Taking the time during the victim interview to document each time the victim offered resistance to the act— whether it was passive, verbal, or physical—is important. If a victim is consenting to the act, then why is there resistance? The consent defense is likely to be the most common defense to sexual assaults. This is why we need to start working on defining signals of nonconsent from the first victim interview all the way through to court.

Counterintuitive Behaviors

These actions of the victim will cause problems unless there are expert witnesses who can explain to the jury that such behavior—although seemingly odd or out of place due to the circumstances—is actually expected and normal with some victims. In fact, counterintuitive behavior can been seen as consistent behavior for someone who has experienced trauma such as a sexual assault. If the behavior is not explained, then this could lead to some problems, particularly if the statement was video recorded and the victim exhibits nervous laughter or giggles or some other behavior that can be misinterpreted.

▶Positives for Prosecutors

There are also several things that can work as positives for the prosecutor and should be emphasized by the detectives as they present their case for consideration.

Defendant Statements

Admissions and denials can be as damaging as a confession when effort is made to validate or refute them. Each denial statement that can be shown to be a lie and every admission statement that agrees with the victim in any way both count as examples of victim corroboration. It is for court presentation that we begin to understand the value of taking a denial or admission statement.

Other Criminal Acts

In many cases the offender was involved in a wide range of other criminal acts, including alcohol-related crimes, drug possession, burglary, kidnapping, or thefts. Juries tend to key in on other criminal acts that the defendant was engaged in prior to or after the sexual act. Forced entry into a residence and theft of personal property are examples of inconsistencies with consensual sex. This is why we want to try to locate any potential stolen property in the offender's possession.

Consistent Victim Statements

Those statements of the victim that we have confirmed or statements from other witnesses that match the victim's are examples of corroboration. Again, they can be invaluable in cases of "he said, she said" where there is no other physical, forensic, or testimonial evidence. This is particularly important when we find multiple persons who had contact with the victim over a period of time and testify that the victim statements were all very similar thus *consistent*.

Medical Examination

This is another form of corroboration. Even when the examination recovers no physical or forensic evidence, the SANE nurse is likely to have talked to the victim about what happened which can provide another example of a consistent statement—providing any statements match what the victim told others. If there are other associative injuries on the victim's body or clothing, then they are also powerful corroboration.

Witnesses

The number of witnesses available to testify is important, especially if they can corroborate the victim's statement or can invalidate any statement made by the defendant.

Expert Witnesses

Because of the *CSI* effect, expert witness testimony may be very well received and probably expected by the jury. Experts who can not only testify factually but are also able to educate the jury about certain aspects of forensic examination such as DNA, toxicology, or the physiological effects of alcohol or drugs on the victim can be very helpful.

▶ Sentencing

The sentencing phase of the trial comes after the defendant is convicted, and in many states this may include yet another hearing to present additional evidence or information to help decide the sentence. During the sentencing phase of a criminal case, the court determines the appropriate punishment for the convicted defendant. In determining a suitable sentence, the court will consider a number of factors, including the nature and severity of the crime, the defendant's criminal history, the defendant's personal circumstances, and the degree of remorse felt by the defendant.

▶ Appeal

An individual convicted of a crime may ask that his or her case be reviewed by a higher court. If that court finds an error in the case or the sentence imposed, the court may reverse the conviction or find that the case should be re-tried.

Appeals and Retrials: Disposal of Evidence

Even after an offender has been convicted, the police are not quite done with the investigation. Generally speaking, it is a police responsibility to safeguard evidence used in criminal trials. Even after the case, however, the evidence must still be maintained until the appeals process is completed. It is very possible for the entire process to be repeated again if the offender is successful in his appeals and an appellate court overturns the conviction and orders a retrial. At that time, the evidence will be needed again.

There is also a new school of thought regarding the keeping of evidence for unresolved cases, especially now that many states have removed the statute of limitations, making prosecution of rape cases possible regardless of the length of time between the incident and the trial. This means that more evidence is liable to be kept and stored until it is needed for court. Because of the constant development of new forensic techniques, the current school of thought is to maintain indefinitely all items of evidence until such time that the case can be solved and someone is tried and convicted or acquitted. This can cause some difficulties for the police, who now have to acquire and maintain long-term evidence storage.

▶ Conclusion

The whole purpose of a criminal investigation is to determine if a criminal offense was committed, who committed it or what happened, and then bring an offender to trial. This is not going to happen if the detective and the prosecutor act independently, so there is a need to work together from the initiation of the case through the end of the trial. This chapter outlines some issues that are likely to cause problems in bringing the case to court. Note that many of the advantages and disadvantages can be influenced or helped by the detective as he is working on the case. We must understand that even during the initial interview of the victim, we are looking for evidence that is going to be used in court, and we should be thinking toward this endgame during every interview and as every piece of evidence is collected.

▶ Further Reading

Cook, P. J., Slawson, D. B., & Gries, L. A., (1993). *The cost of prosecuting murder cases in North Carolina.* Durham, NC: Terry Sanford Institute of Public Policy, Duke University.

Gilbert, D. I., Gilfarb, M. E., & Talpins, S. K. (2005). *Basic trial techniques.* Alexandria, VA: American Prosecutors Research Institute.

Hazelwood, R. R. & Burgess, A. W. (2008). *Practical aspects of rape investigation: A multidisciplinary approach* (4th ed.). Boca Raton, FL: CRC Press.

Scalzo, T. P. (2007). *Prosecuting alcohol-facilitated sexual assault*, Alexandria, VA: National District Attorneys Association, American Prosecutors Research Institute.

CHAPTER FIFTEEN

Common Investigative Mistakes[1]

After reviewing many hundreds of investigations over the course of many years, it is not hard to identify some of the more common investigative mistakes or failures that are found in many different types of investigations. Most, if not all, of the investigative mistakes or failures can be overcome through discipline and reliance on some of the more traditional investigative methods that have been emphasized throughout this text, while avoiding some of the typical pitfalls of criminal investigation. Pitfalls refer to the more common mistakes, and in many cases just bad habits, that detectives routinely fall into. This chapter addresses several of the shortfalls and common mistakes that occur during all forms of criminal investigation, but are especially noticeable in sex crime investigations.

▶ Failing to Believe the Victim

This aspect of conducting sex crime investigation is perhaps the most often encountered. Unfortunately, as noted several times already, there is a natural tendency for many reasons for detectives to view each new report from the prism of past experiences and almost automatically start the investigation with the expectation that the victim is lying. In reviewing many cases, it seems that some detectives are subconsciously going out of their way to prove the complaint is false before they even begin to investigate. **Case Study 15-1** illustrates this point.

---

[1] This chapter is adapted from: Adcock, J. M., & Chancellor, A. S. (2013). *Death Investigations*. Burlington, MA: Jones & Bartlett Learning. Used by permission.

Case Study 15-1

A detective was convinced a victim was lying about being sexually assaulted by an offender who was a friend of a friend and had offered to give her a ride home from a nightclub. The victim statement was rather clear on the circumstances of the event, and she adamantly maintained the incident was nonconsensual and that she resisted the act but was overcome by the force of the offender. There was a time delay in the report, so there was no chance to collect any physical or forensic evidence from the victim or the vehicle. The offender made a denial statement that he had engaged in any sexual activity with the victim. Very little in the way of an investigation was completed because the detective had already determined in his own mind that the victim was lying. When questioned about his suspicions, the detective said that it was based on the victim's identification of the offender's vehicle as a Ford when it was really a Chevrolet, and that she had described the color of the car as black, although it was actually dark green. Based on her lack of an accurate description of the offender's vehicle, the detective concluded the report was made up and was about to discontinue the investigation. After the review, it was pointed out that the event took place late at night, and under certain lighting conditions a dark-colored vehicle may appear to be black if no effort was made to distinguish the color. Additionally, there was no clarifying question to the victim as to her certainty of the vehicle manufacturer or if she had a basis for knowing the vehicle type. Lastly, no other effort had been made to develop any other corroborating evidence to determine whether the victim was lying or not, and no effort was made to confirm any of the offender's denial statements.

In this case above, a suggested re-interview of the victim clarified that she had assumed the vehicle was black because it was a dark color and it was nighttime. She was also not positive that the vehicle was a Ford and had only said she thought it looked like one. The detective then began to look at the case again and started to interview other potential witnesses, eventually gathering enough evidence and information to arrest and prosecute the offender.

The detective in this case study had become so jaded toward sexual assault victims for various reasons that if any victims reported a sexual assault but presented without injury, serious trauma, or other similar evidence, he initially disbelieved them. As stated earlier in the text, such suspicion is not only unwarranted, but it can also be communicated through the detective's actions toward the victims, which then may directly affect their willingness to continue with the investigation. Remember that one of sex crime victims' main concerns and hesitations in reporting an incident in the first place is that they will not be believed. So, whenever a victim recants or decides not to continue with the investigation under these circumstances, it appears to be a self-fulfilling prophecy by the detective that the victim was lying or was about to make a false report. As stated earlier in this text, there are without a doubt a number of false reports that are made to the police; but, even if 90% are false, that means there are still 10% of the reports that are not false. Because there is no way to tell at the initial stage of the investigation that the report is going to be false, each complaint, regardless of the reported circumstances, should be actively pursued to determine the facts. **Case Study 15-2** is a good example of the concept of accepting the complaint and following through regardless of the circumstances.

Case Study 15-2

A 45-year-old male victim reported that when he was 18 and attending a boarding school, he was asked to accompany one of the older male staff members to the school cafeteria to help him pick something up. When they arrived there was no one else around, and the victim reported that the staff member told him to stand up and then knelt down, unzipped the victim's pants, and began to perform oral sex on him. The victim said he was in such shock he did not know what to do and was terrified because the staff member was older and of greater physical stature than he was. The victim said he did ejaculate and the staff member stopped and told him to "zip up" and then they left the area. The victim stated that there had been no other instances with the offender before or after the incident, and although he saw the staff member afterward there was never any further mention of this incident. The victim went on to say that he had never reported that incident out of fear and embarrassment, but that it had caused him great psychological problems over the years and contributed greatly to his marital problems, drug abuse, and inability to hold a job. He had finally come to terms with the situation and began to open up in counseling, and after urging from his counselor, finally told his wife and family about what had happened to him. The last step for him was to make a police report to confront the offender.

At first blush, it may seem somewhat incredulous that an assault as described in this case study could be possible, or that the victim would have remained silent all of these years and only now want to make a complaint. Based on the departmental protocol, the victim was interviewed in detail and the investigation continued. Shortly afterward, the offender was located and discovered to be employed in a teaching position at another school. The victim made pretext phone call to the offender that was recorded by the police. The victim then confronted the offender with the facts of the case and how much the assault had affected his entire life. To the surprise of the detectives, the offender apologized to the victim and said that he had been troubled by that incident the remainder of his life as well. The police later interviewed the offender, who made a complete confession to the act almost exactly as described by the victim. Although prosecution was not possible in this case based on the statute of limitations, the offender was forced to terminate his employment at the school.

The importance of this particular case is that strange things happen all the time, and we cannot simply discount the report of an alleged assault because it does not sound plausible to us at the time. When dealing with any sexual assault we need to rely on and operate by a very simple principle: *The victim is always telling the truth, unless we can prove otherwise.*

This means that we start out every single case with the idea that the victim is telling the truth, and we go through the same investigative process as outlined earlier in this text, regardless of the case facts as initially presented. When we follow the same procedures, it becomes clear relatively quickly whether the victim is telling the truth or is telling a lie. But such a determination should only be made after a thorough review of the facts, and never from our initial impression. This concept will also help develop empathy and sympathy toward victims. Even when cases turn out to be false, it is not a wasted effort because there is experience to be gained in those situations as well.

▶ Handling the Victim

As stated earlier in the text, the first contact with the victim and her interview are the first steps toward making a good witness in court and toward the victim's recovery; establishing trust with the victim also goes long way in helping the prosecution. However, handling the victim is not always about the interview and preliminary investigation; it is often about being able to help the prosecutor control the victim—in particular, to make sure she shows up for court hearings. In some cases, as demonstrated in **Case Study 15-3**, it sometimes takes a Herculean effort to try to keep victims on track and out of trouble.

Case Study 15-3

During the course of actively investigating a suspected serial murderer of at least half a dozen women, the case detective became aware of the suspect being involved in yet another incident where the victim had actually survived being kidnapped, raped, and physically assaulted. During her interview with the detective, the victim was able to identify the suspect almost immediately, and based on her complaint and other information already known about the offender, he was arrested and held without bail. Unfortunately for the police and prosecutor, the victim, like the offender's other victims, was a street prostitute and crack cocaine abuser with an extensive criminal history. Within just a few days of being assaulted and raped, the victim returned to the street and continued working as a prostitute. The detective was unsuccessful in trying to get her off the street, but continued to maintain contact with the victim over a number of weeks, finding her prior to each legal proceedings and managing to bring her to them. Several times during the lengthy process, the victim grew tired of the legal processes and of having to continually testify and be belittled by the defense attorney. There were many heated discussions concerning her request to simply drop the charges because of her frustration over the process and the time involved. Each time, the detective was able to talk to and calm the victim down, and managed to keep her on track with the prosecution. A month before trial, however, the victim disappeared in an effort to avoid going forward with the case. Again, the detective had to go find her in the weeks before trial, and then actually helped her sober up and get cleaned up, including using some money from the prosecutor's office to get her a haircut and buy a new set of clothes for court. The detective was essentially a babysitter during the subsequent trial for this most uncooperative victim. The detective was the only one who had any influence over the victim and who could calm her down and get her to cooperate with the process. The results of all of the detective's personal efforts were worth it, however, and led to the eventual conviction of the suspect and a lengthy prison sentence.

This case study only describes *some* of the difficulties experienced by the detective to control this victim and the extraordinary efforts to bring the offender to justice. Many detectives would not have been willing to take the time or put up with all of the extra trouble, but it is clear if the detective had not made the effort, this offender would have gone free and would certainly (based on his background) have continued to assault, rape, and murder other victims. With the offender now incarcerated for a substantial period of time, the detective was able to pursue the other homicide cases the offender is suspected of committing, without having additional new victims to worry about. This is an example of going the extra mile to get a conviction that many detectives are not willing to make, and thus they end up working more and more cases when the offender is not prosecuted or punished.

▶ Failure to Properly Interview the Offender

Not taking the time to properly interview offenders and lock them into their statements is a common problem, and from an investigative viewpoint it is fairly hard to understand. Unfortunately, there is a school of thought among many detectives that if the offender does not confess, then there is no need to obtain a written or recorded statement. When teaching this course at police academies, students often make such comments as, "So he said he didn't do it? What difference does it make to the case?" However, as discussed earlier in the text, the offender's version of events is critical to establishing what happened, and admissions and denials are sometimes just as important as confessions—especially when his denials can be proven to be lies. So, we want to lock offenders into their statement as early as possible, before they have a chance to construct a different alibi or come up with some other excuse or explanation for their conduct. This also prevents them from changing or adding to their statement at a later time. Some detectives make a conscious decision to delay taking detailed statements from offenders, using a tactic of allowing them to return at a later time and perhaps take a polygraph. The thought process is that the offenders, because they were not actually interrogated, will somehow be lured into thinking they are not really in trouble or the police are sympathetic toward them, and they therefore will voluntarily return for another interview and take a polygraph. Although this tactic may work on occasion, typically the offender does not return and does not make a later statement or take a polygraph. Perhaps the most famous example of this tactic backfiring occurred in the O. J. Simpson murder investigation. Simpson was brought in for questioning and interviewed for only about 20 minutes, without a lawyer present. If there is ever a time for an offender to make admissions or a confession, it is during this initial interview with the police. Unfortunately, the tactic to let him go and then return for an interview and polygraph did not go as anticipated and once he was released, Simpson immediately sought legal counsel and declined to take a polygraph or be interviewed further. Thus, he never adequately explained the cut on his finger or answered the hundreds of other questions police would have wanted to ask if given the chance again.

So, the best advice for offender interviews is to get their statement in writing or recorded, and therefore locked in, as soon as possible. If they will come back for a polygraph or for a re-interview that is great, but this makes it very difficult later on to divert greatly from the original statement. Failing to document their statements could lead to a "he said, he said" type situation, wherein the detective claims the offender said something or made an admission that becomes very important later on in the case, but the offender then says in court, "No, I didn't say that." The question then becomes: Where is the statement or recording, or other evidence to validate the alleged statement? It is also important to document in detail anything that could signify the suspect's consciousness of guilt, including refusing to cooperate, attempts to flee the area, changing his appearance, destroying evidence, or making incriminating statements to others.

▶ Failure to Take Detailed Statements from All Witnesses

In the same manner as with victims and offenders, we should also take written or recorded statements from all significant witnesses. Again, this is to get them locked into their statements and eliminate a chance of them changing their story later after being influenced or threatened by the offender or others. It is also just as important to document their statements when the incident is fresh in their minds, because often there is a substantial period of time between the incident and eventual court testimony. This will allow witnesses to review their initial statements to refresh their memory for court. At the same time, those witnesses who initially report they have no information to provide during the initial stages of the investigation are going to have a difficult time coming into court with some type of exonerating evidence later on. Taking statements from witnesses that they do not know anything or did not see anything may preclude them coming forward at a later time to provide an alibi or evidence for the defense.

▶ Failure to Seek Out Corroborating Evidence

As repeatedly emphasized throughout this text, obtaining corroborating evidence is essential for a successful prosecution, and juries are going to want to see it in some fashion. Luckily, corroboration can take on many forms including witness testimony, physical evidence (e.g., torn clothing), forensic evidence, prompt complaint, the victim's statement, the offender's statement, and even through the victimology assessment. These are only a few of the many examples provided in the text, and there are certainly many others. The problem comes from detectives who are gathering the information and even correctly documenting it, but who do not understand how to properly identify examples of corroboration. Even worse are detectives who go through the investigations with a checklist mentality but do not go out of their way to complete any additional investigative leads that may help to provide even more corroboration. This is how we end up with "he said, she said" situations and no prosecution.

▶ Failure to Work with or Develop Working Relationships with Victim Advocates or SANE Practitioners

As stated earlier, the victim's advocate and SANE practitioners are the best friends detectives working sex crime cases can have, but unfortunately there is often little to no effort to develop these relationships. Whereas detectives are willing and able to interact with them during the conduct of their cases, many generally do not sit down and have a cup of coffee in between cases to work out any problem areas or exchange suggestions on how to work better together. It is assumed that each will do his or her own job, and we miss out on the aspect of a multidisciplinary team that is supposed to be working together. This failure is not always seen in any particular case, but rather can be seen throughout many of their cases as they are worked over time.

▶Developing Tunnel Vision

Tunnel vision is perhaps one of the most prevalent common errors we find in unresolved cases, regardless of the crime. It is essentially a dogged insistence to focus on one aspect of the case or one suspect regardless of whether the evidence points in another direction or to other persons. Tunnel vision can best be understood through the old adage: "Don't confuse me with the facts," wherein detectives are determined to have the outcome they want regardless of the evidence that is presented to them. Another term that is used to describe this concept is known as *cafeteria investigation,* wherein the detective accepts as truthful and viable any evidence or facts fitting into his particular theory of the crime or implicates his particular suspect, but discounts or completely ignores anything that disagrees with his theory. **Case Studies 15-4, 15-5, and 15-6** are good examples of tunnel vision and the problems it can create.

Case Study 15-4

The police were investigating the disappearance of a female teenager who failed to come home from work one evening. Three weeks later, her body was found two counties away. Almost immediately there were detectives who were absolutely certain the crime had been committed by a well-known serial offender who was known to operate in the surrounding counties. Unfortunately, no real suspect was ever identified and the case was relegated to the filing cabinet. Upon reviewing the case and other cases involving the serial offender, along with the investigative reports documenting efforts to link him to the death of the teenager, it was clear that the serial offender was not involved in the disappearance or murder of this particular victim. The serial offender had a very well-established modus operandi (MO) of picking women up at nightclubs, concerts, or other public places; his choice of victims were older; and although he had raped several women, he had never resorted to using physical force. He overcame resistance by simply not stopping his attempt until his victims finally quit resisting. But, most important, the offender had a very good and verified alibi that he was elsewhere at the time of the victim's disappearance, and therefore was not in the area at the time of the offense. However, this did not change the minds of several of the detectives, who still insisted that the offender was involved. Later, when other sex crimes were reported and reviewed, this same offender's name was repeatedly brought up by the same detectives as a potential suspect.

Case Study 15-4 describes a common occurrence in many cases: A possible well-known suspect is identified and every effort is expended to tie him to the crime. It is quite normal and acceptable to consider those known suspects as being potentially involved in other cases. But, when the evidence cannot firmly link the suspect to the crime and or may exonerate him from involvement, continuing to try to link him to the case is the same as developing tunnel vision. It takes great determination to continue through a difficult case with all of the twists, turns, and red herrings that are a part of every investigation. But we should be forming our theory of the crime based on the available evidence, not forming a theory and then seeking out the evidence that supports the theory. Theories and suspects are good to have, but they are always subject to change or refinement as new evidence is collected and evaluated. If we can establish our most viable suspect was not involved with the crime or has an undisputed and verifiable alibi, then we have to eliminate him and move on to look for other suspects. As noted in **Case Study 15-5**, if the facts do not fit we may not have the right suspect.

Case Study 15-5

A review of a cold case showed that the police had initiated an investigation into the rape and murder of an elderly white female from a small rural town. In the course of the investigation, the police had turned to the Federal Bureau of Investigation (FBI) for assistance in "profiling" the offender. The FBI analysis suggested the offender would be local, known to the victim, and most likely a black male with lower education or perhaps mentally handicapped. The investigation shifted and began to focus on likely suspects from the local small town when another suspect, an out-of-state drifter who rode the rails, was identified in a neighboring community. For several reasons, including the fact that the railroad tracks of the small town were just a short distance away from the victim's residence, the focus of the investigation abruptly turned completely toward this new suspect. However, after pursuing this particular suspect for a number of months without success and with the resulting laboratory forensic analysis being inconclusive, the investigation died down and eventually went cold. The department was certain the drifter was their man, but they simply did not have the evidence to prove it. After reviewing the facts and evidence, the reviewer concluded the FBI offender profile would yield a much more likely suspect than the drifter the department had identified, who some 20 years later they were still convinced was involved in the rape and murder. Part of the evidence in the original case was the post mortem rape kit obtained from the victim during her autopsy and a dried blood sample from the drifter. Both were resubmitted to the crime lab for DNA analysis, which was unavailable at the time of the incident. After 20 years a male profile was recovered from the victim's rape kit, but it did not match the drifter suspect.

Again, the police were shocked at the results of the DNA analysis. The investigators' tunnel vision doomed the case to fail almost from the very beginning, because once the drifter was located and identified as a possible suspect, no other effort was expended to locate any other suspects, witnesses, or evidence. The key to these situations is simple: If the suspect cannot be linked to the crime scene or victim regardless of the effort, perhaps we have gotten the wrong suspect and need to step back and reassess the situation and evidence.

Case Study 15-6

During training at a state police academy, the discussion centered on the importance of sending evidence to the lab. A discussion followed with a local detective announcing he had evidence in a sexual assault that he *could* send to the lab, but did not want to because he was concerned with the result. He was convinced he had the correct suspect and therefore did not want the evidence to be examined at the lab and uncover a different result. "If they [the lab] tell me he's not the guy, then I'm out of luck so I'm not taking a chance to send it in."

Case Study 15-6 is the worst scenario of all of these case studies and presents not just an example of tunnel vision, but also of a very serious ethical problem wherein the detective had obviously settled on a good suspect but was not willing to put his theory to the test by sending the evidence to the lab for confirmation. Could this not result in a wrongful conviction? We have also given the defense attorney a great club to use against us in court if there is evidence that could potentially exonerate his client that the police refused to submit. How will this situation play out in court?

▶ Conducting an Incomplete Investigation

One of the major failures in sexual assault investigations is conducting an incomplete investigation. This is seen many times when detectives believe a sexual assault investigation is limited to a victim interview, a suspect interview, the crime scene, and forensic examination. If witnesses are identified by the victim or suspect then they are interviewed, but otherwise these detectives feel they are done. It is unclear how this approach can be successful in any criminal investigation, but it is certainly not possible in sexual assault investigations. For instance, a background investigation on an offender is a good suggestion in every criminal case, but as stated earlier in the text, this is absolutely critical in sexual assaults, especially when we find other similar criminal acts in an offender's past. This is especially useful for acquaintance/date rape type investigations when we discover that the offender has been investigated in the past for a sexual assault, perhaps committed in a dating situation. It becomes potentially valuable evidence if we discover the offender used a similar approach or made a similar claim in the previous incident that he is making in the current investigation. We are looking for any pattern of similar misconduct and any other potential victims. Even if we cannot use the previous incident as direct evidence in court, we may be able to use it when we discuss the case with the prosecutor to show the same pattern of behavior and the reason why the new case should be prosecuted. It stands to reason that if an offender is put through the wringer in one investigation when the victim was misunderstood or he did not pick up on her "no" or her nonconsent signals, it is unlikely he will repeat the mistake and go through the investigative process again.

The main purpose of the background investigation is to locate other potential victims and crimes that the offender may have committed in the past. This is another aspect of tunnel vision, wherein the detective tries to remain totally and singularly focused on the current investigation and has no intention to widen the scope of the inquiry. As stated earlier, the more victims you have, the more evidence you have, especially in cases that amount to "he said, she said" because there are no other witnesses to the event and no forensic evidence is available to establish the facts. A "he said, she said" type incident works to the offender's advantage when there is one incident; but, it starts to weaken when we can show multiple victims who provide similar stories. The case then becomes, "he said, *they* said." But, so many times in training classes detectives report that looking for other victims creates additional work, so they try to stay focused on the one crime.

Likewise, it is imperative that we take some time to locate and interview offenders' (ex-)wives and girlfriends, even if we cannot do so prior to a suspect interview. Like other witnesses, you never know what they may be able to provide in the way of evidence for your case until you ask them.

▶Failure to Maintain Documentation

Perhaps one of the biggest critiques of modern detectives is the lack of proper documentation and written reports detailing the results of their investigative efforts. Many times this comes from the general nature of police officers who love to investigate and do all the action-orientated things associated with being a detective, but seem to avoid putting anything down on paper. This isn't because they don't know how to write or prepare a report, but because it is time consuming and takes away from the "fun" of investigations, of picking up evidence, conducting interrogations, or identifying witnesses. One of prosecutors' biggest complaints is that investigations are not fully documented. The reluctance to make a written report or to properly document investigative activity can have severe ramifications in the life of the investigation, as noted in **Case Study 15-7.**

Case Study 15-7

While reviewing a serial homicide cold case, the detectives were briefed on at least one very good suspect who was associated with at least five of the six known victims. It was especially interesting to learn he had lived next door to the first victim. He was seen in the morning hours at a small park a short distance from the residence of the second victim the morning the victim was found murdered. He had allegedly spent the night in his car about a block away from the residence of the third victim the night before she was found dead in her apartment. He often slept in the woods close by and was observed many times walking by the residence and crime scene location of the fourth victim. He may have had a personal dispute with the fifth victim over the collection and sale of aluminum cans at a local recycling center. During the lengthy briefing prior to reviewing the case documents and scene photographs, the case detectives continued to provide a seemingly never-ending stream of facts and circumstantial evidence they had uncovered. The sum of all of this information clearly painted this particular suspect as the leading person of interest.

However, when the case documents were later reviewed, there were no actual police reports within the file documenting any of the previous information supplied by the detectives during their briefing. The detectives were asked about the missing reports and the source of the information they had provided. Sadly, the detectives explained they had intentionally not prepared any written reports because the suspect was related to someone within the department and they were concerned such information would be compromised. Following this revelation, the detectives were advised to begin to document all of their information, even at that late date. Unfortunately, after an hour or so of discussion, the detectives could not agree concerning the source(s) of information for placement of the suspect at any of these locations. After several hours of honest effort, it was still not clear who exactly had provided the information, and what sounded like such a good suspect with very good circumstantial evidence linking him to five out of six homicides was essentially lost because it was not properly documented. Because it was not documented, it is unclear how many times the telling and retelling of information may have resulted in the inflation of facts, evidence, or event time sequencing.

There is an old adage used to explain the importance of documentation that says: *If it's important enough to do, then it's important enough to write a report about it. If it's not important enough to write a report about it, then why did you do it?* The wisdom of this saying is illustrated in **Case Study 15-8**.

Case Study 15-8

During the initial review of an unsolved case, a new detective was brought in to give the investigation some new life. After the initial review of the case file, the new detective identified more than 100 additional or new investigative leads that needed to be accomplished, including the interview of one particular person of interest. During the initial briefing when this person's name was mentioned as an important interview, one of the original investigating police officers stated the interview was not necessary because he had interviewed the witness already. Since there was no written report reflecting that interview in the file, the new detective asked, "What did he say?" The police officer answered, "Hell, I don't remember, but it must not have been important if I didn't make a report." The person of interest was later interviewed and was eventually determined to be the perpetrator of the double homicide.

There is another old investigative adage that applies to the same concept found in this case study: *If it isn't written down, then it didn't happen.* The point is, we cannot rely on our memory, and many times it becomes just as important to document what we were unsuccessful with as it is to document finding a particularly useful piece of evidence. This is especially true when dealing with interviews and testimonial evidence. The best example is conducting an interview with a witness such as a neighbor or close friend without documenting it, and later finding his name on the defense list for court and discovering he made a statement that is favorable to the defense. These situations are avoided by making sure we have conducted those interviews and thoroughly documented the results. Police work, particularly detective work, is all about documentation and report writing. It is part of the job and those unwilling to make their reports are in the wrong profession.

For sex-related crimes, identification of the offender is a key point; when made through forensic evidence, it is not as difficult to document because there are generally some type of laboratory reports that have made a scientific comparison. However, in incidents in which the offender is identified with a photo or physical lineup, it becomes extremely important to properly document what efforts were made to construct and hold the lineup and its results. For example, if a photo lineup is used, it is necessary to make copies of the lineup, including in what order the various photos were aligned. This is to demonstrate that the lineup was not suggestive or otherwise improper. The same is true when a physical lineup was used; it should also be photographed to show the various participants of the lineup.

One last documentation fallacy is the failure to collect all investigative reports from all participants in the investigation. This is particularly important when multiple agencies may be involved in the same investigation. It is incumbent upon the assigned detective to make sure he has all of those reports. **Case Study 15-9** demonstrates this important area of documentation.

Case Study 15-9

A cold case was reviewed that had been worked initially by the county sheriff, and after a few weeks the state police joined in the investigation. Upon reviewing the file from the county sheriff, it was noted very quickly that only the sheriff's reports were included in the case file, and although the state police had obviously done some work on the case, the two agencies had never exchanged reports with each other. Each followed similar paths and each collected a portion of evidence on persons(s) of interest, but neither agency was sharing with the other. Eventually, the state police case file was located and reviewed. When viewed separately, both files came up with persons of interest or potential suspects, but neither file was able to identify one particular suspect. However, once the files were combined, one suspect was clearly identified almost to the exclusion of anyone else and the remaining effort focused on this suspect.

Any omissions or mistakes within the case file only serve to give defense attorneys fodder for cross-examination, and many times detectives will face questions not about their actual investigation, but rather about what they *did not do*. It is very difficult to criticize the investigation when it was conducted in accordance with established agency protocol and such efforts were clearly documented. Such by-the-book efforts are also greatly approved by juries who want to believe the detective acted in a legal, technical, and professional manner.

▶ Failure to Follow Logical Leads

Many times clear and logical leads for some reason are never pursued. There are always innumerable reasons or excuses for not completing identified leads, but generally the real reason they were never completed is not because the lead was not recognized, but rather that the detective just did not want to follow the lead or did not think it would be beneficial. The traditional thought process has always been that it is always better to run the lead and discover it was not beneficial than to ignore it and find out later that the defense completed the lead themselves and discovered other evidence. Now not only did the defense discover potential evidence and catch you off guard, but it can be argued the investigation must be deficient; the defense might then try to make you seem incompetent, biased, untrained, or unprofessional. Experience has shown it is almost always easier to do the lead and document the results than to try to find a reason or excuse not to run it.

An investigative lead is basically some question, fact, or statement that has come up in the case and needs to be answered, clarified, or verified. If there is an unanswered question or an unverified fact, then it needs to be addressed. Every lead that is run—every fact that is verified, or clarified, or determined not to be true—advances the case. Every suspect who is eliminated advances the case, because at least we know what did or did not happen based on the lead or who was not involved through the elimination of the suspect.

A defense investigator or attorney is not necessarily concerned with what the police did do, but rather, what the police did not do or what the police missed. Therefore, when leads were not pursued or completed, this would likely be the initial thrust and would be aggressively pursued to see if there was something they had missed. The teaching point is clear: What detectives fail to do or fail to document provides a starting point for the defense to start poking holes in the investigation. This is true for sex crimes as well as other investigations.

▶ Failure to Validate Alibis or Statements

One of the more important steps is to validate information found within the various statements or testimonies obtained in the course of the investigation. When dealing with any statement made by any person, including a victim, witness, or the offender: *Believe nothing; verify everything.* That is, we do not ever accept at face value any information we receive, and we always want to go back and validate that information from at least two sources—particularly if the information is used to establish circumstantial type evidence, because circumstantial evidence is basically an assumption based on other facts. In other words, if we can establish that separate facts of A, B, D, and E took place, then we can assume circumstantially that fact C also took place, although we may not have any direct evidence that it is true. However, circumstantial evidence is only good when the series of actions can be linked together; if the link between these actions is ever broken, then the circumstantial evidence probably cannot be established. Therefore, when we seek to confirm our facts, we always seek at least two sources to verify the information, so if one source is invalidated, there is still a second source available to establish that link. This is particularly important for statements that may seem outlandish, confusing, or doubtful. **Case Study 15-10** demonstrates such an example.

Case Study 15-10

A young female soldier claimed she was assaulted in her bed by a fellow soldier. During the assault, she was viciously cut on the side of her neck and along her forearm. The victim was eventually able to identify the offender and the weapon used as a double-edged razor blade that the offender held between his thumb and index finger. However, during the initial crime scene examination it was noted the open-bay type barracks was absolutely pitch black during the night. The victim insisted, however, that she woke up and saw the offender kneeling beside her bed, and that he had shown her the razor blade before she was attacked. The investigating detectives returned to the victim's area of the barracks during the same time of night as the assault and lay on a bunk where her bed had been. They immediately noted that a light from the parking lot next door shone through the window above the bed with such brightness you could actually read a normal print book. It would therefore be no problem at all to identify someone kneeling by the bed, or to see a razor blade held in front of your face as the victim had described. This finding took everyone involved with the investigation by surprise and immediately changed their impressions of the crime.

This reconstruction or validation of the victim's statement in Case Study 15-10 played a pivotal role in the offender's later conviction, because the offender's identification was based solely on the victim's recognition of the offender, as no forensic or physical evidence was ever recovered from the crime scene. The detective testified as to his confirmation of the victim's statement that it was possible to both identify a person and see a razor blade via the light coming through the window, exactly as the victim had described.

For alibis, we suggest at least three independent sources be used to establish an alibi, especially if the alibi is used to eliminate a suspect from involvement in a case. Three sources are needed because whenever a suspect or person of interest is eliminated from involvement in the case, he is no longer going to be investigated. This is a very big step in the investigative process and should not be taken lightly or without good, verifiable reasons. Anyone who cannot be eliminated based on at least three independent sources should remain at least as a person of interest or as someone who has not yet been eliminated. When dealing with a suspect alibi, we consider a family member as only half of a source: If a family member says the suspect was at a certain place at a certain time, he or she is considered as only half of a source, so a full two and a half more sources would be needed to fully eliminate the suspect. This is because family members will routinely and unabashedly lie to police in an effort to help their family members. While reviewing cold cases, we have discovered many times that the main suspect was eliminated very early on in the initial investigations often based on a weak or unsubstantiated alibi that was never checked out or confirmed. Sometimes these alibis consisted of literally no more than a few weak and unqualified statements. For example:

Detective: Where were you when the crime was committed?
Suspect: I was at Johnny's.
Detective: OK.

Following this exchange the detective might make the mistake of moving on to other questions, apparently satisfied the offender has an alibi for his whereabouts at the time of the crime. On more than one occasion, the brief questions and answers as demonstrated above were actually the only mention of the main suspect's whereabouts in the entire case file. Even worse, based on these simple and unverified statements, some were actually eliminated as suspects, without ever framing the alibi with the parameters of the time of the crime or even more important, to establish, "Who is Johnny?" In numerous cold case reinvestigations, the so-called alibi has easily been discounted so that the suspect could eventually be identified as the perpetrator. These cases typically languish and go nowhere when the detectives are out chasing the wrong person(s) because they have erroneously eliminated suspects based on unverified information.

▶"He Said, She Said" Situations

Regardless of the circumstances surrounding the criminal act, any time we as detectives allow the investigation to degenerate into a "he said, she said" situation with no other corroborating evidence, we have really accomplished nothing. As covered earlier in the text: *in he said, she said cases, a tie will always go to the offender.* It is going to be very difficult to convince the prosecutor to go forward with a case when the only evidence we have is the word of the victim that something happened to her. It is even harder to get a conviction if this is the only evidence available. So, the end result is almost always going to be no prosecution and no punishment to the offender. This, of course, leaves him free to reoffend again and again.

▶Investigation Stopped Too Early and Failure to Coordinate with Prosecutors

These two common errors often go hand-in-hand with each other. Whereas the police are responsible for investigating the case, it is ultimately the prosecutor who is going to have to present the case to a jury. Therefore, it is imperative the two agencies work closely together. As stated earlier in the text, it is often better when the prosecutor is brought into the case early on to get him involved and interested in the case. This helps to develop an *ownership* of and a personal interest in the case. Even when the prosecutors become involved later on, the police must realize the case or investigation is not over until the offender has been convicted. There are many occasions when detectives can expect to be actively pursuing leads and interviewing additional witnesses who have surfaced during the course of the trial. Unfortunately, there is sometimes a serious disconnect between the police and the prosecutor over duties and responsibilities. **Case Study 15-11** demonstrates these problems.

Case Study 15-11

A young wife and mother of two was found nude and murdered in the master bedroom of her mobile home; she had been raped and then stabbed repeatedly and then the mobile home was intentionally set afire. A good suspect was quickly identified; he was as a friend of the victim's husband and was staying at the mobile home temporarily until he could find an apartment of his own. The suspect was the last to see her alive, and the fire was determined to have started shortly after he left the residence for work. After a denial interview, he was offered and failed a polygraph examination. He then invoked his rights and never made any other admissions or confession to the rape or murder. Based on the limited available information, the suspect was arrested and jailed for first degree murder and held at the county jail with no bond. The suspect's attorney declined a preliminary hearing and the case went forward to the grand jury where he was promptly indicted. The prosecutor reviewed the file some months later as the case was coming to trial and realized there had been no other investigative activity on the case since the suspect's arrest, now more than 10 months ago. The prosecutor had assumed additional investigative work was being accomplished, but the detective believed he had completed his responsibility by gaining enough evidence for an arrest and indictment and had moved onto other cases. Although there was enough evidence to get probable cause for an arrest and an indictment, there was nowhere near enough information or evidence to proceed to trial. Unfortunately, the evidence was so slim and so much time had passed it was impossible for the case to proceed without a lot of additional work. Based on speedy trial issues, the district attorney was forced to drop the charges and allow the suspect out of jail. Once released, the suspect then left the jurisdiction. The police took great offense at the suspect being released; although they were asked to reinvestigate, their efforts were so unenthusiastically and lackadaisically accomplished that the case was eventually closed as unresolved. It remains unsolved to this day.

Such cases are especially frustrating because it is very likely the police had identified the right suspect. Unfortunately in this case, because of pride or ego, and clearly misunderstanding their duties and responsibilities, the police failed to continue with the investigation and gather the evidence needed for a successful prosecution. Sadly, like so many other cases, there will be no justice for this victim, her husband, or her two children.

Case Study 15-12 provides another example of what can go wrong when police and the prosecutor do not work closely together.

Case Study 15-12

While working on a complicated homicide, the county sheriff's department had very little success until they identified a suspect who made admissions to being an accessory to murder after the fact and identified several of the victim's own family members as being involved in the actual murder. The sheriff met with the county district attorney to discuss the new evidence. However, the DA wanted the sheriff to gather further evidence to substantiate the suspect's information before arresting of any of the family members. The sheriff disagreed and instead obtained arrest warrants for the family members in question. He also made media releases to announce the arrests and the resolution of the case. This led to a great disagreement between the sheriff and the DA, which was played out in the local media for months following the arrests. The sherriff believed they had sufficient evidence based on the suspect's statement and essentially stopped investigating the case. As might be expected, once the suspect obtained legal counsel he immediately recanted his statement. The DA subsequently refused to even present the case to the local grand jury and eventually the charges against the family members were dropped. The prosecutor perceived the sheriff's actions as a direct challenge to his authority and steadfastly refused to prosecute.

In both of the previous two case studies, the police were probably correct in their suspect identifications; but in both cases they disagreed with the prosecutor's opinion that there was not enough information or evidence at the time of arrest to successfully prosecute them. Sadly, in both of these cases, the department compounded the problem by not aggressively continuing the investigation once an arrest was made. Again, there was no justice for the victims or their families. Even worse, at least two murderers were released back to society, perhaps to offend again. In both cases the police learned the reality of the criminal justice system: that is, the police may make an arrest, but it is the prosecutor who takes the case to court.

It is imperative that prosecutors and police work hand-in-hand with each other. It is not enough to for the police to be satisfied with their effort; it is up to the prosecutor to be satisfied with the information and evidence that is available. No prosecutor is going to take a case to court if there is not a good chance of winning. It is not a matter of making an arrest; it is a matter of convincing 12 jury members of the guilt of the offender.

▶Overdependence on Polygraph or Other "Truth" Devices

The polygraph and other truth detection devices such as voice stress analyzers can be useful investigative tools, but they are not the end all; they are only tools. Their importance comes from their invaluable use as interrogation tools and not necessarily for determining involvement in a crime or guilt or innocence. The polygraph is merely an instrument designed to measure various involuntary responses from the body, including blood pressure, breathing, and the galvanic skin response. Theoretically, the polygraph measures the increases and decreases of responses from the body when being put under stress and providing answers to certain questions relating to the offense under investigation. Since most of us have to think about lying or deceiving and we know when we are lying, this causes an increase and decrease in certain bodily responses, which in turn are recorded on the graph paper by the three ink pens.

But the polygraph is only a machine, and therefore it is only as good as the individual operator and the operator's personal training and experience. Unfortunately, not all polygraph training is the same. There is a big difference between a polygraph examiner who completed a 2-week "basic" course and an examiner who has attended a lengthy and formal multi-month course. For instance, there is no such thing as passing a few questions and failing a few questions. The polygraph is an all-or-nothing type of report, in which the examinee either passes or fails. The proper results for a polygraph are either deception indicated (DI)—the examinee failed the test, no deception indicated (NDI)—the examinee passed the test, or inconclusive—no opinion can be made and more testing is needed. This is important because when the questions are formed, they are made to cover all aspects of the incident ranging from any direct knowledge of the crime, any direct participation in the crime, or conspiring with someone to commit the crime. It is difficult to say what part of those questions is going to cause difficulties for the examinee, so even if the examinee fails on only one question it should be interpreted that they failed the entire test.

Since the polygraph is only intended to be an interrogation tool, it might be used in the expected interrogation following the examination, but it has limited value in the remainder of the investigation except to provide confidence the police are on the right track or have the right suspect. The results of a polygraph or any other truth verification instrument should never be solely used as probable cause to make an arrest or to charge a person, nor should they be solely used to eliminate someone from being involved in a crime. In our experience we have seen on more than one occasion the guilty pass an examination and the innocent fail—not very often, but they both happen. However, it can be used as *one* factor among other evidence, but should never be considered on its own. For example, if we have a suspect for whom we can only find one source to validate an alibi, perhaps we can use the polygraph as a means to fully eliminate the suspect or move him lower down the priority line of potential suspects.

It is somewhat surprising how many times the results of the polygraph are ignored. For instance, during a typical "he said, she said" type of investigation, with very little corroborating evidence, the lead detective was leaning toward believing the offender's denial statement that the incident did not really happen. As a way to resolve the situation, the offender was offered a chance to take a polygraph examination to validate his statement. The offender came in, was administered the test by a competent and experienced examiner, and failed. During a subsequent interrogation, he made some minor admissions before he stopped the interrogation and asked for an attorney. The lead detective, however, decided to ignore the polygraph results and thought the offender was still telling the truth, so the case was not presented to a prosecutor. The question becomes: Why was the offender offered the examination in the first place, and why might the detective have accepted the no deception indicated results if he was not going to accept deception indicated results? This is also another example of tunnel vision and the detective using cafeteria evidence to come up with the results he wanted.

▶ Overdependence on Forensic Evidence

If modern detectives have an Achilles heel or weak point, it is in the overreliance and dependence on forensic evidence. This is not to say forensic evidence is not needed or valuable, because it is extremely important. But, what we have found when reviewing cases is that when a detective is confronted with a reported crime in which witnesses are present or physical evidence is recovered, and where forensic examinations are possible, the chance of resolving the case is almost a certainty. Even more important, the detectives know exactly what to do, what remaining leads are necessary, what additional evidence is needed, and how to present the case to the prosecutor.

In contrast, when presented with a situation with no witnesses or a limited amount of physical and forensic evidence, many detectives are lost. It is clear the modern detective has become "spoiled" by and overly dependent on the forensic examinations of evidence. We see evidence of this overreliance on forensic examination as we look through the many cold cases from throughout the country. Typically, this is demonstrated in one of two ways. First, an aggressive initial surge of effort occurs when a case is initiated, including a good effort at the crime scene and initial interviews, but very quickly the activity dies down when eyewitnesses or forensic evidence are not turned up during the initial hours of the investigation. The second typical finding is a near shut down of investigative activity for months at a time, because the detectives are "waiting on the crime lab" before they go any further. Whereas on the surface, this may seem like a good tactic and we certainly believe in the importance of submitting evidence for examination, with the backlog of work in most crime labs, it could easily take between a month and a year or more before the forensic examination is ever completed. Even worse, as the case is stalled because it is "pending lab results," life goes on.

Witnesses may move away, they might die or get into an accident and be unable to testify, their memories may fade, they may change their mind, or they might even marry the suspect and no longer want to cooperate with the police. The same kinds of things might happen with your suspects or a myriad of other factors and evidence.

An even worse consequence of waiting on lab results is that the interest in the case that was so strong during the initial stages—after a year or more in which other cases to work on come up—wanes and it it is difficult to dust off this old investigation and get back to work. It is also possible the forensic examinations will come back with findings that are not helpful to the investigation anyway. Now, the ultimate nightmare is that the case is basically cold and there is nothing else to fall back on. The detective will then have to try to restart the investigation and seek out other forms of evidence a year or so later. Needless to say, the case is now even more difficult. Therefore, reading a file that says the detective was or is waiting on lab results before continuing with the investigation is the equivalent of hearing someone scratching their nails across a chalkboard. As emphasized throughout the text, the vast majority of cases are not solved by fantastic new forensic techniques and technologies, but through the hard work of using traditional methods and techniques. Forensic examination of evidence is without question an imperative and should be sent to the supporting crime lab as soon as possible. But, while the evidence is at the lab, the investigation should continue with the expectation the lab examinations are going to come back negative or without any useful information. So the case continues to progress rather than "pending" and growing old.

There are exceptions to this general rule. For instance, if a good suspect has been identified and needs to be interviewed, but the lab has promised a result within a short period of time, a slight delay is not that harmful and a positive lab result will clearly help out in the interrogation of a suspect. But, if the delay will be in months, we would recommend the interview proceed without the examination results. If the suspect makes admissions or denials during the interview, but the laboratory is able to confirm or refute the suspect's statement, what is the real difference? If he denies and is found to be lying, it might prove to be just as strong evidence as if he confessed in the first place.

The importance of understanding and using the traditional methods of "walking and talking," following investigating leads, developing motives, and verifying statements and alibis can be demonstrated by some statistical findings from a homicide study of some 798 homicides conducted by Wellford and Cronin[2] that noted that physical evidence of some form was discovered in only 72% of the cases and a witness was found in only 80% of the cases.

---

[2] Wellford, C., & Cronin, J. (1999). *An analysis of variables affecting the clearance of homicide: A multistate study.* Washington, DC: National Institute of Justice Programs.

Additional studies documented by Baskin and Sommers[3] tracked the outcomes of some 400 homicide cases through the justice system and noted that although physical evidence had been recovered in 97% of the studied cases, there was an arrest in only about 55% of them. Clearly, physical and forensic evidence are important, but they are not the end all to any investigation.

Based on these two studies, detectives can expect there will be a number of instances when they must investigate a crime where there is little if any physical evidence or any witnesses that can point them in the right direction. Additionally, the evidence they do recover might not necessarily point to a particular person. Therefore, it is incumbent upon detectives to develop these other skills to locate additional evidence needed to resolve the case. Along the same lines of overdependence on forensic evidence, a second aspect of forensic examination presents as just as important a problem: the misunderstanding of forensic results from the crime lab. We have found that over and over again, the police have correctly identified, collected, and forwarded the items of physical evidence to the laboratory for examination. But, once the report of examination is received, detectives often place it into the file as if they are checking off a box in a checklist, but they never take the time to understand the report itself or what exactly the examination revealed. **Case Study 15-13** demonstrates the problems that occur when the detectives do not completely understand the forensic analysis or various lab reports.

Case Study 15-13

The case detectives of a cold case reported they had sent in evidence to the lab for DNA analysis some 18 months before but the lab was unable to find any DNA. When we reviewed the file we noted the crime scene report, photographs, and the evidence collected, and we were also shocked at the negative findings. We looked at the crime lab reports in greater detail, particularly the submission and request and the resulting DNA analysis. We noted there were actually several lab reports dealing with DNA analysis. The first was a lab report that acknowledged request for DNA analysis in one paragraph and in the next paragraph advised the agency they had conducted a preliminary screening of the evidence and noted the presence of blood. The third paragraph, however, advised the agency if they still wanted the DNA analysis to be completed they needed to reconfirm the request with the crime lab. The second lab report simply stated since the agency had not reconfirmed their DNA request, and the evidence was being returned to the agency. The case detective misinterpreted the two reports as a negative finding. However, in reality the evidence was never actually processed for DNA as requested.

---

[3] Baskin, D., & Sommers, I. (2010). The Influence of forensic evidence on case outcomes of homicide incidents. *Journal of Criminal Justice, 38*, 1141–1149.

Because of the expense of completing the DNA analysis, the crime lab had established a protocol requiring the agency to reconfirm the necessity of the analysis after the initial screening, but before it was conducted. Essentially, the crime lab was requiring the same request to be made twice. In this particular case, when the agency did not respond within a certain time period, the evidence was repackaged and sent back to the agency. The detective, not having totally understood the laboratory report, was under the impression no offender DNA was identified from the evidence submitted. Unfortunately, as stated earlier, the detectives were also so convinced the forensic evidence was going to identify their offender, they had paused the investigation pending the results of the crime lab examination. Now, some 18 months later they were discovering it had never actually been examined.

In another example, the detectives believed the latent prints from the crime scene were unidentifiable or did not match their suspect. In reality, the lab report indicated the recovered latent print was a palm print, but the detectives only submitted known fingerprint cards and not major case prints which would include the palms of the suspect's hands. Yet another example dealt with examining documents to compare handwriting, but the lab report indicated they did not have enough known writing of the suspect and the exemplars were improperly taken so therefore they could not complete their examination. The detective interpreted this as a null match, but again the problem was simply that the detective did not take the time to completely read and understand the report.

The only way to stop this problem is to encourage detectives to pick up the phone when they receive a report and talk personally to the lab examiner or talk to their supervisors to make sure they understand exactly what the report says and what it means to the rest of the investigation.

▶ Lack of Supervisory Oversight

Supervising a detective unit is not just about monitoring schedules, assigning cases, and monitoring training, supplies, and equipment. While these are part of the major goals of any supervisor, another very important function is one of the weakest points in U.S. policing today: the review and oversight of individual cases to make certain the detectives are staying on track and accomplishing those things that need to be accomplished. Much of what has been written in this chapter about mistakes and investigative failures in the investigative process could be avoided if proper oversight is conducted by a supervisor who is monitoring the work of his assigned detectives. But this is not a widely held belief among U.S. detectives. In fact, whenever we talk about this aspect of investigations to detectives during service training classes, there is often an open and loud hostility and attitude of rejection of the concept of someone reviewing or supervising their work. This is probably based on the type of personality of the individuals attracted to detective work in the first place—the independent self-starters and logical thinkers. They tend to place themselves in a category of being the exclusive determiner of what is important and what is not important in their particular cases and therefore guard their case file as if it were some sort of top secret, not-yet-copyrighted collection of their genius.

We frequently see this expressed in body language, comments, and definitive statements made during training courses, generally centering on the theme of: "This is my case, and I don't share it with anyone; no one tells me what to do on *my* case." We also see this concept shared by many supervisors who state they do not supervise the conduct of the investigation itself, because "the case belongs to the detective," and this is typically understood as an unofficial but established agency policy.

Until very recently, there was a state police agency with no policy or mechanism for maintaining the original case file once the detective had concluded the investigation, whether or not it resulted in an arrest and conviction or closed as unsolved. The case files were maintained by individual detectives at their office or at their home, and when they retired or left the job, they actually took their original case files home with them, including photos, negatives, and original statements. Years later when working cold cases, one of the first steps was to go find the original detective, or his widow in many cases, and try to get the original file returned so it could be worked again. Whereas we agree with the important general concept of *ownership of a case*—where the detective takes pride in his work, is concerned about the case outcome, and wants to see it through until the end—we also realize the importance of someone outside the investigation looking at the work to make sure the important things are being done.

What exactly is important is usually case or event dependent, but it is certainly necessary to ensure basic investigative steps are being taken in a timely manner. Such steps include making sure that evidence is sent to the lab, witnesses are interviewed on a timely basis, alibis are properly checked out, other investigative leads are completed, and the detective is still engaged throughout the investigation, even after an arrest is made. Many if not all of the investigative failures could be eliminated or limited if such supervision was carried out. If an active supervisory review process is in place in most agencies, there can be no excuse for not having important documents in a file and no reasons for failing to prepare written reports. There are many advantages to conducting a supervisory review of the investigation, and perhaps the biggest one is completeness. If the supervisor can read the file and have no questions or identify no other investigative leads that need to be completed, then there is a good chance the case is going to be acceptable to the prosecutor as well. If the supervisor, however, has questions or does not understand the investigation, it is likely the prosecutor or the jury might not understand it either. It is also important that supervisors are also trained so they know what they are supposed to be looking for when they review the file, and they need to be empowered by the agency to give specific instructions to their detectives to make certain they have a professional product.

▶ Conclusion

There are very few instances where one single error or mistake causes a case to go unresolved. Most of the time, failure to resolve a case is the result of a combination of events or series of mistakes that causes the case to bog down, frustration sets in, and the detective becomes inundated with newer cases, or simply loses interest. Understanding the most common errors hopefully will spark awareness in detectives and their supervisors and help keep them on track and lead to more successful case resolutions. Victims, their families, and our communities are all depending on us to do the right thing, find the bad guys, and bring them to justice.

INDEX

Page references followed by the letters *f* and *t* indicate significant figures and tables.